THE ROMAN
EMPERORS

THE ROMAN EMPERORS

A Biographical Dictionary of Rule and Misrule

Including Usurpers, Rebels and Near-Misses,
48BC-AD602

Maxwell Craven

AMBERLEY

Title page image: Vitellius, plaster library bust after the antique original. (Bamfords Ltd.)

First published 2025

Amberley Publishing
The Hill, Stroud
Gloucestershire, GL5 4EP

www.amberley-books.com

Illustrations are all kindly provided by John Travis. He holds a
Doctorate in Roman Archaeology from the University of Liverpool.
John is an Associate member of the Institute of Field Archaeologists
(AIFA). The illustrations provided here are based upon a careful
examination of all available historic representations of the subjects.
He co-authored the Amberley titles *Roman Helmets*, *Roman Shields*
and *Roman Body Armour*.

British Library Cataloguing in Publication Data.
A catalogue record for this book is available from the British Library.

ISBN 978 1 3981 2625 1 (hardback)
ISBN 978 1 3981 2626 8 (ebook)

1 2 3 4 5 6 7 8 9 10

Typesetting by SJmagic DESIGN SERVICES, India.
Printed in the UK.

Appointed GPSR EU Representative:
Easy Access System Europe Oü, 16879218
Address: Mustamäe tee 50, 10621, Tallinn, Estonia
Contact Details: gpsr.requests@easproject.com, +358 40 500 3575

Contents

Introduction   6

Acknowledgements   17

Nomenclature and Sources   18

The Biographies   20

Appendix I: Chronological List of Entries in the Dictionary   329

Appendix II: Abbreviations of Names   333

Bibliography   334

Index of Persons Excluding the List of Biographical Entries   342

Introduction

Roman Emperors seem to be of perennial interest, especially those whose names are better known. Their lives, excesses, foibles and achievements are matters of enormous fascination, fuelled by films, novels and the revelations of archaeology. Because the empire never perfected any means of ensuring straightforward succession, this led to continual coups, *pronunciamentos* and civil wars, with the inevitable result that the majority of emperors died violently. Of the 198 men and women whose biographies people these pages, no fewer than 101 died violently by assassination or judicial execution, 13 committed suicide, 10 died in battle (not always against an external enemy), 45 died of natural causes and the fate of 29 – mainly obscure usurpers – is not known.

In the face of statistics like these, one might wonder why anyone would wish to rule the Roman Empire at all, let alone risk everything to depose someone else with no guarantee of success and little security thereafter. The usurpers whose lives are set out in this work very nearly outnumber those whose names are listed in the accepted canon of emperors; one wonders why they bothered. Yet, in some cases, blood was thicker than water, and concepts like *dignitas* were hard taskmasters when the competition to bring glory to one's family was intense on most levels of Rome's élite society. And when internal chaos or external threats reared their hydra-like heads, expediency frequently over-rode propriety, especially if the clamour of soldiers was heard rising beyond the doors of the *praetorium*.

Books intended both for the expert and the interested non-academic on the Roman emperors are usually presented chronologically, in some form or another, or less often, thematically. Short of rather more miscellaneous 'Who's Who' type popular books or in the determinedly academic works such as the *Prosopographia Imperii Romani* and the *Prosopography of the Later Roman Empire* – neither of which are easily available and the former being written in Latin – there seemed to be no easily accessible book which lists the emperors (of which there are very many, thanks to the vicissitudes of the empire itself) in alphabetical order for easy reference and in which a biographical account, with references, of each could be read. What follows is an attempt to do this. Gone are the arcana of complex genealogical connections which informed

The Imperial Families of Ancient Rome (Fonthill 2017), but retained are informative and reasonably comprehensive biographies of each man. The timespan of this biographical dictionary runs from Caesar's seizure of power in 49BC to AD602, when the dynasty of Justinian and his successors ended (rather bloodily in a mutiny) and the true Byzantine, much more entirely Greek, character of the empire finally emerged.

Before that, however, it is useful to the reader to give an account of the way the empire evolved constitutionally, essential background to the biographical sketches.

1 From monarchy back to monarchy

Forms of governance tend to evolve through stress testing and adaptation, sometimes in response to crises, sometimes through civil conflict and sometimes just to attain some particular objective; violent revolution, though, tends to be rare, which is probably why dates like 1649, 1789 and 1917 stick in the mind. Rome was no different. According to its earliest history – written down very much later than the events described by later annalists and mostly well beyond the reach of any certain attestation – Rome was a monarchy which had arisen in the eighth century BC and which was swept away by a revolt of the great and good, the patrician aristocracy, and replaced by a Republic administered by these same patricians and therefore best described as an oligarchy.

The patricians, supposedly the descendants of a hundred 'conscript fathers' brought together from the tribes that made up the population, were recruited by the first king, Romulus, but did not have things their own way for too long. By the mid-fifth century BC, those outside the charmed circle of families whose members made up an assembly which evolved into the senate, the plebeians, were agitating effectively for their own involvement. Various compromises were essayed in order to satisfy both elements, a process which appears to have gone on in various forms for a century. A final upheaval, supposedly in 367, seems to have led to the arrival at a *status quo*, in which plebeian families were fully eligible for election to the senate, and could put themselves forward for some of the magistracies which had, by that date, evolved. The consulship – the highest permanent office of the state, consisting of an annually elected pair of senior senators – was henceforth shared between the two castes, so for each year one patrician and one plebeian consul was elected to serve and to bestow their names on the year. By later convention, too, the descendants of a consul, patrician or plebeian, were known as and ranked as *nobiles*, thereby adding lustre to their families. The next rank down, the praetorship, appears to have been open to both more or less equally, but the position of aedile was divided, so that there were henceforth to be a pair of curule aediles held by patricians and, alongside them, a pair of plebeian aediles, filled by members of the plebeian families. Most important of all, ten plebeians were elected as tribunes of the people each year, with the power to veto legislation.

This dispensation, more or less, continued for the remainder of the life of the Republic, along with the three temporary magistracies, the dictator,

elected for six months to cope with serious crises, a master of horse, his effective deputy, and the censors, two being elected from the ranks of senior ex-consuls from time to time (usually at five-year intervals) to hold a census to regulate the membership of the senate, enquire into public morals and evaluate the state of public finances, a proceeding supposedly initiated by King Servius Tullius in 566BC. The censorship was separated from the consuls in the fifth century and the first plebeian censor was C. Marcius Rutilus, elected in 351.

Most early pressures upon the system of government, apart from internal agitation, came from external threats, and as time went by it became apparent that holding senior office for only one year was not sufficient to see through a military campaign and thus one could have one's tenure extended by being voted a pro-consulship (or a pro-praetorship) in order to finish the job, although consuls as such were still elected for the year following, rendering the proconsuls supernumerary magistrates with *imperium*: the power to lead an army.

As Rome expanded its dominance over the Mediterranean periphery, pro-magistrates were required to go to various newly acquired provinces to administer them, usually with military support. Magistracies were held by ambitious senators in a particular order of importance linked to age eligibility: first, the quaestorship. then for plebeians, tribunate of the people, followed by the aedileship, praetorship and the climax of one's career, the consulship.

Yet it was this territorial expansion, and the stresses it brought, that began to put the entire system, evolved to control a modest sized Italian city-state, under insupportable strain. With so many men under arms, their retirement had to be allowed for: this required land to be available to be distributed amongst retiring soldiers, and mainly in Italy, too, for it was still a citizen army, whose retired members were hardly going to welcome being settled in some corner of a far-flung province. This, and other mainly economic stresses, undermined the whole creaking constitutional structure, resulting in conflict and bloodshed in 133 and 122BC, and again in 104, when a single classic 'strong man', the outsider Caius Marius, a successful commander, contrived to be elected as consul in 107 and for a further five uninterrupted years from 104 to 100. He had managed to alienate almost every faction by the time he stepped down, despite defeating a German invasion, and laid the seeds of further discord with the non-Roman nations of the Italian peninsula which led to a further – essentially civil – war in the course of which Marius, after another consulship, died. He was replaced by L. Cornelius Sulla, a patrician who served two consulships (88 and 80) and in 82 revived the dictatorship in order to assert effectively monarchical control before (unexpectedly) retiring – an act which prompted the young Julius Caesar to remark that Sulla 'didn't know his ABC'. These men, Marius and Sulla, were the first glimmerings of a revival of monarchy and the following generations up to the settlement of Augustus saw powerful men almost sleep-walking into monarchy and trying to stretch the constitutional envelope (frequently past its limits) to enable power and continuity to be wielded without a naked revival of the hated institution of kingship.

From this time, Roman politics became highly fractured, and men bent on gaining control of the levers of government began to emerge with increasing frequency, some unsuccessful, like the patrician demagogue L. Sergius Catilina, and others more successfully, like the *arriviste* Cn. Pompeius (Pompey), the *nobilis* M. Licinius Crassus and another patrician, C. Julius Caesar. The last three initiated a semi-monarchical rule by forming, from 59 to 53, a triumvirate, ratified by a coerced senate, to overcome the numerous veto points that had evolved in the Roman constitution by that date, mainly as a result of social tensions and the strains on the system imposed by the actions of previous strong men like Marius and Sulla. This alliance began to crumble from 55, was weakened by the death in battle of Crassus in 53 and finally collapsed as the two remaining power-brokers fell out, leading to the death of Pompey and the final rise of Caesar.

After that, Julius Caesar used repeated consulships in order to stay in control, as had Marius, but decided, like Sulla, to revive the dictatorship, at first renewed every six months as convention required from 49, but from 44 as perpetual dictator – that is, holding office for life – a development his less enthusiastic supporters could not stomach, leading to his assassination in March 44. The story that he had earlier been offered (in an informal context) a crown but had refused it publicly may well be true; clearly, he was aware of the dangers in which his new eminence placed him.

Caesar's death immediately plunged Rome into a further period of instability, with competing successors – Marcus Antonius (Mark Antony), Caesar's nephew C. Octavius (testamentarily adopted as C. Julius Caesar Octavianus), Pompey's younger son, Sextus and a Crassus-like figure, the influential grandee M. Aemilius Lepidus, all jockeying for power. Although Antony, Octavian and Lepidus managed to form a second triumvirate from 43, which placed them on a much more formal footing than the previous triumvirate, it hardly brought peace, what with mopping up operations against the assassins of Caesar, attempts to dislodge Sex. Pompeius from the central Mediterranean, where he had managed to set himself up as a sort of pirate king, and other perturbations. Eventually, Lepidus was sidelined and in the end Octavian and Antony, both unwilling to allow the other to gain superior influence, turned on each other, leading to the latter's defeat at Actium and his death in Egypt with his mistress and ally, Cleopatra VII of Egypt, leaving Octavian as last man standing, as Caesar's heir and effectively sole ruler of a battered and by this time largely ineffective Republic.

2 An Evolutionary Monarchy

Octavian now had to work out how to remain in power, for to lose it would effectively be signing his death warrant; yet the Republic was beyond being able to assert itself as a collective entity, and his departure would inevitably usher in a quasi-monarchical replacement or another bruising civil conflict. He had already held two consulships under the triumvirate – the first in 43 at the age of nineteen and held in an entirely unconstitutional way – and at first, he maintained his grip on power by being elected consul every year

Octavian as a youth; grand
tour copy of an antique bust.
(Bamfords Ltd.)

(echoing Marius and Caesar), usually with a favoured colleague, but this had the unfortunate effect of limiting the number of senators who could hold the consulship, which was hardly popular, especially as the *cursus honorum*, which culminated in the consulship, was effectively an in-house training course for provincial administrators, of which a steady stream was required. Nevertheless, in 27 he took the name Augustus ('the favoured one') combined with the filiation 'son of the God' acknowledging his adoptive parentage and the fact that Caesar had been deified by the senate after his death. He was also elected *princeps senatus* giving him primacy in debate over all other senators.

Nevertheless, this was a trifle make-do-and-mend, and several occurrences made this obvious. Thus in 23, he relinquished the consulship (except for only two other years, 5 and 2BC) and was granted the *imperium* of a proconsul for ten years, combined with the powers of a plebeian tribune as well. These powers were renewed every decade thereafter, giving Augustus direct control over all the armed provinces, power to summon the senate and the power to veto legislation. He was also voted the perpetual power of censor, which enabled him, amongst other things, to decide who could and could not sit in the senate. Caesar had been the precedent for this, for he had purged the senate, adlected new people into it (including provincials) as well as raising some distinguished families to patrician status, to make up for losses in the

turmoil of the preceding decades. Now Augustus could do likewise. His aim on both occasions was to preserve all the usages of the Republican constitution whilst retaining discreet overall control: he was theoretically first amongst equals not an overt dictator, eschewing the trappings of monarchy like the purple toga and other symbols, as latterly adopted by Caesar himself.

This settlement of 23 really defined the position of the emperor for the next 220 years, but although Augustus, as he then became, managed to maintain (with one or two unfortunate exceptions) the balance of the exercise of power whilst treating the senate as a partner and maintaining the *amour propre* of its members. This was mainly successful, and it has to be remembered that the senators were the men who actually led the armies, governed the provinces and administered the empire: partnership was of the essence. Were this partnership to break down, it was the smooth running of the empire that would suffer, with unthinkable consequences. What completed the emperor's powers was that in 12BC, the long-retired ex-triumvir Lepidus died. He had succeeded Caesar in 44 as *pontifex maximus*, chief priest of the Roman state religion, and this enabled Augustus to assume the role once held from an early age by his deified uncle Caesar (allowing a grateful senate to elect him to the role.)

Not every successor was able to strike the right balance between the exercise of power and the maintenance of a semblance of functioning Republican institutions. Yet, on accession, every following emperor was granted renewable proconsular *imperium* by the senate, along with the *tribunicia potestas*, the tribunician power – renewable every year on 10 December, a notion which continued through much of the ensuing centuries, at least in theory – and the office of *pontifex maximus*. Tiberius, Augustus' successor, essentially reluctant, well understood how it worked, but as he retreated from public life he allowed powerful appointees to exercise power on his behalf in a way that Augustus, with his two senior advisors Agrippa and Maecenas, would never have tolerated, although both were closer to Augustus and in a far more trusting relationship that either the manipulative Pretorian Prefects, Sejanus and Macro, were with Tiberius. Both these Pretorian Prefects were allowed to get out of control, threatening the relationship between *princeps* and senate, wrecking what cohesion there was in the Imperial family and setting a precedent for the power that could be exercised by Pretorian Prefects generally, which eventually led to the demise of the relatively effective and symbiotic relationship between emperor and senate. This damage was exacerbated by the accession of Caligula, who had no real interest in ruling, only in exercising power.

The relationship was to a large extent restored under Claudius (who took up the censorship and conducted a *lustrum* in AD48) and under the first half of the reign of Nero but, with the latter's artistic inclinations beginning to take precedent over his interest in ruling the empire (with or without the senate) the relationship once again decayed, a process accelerated by his reaction to the conspiracy of C. Calpurnius Piso in 65 – brutal suppression – and made catastrophically worse by the civil war that followed Nero's death.

Vespasian, who emerged as victor from the upheavals of 68-69, managed to restore something like the relationship which Augustus had evolved with

the senate. Gossipy historian Suetonius emphasised in *The Lives of the Twelve Caesars* that he was a man with a sense of humour, a quality that would doubtless have stood him in good stead in restoring the Augustan settlement and one crucially lacking in most of his successors (as far as we know, at any rate). Vespasian replenished the senate through the exercise of his power as censor in 74, and a good relationship with the senate continued under his son Titus. This became increasingly strained under the younger son, Domitian, but was restored under Nerva and Trajan, whose handling of the senate emerges interestingly from the correspondence of the younger Pliny. Under Hadrian, Antoninus, Lucius Verus and Marcus Aurelius, too, the relationship seems to have continued relatively smoothly, although a pair of senators seem to have caused a problem for Antoninus Pius in 145 and a descendant of an eastern prince acting as governor of Syria likewise caused panic through a misguided attempted *coup* against Marcus Aurelius in 175 in the belief that the emperor had died.

Unfortunately, the great truth, revealed during the notorious 'year of the four emperors' in 68-69, that emperors could be created by other means than through the senate – by superimposition through military force – was hammered home in the aftermath of the assassination of Marcus Aurelius's murderously barmy son, Commodus, on New Year's Eve 192. The Praetorian Guard, a Rome-based élite military unit set up by Augustus to protect the emperor, decided it couldn't endorse the senate's elderly, distinguished, but rather strict Commodus replacement, L. Helvius Pertinax, deposed him and instead sold supreme power to the senator who would offer the highest bounty to the guard's officers and personnel. This set three appalled provincial governors off on a race to grasp power, which resulted in yet another bloody civil war from 193 to 195, the winner, Septimius Severus, a North African of mixed Phoenician and Roman descent, being himself much inclined to resolve problems by violent suppression and a man entirely lacking the tact and emollience required to operate successfully within the constraints of the Augustan settlement.

Severus did not drastically alter the governance of the empire, merely making it less predictable. He was more specifically dynastic, too. Having re-aligned himself after 195 as a *de facto* member of the dynasty of Marcus Aurelius, the relatively large number of the latter's surviving family were in severe jeopardy of being picked off as a threat, as indeed many were; the succession of his sons was Severus's paramount aim, driven by his Syrian second wife and her somewhat exotic family. Once Severus was dead in 211 and his younger son had been killed by the elder, the succession was with a brute (Caracalla), a teenaged weirdo (Elagabalus) and a relatively normal youth under the thumb of his mother (Severus Alexander). The whole period from 211 to the death of the latter in 235 was marked by numerous attempted usurpations, thanks to Severus having set the standard. Eventually, in 235, one of these succeeded in the person of the allegedly uncouth soldier Maximin I, who deposed and killed Alexander.

Yet the Augustan settlement wasn't quite finished. So outraged were the governing class – the senate and the administrative echelons of the equites – that following an abortive attempt to take power by the governor

of Africa, Gordian and his son, the senate attempted to wrest back control and appointed two members of a constitutional grand committee to replace the Gordians and defeat Maximin, by then on the point of invading Italy to neutralize this unexpected opposition. Their appointees somehow managed to defeat Maximin at Aquileia but sabotaged their own cause by falling out and losing the already half-hearted support of the Praetorian Guard. The guard promptly switched their allegiance to the surviving member of Gordian dynasty, killed the two senatorial emperors and elevated to the purple another teenager, Gordian III. 238, therefore, was a year that eclipsed even 68-69 and 193 as the year of the six emperors.

All this coincided with increasing pressure on the empire at the periphery, requiring increased military spending, which in turn led to the progressive debasement of the currency to fund it and then to inflationary pressures, felt most keenly by the commoner sort. A succession of senatorial governors seized power between the fall in 244 of Gordian III and the murder of the most stable of his successors, Gallienus, in 268, which compounded the underlying problems.

Yet it was Gallienus who grasped the nettle of reforming the administration by opening up governorships and senior military posts to non-senators, and by moving the army gradually to a form of unified command under the emperor. This, however, meant that the succession of senatorial usurpers was replaced by a succession of generalissimos vying for power, leaving almost all posts henceforth closed to senators and the problem of inflation uncured. It was only with the Praetorian Guard-aided *coup* of Diocletian in 284 that things began to change.

Diocletian moved completely away from the Augustan settlement (to which only lip-service had been paid since 244 and even less since 268) and instituted direct, autocratic rule by two emperors, one for each half of the empire, split east/west, each aided by a deputy and designated heir, thus four rulers: the tetrarchy. He also overhauled the economy, imposed price controls, re-established the coinage and introduced hereditary succession to most occupations, some of which measures had unintended consequences.

The Tetrarchy as an institution failed to allow for human nature, so that the sons of Tetrarchs, who tended to be overlooked as deputy rulers ('caesars') were thus inclined to attempt usurpations, as with Maxentius and Constantine, the latter far more successfully than the former, whom he eventually and memorably defeated at the Milvian Bridge outside Rome in 312. The system fell apart, being succeeded by one in which the emperor ruled with or without a colleague with no pretention to hereditary succession, as had been the case under the principate. Constantine reformed further, building a mobile, mounted army, the *comitatus,* easing some of Diocletian's more egregious restrictions, re-opening most careers to senators and revising the system of ranks and honours, abolishing the old patriciate, and using the word 'patrician' to define a particularly elevated imperial rank. He also ended all restrictions on Christianity in the Edict of Milan in 313, clearing the way for successors at the end of the fourth century to begin trying to exclude pagan senators from public life.

From the Theodosian dynasty when, from 395, the empire was formally and permanently divided, there came a development in which very young or child emperors reigned under the *de facto* rule of military supremos, usually of barbarian stock, brought in to lead campaigns in lieu of an adult ruler. During the fifth century in the west, so powerful did the barbarian *generalissimos* become that emperors (nearly all back to being drawn from the senatorial aristocracy again) increasingly saw their power attenuated until, in 476, a new child-emperor, Romulus Augustus, was painlessly deposed and replaced by the war-leader who had brought this about and by a nominal re-assertion of authority by the eastern emperor, where this trend had been reversed by a succession of moderately competent adult rulers.

The succession was the single most challenging problem, as John D. Grainger's book *The Roman Imperial Succession* (2020) analyses in detail, covering most of our period. In the time of Augustus and thereafter it had been a given that the succession would go to a member of the family, essentially the wider family of Caesar, Augustus and his wife Livia. The inevitable consequence of this was – again bearing in mind human nature – attrition, as a result of conspiracies, real or imagined. Those dying by natural causes were immediately thought to be the victims of murder: Caius and Lucius Caesar under Augustus and Germanicus under Tiberius. Had Augustus had any sons, things might have been more straightforward, but the absence of male heirs at least gave the emperor the chance of appointing as potential successor someone he felt most suited to the job. This system broke down comprehensively through the Julio-Claudian dynasty amidst much blood-letting, causing the extinction of several distinguished old families.

The Flavians tried hereditary male succession but were thwarted by the third emperor being perceived as too flawed to be allowed to continue and because Domitian had killed almost all of his potential male heirs, although one line seems to have survived to be absorbed into the Antonine dynasty. The succession of eldest sons was almost always a disaster. One only has to look at Commodus (180-192) and Caracalla (211-218) – bad eggs who made the purple – or the sons in waiting who perished with the fall of their parents, like the sons of Maximin, Gordian I, Philip the Arab, Decius and Gallus; only Valerian's son Gallienus would reign on his own account, managing to sustain himself in the face of at least 24 usurpers over almost eight years – fifteen years altogether, including almost seven under his father. Yet even his attempts to be succeeded by a son were foiled by the events leading up to the rise of the secessionist Gallic empire.

Apart from Carus, who was succeeded by two sons and possibly a grandson (all within the space of less than three years), hereditary succession nominally took a back seat under the Tetrarchy, its cohesion depending on complex inter-marital alliances, but the fecundity of the house of Constantine led to a return to a form of male hereditary succession tempered by assassination until the death of Julian the apostate in 363. Thereafter, the dynasties of Valentinian I and Theodosius I (interconnected by the marriage of the latter to the former's daughter), brought some kind of order until 455 in the west and 457 in the east, supplemented by a number of fairly fleeting

reigns by members of the powerful western Anician dynasty bolstered by probable connections with the later third-century soldier emperor Probus and the late fourth-century Magnus Maximus, who emerge, clearly driven partly by conscious heredity, until 472 or even 532. Finally, the dynasty of Justinian and its connections, again largely missing in father-son-successions until the very end, lasted from 518 to 602. In Rome, unlike Medieval Europe and elsewhere, the natural succession of son to father was a rarity and, where it did occur, was usually a disaster. It was only in its Byzantine mutation after 610 that dynastic succession became more standardized, but even then, remained mediated by assassination.

3 Identifying the nearly men

It was largely a third-century problem that disaffected military units might unexpectedly acclaim their general as emperor, leaving the unfortunate commander so marked out that he had little choice but to pick up the ball and run with it; if the general were to demur, it would inevitably leave the soldiers open to an accusation of mutiny, the punishment for which was decimation. Thus, a refusal of imperial honours tended to guarantee a quick assassination, whilst acceptance was a gamble with the likelihood of a similarly fatal outcome – a classic Catch-22. That aside, there remained plenty of men who were, through dynastic connections (often not readily apparent), hunger for power, threat or idealism, driven to attempt to seize the purple.

These, if successful, entered the canon of 'legitimate' emperors and, if unsuccessful, remain branded as usurpers. Amongst the former there are a good number, from Vespasian to Constantine the Great and beyond, whilst a few, like Magnus Maximus were successful, but fell out with others and had their reputation so vigorously attacked *post mortem* as to be somewhat unfairly branded usurpers.

The emperors are listed below alphabetically by their commonly used names, their other names where appropriate being cross-referenced. Where emperors have familiar forms, they are used, eg. Vespasian rather than Vespasianus, Trajan instead of Traianus, Constantine instead of Constantinus or Majorian *in lieu* of Maiorianus, and so on. Those less familiar appear with their names in their full Latin form. The emperors generally acknowledged as being in the main canon of fully acknowledged rulers are listed in bold, whilst those generally accepted as usurpers and others, the full-blooded usurpers, in bold italic. The dividing line between legitimate emperors and usurpers, or peripheral claimants to imperial power, is, however, a narrow and porous one and the judgements are entirely those of the author. Largely, the generally acknowledged emperors are viewed here as those who were in unchallenged power throughout the empire (or in east or west after 295) or who were acknowledged by the senate, even if they turned out to have been ephemeral. Those listed in italics are those generally acknowledged to have been unsuccessful usurpers, never formally recognised and also a handful of people who were neither emperors nor usurpers, but who came close, either

because they were rebels with no apparent aspirations to full power, or by refusal to serve, or in some cases, people who appear in the more dubious sources and probably never existed.

Emperors are listed with their dates in power (years followed by months and days where known) followed by a brief *résumé* of their careers following acclamation. This is then followed by their style as ruler, followed by their original name, family, place of origin, birth, prominent kinsmen and previous career. This is normally followed by an outline of their rule, achievements and other notable matters, followed by any general remarks. Sources are to be found in the footnotes.

Several Roman emperors in the accepted canon bear numbers following their names: the three Gordians, Constantine and his sons (and others bearing their names), Severus the tetrarch and Libius Severus, the Leos, the Justins and so on. But listed alphabetically, much confusion can be engendered with repeated names, so I have taken the liberty of adding numbers where there are more than one, but in brackets, to avoid confusion with emperors normally accepted as being numbered.

Acknowledgements

As a student I enjoyed an immensely valuable amount of academic guidance from emeritus Professor John Rich of Nottingham University who supervised my bachelor's degree dissertation, and emeritus Professor Peter Wiseman, who supervised the next effort, until Derby City Council – who were paying – decreed that to retain my subvention, I should transfer to Museum Studies at the same university. My interest stemmed from having read Sir Ronald Syme's *Roman Revolution* (1939) in my late teens. I was also much encouraged by my relative by marriage and close friend HSH the late Prince Michael Grousinski and by long enjoyable debates with our late friend Tom Glaser. The libraries of the Universities of Leicester and Nottingham, of the Roman Society and the Society of Antiquaries and their ever-patient, friendly and accommodating staff have also been a source of information and support.

Nearer home I have been encouraged by former colleagues at Derby Museum, by the late Robert Innes-Smith and by my wife, Carole, without whose affection and support nothing I have researched or written would have been at all possible.

I also stand in the debt of my publisher, Amberley, for being prepared to see this book into publication, especially Shaun Barrington.

Nomenclature and Sources

Roman nomenclature can be confusing, especially with emperors, who tended to change their style of naming at the drop of a hat. About half the people listed below bore the traditional *tria nomina* (three names): *praenomen*, *gentilicium* (or just *nomen*) and *cognomen*, as in Caius Julius Caesar. The *praenomen* was chosen from a very restricted choice, was invariably abbreviated in written use and I have used these abbreviations throughout, thus saving a lot of ink. However, I have listed them in full in Appendix II, which includes other abbreviations. Otherwise, I have tried to translate Roman appointments, ranks and so on in the text where they occur. Dates are expressed in the traditional BC/AD form, but only where events described are near the year of changeover; otherwise, BC dates are designated but most years referred to herein are AD and will not generally given the AD prefix.

I have ancient accounts of the emperors but have supplemented these with the accounts published in the best academic sources where possible, for these include inscriptional evidence, largely very difficult to access, and other numismatic and written sources. The academic sources here rely heavily on the second edition of the monumental *Prosopographia Imperii Romani* (Dessau, H., Stein, A., Groag, E., *et multi aliis*, Berlin, from 1933-2006) which covers the ground from 27BC to 268 and from that date to 641 – thirty-nine years beyond the parameters of this book – the *Prosopography of the Later Roman Empire* (Jones, A. H. M., Martindale, J R & Morris, J., 3 vols in 4 (Cambridge, 1971, 1980, 1992). The bibliography cites those that have been consulted.

Of the ancient sources, I have used the third-century senatorial author Dio Cassius, generally thought reliable, but by no means contemporary prior to the Severan dynasty, supplemented (with gaps) from 14 to 69 by Tacitus' *Annals*, and from 27BC to AD96 by Suetonius' gossipy (but hugely enjoyable) *Twelve Caesars,* and also Herodian's *History of the Empire* which, like Dio, fails us after 238. Later in the saga, we have Aurelius Victor, and Eutropius' *Breviarum ab Urbe Condita* supplemented by Sozomen's *Ecclesiastical History*, Zonaras' *History* (which takes us from the fall of Elagabalus to the death of Theodosius) and Zosimus' *New History* for the later fourth and part of the fifth century (taking over from Ammianus Marcellinus, who stops with

the accession of Theodosius) and then the three great works of Procopius for the sixth century, with many other important *urtexts* in between.

Some of these works were completed long after the events they describe, but most are thought to include earlier, more reliable sources. The one problematic source is the anonymous (or pseudonymous) *Scriptores Historia Augustae* (HA) which purports to give blow-by-blow accounts of the emperors to the time of Diocletian and to have been written at the end of the third century. The late Sir Ronald Syme established very convincingly that it was really a polemic and to some extent satirical at that, written by someone embedded in the senatorial western élite of the late fourth century. That it was, after its account of the Severan dynasty, packed with fantasy and utterly unreliable, has never really been in dispute. Yet there are credible elements and, where they have been deployed, due caution has been expressed. Coin inscriptions have also been leant on heavily for imperial styles and titles along with relevant commentaries on them.

Secondary sources have been consulted widely, for the insights they bring and every attempt has been made to include the latest research, not least the author's own efforts to rehabilitate Magnus Maximus, published by Amberley in 2023 as *Magnus Maximus: a Forgotten Roman Emperor and his British Legacy*. Again, all are listed in the bibliography. Also there, you can find the abbreviations used in the footnotes at the end of the entries for relevant works.

The Biographies

ACHILLEUS
297, December – 298, July

[M.] Aurelius Achilleus was a *vir perfectissimus* and the *corrector* (equestrian governor) of an unknown Egyptian province in September 297. He is named as a usurper, instead of Domitian (III) in several sources, but was in reality probably the latter's successor after 2nd December 297. As the subsequent siege of Alexandria by Diocletian lasted for eight months[1] his reign must have ended, no doubt bloodily, in June or July 298, depending on exactly when it began.[2] No coins survive from his time if, indeed, any were minted.

AEGIDIUS
461, November – 465 October/November

Aegidius was a competent military commander who unexpectedly found himself ruling most of northern Gaul and what was left of the Rhine frontier on the deposition of Avitus who managed to hand his polity on to his son.

A Gallo-Roman aristocrat, Aegidius was one who adapted to the new opportunities available to senators of distinguished family during the breakdown of central authority in the west by choosing a military career. He was serving in Gaul when Majorian was deposed, but when Severus III was proclaimed he was relieved of his post. He refused to recognise Severus and threatened to invade Italy, only being prevented by attacks apparently on the part of the Visigoths, which he subsequently put down with aplomb. He was distinguished both by his prowess and conduct.[3]

He thus ruled what appears to have been a third breakaway Gallic empire, not dissimilar to that controlled by Constantine III, only somewhat smaller. He faced down the attempt by his replacement (appointed by Severus), Agrippinus, to take over and continued to exercise his authority, winning a

---

1 Eg: Eutropius 9, 22–23 & Orosius VII, 25.4.8
2 PLRE I Achilleus 1
3 See also MacGeorge (2002) 82-110

major encounter with the Visigoths at Aurelianum (Orléans) in 463. At this juncture he could have conquered the Visigothic kingdom, or he could have returned Gaul to Imperial control but, tellingly, he did not; he was content, like Postumus and Constantine III (at first), to hang on to what he had got. Later though, he opened talks with the Vandals with a view to forging an alliance against the Visigoths. He made his capital at Noviodunum (Soissons) and allied himself with the Franks, newly settled in the area. The Franks acknowledged him as their overlord, referring to him as *rex* – King.[4] Professor Fanning, however, has shown that the terminology employed (chiefly by Gregory of Tours[5]) is misleading: 'It would be extremely rash to suggest that Aegidius and Syagrius were in fact Roman Emperors, but it is clear that Gregory of Tours and the *Liber Historiae Francorum* were using language that meant just that.'[6]

The family may have been senatorial before the time of the two 4th-century consuls called Syagrius, at least in the distaff line. Alternatively, they may have been amongst the eminent Gauls who entered public life in the wake of the rise of Ausonius, the tutor of Gratian.[7] The name Afranius might imply a possible blood link with Afranius Hannibalianus, the first husband of the empress Eutropia, wife of Maximian (qv). The name may have come into the family via one or other of the two consuls' mothers as suggested below. There must have been at least one missing generation between the consul Syagrius and Aegidius (qv). This gap could conceivably be filled from a rather later Frankish poetical genealogy quoted by MacGeorge:

> *Primus rex Romanorum Allanius dictus est*
> *Allanius genuit Pabolum*
> *Pabolus Egetium*
> *Egetius genuit Egegium*
> *Egegius genuit Siagrium*
> *per quem Romani regnum perditerunt.*[8]

For 'Pabolus' we should read Paulus. 'Egegius' is clearly Aegidius but, if one reads 'Egetius' as Aëtius, then we are moving inexorably into the realms of fantasy, bearing in mind that Valentinian III's general Aëtius is not known to have had more than one son (called Gaudentius). Furthermore, had Aegidius been a son of Aëtius, it is exceedingly unlikely that no writer of the time mentioned it. Yet the etymology of 'Egetius' seems exceedingly close to 'Aegidius', in which case it is possible that the poem celebrates the fact that Aegidius bore the same name as his father, who was the son of a Paulus, for whom there are a number of possible candidates towards the end of the fourth

---

4 Barnwell (1992) 70

5 Greg. *HF* 2, 27

6 Fanning (1992) 296-297

7 Sivan (1993), 115, 133-134

8 MacGeorge (2002) 80. It ends, 'by whom the Roman kingdom was lost'.

century. If we could accept this, then 'Al[l]an[i]us' would have to have been a brother of one or other of the consular Syagrii to enable the chronology to fit. On the whole it is better to proceed on the basis that the poem is just too untrustworthy to be relied upon, despite its intriguing content.

Through the wife of Tonantius Ferreolus (praetorian Prefect of Gaul in 451), Aegidius and Syagrius were connected with the families of emperors Avitus and probably Petronius Maximus.[9]

Aegidius himself was probably born c. 410, during the upheavals of the period of the rule of Constantine III and must have decided on a career of arms. He is known to have served with Aëtius and following him with Majorian when he was *magister militum* under Avitus. He became *magister utiusque militum* and *comes* in Gaul, appointed by Avitus in 456. The position was something of a poisoned chalice but, despite losing control of Colonia Agrippina (Cologne) in 457 and subsequently Augusta Treverorum (Trier), both to the Franks, he managed to save Arelate (Arles) from the Visigoths.

He was noted for his courage, good character and faith, but died in autumn 465, although accounts vary as to how this came about; one version favouring poison and the other death in an ambush.[10] We know nothing of his style of address, nor whether he had an assembly and nominated consuls; desperate times may have precluded such embellishments to his regime. Nevertheless, by his death he controlled a large part of northern Gaul, which he seems to have ruled as a full-blooded *tyrannus*, and on his demise his son Syagrius (qv) stepped peacefully into his shoes.

AEMILIAN I
253, June – October

Aemilian was governor of Lower Moesia who was declared emperor by the troops under his command in July 253 after he had led them to an unexpectedly emphatic victory over the local Goths under their leader, Kniva, who had rebelled over the payment of an agreed subsidy by the Roman authorities.

News of Aemilian's elevation took a month to reach Rome, but Trebonianus Gallus called upon the future emperor Valerian to come to his aid from the German frontier to neutralise the challenger. However, as the inferior forces of Gallus squared up to the freshly victorious army of Aemilianus, the former's soldiers, reluctant to fight their kin, deserted in numbers to Aemilian, who quickly prevailed, killing Gallus and his son and colleague Volusianus at Interamna Nahars (Terni).

On his arrival at Rome, Aemilian was quickly recognised by the senate and throughout the empire. He took the imperial style Imperator Caesar M. Aemilius Aemilianus Pius Felix Invictus Augustus, being made *pontifex maximus* and granted the tribunician and proconsular powers, renewable

---

9 Tonantius Ferreolus was claimed (not wholly unbelievably) by later chroniclers as an ancestor of Charlemagne.

10 PLRE II Aegidius; McGeorge (2002) 143. He issued coins in the names of the eastern emperors.

on 10 December yearly and made Father of his Country (*pater patriae*); his wife was also recognised as augusta, all this despite the emperor Trebonianus Gallus being still recognised in some parts.

Aemilianus attempted to rule as *primus inter pares* with his fellow senators, but the upheavals in train made such an aspiration a forlorn hope. Valerian, finally arriving in Italy too late to save Gallus, carried on into Italy, despite receiving news of Aemilian's success. His army, specially strengthened to fight the Alemanni on the Upper Danube, seem to have acclaimed him emperor once their objective was clear to all, and in October, as soon as he was in a position to confront Aemilian, the latter's officers killed him near Spoletum (Spoleto, Italy) in a carbon copy of the demise of Gallus a few months before.

M. Aemilius Aemilianus was born at Girba on the island of Meninx off the North African coast either in 206 or 213.[11] His ancestors were Moorish, marking him out as the first Emperor of Moorish origin. It is also assumed that he was the first of his family in the senate, so his promotion would not have been as fast as that of a patrician or a member of an established family like his predecessor, Gallus. Having been appointed governor of Moesia in 251, he must have previously held a suffect consulship, which is unlikely to have been prior to 240/241 (if he was born in 206) or 247/248 (if his date of birth was 213), the latter being more likely. Zonaras calls him grovelling and ignoble, but as he was writing over a century later, such epithets have to be greeted with caution. He married C[aia] Cornelia Supera (her name suggests her father was probably called C. Cornelius Superus, otherwise unrecorded) but no children are known.

Aemilian was appointed governor of the province of Lower Moesia by Gallus, probably in 252, and he responded with celerity when unrest amongst the Goths threatened a breakdown of order. He immediately took to the field, cleared his province of Gothic marauders and then carried the fight into Kniva's territory, winning a great victory, mainly thanks to having caught his enemy off guard. A donative paid to his troops in the wake of this, probably paid for out of the subsidy previously destined for Kniva's cohorts, was surely the catalyst for his elevation.

AEMILIAN II
261, November – 262, 31st March

With the death of Quietus in Emesa at the hands of Odenathus of Palmyra in November 261, Syria and Asia nominally were returned to the control of the Empire. However, in Egypt, L. Mussius Aemilianus Aegippus, the Imperial prefect, who had thrown in his lot with the two usurpers, must have realised that his only hope of escaping a terrible retribution for defecting from Gallienus to Macrianus and Quietus was to seize the purple himself, playing Egypt and its grain supplies as his trump card.[12] According to the *Historia*

---

11 ILS 528; PIR ² A330; *Epit.* 31, 1-3, cf. Zonaras, XII, 22

12 Aurelius Victor (32.4) is the only non-*Historia Augusta* authority for his actually having assumed the purple.

Augusta, he bore the *cognomen* Alexandrinus, possibly a reference to his prefectural capital in Egypt.

Aemilianus was born c. 210/215 although nothing is known of his family, although they were probably of Italian stock.[13] He rose rapidly through a distinguished equestrian career, ending up holding the second most important equestrian appointment after Pretorian Prefect, that of prefect of Egypt in 258, appointed by Valerian.[14] As such he bore the style of *vir perfectissimus* (abbreviated as *vp*) and was a zealous persecutor of Dionysius of Alexandria and the strong Christian community in Egypt generally whilst Valerian was alive. He was still *en poste* when Macrianus and Quietus were proclaimed, for he allowed their coins to be struck at Alexandria, indicating his support for them. Aemilian II was overthrown by his successor as prefect of Egypt, the *dux* (general) Aurelius Theodotus, probably before the end of March 262, certainly by August. It seems strange that he issued no coins in his own name; after all, Gordian I was only emperor for three weeks and still managed an issue (albeit probably posthumous). Perhaps Aemilianus was content to continue to issue those of Quietus, or accepted Alexandrine provincial issues. The alternative is that he never had himself acclaimed emperor at all, but merely held out against Gallienus's forces from necessity. Needless to say, he was killed on the orders of Gallienus.

AGRIPPA POSTUMUS

14, 19–22nd August

Youngest and last surviving of the three sons of M. Agrippa by Augustus' daughter Julia, Agrippa Postumus was technically an heir to his grandfather, but who, having been effectively by-passed subsequent to his siblings' deaths, was made away with following Augustus' demise in 14.

Agrippa [Vipsanius] Postumus was born shortly after Agrippa's death in 12BC. He was the youngest son of Agrippa and Julia and was formally adopted by Augustus following the deaths of his two elder brothers, in AD4, as next heir, becoming Agrippa Julius Aug. f. Caesar Postumus. He appears to have had personality difficulties, being allegedly truculent, uncouth and indifferent, which caused the *princeps* to prefer Tiberius over him as a potential successor, especially as the Empress Livia naturally preferred her own son over Postumus, who was only her step-grandson. He was exiled in 7 to Sorrento and then the island of Planasia where, in the days after the accession of Tiberius, the great Imperial minister Sallustius Crispus had him killed, allegedly without the new emperor's knowledge, aged just 26.[15]

---

13 Syme (1971) 270 & n. 4
14 HA *Tyr. Trig.* 22; PIR² M757; PLRE I. Aemilianus 6; his meteoric career: ILS1433
15 Pettinger (2012) *passim.,* PIR² 214

ALBINUS see CLODIUS ALBINUS

ALEXANDER (I) see SEVERUS ALEXANDER

ALEXANDER
308 – 310, summer

Alexander was a *vicarius* of Africa when he rebelled and allowed himself to be acclaimed by his troops. His imperial style was Imperator Caesar L. Domitius Alexander Pius Felix Augustus. One of his coin issues describes him on the reverse as *optimo principi*, a remarkably old-fashioned conceit. Thanks to the turmoil elsewhere, it seems that he ruled the African provinces peacefully and was not dislodged until Maxentius was able to send a force to Africa under the elderly ex-governor of the senatorial province of Africa Proconsularis, C. Ceionius Rufius Volusianus, made Pretorian Prefect for the purpose and supported by the equestrian commander Zenas, who defeated and killed him, presumably along with his unfortunate son, whose name has not survived.[16]

L. Domitius Alexander was a Phrygian equestrian officer (he was styled *vir perfectissimus*) of fairly advanced years who was appointed *vicarius* of the Diocese of Africa at some stage prior to 308, in all probability from 303. His tenure probably lasted until 308 because in that year emperor Maxentius, doubting the loyalty of the army in the province, demanded that he send his son to Rome as a hostage. An inscription from before his elevation gives his name as Val[erius] Alexander.[17] It has been suggested that he changed his name on being declared emperor; alternatively, he may have had other names, as was still then fashionable even for non-senators. Either way, he may have dropped the 'Valerius' element in order to distance himself from the Tetrarchs, almost all of whom bore this name.

ALLECTUS
293 – 296

The assassination of Carausius may well have been the result of the loss of that ruler's continental possessions. Nevertheless, Allectus, his nemesis, still controlled Britain. The two of them had attempted to reform their currency to match that being undertaken in the wider empire. That he survived for as long as three years is down to the fact that Constantius and the other Tetrarchs had to be sure that the Germanic tribes to the east of the Rhine would not rise to support him or take advantage of an attempt to end the secession by invading Gaul. There having been an attempt to dislodge Carausius earlier in c. 289 which failed dismally, no chances could be taken, and the Tetrachs had

---

16 PLRE Volusianus 4, who was back in Rome by October 310 & Zenas 1.
17 PLRE I Alexander 17, 20. The claimant, also *vicarius* of Africa could conceivably have been a separate person.

to be certain of success before trying again. The fact that Allectus had to be dislodged at all suggests that there was little opposition to his *coup*.

Allectus styled himself Imperator Caesar Allectus Pius Felix Augustus; he held a consulship in 294 and, despite the loss of Bononia (Boulogne) by his predecessor, seems to have still had control of large parts of Gaul. He seems also to have continued work on the Saxon shore forts undertaken by his predecessor and he began the construction of an imperial palace beside the Thames in the SW angle of the city of London.[18] When the invasion did come, Caesar Constantius I sent two fleets, led by his Pretorian Prefect, Julius Asclepiodotus.[19] Allectus, leading the British field army which he strengthened with a large contingent of Frankish mercenaries, seems to have been wrong-footed by being under the impression that only one fleet had arrived, for there had been fog in the Channel and another fleet had by-passed Allectus' scouts and landed further west. He hurried to meet the men disembarked from the fleet of which he *was* aware, but the other contingent outflanked him and he was killed in battle. Constantius then arrived in London and set about restoring the provincial organisation, in the process striking a very fine gold medallion to mark the occasion.

We do not know Allectus's other names, for no inaugural minting of coins has turned up, which, as tradition tended to demand, usually incorporated the ruler's full imperial style.[20] Neither do we know anything of his origins, although if he had been British, it is likely his name might have lived on in the legends and genealogies deriving from post-Roman British literature, as even Carausius's did. We do know that he rose to become Carausius's chief ally and his *rationalis summa rei* (chief financial officer).

AMANDUS
286

In the period of transition from the rule of Carus to that of Diocletian, and with Julianus (II) active in northern Italy, an outbreak of anarchy took place in Gaul led by a man called Amandus and supported by one Aelianus. They were allegedly *bagaudae* or brigands, a phenomenon of late Roman provincial life whenever government was in dispute or weakened in some way. In this case, so entrenched had they become by 286 that Amandus began styling himself Augustus and issuing coins, albeit with rather clumsy legends, like *Imp. C. C. Amandus P. F. Aug.* and *Imp. S. Amandus P. F. Aug.*, from which we might reasonably conclude that his full name may have been something like C. S[ ] Amandus.[21] He was, however, quickly suppressed by Maximian. In later hagiographies he is alleged to have been a Christian.[22]

---

18 Casey (1994) 127, 134
19 PLRE I Asclepiodotus 3. He was consul in 292
20 PLRE I Allectus
21 PLRE Aelianus 1 & Amandus 1. Some older sources credit him with the *nomen* Silvius, for which there is no proof.
22 Abbot Babolenus in Duchesne, *Rerum Franciarum* i., 662

ANASTASIUS I
491, 11ᵗʰ April – 518, 9ᵗʰ July

Anastasius was an emperor who, although in late middle age on his elevation, ushered in a period of stability and consolidation during his unexpectedly long reign of 27 years. He was personally selected by Ariadne, the widow and dowager empress of the emperor Zeno and proclaimed in the senate on 11ᵗʰ April. At the death of Zeno there was a power vacuum, as so often happened in the fifth century, for the old emperor was childless, having previously lost both of his known sons, Leo II and Zeno, leaving his Empress as regent, surrounded by men with good claims to rule, either from close kinship with previous ruling families, ancient nobility or military merit, all of whom she ignored, instead choosing Anastasius, a man not even of senatorial rank, but one whom she felt she would be better able to control.

Anastasius was born in 430 in Dyrrhacium (Durazzo, Albania) and was of a rather heterodox family, his uncle having been an Arian, his mother a Manichaean and having been himself a Monophysite. His father's name is not known, but Alan Cameron has plausibly suggested it was Pompeius, especially in view of its recurrence amongst his descendants.[23] It is likely that the family were in some way influenced by the sojourn of the Goths in the area (who were Arians) although most of his nephews and nieces were Chalcedonians: this in an era in which such things mattered a great deal. His mother's Manichaeanism – a dualistic belief in which the world is considered inherently evil and that access to special knowledge (*gnosis*) was required to access spiritual good – suggests that she may have come from the east, where these beliefs had originated and at one time had seemed likely to challenge Christianity as the displacer of paganism in the Empire. The result was that the new emperor was not an Orthodox, or Chalcedonian Christian, but a Monophysite, a heresy much favoured in the regions of the Empire nearest to Persia. He was keenly interested in religion and at one point had been suggested as Bishop of Antioch. He had also fallen foul of the Patriarch of Constantinople by offering classes in his beliefs.

He managed to join the Imperial court as one of the corps of ushers, the *silentiarii*, who were only some thirty in number and were the officials who enabled the court to function smoothly. He presumably had a family member or patron who enabled him to make this career move, for the corps carried great prestige and by 491 he was one of the three *decuriones* or officers in overall charge and was thus ranked as a *vir spectabilis*. He was nicknamed Dicorus, because the pupils of his eyes were of different colours (blue and black). At 61, he was getting on in years, so was probably thought of as a stop-gap candidate for the purple.

He took the style Dominus Noster Flavius Anastasius Pater Patriae Augustus and he held his first consulship in 492, followed by two further consulships in 497 and 507. On 20 May his rule was further secured by his marriage to the Empress Ariadne, being crowned by the patriarch after

---

23 Cameron (1978) 259-260

having been obliged to sign a declaration that he would reign as an Orthodox Christian.[24]

His first act thereafter was to neutralise opposition. The only serious threat to his rule was the late Emperor's brother Longinus, who, despite being described as 'stupid, arrogant and licentious', enjoyed high esteem amongst his fellow senators and had the support of his namesake, the Isaurian *magister officiorum*, also Longinus (of Cardala). He was promptly exiled, but in their accounts of what happened next, contemporary accounts diverge. That he was merely exiled to southern Egypt and there starved to death seems inherently unlikely. Another account merely labels him as an Isaurian rebel whom the Emperor captured, which implies that Longinus of Cardala was really intended. As his chief cheerleader, the latter indeed immediately rebelled, but as he was nowhere said to have proclaimed himself emperor, one is inclined to favour the account of Zonaras which states that it was Zeno's brother who had proclaimed himself emperor, but who was soon captured at the Battle of Cotyaeum in Phrygia and then exiled to Alexandria, ordained and died in 499. There is, however, little other evidence to support this narrative.[25] The Isaurian revolt continued without him and was not completely extinguished until 498.

Anastasius, having successfully moved the tiresome Ostrogoths on to Italy in 490, found their place taken by the Bulgars (often referred to as Huns in contemporary chronicles) who raided across the Danube from about three years later. The potential and actual destruction they caused prompted the emperor to order the construction of a defensive work to protect the capital from the Propontis to the Black Sea, called the Long Walls and the strengthening of the existing Danube forts. The Persians, under a new king, Cavades I (488-531) finally broke the long peace between the two empires and this led to a war from 502 to 506, from which the Romans emerged generally with the advantage, leading to a new treaty between the two. In the west, Theoderic was recognised as king of Italy at the third attempt in 497, though Anastasius subsequently fell out with him in 505-510 over which of them controlled Pannonia.

Macedonius, Patriarch of Constantinople, was in 511 replaced by a Monophysite on the Emperor's orders, which provoked riots in Constantinople and the revolt of the *magister militum* in Thrace, Vitalianus, who used his army in an attempt to force the religious orthodoxy of the Council of Chalcedon upon the emperor. Negotiations, which involved the Pope, eventually collapsed and Vitalianus was defeated in Thrace in 515, in the wake of which he went on the run (his rebelliousness was to recur again during the following reign). An attempt to replace the Patriarch of Jerusalem with a Monophysite in 516 also provoked riots, but again the Emperor backed down.

Although Anastasius was well known to be careful with his money, on accession he nevertheless remitted two burdensome and unpopular taxes,

---

24 PLRE II Anastasius 4
25 *Op.cit.* 14, 3.20

applied stringency to the imperial finances and improved efficiency in tax collection, with long term beneficial effects, although specific acts of parsimony occasionally led him into difficulties. In 494 he also reformed the coinage, including an increase the availability of bronze, previously in short supply. By the time of his death from natural causes in 518 aged 88 the treasury had a surplus of 320,000 lbs. of gold.

According to the panegyrics composed by the poets Christodorus and Priscianus, the family were alleged to descend from Pompey which would have made him kin to Marcus Aurelius, but this is universally doubted and probably arose from the use of the name Pompeius by the family.[26] Other equally dubious sources suggest that his mother was called (Anastasia) Constantina and that her family descended from Constantius Gallus via an unattested daughter called Anastasia. Anastasius had no children by the Empress Ariadne (who was past child bearing age when they married), but an illegitimate son was killed in a theatre riot in 501.[27] Yet there were plenty of suitable heirs by the time the emperor died in 518 and they had acquired positions at the heart of government and in the highest echelons of the nobility, for Anastasius' brother Paullus married a senatorial *grande dame* called Magna, quite possibly an otherwise unattested daughter of the Emperor Olybrius. The frequency in which the names Magna/Magnus, Proba/Probus and the Placidia/Placidus occur amongst her descendants seems to confirm this, not to mention a probable descent from Theodosius I through Olybrius' wife. (The reign of the emperor Anastasius II, 713-715, lies beyond the parameters of this book.)

ANTHEMIUS
467, 12th April – 472, 11th July

Anthemius was a blue-blooded and patrician eastern Roman, a descendant of the Procopius who had attempted to usurp the throne of Valens in 367. One of a succession of perfectly sound senior high-ranking commanders who emerged to attempt to stem the collapse of the western empire, Anthemius was appointed because on the death of Severus III, the barbarian master of the soldiers Ricimer remained in power in the west but could not function without an emperor in whose name he could act. As with Majorian, Anthemius' eventual failure was down to his having been unable to impose his authority on his barbarian commander, who ultimately discarded him.

On Severus's death, the Vandal king in Africa, Gaiseric, pressed the case for his brother-in-law Olybrius (qv) to be sent to take over by Eastern Emperor Leo I, which presented a problem for the eastern court, for denying him was inevitably going to lead to further raids by Gaiseric on the coasts and hence the supply lines of Italy, whilst imposing Olybrius would risk civil war in Italy. In the end, Leo I decided to endorse Anthemius in spring 467.

26 Cameron (1978) 259-260
27 *Ibid.*, 271 n. 31

The new Western Emperor was the son of the *magister militum* Procopius and was married to Aelia Marcia Euphemia, the daughter and heiress of the late Eastern Emperor, Marcian. Unusually for a high noble, Anthemius had made his career in the army, and by 453 his father-in-law had appointed him *comes rei militaris*, serving on the Danubian frontier. He did a sound job restoring the defences there and on his return in 454 he was promoted to *magister utriusque militum* (commander-in-chief), which post he held until made Western Emperor. He had been Eastern consul in 455, sharing with the Western Emperor Valentinian III. It would have been expected that the husband of the emperor's only daughter would had succeeded seamlessly to the eastern throne on the death of Marcian, but in fact it was said that his reluctance and the opposition of his rival and fellow *magister utriusque militum*, Flavius Ardaburius Aspar, led to the elevation of Leo I as a unity candidate and under whom Anthemius continued to serve, distinguishing himself against the Ostrogoths and then the Huns.[28]

He arrived in Italy by sea with an army and was formally proclaimed on 12 April. The only thing against him was that the Empire had been divided for almost a century and people saw him as a foreigner, calling him *Graeculus* (Greekling). Once arrived in Rome, however, he was invested with the insignia of office, granted the usual powers by the senate and took the style of Dominus Noster Procopius Anthemius Pius Felix Perpetuus Augustus.[29] His wife, who seems to have died shortly after he came to power, was made Augusta.[30] He served a second consulship in 468, followed by his son Marcianus the following year with the future Eastern Emperor Zeno as colleague.[31]

The first development was that Ricimer married the emperor's daughter Alypia, presumably to cement their working relationship. The intention of the entire set up from the point of view of Leo was that with an experienced general as emperor, allied to a ferocious and capable barbarian C-in-C, the war could be taken to the Vandals in Africa so that the running sore of Gaiseric and his raids could be ended. In fact, Anthemius had to fight on two fronts, for his direct hold on Gaul was by this time confined to the Rhône valley and the Auvergne, and the Visigothic king there was the able and determinedly anti-Roman Euric. He reckoned that with the constant changes of emperor, the West would be a pushover, and he was not far off the mark. Anthemius and Ricimer had to neutralise Euric before they could risk moving against Gaiseric.

Twice Anthemius campaigned against Euric, twice gained little or nothing, and in the process lost his son Anthemiolus, killed in action. A following attempt to re-conquer Africa was also a complete failure and inevitably Emperor and patrician fell out, attempts at reconciliation being on the whole fruitless. The last of these attempts was negotiated by the distinguished senator,

---

28 PLRE II Anthemius 3

29 ILS 812, 815 and coin issues, only one of which, uniquely, gives his name as Procop[ius] Anthemius.

30 Coin evidence only.

31 The son Marcianus received a second consulship from his father in 472, this time as eastern nominee.

exiled to Constantinople, Olybrius, brother-in-law of the Vandal ruler. This, too, broke down, resulting in Ricimer proclaiming the mediator emperor, in opposition to his own father-in-law in April 472, and laying siege to Rome for five months, finally entering the City on July 11, at which point Anthemius was killed, according to John of Antioch, in cold blood by Ricimer's nephew, Gundobad, King of the Burgundians. Despite the catastrophic end to his reign, however, it would be unfair to describe Anthemius as Ricimer's puppet. The emperor was a distinguished and competent commander, nominated by Leo, not by the western patrician, and by no means beholden to him. His problem was that neither he nor Ricimer, both experienced soldiers, no longer had the resources (despite the Emperor's eastern detachments) to overcome successfully either Euric or Gaiseric. It was only ever going to end in tears.

ANTIOCHUS
273, February/March – April/May

An ephemeral usurper in the east, probably representing an attempt to revive the influence of Palmyra following the fall of Zenobia. Early in 273, whilst Aurelian was dealing with an uprising amongst the Carpi in the Balkans, Marcellinus, his overlord in the East, appointed to damp things down after the collapse of the Palmyrene empire, was approached by a delegation of powerful Palmyrans led by one Apsaeus, who urged him to assume the purple. Being no fool, he was non-committal and played for time, allowing him to send word of what was afoot to the emperor. However, in the interval, being tired of waiting for his decision, Apsaeus and his *confrères* acclaimed one of their own, Antiochus, as emperor, a man generally thought to have probably been the father of Zenobia (qv).[32]

In the event, Aurelian managed to break off his campaign against the Carpi, return to Antioch rather more rapidly than the insurgents might have anticipated and, within a couple of months, Palmyra was re-taken and the uprising ended. No coins are known, ever a sign of a short-lived regime. Zosimus records that Antiochus was spared because the emperor 'considered him unimportant'.[33] Despite the *Historia Augusta* recording that the city was razed, archaeology tells us that no such thing happened and that it continued to flourish for another three centuries before decline set in.

ANTONINUS (I) PIUS
138, 10th July – 161, 7th March

Antoninus Pius was a ruler generally regarded as a paragon amongst Roman emperors, as the ideal of the enlightened ruler. Indeed, even in his own time he was sufficiently admired, alongside his successor Marcus Aurelius, to be held up as a yardstick against which all who followed him were compared (and

---

32 Southern (2008) 44, 152-153
33 Zosimus 1, 61. 1

inevitably found wanting). Antoninus attempted to rule by consent, reformed further aspects of Roman law and even in the reign's two treason trials, made sure that the proceedings were unbiased and beyond criticism; nor on either occasion did he encourage a witch hunt for co-conspirators, real or imagined. Under Antoninus, the empire was ruled in quite the opposite way to the peripatetic and restless fashion adopted by Hadrian, for Antoninus remained in or near Rome throughout his long reign. He was, in short, the ultimate delegator of authority, a sign of supreme confidence in any ruler in any era.

Antoninus was chosen, it would appear, to hold the stage pending the majority of the two men chosen by Hadrian to succeed him ultimately, the future Marcus Aurelius and Lucius Verus. Such a role would have adversely affected many men, coloured his decisions or even inspired him to diverge from Hadrian's intentions altogether, but not Antoninus. The only fly in the ointment regarding the succession sprang from the senate's extreme reluctance to vote divine honours for Hadrian which, out of filial piety, Antoninus was insistent about, if only to maintain the legitimacy of his own position and the respect he felt was essential to the office of *princeps*. A perceptive and moving speech from the Emperor, a fine orator in any case, swayed the chamber and the vote was passed; hence, probably the addition of Pius to his name in 139, the year in which he served his second consulship and was granted the title *pater patriae* by the senate.[34] On accession, he assumed the role of *pontifex maximus*, was acclaimed *imperator* for the first time and was granted the tribunician and proconsular power. A third consulate followed in 140 and a fourth and final one in 145, eighteen months after his second imperial acclamation, in recognition of the end of a successful campaign in Britain. In 150-151 he briefly added the name 'Hadrianus' after 'Aelius' in his style, moving the name 'Caesar' to precede his *praenomen*, as illustrated on various coin issues of the period.

The Aurelii Fulvi came, on the authority of the *Historia Augusta*, supported by other evidence, from Nemausus (Nîmes), in the province of Gallia Narbonensis. They will have been descended from Roman or enfranchised Latin traders – *negotiatores* – who first settled there, keen for a quick profit in the years following the defeat of Hannibal. The future emperor was born T. Aurelius Fulvus Boionius Arrius Antoninus at Lanuvium on 19 September 86 and inherited an Etruscan estate at Lorium, where he spent as much time as he could throughout his life.[35] There is no evidence of service in the army as a junior officer, and he entered the senate with a quaestorship, but as his family had been made patricians he could avoid serving as either aedile or peoples' tribune and, after a praetorship, was made ordinary consul in 120, confirming that even then, Hadrian must have held him in high esteem. He governed Asia in 135-136, and by that time he had married Annia Galeria Faustina ('the elder'),

---

34 Conceivably, the 'Pius' name was already in the family, for there was an ex-quaestor called Aurelius Pius recorded near the start of Tiberius' reign who could easily have been an ancestor [Tac. *Ann.* I 75] There is no reason why the Tiberian ex-quaestor could not have been from Nemausus, too; he would have been a near contemporary of D. Valerius Asiaticus (suffect consul in AD35 and ordinary consul in 46), generally regarded as having been the first well-attested Gallic consul.

35 PIR² A1513

daughter of thrice ex-consul M. Annius Verus, by Rupilia, daughter of Libo Rupilius Frugi – a likely descendant of Crassus, Pompey and Augustus' kin, the Scribonii Libones – and Vitellius's daughter Galeria Fundana.[36] She died in autumn 140 and was deified. He was adopted by Hadrian on 25 February 136, and the same day himself adopted his nephew M. Annius Verus (later Marcus Aurelius) and L. Ceionius Commodus (later styled Lucius Verus). He was henceforth styled Imperator T. Aelius Caesar Antoninus[37] and succeeded Hadrian on 10 July 138, when he added the name Augustus.

For almost a quarter of a century he reigned self-effacingly, with admirable restraint and enormous dedication. His period wearing the purple was perhaps a favourable one in any case, being relatively free of threats within or from outside the empire, and it could be argued that he flourished in the afterglow of the brilliant military achievements of his two eminent predecessors.

The succession of his two adoptive sons was eventually made less perilous, for all Antoninus's children had died young except for his daughter Faustina, whom he married off to his successor Marcus at the earliest opportunity. As regards external threats, there was plenty of warfare. Southern Scotland was won, probably on the back of a suppressed revolt, and wars were fought in Mauretania, Germany and Dacia. Not only that, but revolts of varying seriousness erupted in Egypt, Greece and even in recently pacified Judaea. Nevertheless, such was Roman prestige after generations of military success, that diplomacy, often as not, was all that was required to achieve a favourable outcome.

Antoninus died at Lorium on 7 March 161, untroubled by any successor problems. His predecessor's scheme of things moved well-oiled into its second phase and he was succeeded by his two adopted sons, having formally delegated power to Marcus during his brief last illness, thus ensuring the primacy of the more competent of the pair without wounding Lucius' *amour propre*.

ANTONINUS (II) see CARACALLA

ANTONINUS (III) see ELAGABALUS

ANTONINUS (IV) see URANIUS ANTONINUS

ANTONINUS (V)
260/262

An Antoninus is mentioned by Zosimus[38] as an usurper at the same time as Memor and Aureolus, but probably he has confused this figure with Uranius Antoninus (qv). Otherwise, location, career, family and fate are totally obscure.[39]

---

36 Birley (1987) 243

37 ILS 331

38 Zosimus, *loc. cit.*

39 PIR² A790; PLRE I. Antoninus 1. HA *Tyr. Trig.* 29 also inserts a fictitious claimant here, **Celsus**.

ARCADIUS
383, 9ᵗʰ January – 408, 1st May

Arcadius was the first in a long line of child emperors that rather defined the late fourth and early fifth centuries. The reason for his elevation was essentially to enable his father Theodosius to signal that he had an heir; it may also have been done as a warning shot across the bows of Magnus Maximus, a kinsman, who was either in the process of declaring himself emperor in Britain or was expected to do so. Subsequently, he reigned as more of a figurehead than any predecessor.

The lad was thus raised to the rank of co-emperor with his father Theodosius I aged just six, although he did not begin actually to rule until he was almost 18. Arcadius succeeded to the eastern empire according to the arrangements devised by his father on his death on 17 January 395. In the meantime, he had been educated by the elderly philosopher and senator Themistius and a monk called Arsenius.[40] Arcadius took the imperial style Imperator Caesar Dominus Noster Flavius Arcadius Perpetuus Augustus.[41] He had held his first consulship in 385, almost two years after having been made co-emperor, and then he served again in 392, 394, 396, and 402.

The new emperor was short and swarthy, indolent and of no great intellect, which left a more than usually extensive power vacuum. Just as Stilicho stepped into the role of unofficial regent in the west, so in the east, Arcadius found support from the dubious abilities of Flavius Rufinus, a Gaul who had been his father's *magister officiorum* (chief minister) and who had been made Pretorian Prefect of the entire Eastern Empire by Theodosius in 392. Although accused of corruption and indeed treason at intervals throughout his tenure, his administration was generally sound. His ambition expressed itself in that he plotted to betroth his daughter to the emperor. However, this was thwarted by his enemy, the elderly eunuch Eutropius, who was *praepositus sacri cubicula* (chief chamberlain of the household).

When Alaric took advantage of the death of Theodosius to ravage Greece, Macedonia and Thrace, Rufinus went without a bodyguard to try and bargain with the Gothic ruler but became alarmed when a western army under Stilicho (who was speciously claiming to have been appointed as guardian of *both* young emperors) appeared, to aid him in repelling the Visigoths. Whilst away from the capital, Eutropius found a beautiful young woman of part barbarian extraction and married her to Arcadius on 27 April 395. This was Aelia Eudoxia, daughter of Bauto, a retired Frankish general who had held the consulship with the young Arcadius in 385. This put Rufinus's nose seriously out of joint, and precipitated his fall; in withdrawing from Thrace, Stilicho had persuaded Rufinus's general Gaïnas to lead the army of the East back to Constantinople and then kill Rufinus, which he duly did on 27 November, in the emperor's presence: hardly an auspicious start to the reign.

---

40 PLRE I Arcadius 5
41 ILS797: *imp.caes.*, 793, 794: *perp aug.* & 795: Flavius Arcadius.

The Eastern government, however, was thereafter undertaken by a triumvirate of Gaïnas, the empress and Eutropius, an alliance stabilised by mutual loathing. Matters came to a head during a rebellion by Gothic settlers in Phrygia (Asia Minor) which Gaïnas used to bring about the fall of the all-powerful eunuch (with the Empress's connivance) in 399. The following year, he over-reached himself in trying to grasp supreme power and rule through a weak emperor and, in staging a *coup,* failed to anticipate the mood of the Constantinopolitan populace, who were fed up with barbarian soldiers all over the place; he was heavily rebuffed. Escaping to the North, he fell in with the Huns, who despatched him and, as a gesture of goodwill, sent his head to the emperor.

The fall of Gaïnas resulted in the Emperor granting the beautiful Eudoxia the style of Augusta (400), but she was never popular and was not trusted by the church, sentiments expressed by the forthright St. John Chrysostom, who called her a Jezebel, and a loose woman. She died on 6 October 404 in childbirth. The religious friction stirred up by Chrysostom was made worse by the hostility and indifference of Arcadius himself, who became particularly unhelpful when the Pope and his brother Honorius sent a delegation from Rome to mediate. They were treated badly and sent back. It was this that persuaded the ever-ambitious Stilicho to declare war on the East in 406, only to have his invasion thwarted by lack of resources, the irruption of barbarian tribes across the Rhine on New Year's Eve that year, and the appearance of three usurpers in Britain. This was just as well, for Arcadius died unexpectedly on 1 May 408.

ATTALUS
409, November – 410, May/June
414 – 415, June

Attalus was essentially a career non-entity, imposed as a puppet emperor upon Italy by the Gothic warlord Alaric. He was notable for remarkably little except that, having fulfilled his purpose in 410, was put back in his box by Alaric for future use and duly re-elevated by him in 414 when it again suited the Gothic leader, but the second occasion ended the hapless usurper's career.

Priscus Attalus was a senior and very distinguished pagan senator whose family had originally come from Greece. He was born c. 360/365, and late in the reign of Theodosius I had served as a provincial governor, for he held the rank of *vir spectabilis* according to his first surviving letter from the senator Symmachus in 394. Four years later he was one of a deputation from the senate to Honorius and fulfilled the same role again in 409 after the first siege of Rome by Alaric. As a result, he was appointed *comes sacrarum largitionum* (chief finance minister) for the western Empire, but about six months later was moved to be prefect of the City of Rome. It was whilst he was in this office that the second siege of Rome began and he was singled out by Alaric to be his puppet emperor late in the year, probably in November. Attalus was extremely wealthy and had estates in Greece as well as a villa at Tibur (Tivoli) and a town house on the Mons Caelius at Rome.[42] There

---

42 PLRE II Attalus 2

is no mention of a wife, so she probably had died or divorced prior to her husband's accession.

As emperor, Attalus was first of all baptised a Christian, although by an Arian Gothic bishop, for most of the migrating tribes which came into the Empire at this period, if they were Christian at all, were of the heretical Arian persuasion. Attalus assumed the rather obsolete style Imp[erator] Priscus Attalus P[ius] F[elix] Aug[ustus] on his coins. One might have assumed that he would have become consul on the next available opportunity, but the western consul in 410 was Tertullus, who was probably a son or brother. This was recognised neither by Honorius at Ravenna nor Constantinople, although no alternative western consul seems to have been appointed. He was acclaimed by the senate (at the command of Alaric), to which he delivered a long and elaborate discourse, and may even have been formally accorded the tribunician and proconsular powers at the same time. One issue of his coins bears the reverse legend *Invicta Roma Aeterna* (Eternal Unconquered Rome) which seems gloriously ironic when one bears in mind that some time after the issue was minted, Alaric sacked the city, even though he pulled his punches, for the more lurid accounts of the incident are all by later Christian writers with an axe to grind. Attalus made some appointments, notably Alaric, who became *magister militum*, a position which he had asked Honorius to grant him but which had been denied, precipitating the sack, during which the princess Galla Placidia was taken hostage. Attalus then sent Alaric to take control of northern Italy and to invest Ravenna, which, coming at a critical period in the affairs of Honorius, forced a recognition of Attalus as co-Augustus.[43] Meanwhile, measures were set in train to secure Africa. In this, the Gothic king believed his emperor was dragging his feet. His disaffection drove him to re-open negotiations with Honorius with the result that in summer 410 Attalus was deposed, although (most unusually) he came to no harm. However, as an Arian who had presided over the sack of Rome as Alaric's creature, he could hardly return home, so remained with the Visigoths, even after their king had died and been succeeded by his brother-in-law Athaulf.

After having supported Jovinus and Sebastianus and subsequently betrayed them, Athaulf remained in Gaul campaigning for Honorius against the Vandals, but in summer 414 after a squabble with the emperor over his unauthorised marriage to Galla Placidia, he once again elevated Attalus to the purple, on this occasion without the prospect of recognition as co-ruler. However, when the Goths retreated into Spain in 415, they abandoned poor Attalus (but not Galla Placidia), leaving him to fall into the hands of the imperial government. He was deposed, mutilated (thumb and forefinger of his right hand only – he was let off rather lightly) and led in a rather empty triumph celebrated by Honorius over Athaulf in June 416 (probably on the first anniversary of Attalus' second deposition) before being exiled to the Lipari Islands, after which no more is heard of him.

---

43 He retains his status as an usurper not because his recognition in 410 was fleeting but because his second reign was completely un-recognised.

AUGUSTUS
27BC–14, 19ᵗʰ August

Augustus was the first in the accepted canon of Roman emperors and in him the transition of Rome from a creaking and overburdened Republican form of government to a form of monarchy was achieved. Augustus was the style settled on Julius Caesar's nephew and heir in 27, when he had finally triumphed over his rivals for power and had established himself. He was to remain in control for forty-one years and his lengthy time in power allowed a new form of governance of the state to emerge relatively gradually. It also encompassed enormous changes throughout the empire, including a measure of expansion.

C. Julius Caesar Octavianus had finally emerged the single most powerful person in Rome after the Battle of Actium, fought on 2 September 31, although it took another four years for him successfully to formulate the way in which he intended to govern the huge empire, so much expanded by both himself and his adoptive father.

Officially styled Imperator Caesar Divi f. Augustus from 27, he was of patrician rank by adoption and prior to that had also been so by Caesar's creation. He came from a family newly risen into the senate from provincial opulence, although it was claimed, no doubt on the instigation of the first *Princeps* himself, that they were a branch of the ancient plebeian senatorial house of the Octavii, an assertion sufficiently current for Suetonius to transmit it as truth.[44] Cn. Octavius, a supposed brother of the praetor of 205BC, served as a military tribune against Hannibal and was the claimed ancestor of Augustus. What makes the connection unlikely was that the senatorial Octavii were in the Aemilian tribe, whereas Augustus' forebears were in the Scaptia.[45]

Augustus himself was born at Rome 23 September 63BC as C. Octavius C. f. C. n. Scapt., but was testamentarily adopted on 8 May 44 by Julius Caesar as C. Julius C. f. C. n. Caesar Octavianus, thus retaining his original identity through the use of the adjectival form of his original name being added to his new identity.

He was granted pro-praetorian *imperium* in January 43 by the senate. After the formation of the Second Triumvirate with Mark Antony and M. Aemilius Lepidus and the deification of his adoptive father in January 42, he changed his style to C. Julius Caesar Divi f. Imperator, having been hailed as *imperator* (*generalissimo*) for the first time by his troops the year before. In 40, purely for propaganda reasons, he further modified it – this time in a totally innovative way with no precedent, legal or otherwise – to Imperator Caesar Divi f., which effectively set the standard of address for most subsequent rulers of the Roman world until the fourth century AD.

At the time of the first constitutional re-ordering of 27BC, designed to confirm him totally in power but to provide a simulacrum of a return to

---

44 *Divus Augustus* 2
45 Taylor (1960) 271, 275

normal (Republican) government, he assumed the style – granted by the senate on 16 January – by which he was known subsequently. He was granted the power of a tribune of the people (but not the actual rank, for, as a patrician, he was ineligible to hold it) for one year – effectively making him a supernumerary tribune – on 26 June 23, renewable yearly thereafter – the basis of his effective power and that of his successors; this enabled him to relinquish holding yearly consulships – he had been consul in 43 and 33 already, and thereafter was consul successively from 31 to 23 – in order to retain complete control.[46] By his death, he had been consul thirteen times, adding additional occasions in 5 and 2BC. He became *pontifex maximus* on the death of the ex-triumvir Lepidus (who had been elected to succeed Caesar) in 12BC and was hailed as *imperator* another twenty times.[47] In 2BC the senate conferred the title *Pater Patriae* ('father of the country') upon him.

The achievements of the first Emperor's reign are such as to defy the cleverest precis. It is possible to apply a whole variety of adjectives to sum up his talents and elusive personality, but he always seems to escape easy categorisation. Sir Ronald Syme was not an admirer, although others accord him praise and endow it with a cohesion which lasted nearly one and a half thousand years. He was certainly a far more astute politician than his uncle but a much less able commander. His achievement was to weld the empire together, to make sense of all is parts.

His mastery of propaganda and his elevation of Rome into a worthy imperial capital lent focus. Early consolidation in Spain and the East was followed by dramatic conquests in the Balkans and on the Danube, although a clear objective in extending Imperial rule from the Rhine to the Elbe received a fatal set-back – despite ringing successes beforehand and afterwards – through the defeat and virtual annihilation in 9AD of three legions under P. Qunictilius Varus in the *Teutoberger Wald* not very far from Osnabrück in Germany.

Augustus married Clodia in late 44BC (whom he divorced less than four years later), daughter of the patrician-turned people's tribune Publius Clodius and Fulvia, who had re-married Mark Antony, but they had had no issue (the marriage was probably not consummated) before Augustus made a second and very brief political marriage in 40 to Scribonia, daughter of L. Scribonius Libo, an equestrian banker who, unlike Augustus's grandfather, was of genuine senatorial descent. Her brother, however, had entered the senate, rising to consul in 34BC, despite politically perilous early alliances with Pompey and then with his freebooter second son, Sextus. Scribonia had been married twice before, her descendants constituting a body of imperial 'connections' – people not close enough to be regarded as part of what we have to call the Imperial family, but close enough to have imperial domestic and political issues affect them. These husbands were first, Cn. Cornelius Lentulus Marcellinus, one of the consuls for 56BC – the son of a Claudius Marcellus adopted into the patrician house of the Lentuli – and second,

---

46 But note that in 43 he was only a suffect (additional) consul.
47 PIR² I 215

P. Cornelius [Scipio], almost certainly the obscure member of the once great patrician clan of the Scipiones, who was suffect consul in 35BC.

In January 38BC, Augustus married for the third time, to Livia Drusilla, previously wife of the patrician Ti. Claudius Nero, *praetor* in 42BC, a supporter of the Republic who had ended up siding with Antonius before returning to Rome in 39. It was, apparently, a love match, but was politically advantageous as well. Livia was born in 58, daughter of M. Livius Drusus Claudianus, *praetor* in 50BC and the son of C. Claudius Pulcher (consul in 92BC) but adopted by the popularist tribune of 91, M. Livius Drusus, a member of an old plebeian family boasting their first magistracy as far back as 323.[48]

Although absent from most accounts, Livia would seem to have had a brother, and thus yet another connection to trouble Augustus' suspicious advisers, like the equestrian fixers C. Maecenas and M. Agrippa. His existence is only implied by the scattered inscriptions of daughters, but C. Livius Drusus must have been a senator under the triumvirate, unless proscribed or killed in battle immediately after Caesar's assassination. His daughters were: Livia C. f. Pulchra – her *cognomen* clearly emphasising her descent from Claudius Pulcher the consul – and Livia C. f. Livilla.[49]

Livia Drusilla was pregnant with their second son, Drusus Claudius Nero, when Augustus married her, yet the marriage was long lasting and successful. A defining element in Livia's life was to line her elder son up as Augustus' chosen successor, to which end her hand was discerned by the cynical in the early demise of M. Claudius Marcellus, Agrippa's sons by Augustus's daughter Julia (Caius and Lucius Caesar) and the exile of the latter's youngest brother Agrippa Postumus. Whether or not the scheming mistress of intrigue she is often portrayed – the evidence is equivocal – she was a constant support for Augustus and the source of much advice, sound or otherwise. She died without having further issue in AD29 aged 86.

Apart from various conspiracies and scandals, the Emperor's last years were marred by shadowy conspiracies, largely hushed up and inadequately disinterred by contemporary chroniclers. The most significant took place in 6/7AD and centred around distinguished grandee L. Aemilius Paulus. This coincided with the relegation from public life and exile of an obvious heir, Agrippa Postumus (qv), the youngest brother of C. and L. Caesar, both of whom had already died unmarried. He was accused of being an unstable character and generally irresponsible, but there was clearly a move to thrust him forward as the true successor at the expense of Livia's elder son Tiberius Claudius Nero. Furthermore, Postumus was not the only person exiled, for Julia the younger, the grand-daughter of Augustus, was also packed off to an island, allegedly for immorality and adultery, just as her mother had been nine years before. She is supposed to have had a child by senator D. Junius Silanus, and may even have married, suggesting, if true, that her husband,

---

48 M. Livius (C. f. Drusus), *magister equitum* that year; *cognomen* possibly applied
   retrospectively, see *Fasti Hydatii* & CIL.I²/130; on Livia herself, see PIR². L 301
49 AE (1969/70) 118, from Formiae and CIL.XIV.3796 from Tibur

By the time of Augustus' death in 14, the Roman Empire was more or less complete. Most of the Empire was created under the Republic.

L. Aemilius Paullus was by then dead, which he was not.[50] The result was that the emperor's stepson Tiberius was brought back into the mainstream in AD12, commended to the senate as senior senator (*princeps senatus*), given full powers by the senate and people and generally made subject of a declaration of succession.[51] By the time the old Emperor died at Nola on 19 August 14, his position was apparently unassailable, but it was less so than supposed.

The descendants of Augustus himself via Julia, his only child and through adopted close relatives were relatively numerous, but almost all had died or been murdered by the reign of Vespasian, having been seen or perceived as the potential focus of plots against various members of the wider family of Augustus reigning after him. Sir Ronald Syme makes a telling distinction here regarding the legacy of Caesar:

> That was all he [Augustus] affected to inherit from Caesar, the halo. The god was useful, but not the dictator: Augustus was careful sharply to discriminate between *dictator* and *princeps*. Under his rule Caesar the dictator was either suppressed outright or called up from time to time to enhance the contrast between the unscrupulous adventurer who destroyed the Free State in his ambition and the modest magistrate who restored the Republic.[52]

Thereafter he ruled essentially with his close friend and brother-in-law M Vipsanius Agrippa, until the General's death in 12BC.[53] The problems Augustus faced thereafter included a longing amongst the senators, despite fairly radical reform of the membership of that body, for a return to 'true' Republican government and the persistence of various factions inimical to him and to the network of familial and political alliances that he forged – and the succession.

The first manifested itself from time to time in plots, beginning with one in 30BC led by the elder son of Augustus' triumviral colleague, M. Aemilius Lepidus, followed by others led by Varro Murena and Egnatius Rufus. The factions set up tensions which tended to come to the fore at times of crisis, as when Augustus' daughter, Julia, was found to be the epicentre of a circle of adultery and treason in 2BC. They also coalesced around the men chosen by Augustus to succeed him.

Thus, the question of who should succeed Augustus was seen as crucial and became increasingly so, as each designated heir predeceased him. Nor did anyone really question the hereditary nature of this succession, such was the prestige of Caesar, despite frequent discussion amongst the senior senators

---

50 Pettinger (2012) 129-132: the child was probably covertly killed. Julia had even been adopted as his daughter by Augustus, *ibid.* 132 n. 36

51 *Ibid.*, 145, 151

52 Syme (1939) 53-54

53 Freudenberg (2014) 105-107

concerning the qualities of men they adjudged to be *capax imperii* – having the capacity to grasp and wield power.

The complex structure of the dynasty was dictated by the lack of male heirs and by the repeated attempts to bind to itself various individuals, singled out by the *Princeps* as current heir. That he had, in the end, to fall back on the stepson, Tiberius, whom he never really liked, indicated the Claudian element in the dynastic designation.

Yet public opinion was found to be insistent on the continuation of the principate at times of transition, when substantial groupings in the senate were seriously minded to try to restore Republican forms, as was especially apparent in 7 and again in 41AD with the murder of Caligula. The choice of the obscure and physically handicapped Claudius also reminded the senate that the family of the *princeps* still commanded prestige and a mystique too powerful to ignore, despite the perceived shortcomings of the surviving candidate. It took the vain incompetence of Nero to alienate them completely.

AURELIAN
270, September – 275, September/October

The emperor Aurelian seized power in the chaotic weeks following the unexpected death of Claudius II and the rather speculative succession of his brother Quintillus, whom Aurelian quickly deposed. He is widely regarded as one of the more successful rulers during the mid-third century, when the twin spectres of political and social instability stalked the empire. His achievements include the building of a new defensive wall around Rome, which now bears his name. He was a votary of the worship of the sun god Sol Invictus, which seems to have been dominant in his native Danubian homeland. His idea seems to have been to unite the other cults of the empire within the monotheistic umbrella of Sol. The fact that the old Republican dynasty of the Aurelii (to which he was totally unrelated) had some role in providing priests for a similar cult at Rome may have influenced him in this.[54]

Aurelian was recognised by the senate as Imperator Caesar L. Domitius Aurelianus Pius Felix Augustus, to which his military prowess was sufficient for him to add the title Invictus. He was confirmed as *pontifex maximus* and granted the tribunician power and the proconsular *imperium*. He assumed the consulship for 271 with a descendant of Marcus Aurelius, Ti. Pomponius Bassus Faustinus, no doubt as a gesture of his intention to co-operate with the senate as well as a nod to the shining example of the rule of Bassus' ancestor. He was consul again in 272 and 273.

Once invested with power, he had no time to stand still, however. He was immediately forced to deal with an incursion of the Iuthungi, a German people, intercepting them on their way back from a devastating raid into Italy. Not that his attentions were on this occasion sufficient, for he was forced to intercept a second invasion of Italy, suffering an initial defeat in the process but ultimately annihilating the raiders. In between, there was an

---

54 White (2005) 132

incursion of Vandals in Pannonia. Thereafter, instead of fire-fighting he was able to go on the offensive, re-organising the Danubian frontier before dealing with the Palmyrene Empire and thereafter the Gallic one. On the Danube he withdrew from the greater part of Dacia, re-creating the reduced province as Dacia Ripensis (Dacia Bankside) on the south of the river and incorporating parts on Moesia and Thrace. To keep the East quiet, papyri seem to indicate that by late 271 he had recognised Vaballathus of Palmyra as joint emperor, but this arrangement appears to have been overtaken by events by the end of August 272 when he was obliged to lead a force there himself in order to deal Vaballathus' mother, Zenobia, after which he had to make a hurried return to the Danube to destroy the Carpi, yet another barbarian grouping. Before this was complete, he had also to deal with the brief resurrection of the Palmyrene polity under Antiochus. The Gallic campaign flared up again, possibly under Faustinus as well as Domitian II. No wonder, then, that Aurelian had already been heaped with celebratory *agnomina*: Arabicus, Carpicus, Parthicus, Palmyricus, Gothicus, Dacicus (all followed by 'Maximus'), the last being bestowed after his seventh renewal of his tribunician power, probably early in 275.[55] His coins acknowledged him as *Restitutor Orbis*, 'the restorer of the world', amongst other laudatory epithets, most of which were, in truth, deserved.

It was widely reported that Aurelian was the preferred and indeed nominated successor of Claudius II and indeed Aurelian subsequently measured his reign from the death of his old colleague-in-arms. The Emperor's *nomen*, Domitius, suggests that his family had held the citizenship since before Caracalla's enfranchisement of the empire in 212, but beyond that little can be said of his origins. His wife, known from coins and an inscription, was Ulpia Severina (whose *nomen* probably gave the author of the *Historia Augusta* the idea to conjure up the entirely fictional senator Ulpius Crinitus), styled Augusta during her husband's reign and *diva* after it.[56] He apparently had a sister who married and had a son, whom Aurelian had killed for some unknown reason. The *Historia Augusta* includes this information, adding that the unfortunate young man also had a sister (who suffered a similar fate) and that there was another sister who left descendants, one of whom was Aurelianus, governor of Cilicia c. 300, but for none of which is there corroborative evidence.[57]

Aurelianus himself was apparently born in Moesia Superior[58] in humble circumstances on 9 December in or around 215. A full career is mapped out for him in the *Historia Augusta*, none of which can be taken at face value, especially a claimed suffect consulship under Valerian shared with the fictional Crinitus 'of the house of Trajan' (by whom he had allegedly been adopted) – quite an achievement for an equestrian officer.[59] Whatever his career before 268, he appears to have been one of the *junta* of senior equestrian officers

---

55 ILS 575, 576, 577, 579, 581, 582
56 PLRE I Severina 2; ILS 587
57 PLRE I Aurelianus 1; HA *V. Aur.* 42.1, cf. Eutropius ix.4.
58 Aurelius Victor, 35, 1. Eutropius says Dacia 'Ripensis', *op.cit.* 9, 13 but cf. Syme (1971) 210.
59 PLRE I Aurelianus 6; HA *V. Aur.* 10, 3, 14 & 38.4.

who encompassed the demise of Gallienus outside Mediolanum (Milan) that year. Yet even they are largely to be discounted; only the Praetorian Prefect Aurelius Heraclianus (who really did plan the assassination of Gallienus) can be identifed for with confidence.

There is confusion amongst the sources, but the death of Quintillus and elevation and recognition of Aurelian seems to have led to a rebellion in Rome. The spark appears to have been a decision by the new emperor to close the Rome mint prior to a re-organisation. The mint-master Felicissimus seems to have led a riot which escalated into a fully fledged revolt, the participants ending up fortifying the Caelian Hill, before being dealt with savagely. The fact that numerous senators were caught up in all this suggests that a pro-Quintillus faction may have been involved and that the matter arose at the beginning of the reign.[60] Having damped down the aftermath of the mint workers' rebellion, the emperor appointed a new mint master, C. Valerius Sabinus, and proceeded to improve the quality of the silver coinage, which had fallen from billon to base metal with only a 2% silver wash over each flan. This was boosted to 5% and the gold *aureus* was increased in weight to fifty per pound. The quality of the dies was also improved.

In 275, the Emperor went to Germany and then east to deal with the Persians, who were showing signs of restiveness after the defeat of Palmyra, which had long acted as a useful deterrent in the area. At Coenofrurium near Perinthus (later Heracleia, now Marmaraereğlisi) in Thrace in late September or early October 275 he was murdered by a faction of the Praetorian Guard at the instigation of his private secretary Eros, probably, like the demise of Gallic emperor Victorinus, as the result of a private quarrel rather than a planned change of regime. There was no obvious successor waiting in the wings, and a brief hiatus followed before the next emperor was identified and acclaimed. Once the succession had been resolved, Aurelianus was promptly deified by the senate, although one inscription suggests that he was briefly subject of a *damnatio memoriae*, perhaps as a consequence of the brutal suppression of Felicissimus' revolt.[61] Perhaps the empress held the line during the negotiations regarding a successor.

AUREOLUS
Autumn/Winter 267 – August/September 268

Aureolus was briefly acclaimed emperor in the midst of a minor civil war waged by a group of Danubian senior officers against Gallienus and possibly involving Gallic Emperor Postumus, too. Aureolus failed to issue any coins and seems to have been quickly suppressed. He did make his mark on history, but that was prior to his defection from Gallienus, whose right-hand man he had been.

---

60 Eutropius 9, 14, 1.
61 ILS 585

M'. Acilius Aureolus was Gallienus' lieutenant even from before Valerian's capture by the Persians in 260. Sir Ronald Syme, the supreme expert on the Danubian provinces, considered that he may well also have come from Dacia Ripensis.[62] With future emperors Claudius, Aurelian and Probus, he seems to have been one of a group of brothers-in-arms, all of Danubian origin and all officers in the élite mobile cavalry corps (*comitatenses*) created by Gallienus to act as the spearhead of a mobile, troubleshooting force based in Mediolanum (Milan), the perfect hub for reaching the likely hot-spots of the Rhine and Danubian frontiers. Aureolus was born c. 225 and is said to have been of humble birth, but his full name suggests that his father or an earlier ancestor was granted Roman citizenship by a member of the old Republican noble family of the Acilii Glabriones, members of which invariably used the archaic *praenomen* Manius (M'.). They were prominent throughout the Imperial period; although none are known from the relatively complete lists of Balkan governors in that period. Nothing further is known of his family.

Aureolus' career comes to notice in 260, when he defeated Ingenuus (qv) and the following year blocked the march west led by Macrianus, whom he killed. In 262, whilst struggling to contain the chaos arising from the aftermath of the numerous usurpers' declarations, it appears from some sources that he was himself acclaimed emperor for a brief time in the Balkans in 262, but seems to have demised his honours to Gallienus and been forgiven. If this train of events is true, then it says much for his loyalty to the Emperor and his effectiveness as a trouble-shooting general.

Nevertheless, sometime in spring 268 he decided to throw in his lot with the Gallic Emperor Postumus, only for this gesture to go unacknowledged. Having done so, he had compromised himself hopelessly with Gallienus. He issued coins, almost all the issues in the name of Postumus.[63] Eventually he was worsted by Gallienus at the Battle of Pontirolo, following which he fell back on Milan. At the siege of the city, Gallienus was assassinated by a group of officers. At a late stage, although according to two sources, before the Emperor's murder, he finally declared himself Augustus.[64] Only one coin of his is known, and unfortunately not seen since it was described in 1718.[65] Yet, *pace* Zosimus and Aurelius Victor, it would make considerably more sense if his declaration had been made *post facto* and not before Gallienus' death. He was promptly declared a public enemy and soon afterwards submitted to Claudius II, only to be killed by the Emperor's men in revenge for his rebellion against Gallienus before Claudius could decide his fate.

---

62 PIR² A1672; Zonaras, 12, 24; Syme (1971) 211
63 Drinkwater (1987) 145-147. Reverse legends, significantly, include slogans extolling the cavalry.
64 If we may accept that testimony of a single late *aureus*, recorded in 1718, since lost: *ibid.* 33, 146, n. 82
65 Drinkwater (1987) 146 n. 82

AVIDIUS CASSIUS
175, 23rd April – 28th July

Avidius Cassius was Marcus Aurelius' military supremo in Syria and had been acclaimed emperor by 23 April 175. It is said that his elevation came in the wake of false news that Marcus had died and was allegedly encouraged by the empress Faustina the younger, supposedly Cassius' lover. Gossip transmitted by the *Historia Augusta* suggests that Faustina was expecting him to marry her, once his accession was assured.[66] The rapid and peaceful acceptance of his *pronunciamento* rather reinforces the claim that he was descended from the princes of Commagene, with all the ramifications of kinship and obligation arising therefrom, bearing in mind that this all happened in Syria. Cassius' continued belief that Marcus Aurelius had died resulted in his having him deified by whatever legitimising apparatus he had by then established.

Avidius Cassius was born c. 128/130 when his equestrian father C. Avidius Heliodorus was Hadrian's *ab epistulis Graecis* (chief secretary for Greek affairs) and was brought up in Alexandria – he could have been born there, for his father had accompanied Hadrian there in 130.[67] Heliodorus was of a family of Syrian nobility from Cyrrhus who credibly claimed descent from the Seleucid Kings of Syria.[68] Cassius' *praenomen* was probably Caius, as was his father's and several of his earlier antecedents. He would have entered the senate as *quaestor* c. 153/154, would have gone on to be *aedile* or people's tribune around 155/156 and *praetor* before 163 – possibly about 158/159 – when legate of *Legio III Gallica*. He was consul in 166 and governor of Syria from the same year as well as the holder of special proconsular powers in the east, c. 172-175.[69] At the time of his *coup*, Cassius – held in high regard by the emperor – was still nominally governor of Syria but with extended powers granted following his suppression of a revolt in Egypt in 172. This included special dispensation, as a senator, to enter Egypt when required.[70] The appointment was so that he could hold the east whilst the emperor campaigned on the German frontier. Because Marcus' male heir, Commodus, was still only 13, the emperor's death would probably have led to a power struggle between various generals and imperial sons-in-law, especially the aged but experienced Ti. Claudius Pompeianus, and clearly, given the misinformation fed to him, Cassius must have thought he had a good chance (but being unrelated to the Imperial house, the influence of Faustina must have played a crucial role) and acted with resolve. His wife's name is unknown, but from her younger son's *cognomen* it may have been

---

66 Dio LXXI. 22.3 & 23.1 has to be the most reliable account.

67 Birley (1987) 186

68 Birley, (1987) 185-186, cf. Syme (1971) 129, n. 3, the details deriving from Greek inscriptions, IGR III 500, OGIS 263 & 766, amplified by Wagner (1974) 168, 172-3, 177 and Astarita (1983) 32. I am also indebted to Prince Kyril Toumanov for further information transmitted via HSH the late Prince Michael Grousinski.

69 PIR² A1402

70 Birley (1987) 174-75 n. 32

Maecia. If the gossip about the empress intending to marry him is true, she may have been dead by 175.

His troops acclaimed him emperor and his Alexandrian origin stood him in good stead as regards support in the east. By the end of April, the whole eastern sector of the empire, including Egypt, was in his control; a papyrus of 3 May confirms this, as does another dated from the previous month. That done, Cassius resolved to set out for Rome to secure his rule, despite having being declared a public enemy by the senate and despite his having eventually become aware that the emperor was still alive. On his eventual departure, therefore, he was assassinated on or before 28 July by soldiers loyal to Marcus and aware that he still lived. His reign, we are told, lasted three months and six days.

Ironically, one alleged cause of all the trouble, the Empress Faustina, died only a month or so afterwards, aged 45 as she and the Emperor moved through the eastern provinces to restore confidence. Unlike most of the imperial claimants who came after him, Cassius appears to have minted no coins – at least none in his own name.

AVITUS
455, 9th July – 456, 17th October

Avitus was a Gallic aristocratic senior commander who was declared emperor in the wake of the sack of Rome and the murder of Petronius Maximus in summer 455. He made valiant efforts to bring order out of the ensuing chaos by enlisting favourably disposed barbarian commanders and with the help of Ricimer, whom he appointed as *magister militum*, a move that in the medium term turned out to have been disastrous for the continuing survival of the western empire.

Eparchius Avitus[71] himself was a member of a very eminent and noble senatorial family with roots in Gaul. They owned an estate called Avitacum near Augustonemetum (Clermont-Ferrand) and, by its alliances both before and after his time, this family managed to act as a genealogical bridge between the Gallic and Roman nobility. We are rich in information about them, simply because his son-in-law Sidonius Apollinaris wrote about his friends and relations in detail, even though he omits occasionally to tell us people's names or specify the degree of kinship they bore to him or to each other. Nevertheless, he is a lot more informative on this topic than St. Ennodius, upon whom we rely for some of the kin of Petronius Maximus, his predecessor.

Avitus was said to be a descendant of Cn. Julius Agricola, famous as the conqueror of Scotland in the 80s, about whose illustrious career his son-in-law Cornelius Tacitus wrote; they, too, were Gauls. This is of course possible, but there is nothing like enough evidence to confirm any such connection. The use of the name Agricola in Avitus' family may have prompted the link,

---

71 The *praenomen* and *nomen* M. Maecilius are given in earlier sources but are now rejected as unsubstantiated.

or may have reflected a genuine belief within the family. We only know of his grandfather, Philagrius, but the probable occurrence of the name Hesychius amongst *his* offspring might lead us to speculate that a daughter or sister of the Flavius Hesychius who was *comes* and *prefectus annonae* (commissioner of the corn supply) under Julian the Apostate, may have married Philagrius and thus have been Avitus' grandmother.[72] Furthermore, the name Maecilius (if we can accept it as authentic) might suggest a descent in some manner from M[a]ecilius Hilarianus who was consul in 332 and a possible descendant of Maecilius Fuscus, who governed Britain under Gordian III.[73] Furthermore, there were almost certainly descendants living in the seventh and early eighth centuries, like Avitus, Bishop of Clermont, who died c. 690. He and his brother St. Bonitus (an ex-prefect of Provence and his successor as bishop) were sons of Theodatus and a Syagria, almost certainly a member of the family of Syagrius and Aegidius (qv).

Avitus was almost certainly an exact contemporary of his kinsman Petronius Maximus, studied law as a youth and, aged about 20, was sent as an envoy to Constantius III, then in Gaul, to seek tax relief for his home region, at that time being harried by various semi-barbarian bands of freebooters, which was granted. Not long afterwards he visited his kinsman Theodorus (possibly an elder brother) who was a hostage with the Visigoths and he swiftly became a close friend of King Theoderic I. In 430-431 he served as an officer under Aëtius against the Juthungi and was appointed to a much more senior command in 436 for that general's campaign against the Burgundians. Although we do not know what post he held, it qualified him as a *vir illustris* (the highest rank in the senates of Rome and Constantinople in late antiquity) and in 437 he was appointed *magister militum* in Gaul, defeating a force of marauding Huns near Clermont and lifting Theoderic's siege of Narbo (Narbonne), which he may have achieved more by diplomacy than by force of arms, given his long-standing friendship with the king. In 439 he was appointed to the less warlike post of Pretorian Prefect of Gaul, after which he retired to his estates c. 440. In 451, he was recalled by his old commander to engineer an alliance between the Romans and the Visigoths to oppose the Huns, which he successfully achieved. He was finally brought out of retirement by Petronius Maximus to become *magister militum* again in order to raise a substantial force of Visigoths to defend Rome, then under threat from Gaiseric.

The fairly restrained sack of Rome by Gaiseric lasted two weeks following the death of Maximus, and the west was left with a power vacuum. Notionally, the Empire was united under the Eastern Emperor, Marcian, yet the need for authority on the spot in Italy to direct the clearing up and re-establish authority, was urgent, for other elements might easily take advantage of the crisis. Normally at this juncture, the senate might have elected an emperor,

---

72 PLRE I Hesychius 5
73 PLRE I Hilarianus 5; Birley (1981) 197, suggesting an Italian or African origin. Note also Pliny the Younger's Gallic friend of praetorian rank, Maecilius Nepos, another Gaul: Plin. *ep.* ii, 3

but some of the most senior and eligible had fled to Constantinople and probably had not had a chance to return; there was probably not a quorum.

Thus Avitus, when the crisis broke, was still at the Gothic court at Tolosa (Toulouse) negotiating with King Theoderic for a force of men wherewith he could relieve Rome. It was the king who urged his to assume the purple. Sidonius, his son-in-law, reported that the king told Avitus: 'We do not force this [honour] upon you but we say to you that we are a friend of Rome; with you as emperor, I am her soldier.'

What Theoderic wanted was Roman support for a planned attempt to dislodge the Sueves from Spain; beyond that, their interest more or less converged. The new emperor of the west was thus acclaimed by the Visigoths at Tolosa and a few days later was officially proclaimed by the Gallic leaders in assembly at Arelate (Arles) 9 July 455, six weeks after the death of his predecessor. He then spent some time gathering a viable army together (with the help of the Visigoths) and set out for Noricum,[74] just freed from Attila and the Huns, chaotic and overrun with other disorganised barbarians, which he recovered and settled before proceeding to Italy, entering Rome on 21 September to a mixed reception. Nevertheless, the senate accepted him and no doubt went through the motions of granting him the usual powers. He took the style Dominus Noster Avitus Perpetuus Felix Augustus. He failed to obtain recognition from the Eastern court, so his serving as Western consul in 456 was not recognised at Constantinople, and two eastern consuls served as well.[75]

He appointed Flavius Ricimer,[76] a Suevic prince with family connections to both the Burgundian and the Visigothic royal houses, and a recently retired Roman commander called Majorian, as *comites*, the former as field army commander and the latter as commander of the Imperial Guard. Both had served with Avitus under Aëtius and were used to working together, although Sidonius rightly described Ricimer as 'a most ferocious' barbarian. By appointing him to a position of power, the new emperor was inviting a cuckoo into the nest.

Ricimer was fiercely ambitious and a Sueve, and thanks to Avitus the Visigoths had been given *carte blanche* to enter Spain and clear them out of the Diocese, which they had accomplished very thoroughly, pushing the Suevic principality back towards the northwest of the peninsula, events which hardly endeared the emperor to his new commander.

Once installed, Avitus needed to get the Vandals out of his hair, for they were still blockading Italy. He therefore issued an ultimatum to Gaiseric, but the onset of winter prevented any retaliation, and by the following spring, Ricimer had managed to defeat him at sea and to clear Sicily of Vandals, too, receiving the appointment as *magister militum* in recognition of his success. The lifting of the Vandal blockade was one thing, but it coincided with a severe famine in Italy, which the emperor and his civil service were hard put to alleviate. The senate had lost faith in him, for all his appointments

---

74 Sidonius claims it was to Pannonia.
75 PLRE II Avitus 5
76 PLRE II Ricimer 2

were of Gallic friends, relations and supporters, denying the Italian senators the career opportunities they expected for themselves and their families, especially as with so many provinces overrun by barbarians, the number of provincial governorships had decreased significantly. Furthermore, the large barbarian element of the army which the emperor had brought with him was using up scarce resources when grain and other supplies were in short supply.

Ricimer and Majorian therefore raised the standard of rebellion, and Avitus' *magister peditum* (infantry commander), a Visigoth called Remistus, was assassinated. Unlike the rebellions of the previous two centuries, however, there was no imperial claimant, suggesting that nominal rule from the east was a possible option, giving more freedom to whichever non-imperial strongman was in the driving seat in Italy. Avitus, however, moved north with what troops he could muster and faced his two disaffected generals before Placentia, where he was roundly defeated, taken prisoner and deposed on 17 October 456. He was subsequently obliged to accept the bishopric of Placentia, and died, apparently of natural causes. in Gaul the following year.

BALBINUS
238, 22nd April – 29th July

238 was the Year of the Six Emperors, like 193 and outdoing 68-69's mere four. In the first seven months of the year, events moved fast. D. Caelius Calvinus Balbinus and Pupienus Maximus were senior senators appointed on 22 April by a twenty-strong executive committee (*vigintiviri*) of a panicky senate reacting to the news from Africa that the *coup* of the two Gordians had failed. This was in the face of an irate emperor Maximin I advancing on Rome intent on cauterising the wound inflicted on his regime by the Gordians' revolt and the senate's support for it. His imperial style was Imperator Caesar D. Caelius Calvinus Balbinus Pius Felix Augustus. With Maximus, he was given tribunician and proconsular power, declared Father of the Senate and appointed as *pontifex maximus*.

Neither the urban plebs nor the Praetorian Guard were keen on being presented with a pair of ageing patricians as joint rulers and consequently the former rioted and the latter failed to make any effort to control them. In the end, it was made clear that the two new Augusti should share their rule with the nephew of Gordian II, who appeared to enjoy some popularity, was exceedingly rich – enabling the Emperors to pay a donative to calm febrile expectations – and who was thenceforth adopted jointly by them before the end of April and nominated Caesar.

Whilst Maximus proceeded north to Aquileia, Balbinus remained in charge in Rome. Whilst Maximus came back to an ovation (*ovatio* – only one stage down from a triumph), Balbinus had been having trouble in Rome with unrest, exacerbated by a pair of senatorial delinquents who, in trying to be helpful, put to death a rebellious group of praetorians without authority.

The two emperors fell out as a result, despite the insistent evidence of their coin issues that they were working in harmony. Discord was apparent and this combined with Maximus' unpopularity from his time as an allegedly severe City Prefect. There was resentment amongst the officers of the Praetorian Guard with emperors appointed by the senate but not approved by themselves, not to mention Balbinus' inaction over the senatorial murder of a number of guards during his colleague's absence. Frustrations came to boiling point. What clinched it was the deployment of Maximus' personal German guards to protect the emperors from a praetorian-led mob, which had turned ugly at the conclusion of the Capitoline Games. Balbinus had opposed their deployment, assuming it was a ploy to get rid of him. Whilst the two emperors were arguing about this, on 29 July 238 the praetorians entered the palace, dragged both of them out and killed them, proclaiming the youthful Caesar Gordian III as emperor in their place.

Our sources tell us very little about Balbinus, despite universal assertions that he was very noble. The exception – inevitably – is the *Historia Augusta*, which tells us that he claimed descent from 'Cornelius Balbus Theophanes', a reference to L. Cornelius Balbus, a low born *élève* of Caesar's.[77] This may merely be to explain the Emperor's additional *cognomen* – a diminutive of Balbus – or it may be the truth. Unfortunately, the name in both forms is fairly common. The father's antecedents may have included Q. Caelius Honoratus, suffect consul in 105, for a man of this name was an exact contemporary of the future Emperor, and could have been his brother or cousin. A rather less likely ancestor might have been L. Cael[ius Calv]inus, suffect consul at an unknown 1st-century date. If his name is not to be restored as L. Cael[ius Ruf]inus (or even [Balb]inus), his mother or grandmother could just possibly have been the last of the noble Republican Domitii Calvini.

That aside, Balbinus was born, probably at Rome, in between 165 and 170, although Zonaras says 174, but this is generally accepted as being too late.[78] He was suffect consul in 203, which would be about right for a man of distinguished family and – as alleged – a patrician. Thus he was a *Salius Palatinus* and would also have been quaestor c. 194/6, praetor c. 196/8. He served a second consulship – also suffect in this case – in 213. The *Historia Augusta* tells us that he governed Asia, Africa, Bithynia, Galatia, Pontus, Thrace and 'The Gauls'.[79] Leaving aside Pontus – only created by Diocletian and thus existing when the statement was written, but not in Balbinus's time – this list is perfectly reasonable given the length of his service, although it seems in approximately reverse order of seniority, the most prestigious coming first rather than last.

BALLISTA
260, June/July

Ballista was a Pretorian Prefect of Germanic extraction acting as C-in-C when the emperor Valerian was taken captive by the Persians, upon hearing of which cataclysmic event, he was urged to assume the purple but demurred in

---

77 *V. Max et Balb.* VII. 3
78 FS1003; PIR² C126; *Op. cit.* xii, 17
79 *V. Max. et Balbin.* 7, 2

favour of the father of Macrianus and Quietus (qqv). The *Historia Augusta* claims that he aided Prince Odaenathus of Palmyra to fend off the triumphant Persians after Valerian's capture but, having labelled him as one of the Thirty Tyrants, the author then declares himself unsure whether after all he 'held any imperial power'. Indeed, there is absolutely no evidence that he did and, even in the fifth century, it was the acknowledged convention that barbarians were not eligible to become emperor. Family and fate unknown.[80]

BASILISCUS (I)
476, 9th January – 477, August

Basiliscus was an incompetent and accident-prone usurper who tried to capitalise on the unpopularity of the emperor Zeno in a time of crisis, who tried to make monphysitism the mainstream Christian belief of the empire and who reigned with the recognition of the senate in the capital for eighteen months before being ousted, having been successful only in alientating all possible avenues of support.

Following his disastrous performance as a general in Africa, attempting to dislodge Gaiseric, Basiliscus had not lost his lust for supreme power, despite his slow-witted and trusting nature. With the help of his sister Aelia Verina, the widow of Leo I, he was able to enter Constantinople unopposed on 9 January 476, proclaiming his son Marcus (qv) as *nobilissimus caesar* – effectively heir. He was recognised universally, including by the senate, of which he was then *princeps*, or *caput*, as the position was by then called.

All we know about the family of Verina and Basiliscus is that they were of distinguished Roman stock. There are other gaps in our knowledge. We know Armatus (consul in 476) was Verina's nephew, but not the names of his parents, so we do not know if his father was a brother or brother-in-law of Verina. It is also known that Julius Nepos (qv) was related by marriage to the Empress; he may have been married to a sister or cousin of Armatus. There is also some reasonably persuasive circumstantial evidence that western warlord Odovacer may also have had a connection; perhaps his father, who spent some time in Constantinople at the crucial period, may have married a sister of the future empress, although one (not wholly reliable) source claims his mother as a Scirian. All this might also explain the role of Odovacer's brother Onoulfus, a *protégé* of Armatus, whom he murdered in 477 on the orders of Zeno.

Flavius Basiliscus had a military career at first, being appointed *magister militum* in Thrace 464-468 during tenure of which he held the consulship in 465. He was also made patrician at about this time, and commanded the abortive anti-Vandal expedition of 468-469. He was pardoned in 471 when he aided the emperor against the powerful courtier Aspar. Nothing is known of his wife Zenonis, and although they seem to have had other children, only Marcus is named.[81]

---

80 *Tyr. Trig.* XVIII; PLRE I Ballista
81 PLRE II Basiliscus 2

Basiliscus, having obtained the recognition of the senate, ought thus perhaps not to be classified as an usurper at all, although truth be told, his elevation by *coup* and downfall bear all the marks of one. That his predecessor was able to return to power emphasises the ephemeral nature of his regime.

He was styled D[ominus] N[oster] Basiliscus P[ater] P[atriae] Aug[ustus][82] and his wife Zenonis was made Augusta. He also held a second consulship in 476. His first act, having alienated Verina by an ill-judged judicial murder, was to raise taxes, which also lost him the support of the population at large. His reaction was to elevate his son Marcus as co-emperor, but his flaunting of his Monophysite religious sympathies thereafter began to worsen an already tense situation. As part of his attempt to make his particular brand of Christian heresy the new orthodoxy, he reinstated Timotheus, the former Bishop of Alexandria, ousted for non-conformity in 460, and attempted on his advice to reverse the decisions of the Council of Chalcedon and abolish the Patriarchate of Constantinople. At this juncture a large area of the capital was razed by a serious fire. By this time too, the general and aspirant king-maker Illus was conspiring with the dowager Empress to bring Zeno back, a happenstance Basiliscus countered by making his unmartial and ne'er-do-well nephew Armatus consul, patrrician and *magister militum* with a commission to nip the planned restoration in the bud on the promise of promotion and the rank of *nobilissimus caesar* for his son Basiliscus Leo, should he succeed. In August 477, Zeno returned to Constantinople in triumph, and Basiliscus, Marcus and their families were exiled to Limnae in Cappadocia (Gaziri, Turkey) where they were confined in a dried-up reservoir and allowed to starve to death.[83] Basiliscus Leo briefly succeeded Basiliscus but was deposed in 478.

BASILISCUS (II) LEO
477, August – 478

Son of Basilscus' nephew Armatus, Basiliscus Leo was nominated Caesar by his great uncle Basiliscus in the crisis of summer 477 and, on the deposition of the latter, briefly succeeded him whilst essentially on the run until deposed, ordained and made Bishop of Cyzicus by Zeno.[84]

BONOSUS
280

At some stage in the reign of Probus, two Rhine commanders had themselves proclaimed emperor, most probably in spring 280. Bonosus was commander of the army on the Rhine and the acclamation took place at Colonia Agrippina (Cologne). Quite how the other usurper, Proculus (qv), fitted in is obscure. They may have commanded the armies in the two Germanies and perhaps thought to make their bid jointly. To confuse matters, author Aurelius Victor

---

82 Coin evidence.
83 PLRE II Marcus 4
84 PLRE II Basiliscus 1

omits Proculus entirely, although he is mentioned by Eutropius.[85] Most of our information comes from the *Historia Augusta* and is thus not to be relied upon. Included is the fact that Bonosus was a career soldier, said to have been of British descent, son of a schoolmaster or similar, who had married a Goth and settled in Spain. Both usurpers were quickly suppressed and killed by Probus, so probably their reign lasted only a month or six weeks; there was apparently no time for any coins to be minted, for instance.

Predictably, the *Historia Augusta* provides him with a family, stating that his Gothic wife was called Hunila and that they had two sons, both apparently spared by Probus.[86]

BRITANNICUS
54, 13 Oct. – 55, 11 Feb.

Ti. Claudius Caesar Britannicus was the son of Claudius, born into the purple on 12 February 41, acquiring his *agnomen* a little later, from his father's triumph as conqueror of Britain. He was only seven when his mother was executed for her insane fling with ex-consul C. Silius. Once Nero had been formally adopted by Claudius in 54, Britannicus' name was changed to Britannicus Claudius Caesar. He was never granted the usual powers by the senate, being under age, unlike Nero, who was nearly 17 on accession and thus technically of age. Named in the Emperor's (suppressed) will as joint heir with Nero, he was only nominally therefore in power until he died at the dinner table, probably from poisoning but allegedly of an epileptic fit, on 11 February AD55. Needless to say, nobody failed to see his imperial colleague's hand in the matter.

BURDUNELLUS
496

Burdunellus (meaning 'little mule') was a Roman usurper of the late fifth century, recorded only briefly in the *Consularia Caesaraugustana*. Under 496 it is recorded that 'he became a tyrant in Hispania', a phrase which, in the political language of the time and considering the nature of the source, must mean he tried to claim the imperial dignity and authority there. He was eventually abandoned by his own supporters, who turned him over to the legitimate authorities. They sent him to Tolosa, where he was apparently burned to death inside a bronze bull, a unique fate for a usurper but typically horrible and humiliating. The location of Burdunellus' petty tyranny is unknown, but was probably the valley of the Ebro centred on Caesaraugusta (Zaragoza, Spain).[87]

85 *Op. cit.* 9, 17
86 PLRE I Bonosus 1 & Hunila based on HA *V. Firmi* 15, 2, 3 & 7
87 Collins, Roger. *Visigothic Spain, 409–711*. Oxford: Blackwell Publishing, 2004; Thompson, E. A. 'The End of Roman Spain: Part III.' *Nottingham Mediaeval Studies*, xxii (1978), pp. 3–22. Reprinted as 'The Gothic Kingdom and the Dark Age of Spain' in *Romans and Barbarians: The Decline of the Western Empire*. Madison: University of Wisconsin Press, 1982. pp. 161–187.

CAESAR see JULIUS CAESAR

CAIUS see CALIGULA

CALIGULA
37, 16th March – 41, 17th January

Tiberius' successor, Caligula, is frequently held up as the epitome of a 'bad' Roman emperor and mitigating factors are certainly hard to discern. He ascended the throne very young and mainly by default, for the sanguinary scheming of Tiberius' Pretorian Prefects Sejanus and Macro had decimated his family, leaving him almost the last one standing. Yet such were his propensities for irrational and indeed murderous behaviour, most of those remaining were also despatched during his short period in power.

C. [Julius] Caesar is better known as Caligula, a name meaning 'little boots', given to him by the soldiers when he accompanied his father Germanicus on campaign as a child.[88] He was born a patrician by descent and by adoption on 31 August, 12; he was *quaestor* in 34 and was designated Tiberius's heir in 35 along with Tiberius Gemellus, whom he had killed after his accession in March 37. He was brought up by the women in his family, surrounded by the sons of various foreign client kings, notably M. Julius [Herodes] Agrippa, the future King of Judaea, and enjoyed immense popularity as his father's son. He was given absolutely no responsibility by Tiberius, whose last Praetorian Prefect, Q. Naevius Cordus Sutorius Macro, seeing which way the wind was blowing, attached himself to his cause (aided by his wife, Ennia Thrasylla, who connived at his adultery with her) only to be disposed of after Caligula's succession.

As emperor, he took the style C. Caesar Germanicus Augustus and was acknowledged as *Pontifex Maximus*. He entered upon a suffect consulship without delay and held further consulships in 39, 40 and 41, the latter two irregularly as sole (ordinary) consul. He was also granted the tribunician and proconsular power by the senate on accession and (rather improbably for someone so divorced from military affairs) hailed as *imperator*, an embarrassment not repeated. His lack of higher public office distanced him from the constitutional niceties observed by Augustus and Tiberius and his personality, wayward and possibly manic, inclined him increasingly towards the sort of autocratic behaviour expected of his friend Herod Agrippa. He scandalised the governing class by allegations against him of incest and murder, and the threat (or joke) to make his horse, Inchitatus, ordinary consul with him for 40. In foreign relations – especially with the Jews – his policies were disastrous, his profligacy extraordinary and his behaviour outrageous. A planned invasion of Britain in 40 failed to materialise and ended in a lot of expensive posturing. Nevertheless, he is only accused of having brought about the deaths of 27 leading people, 14 being senators' over only four years

---

88 Tacitus, *Annales* 1.41.2; PIR² I 217

this may be regarded as fairly restrained. A psychologist might convincingly argue that he was not wholly stable mentally and conclude that the emperor was suffering from acute attention deficit disorder, a condition made obvious (but the conclusion not drawn) in Winterling's succinct account of his life.[89]

During his brief reign, he managed to marry four times – one per year a high turnover by any reckoning. His first marriage was in 33 to Junia Claudi[ll]a, daughter of M. Junius Silanus, suffect consul in AD15 whose unknown wife may well have been a relative of Tiberius's, bearing in mind Junia's second name, a feminine diminutive of Claudius.[90] She died in childbirth prior to Caligula's accession. His second wife was Livia Orestilla (according to Suetonius)[91] or Cornelia Orestina (according to Dio)[92] whom he married before the end of 37 but had put aside either after a few days (or again, according to Dio, after two months), after which he divorced her, apparently for showing no signs of pregnancy. She was in fact probably called Cornelia Livia Orestilla and was the daughter of a senator called Scipio Orestinus, descended not only from a branch of the the Cornelii Lentuli (Scipios by adoption), but also from obscure kinsmen of the Empress Livia, the Livii Ocellae, and the grand Republican house of the Mucii.[93] Her ultimate fate is unknown. In September 38, Caligula married his third wife Lollia Paulina, the granddaughter of the consul of 21BC, M. Lollius. Lollia's sister, Lollia Saturnina, married Gallic senator D. Valerius Asiaticus, whose descendants can be traced well into the second century, if not beyond. Lollia was formerly the wife of P. Memmius Regulus, suffect consul in 31. Caligula divorced her around March 39 and she was banished but only put to death in exile in 48 through the machinations of Empress Messallina. Not long after this divorce, Caligula married as his fourth wife Milonia Caesonia, born around 5, the daughter of the sixth and last marriage of a much-married matron of modest extraction called Vistilia, who had had three daughters by a previous marriage. Her husband's name is lost to us. She was, as a result, a half-sister of Nero's great general, Corbulo, father of the Empress Domitia Longina (qv. Domitian). They had a daughter, Julia Drusilla, born within about a month of their wedding.

Caligula had numerous other *affaires* with members of both sexes. He was said on occasion to have had sex with the wives of guests at private dinners and then returned to the table to regale the party with an account of the experience. He was accused of incest, allegedly with all three of his sisters, especially Julia Drusilla; also of having affairs with Ennia, the wife of his predecessor's Praetorian Prefect, Macro, and Pyrallis, a concubine. The only one alleged to have produced recorded named offspring was Nymphidia, daughter of C. Julius Callistus, a freedman of the emperor, who became a trusted member of the his staff and was later a senior civil servant

---

89 I am indebted to Carole Craven for this diagnosis derived from a close reading of the sources.
90 Syme (1986) 195
91 *Caligula* 25.1
92 *op. cit.* 59.8.2
93 PIR² C1492, C1441 – conceivably related to the adoptive mother of Galba.

(*a libellis*) under Claudius.[94] She was married to a man called Asiaticus – not the consular married to empress Lollia Paulina's sister, however – but by Caligula had, so it was later claimed, a son, C. Nymphidius Sabinus, who after service as a junior equestrian officer was appointed Pretorian Prefect by the emperor Nero in 65. On Nero's fall in 68, he persuaded the Guard to support the emperor Galba but was eventually killed making a futile attempt – based on his claimed ancestry – to assume the imperial purple himself.[95] Strangely, all Caligula's promiscuity seems to have stopped once he had married Caesonia and fathered Drusilla: could he have finally found true love?

If so, it was too late. The first serious plot against him, that of Lentulus Gaetulicus (the details of which are obscure, but which involved Caligula's brother-in-law Lepidus in some way), failed and ended in the conspirators' deaths; it was the second of 17 January 41, which succeeded, and he was replaced by his uncle, Claudius.

CALOCAERUS
334

Calocaerus was an adventurer who led a revolt in Cyprus, but whose time in the sun lasted long enough only for his disturbances to reach the Levantine littoral, where he and his followers were caught up with by the ex-consul Dalmatius (father of Dalmatius Caesar qv) at Tarsus, where he and his leading supporters were caught, tried and burnt alive.[96]

CAMILLUS (I)
41, March(?)

Camillus was a kinsman of the Imperial family who made a somewhat wayward and failed attempt to topple Claudius, possibly with the original intention of restoring the Republic.

At the juncture of change from Caligula to Claudius, there was an attempted military *coup* led by a grandee whose full name was L. Arruntius L. f. Ani. Camillus Scribonianus, who had been consul in 32 and who was then governing Dalmatia. It seems to have been precipitated by the execution of the Julio-Claudian kinsman C. Ap. Junius Silanus in Rome shortly before. That Camillus was put up to it by M. Annius Vinicianus, the man who instigated the plot against Caligula, seems likely, however, and there is some doubt as to whether the idea was to march on Rome and re-establish the Republic or merely to declare himself *princeps*. The *pronunciamento* seems to have had the latter effect, but at the religious ceremony to inaugurate the attempt, the omens were very poor and that, with other unfavourable portents, persuaded the enthusiastic soldiers in his legions to change their

---

94 PIR² I229
95 Plutarch, *Galba* ix. 1
96 PLRE I Calocaerus

minds and declare themselves loyal to the dynasty after all. Camillus fled to the island of Issa and was there killed by a soldier called Volaginius. The entire affair lasted but five days, although the actual dates are lost to us. The result at Rome was a series of savage prosecutions and executions of those connected with it.

Camillus himself was a younger son, born into the ancient patrician family of the Furii, his father being M. Furius Camillus, consul in 8, who had defeated Tacfarinas in Africa and who had been a friend of Tiberius. The family's first consulship had been in 488BC but the last, before Scribonianus' father's, had been in 136BC: like Caesar's family, the Furii thereafter fell into eclipse. His mother was the daughter of M. Livius Drusus Libo, consul in 15BC and a nephew of Scribonia, ex-wife of Augustus. Camillus himself had been testamentarily adopted by L. Arruntius (consul AD6) whose mother brought descent from Pompey and Sulla. Finally, he had married the conspirator Vinicianus's cousin, making him highly eligible for power and marking him out for treason. Nevertheless, his sons were spared and there is evidence for the long survival of his stock, albeit in the distaff line.[97]

CAMILLUS (II)

c. 230

Camillus was an elderly and aristocratic pretender of very dubious veracity who, it was claimed, planned in Rome to seize power from Alexander Severus (qv) at an unknown point in his reign. If true, this seems to have occurred probably in the early 230s. The story appears only in the *Historia Augusta* (needless to say) and concerns one Ovinius Camillus, 'a senator of very ancient family'. When intelligence concerning Camillus' intentions reached the Palatine, Alexander invited him to his presence, and basically killed him with kindness, inviting him to share power, accompany the emperor on campaign and so forth, all of which Camillus was too fearful, suspicious and decrepit to undertake. As a consequence, he was allowed to retire to his villa, deeply humiliated.[98]

The family only acquired senatorial rank in the late second century, and L. Ovinius Rusticus Cornelianus, an early 3rd-century suffect consul, would have been of the correct generation to have been this man's father – assuming he is not entirely fictitious. The antiquity of the family would be implied by the *cognomen*, borne by the ancient patrician Furii (cf Camillus I), but no such alliance is recorded. One has to bear in mind, however, that the *Historia* was written in the late 4th century, when there were then flourishing one or two fairly eminent senators bearing the name Camillus, which may have prompted the author to conjure up the name. The Ovinii, nevertheless, managed to continue to flourish.

---

97 ILS 5032; FS 1789; PIR² A1140; Rutledge (2002) 164-165
98 HA *Sev. Alexr.* 48, 1-7.

CARACALLA
198, 28ᵗʰ January – 217, 8ᵗʰ April

Caracalla was the soubriquet of the elder son of emperor Septimius Severus, a ruthless and uncompromising man of military pretensions who, throughout a sole reign of only five years, managed to achieve very little of note except the enfranchisement of all the free inhabitants of the empire – and that was to have lasting effects.

L. Septimius Bassianus was born the elder son of Septimius Severus on 4 April 188 and named after his maternal grandfather. Although a promising youth, rivalry with his younger brother Geta, his mother's favourite, permeated his every action and caused deep bitterness. It is assumed, but not attested, that his *praenomen* was Lucius, but this is most likely in the tradition of the Roman élite of the time. In 195 he was re-named, to accord with his father's self-appointment as a son of Marcus Aurelius, as M. Aurelius Antoninus Caesar.[99]

At the age of only nine, on 28 January 198 he was made co-emperor with his father as Imperator Caesar M. Aurelius Antoninus Augustus, receiving his first imperial acclamation, the proconsular and tribunician powers along with the pontificate – the third time this single office had been divided, although on his younger brother's elevation to the purple in 210 it was actually held briefly by three people! Later in the same year he added Pius to his style, after Antoninus. The senate voted him the title of *pater patriae* the following year and in 200 the name Felix was added after Pius, this combination of 'Pius Felix' setting a trend (when borne *before* 'Augustus') that became increasingly popular in the 3ʳᵈ century and which survived until the end of the 6ᵗʰ century.[100]

He was consul first in 202, then in 205 and again in 208, with a further imperial acclamation on 207. As his father's lieutenant in their campaigns in Scotland in 209-210, he assumed, jointly with Severus, the additional honorific of Britannicus Maximus. In a clear attempt to consolidate an old family alliance, he was betrothed in 200 and in 202 married (on his father's orders) Publia Fulvia Plautilla, the daughter of his father's henchman, fellow-townsman and cousin, P. Fulvius Plautianus, whom he divorced and exiled in 205 on the fall of her father. Recent analysis of coin evidence suggests that they had a short-lived daughter c. 204, whose demise perhaps lay behind the divorce.[101]

On succeeding his father at York in February 211, his style again changed, to Imperator Caesar M. Aurelius Severus Antoninus Pius Augustus Britannicus Maximus.[102] His public assassination of his brother in December 211, who had his own faction and supporters in all walks of Roman life, left Caracalla exposed and he felt consequently that it was necessary to bribe the

---

99 ILS 419

100 ILS 425 which also includes 'L. f.'

101 Bronze *As* (24mm, 10.26 g, 12h). Rome mint 202-203; rev. shows Plautilla as Pietas standing R. holding sceptre and her daughter, RIC IV 581

102 ILS 448

Caracalla, plaster library
bust after the antique
original in Rome.
(Bamfords Ltd.)

Praetorian Guard and cow the Senate into acquiescence, although he was clearly unconvinced by the effectiveness of either tactic. He therefore had recourse during 212 and 213 to a widespread proscription in which, we are told, 20,000 supporters or suspected supporters of Geta were massacred, from all ranks of Roman society. These actions wrecked any hope there might have been for the acceptance, from the senate downwards, of his rule.

On the other hand, as good tyrants do, he quickly made it his business to curry favour with the army, in which he succeeded brilliantly – at crushing expense to the treasury – by giving them an immediate pay rise of nearly 50%. Setting out for Germany on campaign, he increased their esteem by sharing the soldiers' discomforts and disdaining the luxuries usually enjoyed even by field commanders – hence his universally adopted nickname 'Caracalla', derived from the term for a particular type of hooded military cloak that he habitually wore. This German campaign was a success, earning him a fourth imperial acclamation and the additional titles of Germanicus Maximus the same year, in which he was also consul for the fourth time.

As indicated above, his most lasting legacy to the empire was his edict of 212 granting full Roman citizenship to all free citizens of the Empire. Although the short-term idea was to increase tax revenues to fund military spending (especially his universal military donative), the long-term effect was to endow all the inhabitants of the Empire with a sense of belonging, thus binding it together. The other long-term effect was to completely change the way names were applied; it spelt the death of the *praenomen* and the *gentilicium*, the bearing of which were no longer a prerequisite of citizenship. Vast numbers of citizens so enfranchised, however, adopted Caracalla's *praenomen* and *nomen,* 'M. Aurelius', if only to accord with convention; several of the emperors and imperial claimants in the chaotic period following c. 260 were so styled.

These matters settled, Caracalla set out for the east but rather spoilt his no-nonsense image by becoming increasingly intoxicated with the mystique of Alexander the Great, culminating in absurd ceremonies performed at the site of Troy and at Alexandria, where, in the end, it all went very sour, the emperor on a whim ordering the massacre of thousands of unarmed civilians early in 216. He had a long-term physical ailment as well as a serious inferiority complex, fuelled by his clash with and murder of his brother, and had probably reached a stage where he was beginning to become completely unbalanced; the disease, bearing in mind his lack of children and the paucity of stories about any promiscuity, may have been of a sexual nature.

From Alexandria, Caracalla carried out a well-planned and successful campaign against Parthia, earning himself the additional style Parthicus Maximus. During the run-up to the opening of the campaigning season of 217, however, his efforts to buy the loyalty of the troops proved to have been ineffective and he was assassinated in Osrhoëne, whilst taking a comfort break, *en route* from Edessa to Carrhae on 8 April.

The Empress Plautilla was killed in 212 after Geta's execution, her brother C. Fulvius Plautius Hortensianus sharing her fate.[103] Caracalla was also accused of 'marrying' his mother, or at least committing incest with her, a story which occurs in the *Historia Augusta* and several other later sources but which is dismissed by modern scholarship. Caracalla was deified by a reluctant senate at the prompting of his successor, Macrinus.

CARAUSIUS (I)
285, October/November – 293

Carausius is remembered chiefly for having seized power in Britain and northern Gaul and brought about what might be described as the first Brexit by breaking away from the direct control of the empire and successfully maintaining his position.

Carausius was born in the low countries of a people called the Menapii and became an experienced mariner. He proved himself a capable soldier, too, serving under Maximian against Amandus (qv) and his *bagaudae*. At some stage, he had received a commission to equip a fleet and suppress the German pirates in the Channel and North Sea. There is some suggestion that this may have been a commission from emperor Carinus, if not, it would have been

---

103 Birley (1988) Appendix 2, nos. 29, 33

Carausius (I), obverse image of a gold aureus, found in Derbyshire and now on display in Derby Museum. The legend reads: Imp[erator] Carausius Aug[ustus] (Derby Museums Trust)

under Maximian. His exact position cannot be determined, despite plentiful contemporary references to him: he may have been prefect of the *Classis Britannica* (British Fleet, but a unit not recorded at this late date) and then have had a wider brief as *dux* (general).[104] Carausius then, operating out of Bononia (Boulogne), cleared the seas of pirates, and recovered much booty, but instead of returning the stolen property either to those from whom it had been taken or to the imperial fisc, he kept most of it himself, lavishly rewarding his men. Having been tipped off about his impending arrest on Maximian's orders for this piece of *lèse majesté,* he thereupon technically became a pirate himself,[105] being acclaimed emperor in 285 and seizing northern Gaul and the whole of Britain.[106] It may even be that this *coup* was the spur that led Diocletian to promote Maximian from Caesar to Augustus in April 286, in which case Carausius's acclamation may have taken place in autumn 285.

This bold adventurer's actual nomenclature is not wholly clear, as it is given (in its fullest form) as M. Aurelius Ma[ ] Carausius, where the Ma[ ] element may or may not be expanded to the Gallic name Mausaeus, although Maius, Magius or Marius are all possible.[107] The name Carausius seems to be of Celtic origin, and in him it makes its first appearance in the pages of history. The claimant's style appears to have been Imperator Caesar M. Aurelius Carausius Pius Felix Invictus Augustus, and he probably assumed the M. Aurelius element on his acclamation, as Carus (qv) also probably did. Whether he assumed the title of *pontifex maximus* is not clear, but he did

---

104 Birley (1981) 311-312
105 He was referred to as *archipirata* in a hostile panegyric.
106 PLRE I Carausius
107 *Roman Inscriptions of Britain* (RIB) 2291

award himself two consulships during his seven years in power.[108] He also attempted to gain acceptance as co-ruler with Maximian and Diocletian, possibly before the former mounted his first attempt to dislodge him, which failed, perhaps owing to the weather in the Channel (his excuse) but more likely because Carausius had defeated him in northern Gaul. Whether his overtures were accepted (presumably to buy time in which to regroup and mount another campaign) we do not know, for the sources are universally hostile after the event, but the British claimant did produce a famous issue of coins bearing the profiles of himself, Maximian and Diocletian with a legend *Carausius et fratres sui* (Carausius and his brothers). In any case, it would appear that during his reign Britain was quiet and local memories of him must have been most favourable, for one finds British aristocrats bearing his name in the 5ᵗʰ and 6ᵗʰ centuries, most notably on an inscription from remote Penmachno, in North Wales: *Carausius hic iacit in hoc congeries lapidum* (Here lies Carausius in this heap of stones).[109] The spectacular sequence of stone-built and multi-towered shore forts stretching from Cardiff to Brancaster (Norfolk) may well partly be a legacy of Carausius' reign, although whether built as part of the campaign against the German pirates or as a security measure after his Britannic Empire had come into existence is not clear. Two or three were already in existence, but the remainder form a coherent strategic pattern, and the balance of evidence is in favour of them have been built at this period.[110]

His loss of the continental port of Boulogne to the Caesar Constantius c. 292/293 may however have been the trigger for the seizure of power by Allectus, which resulted in Carausius's murder in the latter year. Then again, the panegyricists would have us believe that the ambitious Allectus thought he would be recognised in some way by Constantius if he rid the island of the tyrant. Perhaps he believed he would be made Caesar in gratitude. In the event, of course, he was deluding himself. Nothing is known of the usurper's family nor of any wife or children – unless of course the survival of his rare name implies progeny.

CARAUSIUS (II)

c. 354/358

Carausius II appears to have been an ephemeral usurper nowhere attested apart from a coin found at Rutupiae (Richborough, Kent) of a familiar *fel[ix] temp[orum] reparatio* ('return of happy times') type that could only date from the mid-350s, but the authenticity of which was long doubted.[111] The recent discovery of about twenty further examples, some from primary deposits,

---

108 Coin evidence.

109 Thomas (1994) 205, where he suggests this man was a priest and the date as c. 500.

110 Casey (1994) 115-126.

111 *Numismatic Chronicle*, 3rd ser. vol. VII (1887) 191 and cf. C.H.V. Southerland, 'Carausius II', 'Censeris', and the Barbarous Fel. Temp. Reparatio *Overstrikes, ibid.* 4ᵗʰ ser. Vol. IV/V (1945)

and all from Britain, suggests that this man and his possible successor has to be added to the list of fourth-century usurpers. The likelihood is that he was acclaimed in Britain or Northern Gaul in the wake of the elimination of Decentius (qv) and if so, probably before the incident of Silvanus (qv). The coins read *Domino [Nostro] Carausio C[a]es[ar]* a unique way of styling an usurper or even a recognised emperor for that matter. The lack of the epithet 'Augustus' in inexplicable, although the use of *caesar* suggests that he was appointed by an *augustus* as Decentius had been by Magnentius (qv). Could he have been made Caesar by the latter in his brief period ruling Gaul alone, or was he a true independent usurper? Additionally, the name might suggest either descent, perhaps as a grandson, of Carausius I, or a man wishing to identify himself with his namesake, itself suggesting that this was a British usurper who wished to go it alone, as had been the case in 285. However, the reverse inscription would seem to run counter to this. It presents a familiar bronze type of Constantius II coin with the emperor holding a phoenix and *labarum* standard on the prow of a vessel, the rudder of which is held by Victory. The inscription, uniquely, reads: *domin/conta/no* suggesting a blundered attempt at Domino Con[s]tan[ti]o which, contrary to any successionist ideas, might betoken an usurper rebelling against other usurpers and proclaiming his support for Constantius II. Several further coins again have the legend altered. He has even been furnished with a wife, Oriuna, and daughter Flavia, but these are very much in the *Historia Augusta* mould and should be discarded; hence, the man himself is still clouded in doubt.

CARINUS
282 – 285, July/August

Elder son and joint ruler with Carus (qv) where he enjoyed some significant military successes on both the Rhine and Danube frontiers before being assassinated by a group of his own officers due to his unpredictable nature and his penchant for seducing other men's wives – if we believe the *Historia Augusta*.

Carinus was styled *nobilissimus Caesar* when his father was proclaimed emperor, and on accession M. Aurelius Carinus Pius Felix Augustus.[112] Subsequently, he was left in charge of the western portion of the Empire when his father departed east to campaign against the Persians. On gaining his considerable victory over the Germans, he added Germanicus Maximus to his imperial style. He also defeated the Quadi on the Danube, leading him to return to Rome in 284 to celebrate a triumph. He then seems to have proceeded to Britain, although there seems to be little independent record of why exactly he felt obliged to do so. As a result, he also added the style Britannicus Maximus to his name.[113] At this stage, he had to deal with a usurper, Julianus (III, qv) in northern Italy, possibly following the rebellion of another pretender, also Julian (II qv) in Illyricum, which he had dealt with early in 285. This done, he was left clear to face the advancing Diocletian

---

112 ILS607
113 ILS608. This could have been as a result of one of Carausius's early successes.

at the head of what was essentially a victorious but smaller army. In July they met in battle on the river Margus (Great Morava, Serbia), during which Carinus seems to have been victorious but, at the crucial moment of victory, he was struck down by a group of officers fearful of what the future might hold with him victorious, for he was reported by Eutropius to have put to death many innocent men through false accusations.[114] It may be his staff saw the makings of another Commodus in him. In either case, his army went over to Diocletian without hesitation, and although no one knew it at the time, a whole new era was about to dawn; the chaos of the previous five decades was shortly to end. All three members of this, Rome's shortest-lived dynasty, suffered a *damnatio memoriae* and had their inscriptions erased.

CARUS
282, September – 283, May

Carus was the nemesis of the unfortunate but generally well-liked Probus, who raised his two sons to the rank of *Caesar,* led an outstandingly successful raid into Persia and was the first emperor to style himself *Deo et Dominus* (God and Lord) without the benefit of being dead before being recognised as the former.

M. Aurelius [Numerius] Carus had been born in Narbo (Narbonne) in Gaul c. 225, so was not of the charmed circle of Danubian or Illyrian officers who had dominated the purple since the fall of Gallienus, although like them he was a non-senatorial, career officer, but one who had previously enjoyed a civil career according to the *Historia Augusta*.[115] We do not know who Carus's father was, but he is assumed to have been a Gaul, and the occurrence of the name Numerius in the younger son's nomenclature has suggested to some that the Emperor's original *nomen* may have been Numerius and that he assumed 'M. Aurelius' as an imperial style on acclamation, just as most emperors from the fourth century adopted Flavius. By his wife, Magnia Urbica (whose later fate in unclear), he had a daughter, Paulina, who may have been twice married.[116] One of Carus' children produced a son, known only as *Divus Nigrinianus nepos Cari* (the deified Nigrinianus grandson of Carus). The lack of imperial titulature for Nigrinianus has led to the suggestion that he survived into Diocletian's reign and was deified on his death as a gesture of conciliation towards the supporters of the short-lived dynasty.[117] A possible relation or descendant was Numeri[an]us, significantly, governor of Gallia Narbonensis in 358/359.[118] Later hagiography mentioned by St. Ambrose has also connected saints Cantius, Cantianus and Cantianilla (martyred near Aquileia c. 304/306) with the family of Carus, although one might be more tempted to assume their origin to have been the modern county of Kent.

---

114 *Op. cit.,* 9, 19
115 PLRE I. Carus/PIR² A1473; HA *V. Cari* 5, 2 (a senator) cf. 5.3 (Pretorian Prefect).
116 PLRE I Paulina 1/2; Urbica 1. HA claims he had 9 wives! [*V. Cari* 16, 7]
117 PLRE I Nigrinianus 1; also mentioned on an inscription CIL VI. 31380
118 PLRE I Numerius 1. His name is given as Numerius by Ammianus but by John of Antioch.

Carus was soon in Rome, where he obtained from a compliant senate the tribunician and proconsular powers, renewable annually, was confirmed as *pontifex maximus* and held a suffect consulship, followed by an ordinary one with his elder son Carinus at the beginning of 283. Both sons were initially styled *nobilissimus Caesar*[119] and the elder had also become co-Augustus with his father, probably by the beginning of 283. Carus's style was Imperator Caesar M. Aurelius Carus Invictus Pius Felix Augustus.[120] His additional style of *Deo et Dominus* (God and Lord) appears on an issue of gold coins (*aurei*).

Carus and Numerianus, the younger son, departed for the east to mount a punitive expedition to Persia. As the frontier had previously been quiet, Saturninus (qv) not excepted, this was probably mounted more for prestige building than anything else. With the army well inside the Persian empire after a successful invasion and the capture of the capital, Ctesiphon, Carus died nearby, allegedly from a lightning strike. Others thought that he was murdered either by his son or, more likely, by the scheming Pretorian Prefect, L. Flavius Aper (Numerianus's father-in-law).[121] The sheer unlikeliness of death by lightning might suggest that this is what indeed happened. A third possibility is that his death was brought about by some kind of Persian fifth columnist. The result was that Numerianus was now declared co-Augustus with his brother. His father was deified by the senate and granted the posthumous suffixes Persicus Maximus and Germanicus Maximus.[122]

CASSIUS see *AVIDIUS CASSIUS*

CELSUS
260/268

Celsus was allegedly an ex-tribune who, according to the *Historia Augusta*, usurped in Libya, at Sicca (El-Kef, Libya) but was soon eliminated by a *comes* of Gallienus and his body 'eaten by dogs'.[123]

CENSORINUS
269(?)

The *Historia Augusta* claims that Claudius II was obliged to deal with an usurper called Ap. Claudius Censorinus, apparently an aged senator, twice consul and terribly distinguished. He was apparently acclaimed at Bononia (Bologna) and was later killed by his own troops. Bearing in mind Gallienus'

---

119 ILS601; PLRE I Carinus & Numerianus; PIR² A1473 & 1564
120 ILS598
121 PLRE I. Aper 2/3. If these men are one and the same, Aper had previously been governor (*praeses*) of Pannonia Inferior. He was probably also an Illyrian. *Historia Augusta* says he was murdered.
122 ILS596, 609; he had had his tribunician power renewed for the first time prior to his demise.
123 HA *Tyr. Trig.* XXIX

reforms, the likelihood that a distinguished ex-consul would be leading troops at this juncture seems vanishingly small. The name suggests descent from the Republican patrician family of the Claudii Pulchres, but there is no trace of his many magistracies on the record and his is dismissed by all commentators as fictional.[124]

CIVILIS
69–70

[C.] Julius Civilis was a Batavian prince of a family emancipated by Augustus or Germanicus and an army officer, who had been detained in Rome following the conviction, on trumped up charges, of his kinsman Julius Paulus under Nero. However, Galba pardoned him of all taint of treason and he returned to his native parts, near the mouth of the Rhine.

However, considerable resentment appears to have been built up in him in response to these events, and he soon raised his people in rebellion in 69, mobilising at first under the pretext of supporting Vespasian against Vitellius in the civil war fast unfolding before him. He was joined by a number of German tribes, defeated a force sent against him at Castra Vetera (Xanten) and went on to raise the northern Gauls, too, who in their turn killed their governor Hordeonius Flaccus.[125] It is thought that Civilis was probably aiming to create a rival political entity rather than attempting to displace the reigning emperor.

With Vespasian finally triumphant in Rome and able to stabilise matters, his general Q, Petillius Cerealis Caesius Rufus, who had earlier gained fame by putting down Boudicca's revolt in Britain, managed to defeat Civilis, round up his allies and, by offering clemency, managed to defuse the situation and settle matters down. Civilis was allowed to return to his estates and we hear no more of him.[126]

CLAUDIUS I
41, 17th January – 54, 13th October

Claudius was the fourth Julio-Claudian emperor whose life was preserved during the unpredictable events of Caligula's reign by his having lived below the radar and having been generally perceived as mentally weak. On the murder of Caligula, Claudius was dragged out from behind a curtain where he had been hiding in terror by the Praetorian Guard who promptly proclaimed him emperor in Caligula's place. Modern historians are not wholly convinced of his innocence of the plot that removed his predecessor; there are grounds for thinking he was wholly or partly complicit.[127] He it

---

124 HA XXXIII, cf. Syme (1968) 157
125 PIR² H202
126 PIR² I.264 Tac. *Hist.* iv & v *passim*; Josephus, *BJ.* vii. 4
127 Levick (1990) 35

was, though, who initiated the conquest of Britain and ruled with moderate competence, vitiated only by the thoroughgoing awfulness of his empresses.

Born into the old patrician family of the Claudii Nerones in 10, his sheltered life, mainly amongst the women of his family, kept him out of public life mainly because of his perceived disabilities: a severe stammer, slight malformation of the body, bouts of illness, often apparently serious and, so it was thought, mental torpor. In fact, he was intellectually gifted and a keen antiquarian, especially concerning the early history of Rome. He continued Livy and wrote histories of Etruria and Carthage. Caligula had made him (suffect) consul for 37 and kept him at court, although he seems to have been denied any other role in the senate, attendance at which he seems to have eschewed.

As a youth, the new emperor was betrothed to Aemilia Lepida, but this was broken off when her mother Julia was disgraced in 7. He was subsequently due to marry Livia Medullina Camilla,[128] daughter of the very grand patrician *protégé* of Tiberius, M. Furius Camillus, consul in 8 and sister of the usurper Camillus (qv). Tragically, she died on their wedding day. He eventually married Plautia Urgulanilla, a friend of the empress Livia, whom he divorced not so long afterwards in AD24 through allegations of adultery. His next essay in matrimony (by 28) was Aelia Paetina,[129] daughter of a jurist of noble descent, Q. Aelius Tubero, and a relation of Tiberius' poisonous Pretorian Prefect, L. Aelius Seianus (Sejanus). The union survived the fall of Sejanus but foundered in the wake of the accession of Caligula, and they appear to have divorced in AD37. He then married c. AD38 a woman with much closer links to the Imperial house (she was his cousin once removed) and splendidly well connected: Valeria Messallina. She was great-grand-daughter of Augustus' sister Octavia twice over.

After his accession, to strengthen her position and to secure the succession of her infant son Britannicus (qv), she resorted to a murderous regime of eliminating perceived threats, which thinned the imperial house out alarmingly before she lost control completely, took a lover, C. Silius, and went through a semi-public form of marriage with him as part of a sort of rolling orgy in AD48, which promptly resulted in her demise. She was replaced the following year by another virago, Agrippina, another member of the imperial house, who proved just as effective an attritional factor in respect of the surviving members of the imperial house as Messallina, being determined to secure the succession for her son Lucius by her previous husband Cn. Domitius Ahenobarbus, whom she ultimately persuaded the emperor to adopt (as Ti. Claudius Nero) as joint heir with Britannicus, laying the groundwork for further blood-letting.

Ti. Claudius Nero Germanicus[130] succeeded to the Empire in January 41 and was granted the tribunician power by the senate and hailed as *imperator* on accession and on twenty-six further occasions, despite his

---

128 PIR² L304; her connection with the Livii defies identification - perhaps through her
        mother.
129 PIR² A305
130 PIR² C942

unmartial nature. He was also acknowledged as *pontifex maximus* and *pater patriae*. Thereafter re-styled himself Ti. Claudius Caesar Augustus during the census he held under his own auspices when, for antiquarian reasons, he had himself transferred to the Quirinian voting tribe. This was the first time the name Caesar had been assumed for no genealogical or adoptive reason. From this point on 'Caesar' like 'Augustus' effectively became a title. On this occasion he also raised a number of families to patrician status, the first time this had been done since the early part of Augustus's reign. Seven families – *gentes* – were certainly so elevated, with another eight probables, including the families of the future emperors Otho and Vitellius. He held the consulship in 37 and 41 (both as suffect consul), in 42, 43, 47 and 51 and was intending to hold it in 55, crucially the year his sons, natural and adopted, would attain the age of majority – 14, the *toga virilis* – and could be formally designated his heirs, as they were in his will, which was (naturally) not made public by Nero in case people would realise that he was technically supposed to share power with Britannicus.

Claudius' first task on succeeding to the purple was to put down – rather heavy-handedly – a group of prime movers in the assassination of Caligula and other idealistic (or arch-conservative) senators who were planning to govern without a *princeps* at all. A further revolt by a descendant of the family of Augustus's second wife, Scribonia, Camillus (qv), governor of Dalmatia, had to be suppressed as well.

Relations with the senate were difficult and fraught with uncertainties, the emperor's inexperience, insecurity and the unreliability of certain senatorial elements combining to make dealing with the governing élite difficult. He had no faction of supporters in the senate, which forced him to rely not only on a very few senatorial toadies like L. Vitellius, but more upon powerful freedmen and equestrian advisers, further putting the senate's nose out of joint, building up resentment and in the process laying the foundations of the imperial bureaucracy, which subsequently expanded in the control of *equites* and freedmen. Nevertheless, the governance of the empire remained stable and military success was again achieved, in Germany, Mauretania and, of course, setting in train the final conquest and annexation of Britain.

Claudius was a contradictory character, as revealed in his surviving edicts; 'pedantic and idiosyncratic' and a 'donnish buffoon' are both valid comments, and he exhibited the cruelty found in most members of his family. Furthermore, relations with the élite were additionally compromised by his two empresses, the last of whom allegedly had him fatally poisoned through the agency of a crone called Lucusta and a plate of mushrooms on 13 October 54. Power and self-interest once again supervened over the legal niceties of established politics and conventions. As Barbara Levick so aptly observes, legality in the early principate was 'stretched to breaking point by the very existence of the emperor'. Indeed, she makes the point that it was in Claudius's reign the head of state progressed from *princeps* to emperor, a transition more often attributed to Septimius Severus.[131]

---

131 Levick (1990) 76-77, 78

CLAUDIUS II GOTHICUS
268, September 268 – 270, September

Claudius II was one of a number of Illyrian (Balkan) soldier emperors who seized power in the later third century. Claudius himself was famous for achieving a stunning victory over a serious incursion by Goths before dying unexpectedly of natural causes before he was able to achieve anything else.

M. Aurelius Valerius Claudius was born in Illyria on 10 May, probably in 214 (he was 56 when he died), one of a group of cavalry generals under Gallienus, which marked the beginning of a move away from an infantry-based army to a largely mounted mobile one, leaving the infantry increasingly to man the frontiers (*limes*). Sir Ronald Syme described them as 'brothers-in-arms...some perhaps from the same locality and related by ties of blood or marriage'.[132] Claudius had been a tribune under Gallienus, serving at Ticinum (Pavia), although the *Historia Augusta* adds that he was first appointed tribune earlier, under Decius. He served in a legion (almost inevitably not one otherwise known to history) and under Valerian was appointed *dux* of the whole of Illyria, which sounds credible.[133] Certainly, the plotters who assassinated Gallienus may well have started out with a view to putting Claudius in his place, presumably because they thought him temperamentally suited and with and a man they could do business with. They struck when Gallienus was dealing with Aureolus (qv) outside Milan.

Claudius immediately to a stop to the senatorially inspired extirpation of the surviving family of Gallienus and insisted the senate should accord the late emperor divine honours, which they reluctantly did. Subsequently, Claudius refused to come to terms with Aureolus, but he surrendered anyway, being later murdered by some soldiers because of his betrayal of Gallienus, whom they had apparently admired.

Despite his strictures against the senate proscribing Gallienus' family, that body was quick to recognise the new emperor, and he took the style Imperator Caesar M. Aurelius Claudius Augustus, was granted the tribunician and proconsular powers and he was designated ordinary consul for the beginning of the year following (269).

Quite early in his reign Zenobia appears to have annexed Egypt and she had added Syria and southern Asia Minor by the time he died. This was mainly because the new emperor was obliged to turn his attention to events on the German frontier, where a victory early in 269 over a horde of Germanic Alamanni who had crossed Postumus' breakaway Gallic realm and penetrated far into the empire, accorded him an acclamation and the honorific Germanicus.[134] He also managed to detach Spain from the Gallic empire. A year later he was further acclaimed as Gothicus (which adhered to his name ever afterwards) after inflicting a crushing military defeat on a vast horde of Goths near Marcianopolis (Devnya, Bulgaria) on the lower Danube,

---

132 Syme (1971) 211. If only we knew the ties of blood and marriage in detail, it might throw more light on events between 268 and 284.
133 PLRE I. Claudius 11
134 ILS 570. He was acclaimed Parthicus, too: ILS 571

completing a campaign started by Gallienus but against an enemy which had become much more of a threat in the intervening period. Thereafter, he was almost immediately obliged to move to Sirmium (Sremska Mitrovika, Serbia) in preparation for a campaign against the Juthungi who had also made a threatening foray across the upper Danube, but he died there of plague in September (some sources claim May) 270, although at least one account (inevitably) alleges murder. Eutropius said of him that he was a 'frugal and moderate man, a steadfast upholder of justice and well qualified to administer the state'.[135] His victory against the Goths earned him a golden shield and statue, and he was deified on his death by the senate on their own initiative.[136]

Nothing is known about his family except that his brother (who briefly succeeded him) was Quintillus (qv). Nevertheless, the House of Constantine invariably claimed to descend from him, the first direct reference to which occurs in 310, forty years later, although an argument has been advanced for its appearance as early as 297.[137] Although both families appear to have come from Illyria, and some connection is of course possible, descent from Claudius, a mythical brother called Crispus or even a sister, is universally considered to have been adopted or exaggerated as a legitimating stratagem by Constantine or his father. The *Historia Augusta*, however, supplies Claudius with Illus, King of Troy and Dardanus as ancestors, not to mention other kinsmen: Constantius I here being the son of Eutropius, Dardanian husband of Claudia, daughter of Crispus, an alleged brother of Claudius.[138] As Constantine I was probably born c. 250, this descent is impossibly long from a man (Crispus) who would have been born somewhere around 220. If the panegyricists of Constantine had thought about it, they could have declared that Constantius I's father had married the sister of Claudius II; that at least would have fitted the tight time-frame. Presumably, there was enough genuine information then known to preclude deploying this hypothesis. It also alleges that Quintillus had two sons (un-named) and a sister, Claudia Constantina, but at least agrees that the emperor himself had no issue.

CLODIUS ALBINUS
95, c. June 195 – 197, 19th February

Clodius Albinus was one of a select band of emperors elevated to the purple in Britain, and one of the contenders for the purple who declared themselves when news of the elevation of Didius Julianus reached the provinces. With Pescennius Niger and Septimius Severus, he was one of three generals keen to take advantage of the chaos arising from the brief reigns of Pertinax and Julianus.

---

135 *Op. cit.*, 9, 11
136 ILS 572
137 See Drinkwater (1987) 79-80 & n. 171
138 HA *V. Claud.* 11, 10, 13, 1-3, 9. Another sister, Constantia, allegedly married an 'Assyrian tribune'.

The family of the new Emperor, whose full name originally was D. Clodius Albinus, is only recorded in any detail in the pages of the *Historia Augusta* and is thus exceedingly suspect. The only things other sources attest is that his family was noble (that is senatorial),[139] came from Africa (Hadrumetum)[140] and that he was married with children. Dio tells us that he was closely related to Asellius Aemilianus, Niger's chief lieutenant.[141] The remaining reliable facts about him come from Dio and Herodian.[142] The reliable elements in the *Historia Augusta* probably came from the lost history by Marius Maximus. The book claims a descent for him from the Ceionii and Postumii Albini[143] whilst going on to explain the name Albinus in the light of Albinus' whiteness (Latin *albus* = white) both as an infant and as an adult. This is thought by Sir Ronald Syme, perfectly reasonably, to be a satirical reference to the pretensions of the rather grand Ceionii Albini of the later fourth century when the *Historia* was actually compiled.[144] There was no senatorial family of Clodii using the *praenomen* Decimus, however, although it could have been adopted from a marriage alliance with a D. Junius (much commoner). Africa, however, also produced the near contemporary equestrian official D. Clodius Galba.

Albinus himself must have been born about 147, since he appears to have become a senator c. 175. His quaestorship might just have preceded this date, although the outline given in the *Historia Augusta* is not to be trusteed, as Birley points out.[145] Prior to that, he would have served on one of the various boards of young careerists who made up the vigintivirate, followed – it would certainly appear – by a period as military tribune. His praetorship would have fallen in the earlier 180s (it is impossible to determine if he held an aedileship or a peoples' tribunate) followed by the command of a legion and/ or governorship of a minor province. The *Historia* tells us that his military tribunate was in command of Dacian cavalry, that his minor governorship was Bithynia and that he was governor of Lower Germany, none of which can be otherwise attested.[146] Modern scholarship suggests that the Lower Germany appointment is likely and that it would have immediately preceded his certain appointment to Britain in 191, thus falling in 189/190. This would put his suffect first consulship in 187 or 188. If the German governorship is rejected, the consulship can be safely re-allocated to 190, in which year there were, in addition to the two ordinary consuls, no less than 22 suffect ones, of whom the names of only about eight are known for certain.

Albinus married a wife whose name is not known for certain, although the *Historia Augusta* claims Marcus Aurelius' son-in-law M. Peducaeus Plautius

---

139 *Ibid.*, 3, 5, 2
140 Coin evidence confirms this.
141 Dio LXXIV, 6.2
142 *Ibid.*, LXXIII 14, 3 Herodian, 2, 15, 3, 6, 6, 3 & 7.1
143 V. *Albini*, 4. 1. Unlikely, and unattested as an alliance at any period.
144 Syme (1968) 163, supported by Settipani (2000) 284 n
145 Birley (1981) 147
146 V. *Albini* 6. 1-6

Quintillus as Albinus' father-in-law, which would make her a Peducaea Plautia.[147] Whilst one might have expected so momentous a fact to have been recorded elsewhere, the effectiveness of Albinus' subsequent condemnation may have eradicated this 'slur' on the family of the divine Marcus, especially once Severus had attached himself to it in 195; the connection is supported by T. D. Barnes.[148] Thus perhaps Albinus' wife was indeed a daughter of Quintillus but by a previous marriage. The couple are known to have had two sons, either killed on 19 February 197 or exiled then and killed later with their mother, when the victorious Severus carried out his ruthless and bloody cull of the senate.[149]

He was not acclaimed *imperator* by his soldiers as far as we know – although such an event is quite possible and is said to have happened (abortively) twice in Britain during the reign of Commodus – but was appointed Caesar by Severus in early April 193 in order to secure his flank against a potential rival. He took the style D. Clodius Albinus Caesar[150] and we may assume that the senate ratified this state of affairs after 1 June and no doubt granted him, with Severus, the tribunician and proconsular power, renewable every 10 December in the usual way. He probably acquired an imperial acclamation from his army, too. June 193 probably also marks the change in his style to D. Clodius Septimius Albinus Caesar,[151] the addition of 'Septimius' being to set out the more clearly his position as notional heir of Severus. He was (ordinary) consul with Severus for 194. Through most of his subsequent period in power he was effectively ruling and administering the northern European provinces – the Gauls, Germanies, Britain, Spain – almost as a forerunner of the Gallic Empire which arose under Gallienus and underwent further recrudescence under Carausius, Magnus Maximus and Constantine III.

Nobody can tell what Clodius Albinus' true intentions were when he heard about the murder of Pertinax in April 193. Furthermore, his mother was from Hadrumetum (Sousse) in Africa, from whence also came some of Julianus' family, which might have inclined Severus, as a fellow African, to consider him unreliable. Another factor was that Asellius Aemilianus, who had swung his considerable influence behind Niger, was (according to the *Historia Augusta* at least) related to Albinus. For Severus to drive a wedge between them might also have seemed prudent; more to the point, it might even open Aemilianus to offers.

Judging by the speed of events, little discussion through messages passing along the *cursus publicus* (postal system) can have taken place. The likelihood is that Severus sent a message saying that he had been proclaimed and

---

147 HA, V. *Albini* 10.7

148 *The Sources of the Historia Augusta* (Brussels 1978) 52; but preremptorily denied by Birley (1988) 244 n. 26, who is happier going along with one of the Asellia gens. (Maybe he's bats.)

149 Marius Maximus, quoted in HA, V. *Albini* VII. 3, IX. 4

150 Coin evidence.

151 ILS 414, 415

offering Albinus the role of junior colleague and eventual successor. This would have been perfectly convincing, bearing in mind that Severus' two sons were then five and four years old respectively and that infant mortality was high. On the other hand, there must always have been the fear that Severus would eventually dump his fellow African, an eventuality for which no doubt Albinus prepared over the years of their partnership. Initially, however, whilst Severus advanced rapidly on Rome against Didius Julianus, and then east to deal with Niger and the Parthians, Albinus held northern Europe for him.

Albinus was apparently regarded as a good-natured man and seems happy to have remained in Britain as Caesar for the two years following his appointment, although in regular contact with Rome, presumably for administrative purposes; in the capital he received significant support from senators, who preferred him to Severus. Had he any serious suspicions of his senior colleague, he would surely have crossed the Channel and marched on Rome himself, a relatively safe option as Severus was for a long time away, following up his victory over Niger with a punitive expedition against Parthia.

However, in the middle of this campaign, about May 195, Severus announced that he was the 'son of the Divine Marcus' (Aurelius) and at the same time proclaimed as Caesar his elder son Bassianus, renaming him, in accordance with his bizarre self-adoption into the Antonines, M. Aurelius Antoninus Caesar. As soon as this news reached Albinus, his position must suddenly have appeared precarious.

Yet Severus could not yet risk a war against Albinus whilst advancing on Nisibis, the Parthian capital; perhaps he wanted the news that there was another official heir to force Albinus' hand so that, by the time he was back in the west, he had a ready-made *casus belli* to use against his erstwhile colleague. He had apparently already attempted covertly to have Albinus assassinated.

Albinus could thus either resign and hope to be allowed to retire, or fight. He chose the latter and, crossing the Channel, declared himself Augustus in opposition to Severus. He was henceforth styled Imperator Caesar D. Clodius Septimius Albinus Augustus and whilst one might have expected him to have dropped the Septimius element from his name pretty quickly, it appears on three versions of his coinage titulature before being dropped. It is possible, in the light of the savagery meted out to over sixty senators after his fall, that the senate may – at least for a time – have recognised him as co-emperor, but this would have ceased before Severus returned to Rome in May 196. He does not appear to have held or claimed the pontificate.

This proclamation on Albinus' part provoked Severus to call upon a cowed senate to declare his former co-emperor a public enemy, which they did on 15 December 195; this was his 'official' deposition. Severus eventually arrived back in Rome by the end of August 196, having taken measures to bottle Albinus up in northern Europe, although one *arriviste* general, Virius Lupus – ancestor of a long line of senators – was given a drubbing by Albinus' forces. Nevertheless, by autumn, Severus had gone north again and was heading a campaign to finish the matter.

Despite heading a much superior force against Albinus, it took Severus until February 197 to bring the matter to a resolution. Severus came within an ace of losing the final battle outside Lugdunum (Lyon) in Gaul on the 19th before fortune swung his way; Albinus' forces were eventually crushed, the city burned, plundered and the corpse of the unfortunate co-emperor brought to him to be humiliatingly mutilated and thrown into the Rhône. The *Historia Augusta* claims the Empress and those of his children who were present also died, but there is a suspicion that his wife may have died prior to his elevation, otherwise she would have appeared on coins; neither do Dio or Herodian mention them.[152]

CLODIUS MACER see MACER

COMMODUS
180, 17th March – 192, 31st December

Commodus is most commonly recognised as being amongst the coterie of truly ghastly emperors, alongside Caligula, Domitian and Caracalla, a view advanced by the classical historians and arising out of long-remembered senatorial antipathy to each. Commodus is remembered for his cruelty, uninterest in his inherited role and as a libertine who lived his life in blithe disregard for any of the conventions of Roman society or Roman *mores*. Consequently, he achieved nothing except what others managed in his name. He ascended the throne so distinguished by his father Marcus Aurelius at eighteen, was the first emperor to have been *porphyrogenitus* – born in the purple – son of an emperor reigning at the time of his birth, bar poor, tragic and ephemeral Britannicus. Yet it was the misfortune of Rome in the first three centuries of empire that almost all sons succeeding fathers turned out badly, although we must in all conscience exclude Gallienus, who held the entire polity together through a decade of apparent collapse. One reason, it could be argued, was that the fathers, all strong, effective rulers, were such a hard act to follow – but in reality, all seem to have been cursed with various forms of personality disorder.

L. Aurelius Commodus was born on 31 August 161 at Lanuvium and on 12 October 166 was raised to the rank of *caesar*, which name he added to his own. As early as 15 October 172 he was allowed to add the style Germanicus, followed in March/April 175 by Sarmaticus. He had been received into all the priestly colleges on January 20 the same year. He was hailed *imperator* in 176 and again the following year, when he also held the consulship and was made joint ruler with his father as Imperator Caesar Lucius Aurelius Commodus Augustus,[153] being given the title *pater patriae* as well as the tribunician and proconsular powers. He was consul for the second time in 179 and gained his third imperial acclamation with another (his fourth) in 180, prior to his accession. For his antecedents these are touched upon in the biographies of

---

152 Eg., Herodian, 3, 7, 7-8
153 ILS 375

Antoninus Pius and Marcus Aurelius. His wife Bruttia Crispina was, on the distaff, also of ancient lineage, He had married her prior to setting out for Germany with his father. She was the daughter of C. Bruttius Praesens[154] who had been consul in 153 and served again in 180 and she was descended from the ancient patrician house of the Quinctii Crispini through the female line.

On accession, he was styled Imperator Caesar L. Aurelius Commodus Antoninus Augustus[155] becoming *Pontifex Maximus* seven months later. In October 180 he assumed the *praenomen* Marcus *in lieu* of Lucius,[156] adding 'Pius' after 'Antoninus' two years later and three years on from that also added 'Felix', probably as a reflection of the sort of feel-good factor he hoped emanated from himself than from his descent from the dictator Sulla. Despite all this, in 191 he reverted to the simpler style of Imperator Caesar L. Aelius Aurelius Commodus Augustus,[157] evoking more the nomenclature of his late adoptive uncle, Lucius Verus. In 182, having thrown away all the advantages won through his father's final campaign in Germany, he ironically added 'Maximus' to his 'Germanicus' and, just over two years later, assumed the triumphal *cognomen* of Britannicus, too, although the (nominal) cause of this on the ground has not been identified. His third consulship came in 181, fourth in 183, fifth in 186, sixth in 190 and finally his seventh in 192. His remaining imperial acclamations came in 182, 183, 184 and 186. Later in his reign he also took the additional names 'Hercules Romanus', reflecting his increasing obsession with himself as a re-born Hercules.

It all started to go wrong on his father's death. He made a neat, appropriate speech to the legions in Germany, but immediately ended a successful and promising campaign on the frontier which could have left most of modern Germany a former Roman province and the borders of empire arguably much more secure, but campaigning was not his style; he was a sybarite at heart. He thus returned home to sully his already slightly dubious reputation with acts of astounding cruelty, caprice and perversity that saw his reign begin with his obsession with gladiators and end with his being worshipped as a god, and in particular as the personification of Hercules. The running of the empire was left to a succession of egregious favourites.

Nor had he had any contact with the workings of the senate and consequently, like Domitian, he placed little value on the formal proceedings of that body which underpinned the delicate balance between the ruler and the governing class. As before, this made the extirpation of members of the senate easier for Commodus, who cared little for legal niceties, even less for the élite, who essentially kept the huge ramshackle machinery of empire creaking along surprisingly effectively. In fact, the impact of a half-mad emperor tended to be on the individuals at the highest level of the governing class, the senior senators and courtiers, not so much on the bureaucracy and

---

154 His full name was L.Fulvius C. f. Pompt. [Rusticus] C. Bruttius Praesens Min[   ] Valerius Maximus Pompeius L[onginus Aburnius] Valens Cornelius Proculus [   ] Aquilius Veiento: ILS 8265

155 ILS 376

156 ILS 177

157 ILS 400; PIR² A1482

individual commanders. And, as the historians who recorded these doleful events were usually themselves from that background, the impact of the wayward head of state is inevitably emphasised, perhaps even exaggerated.

Commodus bothered little with the minutiae of imperial government; indeed, he bothered very little with it at all. He also surrounded himself with rather strange and, to his peers, unacceptable people: charioteers, gladiators, catamites and other oddballs. The atmosphere created of fear, loathing and unpredictability led to frequent conspiracies, some imaginary, others perfectly real, as that of Commodus' sister Lucilla, using her husband's nephew, Ti. Claudius Pompeianus Quintianus and M. Ummidius Quadratus as cat's paws. The attempt was hopelessly bungled and the participants duly executed. This was followed by the murder of his first favourite, Saoterus, which led to a bloodbath of possible accomplices, many his kin, and to a complete withdrawal by the emperor from public life, his contact with reality being maintained by his Pretorian Prefects, Sex. Tigidius Perennis and his successor, the freedman's son, M. Aurelius Cleander.

Thereafter Commodus, clearly a bisexual satyromaniac, revelled in private orgies and was largely protected from all diversions. Plots continued, and in 191 large parts of Rome burned down, giving the emperor the chance to appear bountiful and undertake extensive restoration works, though these were not completed for a decade or so. There was also unrest in the army and in 185 the garrison in Britain attempted to elevate a senior commander called Priscus (qv) to the purple, the selected victim wisely declining. Nevertheless, the Prefect of the Praetorian Guard, effectively in control of the government, sacked all the British legionary legates as a precaution and sent the future emperor Pertinax out to take control. Later, one Maternus, the leader of some deserters who had been roaming Gaul since the abrupt end of the war in Germany, tried to assassinate the Emperor in Rome.

A successful attempt to eliminate Commodus became, it seemed, inevitable. It came in 192. Having decided to re-name the months of the calendar after himself (nothing new there, *pace* Domitian), he now re-styled himself as the putative founder of Rome, which itself he intended to re-name Colonia Commodiana at a ceremony in new year 193, an occasion which was to be accompanied by games at which he would emerge as both sole perpetual consul and gladiator, having murdered the consuls elect beforehand.

The conspirators felt it imperative to kill the Emperor on the night before the planned games, on New Year's Eve 192. The plot succeeded and Commodus was finally despatched. The problem thereafter was of course to install an agreed replacement and avoid a power-struggle, for there had been no children from his marriage to Crispina, who in any case had soon been put away as a result in a (probably specious) accusation of adultery; she was killed in 182.

After his death his memory was erased (*damnatio memoriae*) by the senate. But this was reversed by Severus in 196, who also then had him deified within the Antonine cult, mainly because he wanted his own successful bid for power to be read as an act avenging the deposition of the last of the Antonines, in the remembered glory of whose rule he wished to bask.

In the event, installing an agreed replacement ruler did not prove so simple, and a four-year period of upheaval ensued, including two bloody civil wars. The appointment of Pertinax after the murder resulted in the year 193 becoming the Year of the Five Emperors and made the Year of the Four Emperors 124 years before look like the dimmest avatar.

CONSTANS I

337, 9th September – 350, 18th January

Constans was one of the sons of Constantine I, and a moderately competent ruler of much of the west following his father's death in 337. However, his shortcomings, which included rampant immorality, physical frailty and a predilection for the chase, saw him perceived as becoming too detached from events. He was eventually murdered in 350 at the instigation of his army commander, who clearly thought he could do a better job.

Flavius Julius Constans was born to the Empress Fausta in 320, was educated at Constantinople and taught Latin by Arborius, the uncle of the eminent Gallic author and statesman Ausonius. He was proclaimed Caesar on Christmas day 333 at Constantinople as Flavius Julius Constans Nobilissimus Caesar.[158] On elevation to the purple on Constantine's death in 337, he was styled Dominus Noster Flavius Julius Constans Pius Felix Augustus. Like his brothers, he received the usual powers from the senate. He took the additional style of Sarmaticus following a successful military campaign on the Danube in 338.[159] He was also consul in 339 and 346. Having fought off his elder brother's attempt at controlling his part of the empire – southern Europe and Africa – he was soon afterwards able to enlarge his own share with the addition of the remarkably short-lived Gallic portion over which the unfortunate Constantine II (qv) had held sway. He was thereafter, also by default, notionally senior Augustus, and the empire was once again, as from 313 to 324, divided between east and west.

Whilst the attention of the Eastern Emperor, Constantius II, was diverted by a hard campaign against the Persians, in mid-January 350 Constans was murdered in the Palace as a result of a conspiracy organised by his army commander Magnentius (qv), who promptly declared himself Augustus in his place. Constans had no wife or children.

CONSTANS II

410, c. February – 411, March

Constans was the elder son of British-based usurper Constantine III, elevated to be co-ruler with his father to hold the fort in Gaul whilst Constantine moved into Italy, and whose demise shortly preceded the collapse of his parent's regime in 411.

---

158 PLRE I Constans 3, where the possibility is expressed that his date of birth was actually 323, making him just 14 rather than 17 when he acceded to power.

159 ILS724; campaign, Zonaras 13, 5. 28

Constans was allegedly a former monk, called from the cloister and elevated to the rank of *nobilissimus caesar* by his father after his revolt in Britain. Whether he had ever really been a monk is doubtful, as he appears to have had a wife and family by the time of his demise. He was sent by Constantine III in 408, with the *magister militum* Gerontius as his *comes*, into Spain to settle matters with the barbarians who had arrived there after the incursion across the Rhine in 406. They swiftly put down all resistance and then garrisoned the Pyrenean passes to prevent other barbarian tribes, by this time in western Gaul, from entering Spain. Constans then returned to Gaul. Yet it was in that year, probably in the summer, that things began to unravel. He again returned to Spain with another *magister militum*, Justus, to relieve Gerontius. The handover somehow went seriously wrong; Gerontius took offence and, having won the support of his troops, began plotting against Constantine by colluding with the barbarians whom the latter had finally managed to settle in Gaul. He enrolled many of them into his forces in Spain, which was the thin end of the wedge for the breakaway regime for, from that year, the Pyrenean border became dangerously porous.

In spring 410, Constantine made the same mistake as Magnus Maximus and crossed into Italy, leaving Constans behind at Arelatum (Arles) to hold the fort. It was presumably at this stage that Constans was elevated to the rank of co-Augustus with his father, bearing the style of D[ominus] N[oster] Constans P[ius] F[elix] Augustus; his younger brother Julianus, who was probably only in his early 20s, was made *nobilissimus caesar*. From coins, it would appear that both he and his father still considered themselves recognised co-rulers of the West with Honorius, who had been obliged to recognise Constantine the year before any thereby legitimising their regime. In spring 411, Gerontius and his puppet emperor Maximus (IV, qv) taking advantage of the absence of Constantine, crossed the Pyrenees and besieged Viennensis (Vienne) on the fall of which Constans was killed. Nothing is known of the fate of his wife and family. (The reign of the emperor Constans III, 641-668, lies beyond the parameters of this book.)

CONSTANTINE I
306, 25ᵗʰ July – 337, 22ⁿᵈ May

Constantine the Great's chief claim to fame is that he was the first emperor to have embraced Christianity and the first to have accepted baptism, albeit on his death bed. He also finally united the empire, established a new capital, reformed its governance and successfully handed it on to his sons. He also bridged the transition from the chaos of the mid-third century to the very different empire that emerged from the period in which his dynasty dominated into the late fourth century.

C. Valerius Flavius Constantinus was born at Naissus (Niš, Serrbia) on 27 February 272, only three years after Claudius II had defeated the Goths there – which may explain his later desire to be acknowledged, through a panegyric of 310, as one of that ruler's kinsmen – and followed his father into the army. In that sense he was the last of the Illyrian soldier-emperors

Constantine, bronze
statue of 1998 by
Philip Jackson at York.
(Leila Appleton)

who had dominated the empire from the fall of Gallienus to the collapse of
the Tetrarchy.

As a young, keen cavalry commander, he served under Diocletian as a
senior tribune in Asia and Palestine, later acting as a commander (probably as
a *dux*) under Galerius against the Sarmatians.[160] In this early part of his career
he probably married Minervina, by whom he had a son, Crispus. After his
elevation and later recognition by Galerius, in March 307 he married Fausta,
by whom he had the future Emperors Constans I and Constantius II; his son
Constantine II was born in the same year as Constantius, so was probably
illegitimate and the son of a concubine. There were also two daughters,
both married to cousins: Constantina, who married Hannibalianus (qv) and
after his death in 337 Constantius Gallus (from 354 appointed *nobilissimus
caesar*) and Helena who married Julian the Apostate.

In the wake of the elimination of the errant ex-tetrarch Maximian,
Constantine decided to publicise his supposed descent from the family of
Claudius II, which later ages tended to treat as fact.[161] It may well be asked

---

160 PLRE I Constantinus 4

161 The HA gives Claudius II a sister Constantia and a third brother, Crispus,
whose daughter Claudia marries the Dardanian Eutropius, parents of Constantius I:
V. Claud. 13, 9; Eutropius and Zonaras make Claudia the daughter of Claudius II:
Eutropius 9, 22; Zonaras 12, 26f

why he chose Claudius and not Aurelian or Probus from whom to forge a descent; the answer (apart from, perhaps, his birth in the city where the Goths received their come-uppance) may be that the two families did have some kind of connection and that Constantine merely chose to magnify and embroider it to bolster his own prestige at the expense of his rival Maximian's son Maxentius (qv). His embrace of Christianity, allegedly as a result of a vision on the eve of the Battle of the Milvian Bridge in 312 was just another astute move, and one that might not be so ground-breaking as might seem at first sight, for the name of his younger half-sister, Anastasia (born between 293 and 306) has peculiarly Christian overtones. The thought occurs that she might have been a sibling of the full blood and that his mother Helena's family may have had some Christian connections, which could explain the later assiduity of Helena in her antiquarian quest for the True Cross. The Milvian Bridge victory was, however, followed by the so-called Edict of Milan of 313 which gave Christianity legal status and freed it from persecution by the state.

After he had himself proclaimed emperor at Eboracum (York) on the death of his father, the Tetrarch Constantius I, his *praenomen* changed, first to Marcus and then to Lucius.[162] After elevation (as Augustus) he was recognised by the Tetrarchs as caesar as Fl. Valerius Constantinus Nobilissimus Caesar, but a year later this was modified on his recognition as Augustus to Imperator Caesar Divi Constantii f[ilius] Flavius Valerius Constantinus Pius Felix Invictus Augustus, to which were added *pater patriae* and *pontifex maximus*, with the senate granting the usual tribunician and proconsular powers. In 312 he added the *agnomen* Maximus and in 324 Victor in lieu of Invictus.[163] From that year he shared power with the surviving Tetrarch, Licinius, who controlled the east.

On his recognition as Augustus, Constantine was saluted as Germanicus Maximus, this title being re-conferred thrice more in 308, 314 and 328, along with Sarmaticus Maximus (323 and 334) Gothicus Maximus (328, 332) and finally Dacicus Maximus in 336, reflecting the continual need to pacify the more volatile border regions of the empire. He was also made consul on recognition in 307, holding the consulship again in 312, 313, 315, 319, 320, 326 ad 329 – eight times in all.

Following the Edict of Milan, Constantine patronised churches and expended much time and effort attempting to bring unity to the fissiparous church through councils, inducements and diplomacy. With the defeat of Licinius and Martinianus in 325, the now sole emperor decided to establish a new imperial capital at Byzantium on the Bosphorus, in a sense, the virtual pivot between Europe on one hand and Asia and Africa on the other. This was henceforward to be called Constantinopolis (Constantinople, since 1923, Istanbul) and would be the seat of power, armed with a second senate, mirroring this and other institutions in the old capital. This made strategic sense and also set the scene for the division of the Empire, later to become permanent. The new city was inaugurated with great ceremony in May 330.

---

162 CL.VIII. 1781 (Marcus); *ibid.* 9042, 10064 (Caius) and ILS 690 (Lucius)
163 ILS699, 702; done probably to distance himself from the worship of Sol Invictus.

Constantine completed the military and administrative reforms begun by Gallienus and refined by Diocletian, separating the military and civilian spheres completely. The title of Pretorian Prefect was henceforth applied to a civilian regional supremo with oversight of a group of provinces called a diocese. Likewise, the army, already divided between border troops (including the remnants of the old Imperial legions) and a mobile centrally based trouble-shooting force (along with the Emperor's personal troops, replacing the Praetorian Guard, now finally abolished), were placed respectively under a Master of the Soldiers (infantry: *magister militum*) and a Master of Cavalry (*magister equitum*) both answering to the Emperor and under whom were the commanders (*duces*).

He completely reversed the policy of Gallienus and Diocletian of excluding senators from office, re-opening to them administrative careers and employing them in the highest offices, also up-grading the equestrian governor's rank (*praeses*) to consular status, to entice the senatorial aristocracy back into the mainstream administration of the Empire, a policy which his successors continued, although its effects were less apparent at first in the East.[164] Meanwhile, the reach of hereditary trades established under Diocletian's reform of the currency was extended, even to the army, which was designed to make up for the shortage of manpower caused by the wars of the later 3rd century and major outbreaks of plague, but the longer term and unintended consequences of which went unconsidered. On the other hand, a successful re-organisation of the currency was promulgated. The *aureus* was replaced by the *solidus* (although this *may* have happened as early as 301)[165]. In 309, this was standardised at 72 *denarii* to the (Roman) pound, a rate which continued unchanged throughout the empire until the eleventh century. Nevertheless, the *denarius* had long ceased to exist as a coin and was reduced to a unit of account, with 4 and 25 *denarii* being the value of the two base metal denominations, the latter being the *nummus* which was fixed as the maximum daily wage of a labourer in 301. The silver coin, briefly the *aurelianus,* was re-graded as the *argenteus,* fixed at the same weight in silver as a first-century *denarius* but actually worth 100 of them.

The old definition of a patrician (*patricius*) as a member of a family descended from one of the original members of the Regal senate and entitled to certain privileges, or as a member of a family subsequently raised to that status by one of the dynasts or emperors, also ceased to apply, although its social cachet and importance must have been in steep decline from the later third century with the ending of the senate's leading role in running the Empire

Constantine opened up all official posts to senators' sons (which led to the virtual disappearance of the equestrian order), graded the enlarged senate into ranks, in ascending order, *vir clarissimus* (as all senators from the 2nd century), *vir spectabilis* and *vir illustris* or *inlustris*. The very highest rank to which a person outside the Imperial family could aspire was the new rank of

---

164 Arnheim (1972) *passim*
165 Hartley *et al* (2006) 57

patrician, held only for life. One of the first Constantine ever created was his unfortunate cousin Julius Constantius, killed in 337.

Constantine also wove a cocoon of ritual around his person, giving the emperor near sacred status and surrounding himself with a hierarchy of courtiers, with suppliants prostrating themselves before his person (*proskynesis*), viewing himself as God's vice-regent on earth. The evolution of this (which may have begun to some extent as early as the reign of Septimius Severus) was in part to raise the status of the 'monarch' from the first among equals (*primus inter pares*) of Augustus to a remote and awesome figure making revolt or assassination all the more difficult and heinous. Hence his coin image moved from a 3rd-century-style radiate crown, or laureate head, to the use of a diadem, occasionally a plain-looking band around the head, but more often decorated with a double row of pearls and sometimes with plaques.

Despite this, he continued to encourage his subjects to come to him with petitions and appeals. Constantine was generous but hot-tempered, which occasionally led to rash decisions, and he was especially impatient with the theological disputes amongst his Christian subjects, but he was also a reformer who laid the foundations that enabled the empire to renew and survive a further 1,100 years in the east and 150 years in the west, a considerable achievement when viewed in the context of the near chaos of the third quarter of the previous century.

The Emperor's family was fairly young and, until his elimination in 326 as the result of what appears to have been a plot on the part of the Empress Fausta (mother of two of his half-brothers), his eldest son Crispus was the obvious heir.[166] Crispus is known to have had at least one child, although no names have survived and their fate is unknown. If they did survive early childhood, the likelihood is that they would have been killed at about the same time as their father. Several half-siblings and nephews of the Emperor were appointed Caesars in a pallid reflection of the tetrarchic system and was a clear recipe for the trouble that loomed as he breathed his last at his palace at Ankyrona (near Izmit, Turkey) on 22 May 337.

After his death, Constantine was deified by the senate, although it might seem anomalous that a man who died a Christian should be drafted into a pagan pantheon, but then he was also *Pontifex Maximus* throughout his reign. A coin type was even issued with the late emperor's veiled head as a god and on the obverse the deceased ruler galloping heavenward in a quadriga, the hand of God emerging to gather him up; talk about hedging one's bets.

There was an interregnum of almost four months, during which the Caesars Hannibalianus and Dalmatius, realising that they were being sidelined by the Emperor's surviving sons, were involved in a mutiny at Constantinople along with Julius Constantius, another cousin, ex-consul and patrician (but not actually a Caesar), but this was nipped in the bud by the late Emperor's

---

166 PLRE I Crispus 4; he was consul in 318, 321 and 324.

last right-hand man, the Praetorian Prefect Ablabius.[167] Julius Constantius, Hannabalianus and Dalmatius were all put to death along with other members of the family on 3 September. Consequently, the surviving sons, Constantius II, Constans and Constantinus II were jointly declared co-emperors on 9 September. The dynasty had 23 years to run in the male line.

CONSTANTINE II
337, 9th September – 340, March

Constantine II was the shortest-lived emperor amongst Constantine I's three sons and successors, and in the fallout from the events of September 337 was allocated Britain, Gaul (including the eastern frontier) and Spain in the carve-up organised by their father's kingmaker, Ablabius; in effect, a sort of revival of the Gallic empire of 260-272.

Flavius Claudius Constantinus was born at Arelate (Arles, Gaul) in February 317, probably to a concubine of Constantine, as his next brother Constantius II was born only six months later to the Empress. The use of the name Claudius in this generation of the family is an expression of the claim made on behalf of Constantine that he was descended from the family of the emperor Claudius II. He was declared *nobilissimus caesar* at less than a month old in March 317 as Flavius Claudius Constantinus Nobilissimus Caesar. His first consulship was in 320, and he held the office again in 321, 324, 324, 329 and 339. He married before 335, but we know neither the name of his empress (who may therefore have died or been divorced before his accession) nor of any children. When Constantine I died on 22 May 337 the three brothers and their two cousins Dalmatius and Hannibalianus were all in a kind of limbo: succeeded, but not acknowledged and legal constituted, a situation which pertained until their cousins were extirpated on 3 September and they were duly proclaimed co-emperors on 9 September 337.

As emperor, Constantine took the style Dominus Noster Flavius Claudius Constantinus Pius Felix Augustus, and all three brothers were granted tribunician and proconsular power by the senates of Rome and Constantinople. We are not told, however, whether any of the brothers were recognised as *pontifiex maximus* at this juncture; with the pre-eminence of Christianity, it may have been assumed that this office was in abeyance.[168] He rapidly added Alamannicus to his style after pacifying the tribes on the Rhine frontier.[169]

Soon becoming resentful of being unable to exercise his authority over parts of the Empire beyond those under his immediate control, and in order to assert himself over (or rid himself of) his brother Constans, he invaded Italy in spring 340 but was killed in an ambush near Aquileia, thus allowing Constans to become, by default, undisputed ruler of the entire west.

---

167 PLRE I. Ablabius 4. He was an upwardly mobile Cretan, who rose to the senate and a consulship in 331; his daughter became Queen of Armenia and his granddaughter was a sister-in-law of Theodosius I (qv).

168 FS p. 689

169 ILS724

CONSTANTINE III
407, April – 411, August

Constantine III was a British-based army commander proclaimed emperor in the wake of the crossing of the frozen Rhine on New Year's Eve 406 of many thousands of barbarians. He seems to have taken control effectively, unlike two ephemeral predecessors, and soon crossed to the Continent in an attempt to stem the tide, the Imperial western court at Ravenna being at that time powerless to do so. His European empire – effectively once more a re-creation of the north-western polity created under Postumus (qv) from 260 and Constantine II from 337-340 – was at first successful in achieving its objectives, but after two years became victim to internal dissension, despite recognition by Honorius (albeit *force majeure*) which ultimately resulted in Constantine's death.

Claudius Constantinus must have been born no later than 360, in view of the fact that he had a mature elder son and a grown up, if still youthful, younger one. He may therefore have cut his teeth serving under Magnus Maximus in Britain and in Gaul, perhaps afterwards serving in a variety of theatres in the wider Empire. The magic of the name Constantine may indeed have impelled him into the purple, yet it might seem more plausible to suppose that he had probably engineered a *coup* against his insular predecessor, Gratian (II, qv) probably in April 407, as a result of previous lack of action in a developing crisis. He is said, however, to have been *infima militia* (of the meanest soldiery) which does not seem at all likely. His entire career and the competence of his rule suggests that he was probably an experienced officer dealing with equals.

He probably crossed to the continent in early summer of 407. His dispositions included the appointment of joint *magistri militum*: one of his commanders, Justinianus, and a Frankish officer, Nebiogastes, sending them across the Channel in advance to take command of what remained of the Gallic army.[170] In the event, they had to deal not only with the barbarians roaming around northern and western Gaul, but attempts by Honorius to dislodge him. Had the government in Ravenna recognised Constantine more immediately, more might have been achieved. Instead, within a few months, Honorius' general Sarus had defeated and killed Justinianus and later killed Nebiogastes after tricking him into a parley, instead of allowing them to sort out the barbarians first.[171]

The ursurper's full style was D[ominus] N[oster] Flavius Claudius Constantinus P[ius] F[elix] Aug[ustus] but we are even less well informed about the underpinning of his regime than we were about that of Postumus a century and a half before: did he call a council or senate of Gallic grandees? Did he nominate consuls and so forth? The course of events probably suggests that some kind of assembly of the great and good was constituted, but no consuls have ever been identified except for Constantine himself.

---

170 PLRE I Justianianus 1, PLRE II Justinianus 1 & Nebiogastes
171 Drinkwater (1998) 284 ff.

In 409, the 3rd consulship of Eastern Emperor Theodosius II was not recognised, and Constantine himself held his first in lieu. Towards the end of 407, Justinianus was replaced by another Frank, Edobichus, and Nebiogastes by a Briton, Gerontius, both perhaps more competent and probably fellow officers of Constantine.[172] They soon forced Sarus to lift the siege of Valentia (Valence) which he had invested after disposing of Nebiogastes, as drove him back into Italy.

Most accounts of what transpired thereafter give a highly confused picture, and as such probably represented the situation on the ground fairly accurately. The Barbarian hordes seem to have ravaged westwards rather than southwards, leaving Constantine to move south to secure those parts of Gaul untouched by the chaos, finally fixing his capital at Arelate (Arles). That he lasted as long as he did suggests that he did a fairly competent job in the circumstances. He was only really challenged when the going became rough. He must have also undertaken some stabilisation of the Rhine frontier, which, although more notional than actual after 407, still seems to have been manned to some extent.

Having secured Gaul as well as he could, in 408 Constantine elevated his elder son Constans to the rank of *nobilissimus caesar*, He then sent him, with Gerontius as his *comes*, into Spain to settle matters with the barbarians there. He swiftly put down all resistance and then garrisoned the Pyrenean passes to prevent those barbarians, by this time in western Gaul, from entering Spain. Constans then returned to Gaul.

This period of stability, combined with a period of extreme weakness and peril on the part of the official western government in Ravenna, led Honorius grudgingly to recognise Constantine as co-emperor, sending him an imperial robe and agreeing to serve with him as joint consul for 409. Yet it was in that year, probably in the summer, that things began to unravel. Constans returned to Spain with another *magister militum*, Justus – conceivably a son of the unfortunate Justinianus[173] – to relieve Gerontius. As previously noted (see Constans II, above), Gerontius was stung into action and with the support of his troops, began plotting against Constantine by colluding with the barbarians. He enrolled a large number of them in Spain and from that year the Pyrenean border collapsed.

These events were read at Arelate as an act of rebellion, whereupon Gerontius, an 'experienced soldier and stern disciplinarian' raised his *domesticus* (second in command) Maximus to the purple in 409. Yet despite this, Constantine and Maximus successfully maintained an uneasy peace in Gaul and Spain, although it would appear that in 409 or 410 the regime of the Gallic emperor suffered a set-back; control of Britain slipped out of Constantine's grasp.

From the very confusing accounts, it would appear that the administration he had left behind was ousted by an anti-Constantinian *putsch* (presumably

---

172 PLRE II Edobichus & Gerontius 5
173 The concordance in their nomenclature, as with Constantinus and Constans, is highly suggestive.

led by another usurper – conceivably the Eugenius named in early British pedigrees as Owein, a 'son' of Magnus Maximus – but whose name has not been certainly preserved,[174] and the new administration then appears to have written to Honorius pledging loyalty to him and asking for help in defending their shores and borders. The response was the famous rescript of 410 (fixing the chronology), bidding the cities of the Diocese to look to their own defence for the time being. That 'time being' turned out to be a trifle open-ended and direct control appears never to have been resumed over the British provinces.[175]

Late in 409 or early 410, one of Honorius' disloyal commanders, Allobichus – another Frank – encouraged the Gallic rulers to join him in overthrowing Honorius, and in spring 410 Constantine made the same mistake as Magnus Maximus and crossed into Italy, leaving Constans holding the fort. From coins, it would appear that both he and his father still considered themselves as accepted and recognised co-rulers of the West with Honorius.

Meanwhile, in Italy, the claimant beat a hasty retreat after the plot against Honorius was uncovered and the disloyal Frank executed. However, the temporary absence of Constantine in Italy had encouraged Gerontius and Maximus to attempt to take control of Gaul from him. They crossed the Pyrenees and attacked besieged Viennensis (Vienne), on the fall of which Constans was killed.

These upheavals provided the government in Ravenna with an opportunity to pull things round, and Allobichus's much more competent successor as *magister militum*, Constantius (qv Constantius III), was sent to attack Constantine's capital, Arles. As he approached, the city was already being invested by Maximus, who, on realising this, raised the siege and retreated back to Spain in 411. With things going wrong, Constantine's Pretorian Prefect Decimius Rusticus connived with a Gallic notable called Jovinus, posted on the Rhine frontier to keep order there, to have the latter declared emperor in Constantine's place.[176] Meanwhile, the latter's last hope was the arrival of reinforcements from the Rhine under the ever-loyal Edobichus, but Constantius, perceiving this, made a lightning march up the Rhône valley and confronted the Frank, whose forces handed him over and deserted to Jovinus.

Realising that the game was up, the Gallic ruler took holy orders and then negotiated a surrender with Constantius, including a safe conduct for himself and his younger son, Julianus. On nearing Ravenna, however, the

---

174 Some commentators who have risked speculating on British events from this point suggest the person who has come down to us as Vortigern was the claimant, but it need not be so. Events may have been a lot more complex at this stage: Craven (2023) 270-275

175 The rescript has been challenged. It may refer to Bruttium in Italy, and the date of the revolt plausibly put back a year to 409, perhaps reflecting news of the breach with Gerontius, who may have left behind a following in Britain.

176 PLRE II Rusticus 9. He was a friend of Sidonius Apollinaris's family, and quite probably a close relative of the poet and politician Decimius Magnus Ausonius (consul in 379): Sivan (1993) 60 f.

party was intercepted, and the two were executed on the spot.[177] Despite having received a bad press as being the catalyst for the abandonment by the empire of the Diocese of Britain, Prosper of Aquitaine could write of him that Constantine III defended the frontiers of Gaul better than any emperor since Magnus Maximus, Zosimus adding that until this crisis, the Rhine frontier had been neglected since the time of Julian.[178]

Constantine may have been a Briton, but we certainly cannot be sure, although his name suggested to those who were familiar with the early Welsh pedigrees that he might have belonged to the post-Roman ruling dynasty of Dumnonia. Indeed, from that perspective, with the name Geraint (Gerontius) alternating with Custennin (Constantinus) in the king-lists, it could be argued (or not denied with any certainty) that the *magister militum* Gerontius was a fairly close relation of Constantine himself. There is plenty of precedent. All we can tell for certain is that the usurper had no living wife (or he would surely have named her Augusta and issued coins bearing her image), two sons, one of whom, Constans II, was married, as after the defeat of rebel forces in Spain in 408 we are told that he left his wife and household in Caesaraugusta (Zaragosa) whilst he returned to Arelate. (The reign of Constantine IV (641) and those so named who followed, lie outside the parameters of this book.)

CONSTANTIUS I CHLORUS
305, 1st April – 306, 25th July

Appointed by Diocletian and Maximian as one of the first pair of Caesars under the new Tetrarchic dispensation, Constantius Chlorus is best remembered for emulating Septimius Severus in subduing a rebellion in Britain, dying in York and being succeeded by his son – strictly against the conventions the Tetrarchs had laid down. He was also an outstanding military commander, with responsibility of the Rhine frontier.

Flavius Valerius Constantius was born in Illyria on 31 March in an unknown year, probably around 250. The supposed descent from Eutropius and a sister of Claudius II may be discounted, early though it appears; there is no hint as to the names of his parents, although the recurrence of Julius amongst his descendants may suggest a likely name for one of them.[179] Neither do his origins have to be that humble, for after military service as a member of the *protectores* and then as a senior tribune, he was made *praeses* (governor) of Dalmatia, possibly by Aurelianus, where an inscription supplies his original full name as above.[180] He served as a *dux* (general) under Probus if we may trust the *Historia Augusta*.[181] He married Flavia Julia Helena, a Bithynian, and mother of his son Constantine I (and later

---

177 PLRE II Constantinus 21; Constans 1 & Julianus 7
178 Prosper, year 412, Zosimus 6, 3, both quoted in Knight (2014) 167
179 The earliest appearance of the claim to descent from Claudius II is in a panegyric delivered at Trier in 310: Panegyricus VI (7)
180 PLRE I Constantius 12
181 *V. Probi* 22, 3. Plausible, but unproven.

St Helena, discoverer of the True Cross) and quite possibly a Christian, too, which may explain her son's early embrace of that faith. Helena was divorced by Constantius on the orders of the Tetrarchs in order to marry Maximian's daughter Flavia Maximiana Theodora (by whom he had six more children) when he was made Caesar in March 293. Thereafter he called himself C. Flavius Valerius Constantius Nobilissimus Caesar *signo* Herculius and was given responsibility for NW Europe, being endowed with the tribunician and proconsular power.[182] His first task as Caesar was to eliminate Carausius and Allectus, which he succeeded in doing in 296, having also won two victories over the German tribes on the east bank of the Rhine, mainly Alemanni, recruiting one of their princes, Crocus and his men, into his auxiliaries or his *protectores*.

Constantius was called Chlorus (pallid) only from the 6th century, but he won a favourable reputation amongst Christian writers of the 4th century through his attempts to ameliorate the consequences of the anti-Christian edicts of his colleague Galerius. He was named western Augustus in succession to the retiring Maximian in April 305, thereafter being styled Imperator Caesar C. Flavius Valerius Constantius Augustus, becoming *pontifex maximus*, later adding the *agnomina* Germanicus Maximus II, Sarmaticus Maximus II, Persicus Maximus II, Britannicus Maximus, Carpicus Maximus, Armeniacus Maximus, Medicus Maximus, and Adiabenicus Maximus. The following year he campaigned particularly successfully against the Picts in Britain. Having come back to Eboracum (York) after the conclusion of the Pictish campaign, he became ill and died there on 25 July 306, in only his second year of extraordinary powers. His son Constantine, serving in the east under the beady eye of Galerius (to ensure no coup was formulated by him whilst together with his father) hearing that his father was ill, managed to elude the eastern tetrarch and escape to the Channel coast, arriving in York in time to be acclaimed – not merely *caesar*, but augustus – in his place. Constantius was six times consul in 294, 296, 300, 302, 305 and 306. After his death he was deified by the senate.[183]

CONSTANTIUS II
337, 9th September – 361, 3rd November

Perhaps the most successful of the sons of Constantine the Great, the first part of his reign was spent fighting the Persians on the eastern frontier, not always successfully. From 354 sole emperor, he ruled with moderate success before managing to die of natural causes after the acclamation of his nephew Julian in 361. A century or so before, and some of his military predicaments would have led to an immediate rash of imperial claimants, but it is to his credit and to the respect generated around the dynasty that this hardly happened.

Flavius Julius Constantius was *porphyrogenitus*, having been born on 7 August 317 in Illyricum, son of Constantine I and the Empress Fausta.

---

182 ILS 648/649; ILS 637 gives his *praenomen* (erroneously) as Marcus.
183 ILS652

He was proclaimed *caesar* on 8 November 324 and held the first of his consulships two years later, aged nine; in other words, his promotion as a child was not nearly so fast-tracked as that of his (half) brother Constantine II. Constantius was thrice married: in 335 he wed a daughter (whose name is not known) of his kinsman Julius Constantius. She had either died or had been divorced by 353 when he married Eusebia. She was the daughter of Flavius Eusebius, consul in 347, and her two brothers, Flavius Eusebius junior and Flavius Hypatius, undoubtedly benefitted from her new station, being also made consul together in 359 and appointed patricians.[184] An Arian Christian, she died c. 360 and in the year of his death the Emperor married Faustina, by whom he had his only surviving child, the posthumously born Constantia, who later married the emperor Gratian, linking the house of Constantine with that of Valentinian.[185]

Constantius was elevated to the rank of Augustus on 9 September 337, when his style became Imperator Caesar Flavius Julius Constantius Pius Felix Augustus.[186] He also styled himself similarly but more formally on occasion, inserting Divi Const[antini] f. Val[erius] Maximian[us] n[epos] Divi Claud[ii] pron[epos] after Constantius and adding Sarmaticus and Persicus to mark his eastern exploits.[187] He held the consulship in 326 aged nine, and thereafter in 335, 342, 346, 352, 353, 354, 356, 357 and 360. Once his sole reign had begun in 354, he assumed the venerable title of *pontifex maximus*.[188] One shaky moment early on was the acclamation as emperor of Vetranio, the *magister peditum* of Constans in Illyricum in 350. This was dealt with following the death of Constans by Constantius, ending, most unusually, with the usurper's abdication and pardon; no blood was shed, unlike the battle of Mursa against the next usurper, Magnentius, a year later, the casualties of which were so severe as to leave the Roman army fatally weakened and henceforth increasingly dependent on barbarian mercenary units.

The overthrow of his brother Constans was such as to incline Constantius to appoint a new colleague and in 351 he made his cousin and brother-in-law Flavius Claudius Constantius Gallus Caesar, thereafter styled Flavius Claudius Constantius *nobilissimus caesar*. This was not a wholly successful choice: he was consul in three consecutive years, 352-354 and the arrangement was sealed with Gallus's marriage to the emperor's sister Constantia. However, thanks to his 'cruelty and violent disposition' he proved a broken reed and was degraded from office in 354, subsequently being executed.[189]

Having had to dispense with the dubious assistance of Gallus, it became clear to Constantius that he needed another co-emperor and on 6 November 355 he appointed Gallus's pagan younger half-brother Flavius

184 PLRE I Eusebia; Eusebius 39 & 40; Hypatius 4. The family were from Thessalonica.
185 PLRE I Faustina & Constantia 2
186 ILS732; PLRE I Constantius 8
187 ILS725
188 FS1694
189 Aurelius Victor 42, 9

Claudius Julianus as Caesar.[190] This was probably in immediate response to the appearance of yet another usurper, Silvanus at Cologne (Colonia Agrippina) in Lower Germany on the Rhine frontier earlier in 355. Both he and another shadowy possible usurper, Carausius II in Britain, were probably elevated by their troops in response to the destruction of Magnentius and Decentius in 353 and Constantius' subsequent return to the east. The new Caesar Julian was in consequence sent to the Rhine to sort matters out, which he did with considerable success, becoming popular as a result with both the army and the local élite. Needless to say, this left Constantius feeling threatened. His response was to attempt to curb Julian's power, which had the predictable result of his being acclaimed augustus by his forces in 360. On his way to deal with his presumptuous kinsman, however, the emperor died on 3 November 361, apparently of disease, leaving Julian sole emperor.

CONSTANTIUS III
421, 8th February – 2nd September

Constantius III was a competent senior commander under Honorius who was instrumental in mopping up after the incursion under Alaric and in putting down the resurgent Gallic empire of Constantine III and Jovinus. Having been rewarded by Honorius with the hand of his sister and elevation to the rank of co-emperor, he soon died of natural causes.

Flavius Constantius was yet another Danubian general, albeit of Roman descent, having been born at Naissus in Dacia Ripensis (Niš, Serbia) c. 366, becoming a junior officer under Theodosius I, and who distinguished himself in numerous campaigns. He appears at court in 409, where he had one of Stilicho's assassins killed. By 411, he was a *comes* and *magister militum* throughout the western empire, a post he held until 421. He was also made *vir illustris* and held the western consulship in 414. The following year or a little before, he was made a patrician.

He was an implacable foe of the Visigoths, especially Athaulf, of whom he was jealous for having married Galla Placidia, whom he coveted; this coloured his military policy. He attacked them in Gaul, driving them from Narbo (Narbonne) and forcing them across the Pyrenees, making them again abandon Maximus (IV). When Athaulf died, his successor, Walia, made a treaty with him and repatriated Galla, whom Constantius promptly wed (largely against her will, one suspects) on 1 January 417, at which juncture he entered into his second consulship. She was made Augusta and they had two children, Pulcheria and the future emperor Valentinian III. Meanwhile, he negotiated the settlement of the Visigoths in Aquitania (418) following which he was made consul a third time in 420.[191] At Galla's insistence he was elevated to be co-emperor with Honorius on 8 February 421.

---

190 PLRE I Julianus 29
191 ILS801

He took the style Dominus Noster Invictus Princeps Constantius [Augustus] on accession.[192] The convention when a new emperor was acclaimed was that his statues were sent to the senate and court of the other half of the empire for formal recognition. The unilateral elevation of Constantius and the influence over the young emperor of his sister Pulcheria ensured that these were rejected in Constantinople, a slight which humiliated the new augustus. He therefore made preparations to impose himself in the east by force, thereby re-uniting the Empire but, perhaps mercifully, he died of pleurisy on 2 September. He was known for his incorruptibility and stern demeanour, although it appears he also enjoyed social occasions and found life at court after his accession stifling and confining. Yet for a decade or more he had dominated political and military life, seen off five usurpers and stabilised the rule of Honorius.

CYRIADES
253

At some stage during the chaos surrounding the campaign by Aemilian in displacing Gallus and Volusianus, the *Historia Augusta* alleges that another imperial claimant arose called Cyriades.[193] Almost certainly he is to be indentified with one Mereades who betrayed Antioch to the Persians and ended up being killed by them. No other source suggests that either he or Meriades ever assumed the purple. Either way, he was subsequently killed through treachery amongst his own supporters. The revelation that he was thoroughly unpleasant, although 'rich and well-born' might go some way to explaining his demise but he is not known in any other source and is generally accepted as having been conjured up by the author of the *Historia Augusta* to make up numbers for his section called *The Thirty Tyrants*.

DALMATIUS
337, 22nd May – 3rd September

A grandson of Constantius I Chlorus by his second wife, Theodora, Dalmatius' father was Flavius Dalmatius, consul in 333 and he was the elder brother of Hannibalianus (qv). He was made *nobilissimus caesar* on 18 September 335, and he even issued coins. Along with his brother and three cousins of the half blood (the surviving sons of Constantine) he notionally succeeded to joint power on Constantine's death on 22 May 337. Soon realising that he and his brother were being side-lined by the Emperor's surviving sons, both were involved in a mutiny at Constantinople along with Julius Constantius, another cousin, ex-consul and patrician (but not actually a *caesar*). This was stifled by the late Emperor's last right-hand man, the Praetorian Prefect

---

192 ILS809; PLRE II Constantius 17
193 HA *Trig. Tyr.* II. 1-4

Ablabius and Dalmatius was killed on 3 September, leaving the field clear for Constantine's sons.[194]

DECENTIUS
353, May – 18th August

Decentius was named as the younger brother of Magnentius, who was left in charge in NW Europe whilst his brother contended with Constantius II, but having suffered a defeat on the Rhine he found his position undermined and shortly after Magnentius' death he committed suicide. He was probably made *caesar* by his brother in the wake of the revolt of Nepotianus (qv) and prior to the refusal of Constantius II to acknowledge Magnentius. He was styled Dominus Noster Flavius Decentius Nobilissimus Caesar, the Flavius again suggesting that his appointment preceded the refusal of Constantius to countenance such impertinence.[195] He was consul (recognised only in the area of the former Gallic empire) with his brother in 353. He suffered a reverse against the Franks in his brother's absence and found Trier, to which he had fallen back, closed to him thanks to a *dux*, Poemenius (qv), changing his allegiance and who is thought by some, on numismatic evidence, to have also set himself up as an usurper, although this is highly unlikely.[196]

It is probable that with the Eastern Emperor advancing toward Gaul in spring 353, Decentius was appointed co-ruler with his brother; had he declared himself augustus only after Magnentius' death, it is unlikely we would have the one inscription styling him Dominus Noster Magnus Decentius Caesar Pius Felix Semper Augustus (the Flavius seems to have been dropped once Eastern recognition had eluded the two western rulers).[197] With Magnentius dead, he escaped with some other units, no doubt aiming as successor to rescue the situation, but soon realised his cause was hopeless and also took his own life near Agedin[c]um (Sens) eight days later. It is possible that it was in the context of this usurpation that the bids for power were made by Silvanus, and Carausius II.

DECIUS
249, June – 251, 27th May/1st June

Decius was a senior senator of Pannonian origin, the second, after Maximin Thrax, of a long line of military men from what later became known as Illyricum, the region being so called on some of the Emperor's coinage (which makes up much of his home area), although the only one of senatorial rank.

---

194 PLRE Dalmatius 6 & 7; PLRE I. Ablabius 4. Ablabius was an upwardly mobile Cretan, who rose to the senate and a consulship in 331; his daughter became Queen of Armenia and his granddaughter was a sister-in-law of Theodosius I.
195 ILS746
196 Ammianus 15, 6; Kent (1959) 105-108
197 ILS747

He was known as a persecutor of Christians and also as the first Roman emperor to have been killed in action fighting against an external enemy.

Decius' family came from Lower Pannnonia, and he himself from Budalia near Sirmium (Sremska Mitrovica, Serbia). The fact that he was able to have a long and distinguished senatorial career suggests that the Decii were probably well-to-do and of Roman stock, settled in the province, although arguing from names Sir Ronald Syme thought he was of native stock, long holding the citizenship, and this part of the empire was one in which Syme had long taken a particular interest.[198] He was said by the *Historia Augusta* to have been of 'consular descent', so the family may have reached high office after Marcus Aurelius' Danubian wars. For his son to qualify for the senate, the father, whose name is unknown, must have had a distinguished equestrian career; Syme proposed Q. Decius Vindex, procurator of Dacia in the late 2nd century as his father.[199] Decius was thus probably born in Budalia simply because the family had travelled there to look after their estates.

The new emperor was at first called Q. Decius Valerinus. Subsequently, presumably by virtue of adoption by an otherwise unidentified Caius Messius, he became C. Messius Q. Decius Valerianus.[200] He was born c. 190 and rose to become suffect consul in 232. He was subsequently appointed governor of Lower Moesia (c. 234), Lower Germany and Tarraconensis (Spain), the latter in 237/238. After this, he underwent his change of name before being appointed Prefect of the City of Rome by Philip in 247.

Decius had married Herennia Cupressenia Etruscilla, and the senate made her Augusta on his accession. She was the daughter of Q. Herennius Etruscus, a Severan senator, perhaps by a daughter or granddaughter of Cupressenius Gallus, suffect consul in 147. The name Perperna, one of those bestowed on the younger son, also suggests that the Empress was descended from M. Perperna, consul in 92 BC, although there is no certain senatorial trace of that old Etruscan family beyond the reign of Augustus.[201] They had two sons, Etruscus and Hostilianus, both of whom were briefly Augusti.

Decius was thus still *en poste* in Rome when Philip selected him – because of his local origins – to go to the Danube frontier with oversight of the Moesias and Pannonia, to deal with usurper Pacatianus and the Gothic incursions which had taken place in its wake, which he did with ruthless efficiency, although he had warned the emperor before departing that his own elevation might result, which it duly did in June 249. Once installed as emperor, Decius is said to have written to Philip promising to return to Rome and resume his role as a private citizen. This story of the reluctantly acclaimed but high-minded usurper is not uncommon during the period, and little credence is to be attached to it, especially in that, as a senator,

---

198 Syme (1971) 194-196

199 Syme, *loc.cit.* The consular descent may have been hyperbole, although the Empress could boast of it.

200 FS 2440; ILS 490; PIR² D28 & JRS XCIII (2003) 233

201 ILS 521, 7043, cf. Syme (1971) 197. The *Vita* of SS Calocerus & Parthenius calls her, erroneously, Tryphonia.

Decius probably looked down his nose at the upstart Philip, leaving aside any suspicions the senate might have held about his role in the deposition of Gordian III.

He reached Rome before the end of September and was recognised as Augustus by the senate. He was thereupon granted the tribunician and proconsular power,[202] made *pontifex maximus* and granted the extra name of Traianus, the latter not necessarily at once, but certainly by 250, by his admiring former colleagues in the senate, which gave him rather a lot to live up to.[203]

Decius' imperial style was therefore Imperator Caesar C. Messius Q. Traianus Decius Pius Felix Augustus, to which Invictus was quickly added.[204] He was consul again in 250 and in 251.[205] As recognition of his military efforts prior to his accession, he was later granted the additional epithet Dacicus Maximus.

Nevertheless, much of the good work Decius had done on the Danube was put at risk by his having had to fight it out with Philip outside Verona and his accession was marred by further problems on the Danube, caused by the Gothic king Kniva leading a horde of followers into Roman territory and creating havoc, resulting in the desperate usurpation of Priscus at Philippopolis. This was a blow to Decius, for he was busy numismatically trumpeting his Pannonian or – as on his coins, Illyrian – origins, just as Kniva's people were reducing the area to chaos.[206]

He nevertheless initiated a number of reforms, appealed extensively to imperial nostalgia, invoking the names of past deified emperors and tried to breathe new life into the pantheon of Roman gods, under threat from a number of monotheistic cults. To help achieve this, his regime required certificates of sacrifice from citizens to prove their pagan *bona fides*, which most monotheists, like the worshippers of the Sun, or of Isis or Mithras, were happy to go along with, but not the Christians, who largely refused. This inevitably led to a widespread persecution, long remembered by the church.

The Danubian crisis, despite being somewhat alleviated by a victory gained by Decius' successor as C-in-C of both the Moesias, Trebonianus Gallus, kept rumbling on and the emperor decided to take an expeditionary force there to deal with Kniva once and for all. He left a senior senator, P. Licinius Valerianus (qv), in Rome with special powers to hold the fort, bestowed upon his sons the rank of *caesar* and took off for the Balkans with the elder, who shortly after arrival was made co-emperor.

The Balkan campaign had mixed fortunes, news of which seems to have prompted a rash of imperial claimants. But in the end the campaign came unstuck, for a trap laid by the Emperor with Gallus to crush Kniva as he returned to cross the Danube went completely awry and both father and son

202 ILS 518
203 Syme (1971) 220
204 ILS 514, 515
205 AE (2003) 1415
206 Seaby (1971) IV p. 25 No. 43: the rev. legend reads Gen[ius] Illurici.

fell in battle at Abrittus (Razgrad, Bulgaria) in lesser Scythia on the far north-eastern edge of the Empire, not far inland from the Black Sea coast, between 27 May and 1 June 251.[207] Cynics claimed that Gallus had betrayed them, but this seems unlikely, for the battle was going well until Kniva unexpectedly turned the tables. The senate, on receiving this news, deified both Decius and the elder son, Etruscus.

Gallus, whether he liked it or not, was immediately acclaimed emperor and, as with the deaths of Marcus Aurelius, Septimius Severuys, Alexander and Gordian III, a promising military situation was settled disadvantageously and in haste, in order for him to hot-foot it back to Rome to legitimise his regime.

DIADUMENIANUS
218, 16th May – c. 11th June

Diadumenianus was the son of and latterly co-ruler with Macrinus, who had organised the demise of Caracalla. He did not long succeed him. M. Opellius Diadumenianus had been recognised as M. Opellius Severus Diadumenianus Caesar by June 217.[208] His name was changed again later by the insertion of Antoninus in lieu of Severus.[209] He was born 14 December, 208 and was thus but 9 years old on his father's accession. On appointment as *caesar*, he was also styled *princeps iuventutis* ('prince of youth') as Caracalla had once been.[210] However, his style was soon up-graded with the addition before *caesar* of *nobilissimus* ('most noble').[211] After the revolt instigated by Elagabalus' mother had broken out in Syria, on 16 May 218 Diadumenianus was raised to the rank of Augustus – a move never ratified by the senate, but immortalised on his coinage – as Imperator Caesar M. Opellius Antoninus Diadumenianus Augustus. After Macrinus was defeated on 8 June 218 at the Battle of Antioch, the emperor fled north and then to the Bosporus, but before departing he entrusted Diadumenianus to loyal members of his staff to take him to Parthia. The lad was captured en route at Zeugma on the Euphrates, not far from Samosata (Turkey) and killed a few days after his father's demise, probably in the second week in June. His head was brought to Elagabalus, who reportedly displayed it as a trophy. Both he and his father were subject to a *damnatio memoriae* by a compliant senate.

DIDIUS IULIANUS (I)
193, 28th March – 1st June

Didius Julianus was the ambitious senator who, on the murder of Pertinax, believed he could bribe the Praetorian Guard into supporting his bid to become the next emperor. He was right, they did, but Julianus, a notably

---

207 JRS XCII (2007) & AE (2003) 1415
208 FS 2578 ; ILS 461; PIR² O107
209 ILS 8919
210 ILS 462A
211 ILS 465

venal creature, failed to pay up in full and the monster he promised to feed with money consumed him utterly after a reign of only a fraction over two months. The legacy of his opportunism was a civil war and the demise of two further aspirant claimants to empire.

M. Didius Petronius Severus Julianus[212] was born at Mediolanum (Milan) on 30 January 133. The father was probably called L. Petronius Didius Severus, but unravelling the ramifications of the family presents considerable problems, mainly stemming from the beginning of the Emperor's unreliable Life in the *Historia Augusta,* which provides too many ancestors living within too close a time-frame and has to be carefully disentangled to produce a coherent impression of his family history.[213]

Julianus was clearly of a Roman family from Bixia, but if in fact from Hadrumentum, as the *Historia* claims, the family were recent migrants to Africa. The future Emperor was born in 133. The *Historia* also makes much of the emperor's claim to descent from the jurist Salvius Julianus, which we know to have been unlikely. The most satisfactory answer is that a sister of the jurist married the Emperor's grandfather, C. Fulvius Rusticus Aemilianus, and his daughter later married Julianus' father, the Milanese *eques* Didius Severus.

Julianus was brought up in the household of Domitia Lucilla, Marcus Aurelius' mother and, with her support was elected one of the Board of Twenty, c. 153/4, and designated quaestor a year before the legal minimum age, so served in 162. He was aedile in 164, praetor in 166 – all with the Emperor's support, then went off to Germany to become legate of *Legio* XXII *Primigenia.* Following that, he was appointed governor of Belgica, during which longish tenure he defeated a barbarian incursion. This got him an ordinary consulship with the future emperor Pertinax as colleague – once again with the emperor's support – in 175. At some stage after 180, he was also made a *sodalis Antoniniano* (priest of the cult of Antoninus Pius and Marcus Aurelius). Thereafter he governed Dalmatia, followed by Lower Germany. At some stage after Commodus' accession, he was accused of conspiring against the emperor with a certain Salvius – perhaps an uncle, an ex-consul – but nothing more is heard of it. Thereafter he governed Bithynia and followed Pertinax in the proconsulship of Africa, leading him presciently to call him on one occasion, 'My colleague and successor' – thereby creating an omen ripe for fulfilment.

Having killed Pertinax, the Praetorian commanders were on the one hand fearful that the mob might take a hand and attack them, but at the same time realised that the imperial dignity was entirely in their hands with no obvious successor, despite several members of the family of Marcus Aurelius being alive. To avoid trouble with the populace, the gates of the praetorian camp were closed and word was sent out that the Guards officers were prepared to hear proposals regarding Pertinax's successor.

---

212 ILS 412; PIR² D77
213 For which see Craven (2019) 232 & table XXVII

In the event, two men came forward and both were essentially prepared to offer generous donatives for each soldier. Instead of attempting to decide on the candidates' merits, the guard commanders instead decided to see who would offer the most generous donative. It was simple auctioneering. The two candidates were Julianus and the father-in-law of the late lamented Emperor Pertinax, T. Flavius Sulpicianus. Both were distinguished senators, well into middle life. After several hours of negotiations, the praetorian commanders accepted Julianus' bid, not only because he was able to offer more money per head, but because he artfully suggested that Sulpicianus, as Pertinax's father-in-law, was likely to seek revenge on certain elements within the Guard for their actions.

Although in most ways well qualified for the purple, being the second most senior ex-consul then living and with a highly distinguished career behind him, Julianus' every action thenceforward was influenced by his being beholden to the praetorians; he was a prisoner of his own overarching ambition and lust for power.

Julianus was finally acclaimed emperor by the praetorians on 28 March 193 and on the same day was, by decree of the senate, named emperor, given the tribunician and proconsular powers and his family adlected into the patriciate. He was thenceforth styled Imperator Caesar M. Didius Severus Julianus Augustus. His wife Manlia Scantilla was named Augusta, as was his daughter, Didia Clara. He was hailed *imperator* on 9 April and coin evidence confirms that he was also *pontifex maximus* and (suffect) consul, for the second time.

Once the news of the death of Pertinax had reached the provinces, others, considering that they had as good a claim as Julianus if not better (through being backed by a sizeable military force), immediately made rival bids for the supreme office. This ultimately led to the appearance during April of three imperial claimants: C. Pescennius Niger (governor of Syria), D. Clodius Albinus (governor of Britain) and L. Septimius Severus (governor of Pannnonia Superior). Julianus was suddenly presented with an appalling crisis. He found himself faced with three rivals, each backed by an army, not to mention formidable domestic problems: unpopularity amongst the populace in Rome, a great deal of un-co-operative cynicism amongst his fellow senators and further problems with the praetorians caused by his inability to pay the promised donative in full and on time.

Before the end of April, Julianus was forced to take defensive measures against Severus, who had temporarily neutralised Albinus by negotiation and had acted more decisively than Niger, whom he had by-passed, and had marched on Rome. These preparations were hampered by the reluctance of the praetorians to dirty their hands, especially in the cause of an emperor rapidly looking like a lame duck and who in any case had not fully discharged his fiscal obligations to them. Julianus therefore turned to the senate to suggest that they appoint Severus as joint ruler, but this otherwise prudent move came too late, for Severus' progress was by this stage in late May too well advanced for there to be any doubt about the outcome.

On 1 June, the senators, doubtless fearing for themselves in the event of not having been seen to have supported Severus from as early on in the proceedings as possible, decided to ditch Julianus. They elected Severus as Emperor (with Albinus as Caesar), deified Pertinax and declared the unfortunate incumbent a public enemy, passing a decree of death on him.

The hapless 'cash-and-carry' emperor was found by the senate's emissary, deserted and alone in the palace. Amid much abject pleading, the sentence was pronounced and the unfortunate ruler killed. Now all that the Empire had to do was to watch the bloody contest for power amongst the three marshals unfold, taking the story into the next era of imperial history. The Year of the Five Emperors was about to beome even more complex.

DIOCLETIAN
284, 20ᵗʰ November – 305, 1ˢᵗ May

Whilst Aurelian and Probus can take some credit for stabilising the chaos into which the empire had been plunged following the death of Gordian III, Diocletian, who succeeded Carus and probably disposed of his son, was the man who finally brought order out of that chaos, buttressed the economy, reordered the administration, divided the empire and set up a new system of imperial succession designed to avoid civil wars. Diocletian also went on to become the first man to assume the purple since Antoninus Pius to manage two whole decades of rule. His successes were notable, but he failed over the succession. He retired after 20 years and expected the system to work. He did not reckon with human nature.

When Carus was killed in battle against the Persians, his son Numerianus managed to claim a victory, mopped up and slowly withdrew under a favourable treaty, supported by his father-in-law, the Pretorian Prefect Aper. The expeditionary force then withdrew west, before it was discovered that Numerianus, confined to his litter due to an eye wound, had died, whereupon Aper was apprehended on suspicion of murder. A kangaroo court of senior officers then put him on trial but he hardly had time to be heard before, on 20 November, the troops acclaimed Diocles, commander of the household mounted guard (*protectores domestici*) as emperor. He moved swiftly to have Aper disposed of. Of course, a dispassionate eye might discern the hand of Diocles, now elevated to the purple as Diocletianus, in the entire sequence of events, with Aper – who after all was a member of the Imperial family – framed and conveniently removed.

Born probably in 236 or 237 on 22 December in Illyria, at a village in Dalmatia later re-named Diocleia in his honour, it is unclear what his full name actually was prior to his accession. Various accounts of his origin exist: that he was of obscure birth; that he was the son of a *scriba* (clerk) and that he was the freedman of a senator called Anullinus. In fact, all three could be true. His name, as assumed in 284, was C. Aurelius Valerius Diocletianus.

Diocles had served as a soldier from before 270, rising in rank through service under Aurelian and Probus, possibly including an important command in Moesia. He is also thought to have served as suffect consul or have been granted consular rank in 283 by Carus, when he was also probably made commander of the *protectores*. He was thus the first acknowledged emperor to come to the purple when of senatorial rank possibly since Tacitus, certainly since Gallienus. He was also probably the first freedman to become emperor.

Following his elevation, he seems to have very sensibly sat tight and waited for Carinus to come and challenge him, just as Julianus (III) was doing in Pannonia. Neither seems to have been tempted to confront the other. Patience was its own reward, however, for ten months after his acclamation, he was the beneficiary of the assassination of Carinus. He was sensible enough to seek reconciliation with those who backed his dead rival (hence no doubt the deification of Carus's grandson Nigrinianus) although he did not stop the senate from pronouncing a *damnatio memoriae* upon all three of his predecessors.

Diocletian hardly ever set foot in Rome, although the senate was quick to recognise him, grant him the tribunician and proconsular power, acknowledging him as *pater patriae* and making him *pontifex maximus*.[214] He nevertheless repaid them by continuing the trend of his predecessors and excluding them completely from the administration of the Empire.[215] His formal style was Imperator Caesar, C. Aurelius Valerius Diocletianus Pius Felix Invictus Augustus.[216] He was suffect consul in 285 in the place of the deceased Carus and ordinary consul in 287, holding seven further such consulships in 290, 293, 296, 399, 303, 304 and 308. His wife was called Prisca and they had a daughter, Valeria.[217] After only a few months in power, during which he made a successful punitive expedition against the German tribes on the Rhine frontier (earning himself the additional style of Germanicus Maximus), he nominated an old comrade-in-arms, Maximian, as *caesar* and thus co-ruler, although he himself remained the senior of the two and his colleague always dutifully deferred to him. This clearly worked well and, on 1 April 286 his new colleague was raised to the rank of Augustus. Diocletian adopted the *signum* (extra name) Jovius, bestowing that of Herculius on his colleague.

The constitutional settlement was that he and Maximian would rule east and west, with a deputy each, to be styled *caesar*. The two senior members of this Tetrarchy would retire after 20 years and the two *caesars* would succeed them, appointing two new ones in their place. Needless to say, the urge to hereditary succession and the reluctance to retire from a position of such power was guaranteed to make the arrangement unworkable; it would only be a matter of time before it all began to fall apart.

Diocletian now turned his attention to the re-organisation of the Empire itself. The size of the provinces was reduced (to avoid governors having too much power and thus providing them with the military and financial wherewithal to become usurpers) and they were grouped in twelve Dioceses, each under the control of a civilian governor called a *vicarius*. One result was

---

214 His only certain visit was in late autumn 303.

215 Arnheim (1972) *passim*

216 ILS616

217 PLRE I Prisca 1; a suspect source names her as Eleutheria; conceivably she could have borne this name as well.

that Italy, previously long free of taxes, lost its tax-free status (except for the immediate environs of Rome itself); another was to increase the impotence of the senate, which was left with only two of the provinces assigned to it by Augustus and they were much reduced in size. The armed forces were taken out of the hands of the provincial governors and diocesan *vicarii* completely and were henceforth to be controlled independently. The military was also divided between the border garrisons (*limitanei*) and the more mobile reserve field army which had a preponderance of cavalry and could be sent on demand to tackle problems that needed more than just the border units. These were the largely mounted *comitatenses*, notionally part of the emperor's personal bodyguard (although they were in fact much more numerous than that), and the *palatini*, élite infantry. Personnel were increasingly drawn from the wilder provinces and from barbarian tribes due to the exemptions allowed to citizens.

Price-fixing was introduced in an attempt to stabilise the currency and the coinage was reformed; the revised coinage included a gold *aureus* struck at the standard of 60 to the pound, a new silver coin of drastically improved silver content known as the *argenteus*, and a new large bronze coin, the *Aurelianus* valued at 10 *denarii*. The edict issued in 301 attempted to establish the legal maximum prices that could be charged for goods and services. This was an exercise in futility as maximum prices proved impossible to enforce. Worse, the edict was reckoned in terms of *denarii*, although no such coin had been struck for over 50 years. On top of that, occupations were made practically hereditary, as were town councillorships.

All this achieved some stability, but price-fixing is invariably deleterious in the longer term and fixing people in places and professions prevents the free movement of personnel to wherever they might be needed, which was one of the problems that lay behind the difficulty of army recruitment. Christianity, then rapidly gaining ground in the east and to a lesser extent in the west, was leading people to opt out of mainstream life completely, mainly by taking the tonsure or holy orders and refusing military service. This eventually led to a decree of 298 requiring all in imperial service to publicly sacrifice to the gods on pain of dismissal. Then in 304 a further edict or rescript required everyone, Christians included, to offer sacrifice on pain of death, which triggered the last great persecution of the Christians, although it was enforced a lot more harshly in the east than in the west. The Caesar Galerius has subsequently received most of the blame for this, but one can hardly absolve Diocletian himself.

On the whole, however, the Tetrarchy worked remarkably well at first – until Diocletian decided, in 305, to abdicate, and persuaded the ever-loyal Maximian to follow suit. Thereafter, things began to fall apart rather messily, although the concept of Tetrarchy survived to some extent until after 337.

Having retired to his enormous palace at Spoletum (Split, in Dalmatia), close to his birthplace, the emperor re-entered public life briefly only once, to attend a conference of the tetrarchs at Carnuntum (Bad Deutsch-Altenburg, Austria) in November 308, the year in which he held his final consulship. The tetrarchic system was showing signs of dissolution even then, mainly thanks to the acclamation of Constantine at York in 306 and the taste for power exhibited by Maximian, who attempted to resume the purple to counterbalance this threat in support of his son Maxentius, who had also seized power in the west. Diocletian was asked to re-assume the purple, but he refused point blank. He returned to his palace and died there on 3 December 311.

DOMITIAN (I)
81, 13th September 81 – 96, 18th September

Domitian, as the younger son of Vespasian, grew up not expecting to be called upon to rule, but the unexpected and premature death of his elder brother Titus propelled him unprepared to supreme power, which by all accounts he used deplorably and unpredictably. Nor was he at all charismatic. He had a quirky sense of humour and, as his reign progressed, recused himself from day-to-day affairs, none of which endeared him to the governing class, although he was clearly intelligent and capable when he chose to be.

T. Flavius Domitianus was born on 24 October AD51 at Rome and brought up separately from his elder brother Titus, probably with his uncle T. Flavius Sabinus, with whom he most certainly was on 18 December AD69 when the forces of Vitellius had them surrounded on the Capitol; he was fortunate to escape unscathed (unlike Sabinus), probably shielded by his youth. On his father's accession he was re-styled simply Caesar Domitianus, later adding *Princeps Iuventutis*.[218] His first consulship came in 71, before he was twenty – strictly against convention, but not the first example – and he followed with further consulships in 73, 75, 76, 77, 79, 80 and, after his accession, every year from 82 to 88, then in 90, 92 and 95, seventeen in all.

Domitian is not seriously suspected of having either killed his brother or hastening his end, despite little evidence of any particular warmth between them. Nevertheless, when it became clear that Titus was dying, Domitian repaired immediately to the praetorian camp to promise donatives and exact oaths of fidelity. He was duly acclaimed on 14 September 81 taking the style Imperator Caesar Divi f. Domitianus Augustus. He became *pontifex maximus*, was invested with the tribunician and proconsular power and was hailed as *imperator*, being so hailed another twenty-two times during his reign. His aristocratic wife was Domitia Longina (daughter of Nero's dashing commander Corbulo by the daughter of a Cassius Longinus, one of whose forebears, of course, was an assassin of Julius Caesar. She was also probably the last surviving descendant of Augustus. Domitian had enticed her away from her very upper-class husband. She was hailed as Augusta at the end of September 81 and their infant son, who had died some time before, was deified. Later on, Domitian was elected consul for ten years in succession and made censor for life, albeit that he subsequently declined to enter into many of the consulships.[219]

As with Nero, he started well and instituted a number of governmental reforms that were generally welcomed. Indeed, even after the first few years,

---

218 ILS 246
219 Dio 67, 4.3

when the worst side of his nature had begun to take hold, he was a competent and reliable administrator. Yet he never warmed to the partnership Augustus had tried to maintain between *princeps* and senate, holding that body in contempt – after all (also like Nero) he had never been a member of it as a private citizen – and although he chose some competent senators to do the work of governing the empire and fighting its wars, they were treated more like courtiers, setting a trend for the future, and they tended to be liquidated if they became too successful.

Domitian waged a successful war against some German tribes in 82-83, awarding himself a triumph and the additional name Germanicus, despite having remained in his litter throughout most of the campaign. More serious was a revolt in 85 of the Dacians in the Balkans, who crossed the Danube and killed the local governor. It took two years hard fighting to restore order and three more to secure the region. A negotiated peace had to be settled in 89 in order to switch forces to deal with an incursion of two other tribes in the area of the upper Danube. In the end, troubles along much of the Danube led to a series of campaigns right up to the time of Domitian's death.

Unfortunately, as time went on, his autocratic style also meant that competent magistrates and generals became more than a little nervous at

Domitian, fragment of an antique bust, unknown provenance. (Bamfords Ltd)

their call to serve, since the casualty rate of senators condemned to death was Neronically high, including by the time of his death all the surviving males in his own family, probably except one of the children of his cousin, T. Flavius Clemens, the consul of 95 who was executed not long afterwards for 'atheism'.[220]

After a while, paranoia seems to have taken a grip, leading him to style himself in correspondence as *dominus et deus* (Lord and God), to rename September and October 'Germanicus' and 'Domitianus' after himself and institute a regime of spies and informers with a reliance upon torture, some particularly unpleasant.[221] Also, as perpetual censor, he had a free hand in manipulating the lives of the élite. He was solitary, had become humourless, timorous and insecure, which led to a cycle of plots, the suppression of which resulted in further conspiracies against him. Domitian's worst scare was on the twentieth anniversary of the acclamation of Vitellius, 1 January 89, when Saturninus (qv), suffect consul probably in 82 and at the time governor of Upper Germany, headed a military uprising which was actually quickly put down by the rebel's opposite number in Lower Germany, supported by the future emperor Trajan, whose consulship the following year is unlikely to have been a coincidence. The effect on Domitian's insecure and suspicious mind was doubtless profound. The casualty rate amongst the senate, court and administrators only began to accelerate, becoming almost a 'terror' from 93 until his death. These plots culminated in the killing of his 'atheistical' nephew Clemens (so called because of a rumoured inclination towards Christianity) and the exile of his widow and surviving child, a tragedy which appears to have triggered the further conspiracy which resulted in his assassination on 18 September 96 after a reign of fifteen years and four days. He was not deified but suffered a *damnatio memoriae* (erasure of memory) in the senate, in which his statues – only in gold or silver according to his own edict – were melted down and his inscriptions erased.

Domitian was said to have been a voluptuary and a seducer of women, although the alleged affair with his niece Julia, widow of his cousin Sabinus – killed as the result of a ceremonial solecism in 82 or 83 – is largely discounted by modern scholarship. Neither of his two sons by Domitia survived infancy, although the younger was briefly styled Caesar.

DOMITIAN (II)

271, February – March

Although the transition of power from Claudius II to Aurelian had all the appearance of having been smooth and trouble-free, there were nonetheless others trying to establish themselves in opposition. Domitian II was acclaimed

---

220 A term taken by Eusebius (in reference to his wife) as indicating a conversion to Christianity, a happenstance not these days given much credence: Eusebius *Hist. Eccl.* III.18.4; the surviving male was probably a forebear of M. Annius Sabinus Libo, a cousin of Commodus.

221 ILS 268 & 269 on the additional honorific.

in 271, possibly in Gaul.[222] Conceivably his bid for the purple really belongs to the story of the Gallic Empire (qv above). Little is known of it beyond a brief report by Zosimus (not naming the claimant[223]), and a coin, then not universally accepted as authentic, bearing the legend Imp[erator] C[aesar] Domitianus P[ius] F[elix] Aug[ustus]. Subsequent to its discovery, a second one turned up in Oxfordshire dateable to 271.[224] Nothing else is known of this man, bar the spurious claim in the *Historia Augusta* that he was descended from his first-century namesake.[225]

DOMITIAN (III)
296 August – 297, 2nd December

L. Domitius Domitianus appears as an eastern usurper, passing from his year one to his second year in August 297, so it must be assumed he seized power in Egypt when Galerius was experiencing his difficulties with the Persians. He was probably prefect of Egypt at the time, although we have no record of him in this office, but the sources for the period are scrappy in any case. He may have died in early December 297, when his ally Achilleus (qv) seems to have taken over, by which time he was under siege at Alexandria by Diocletian. The sources do not mention that he was killed by his own men, as usually happened in such circumstances, so he may have died of natural causes or in battle.[226] We know nothing of his origin or family.

ELAGABALUS
218, 16th May – 222, 11th March

Elagabalus was the soubriquet of the Syrian youth whose Severan connections enabled the family of Septimius Severus' wife to regain the power they had lost with the deposition of Caracalla. He was essentially a pawn put in power to enable them to pursue their machinations and enjoy the benefits thereof with neither let nor hindrance. As for the emperor, he was a spoiled and seemingly deranged youth, too callow to be entrusted with rule and too divorced from mainstream imperial culture as experienced in the capital to be able to adapt to his role.

The young man used as the centrepiece of the plot to topple Macrinus was actually called Varius Bassianus but was acclaimed emperor as Antoninus, officially the third to bear that name. He was already hereditary high priest of the local cult at Emesa as, like Severus' empress Julia Domna, he was of the blood line of the priest-kings of that place. The sacred black meteoritic stone which was the centrepiece of worship at Emesa was called after the god it represented, Ela-Gabal. The prestige conferred on its high priest made a deep

---

222 The design of the coin and the quality of the imperial portrait suggest this strongly.
223 *Op.cit.* I. 49, 2, cf. HA *V. Gall.* 2, 6 & 13, 2; *TT.* 12, 14 & 13, 3
224 *Daily Telegraph* 25/2/2004
225 PIR ²D114; PLRE I Domitianus 1; HA *Tyr. Trig.* 12, 14
226 PLRE I Domitianus 6

impression on the 14-year-old Bassianus, to the extent that he required people to address him by it; hence its subsequent use to identify him as Elagabalus despite his formal throne name of Antoninus.

[Sex.] Varius Avitus Bassianus was probably born at Emesa in March 204 and had succeeded to the position of High Priest of Emesa in or by 218; presumably the senior male line was extinct by 218, possibly as a result of Macrinus' elimination of many of the family as potential rivals. The name Bassianus derived from the Arabic *basus,* itself a priestly title.

He was, prior to his arrival in Rome in the early summer of 219, much under the influence of the women of his family, all powerful, and with their ambitions unfettered by the lack of living male kin, the new emperor's father having died a couple of years previously, his grandfather a year later and his uncle having been killed by Macrinus as a result of the *coup*. This dramatic turn of events had been brought about by his mother and her lover Eutychianus, also known as Gannys, but he, too, was executed before the end of the year, mainly because his increasing influence was too threatening for Elagabalus; he also clashed with the young man in an attempt to persuade him into leading a temperate lifestyle.

Elagabalus was acclaimed emperor on 16 May 218, taking the name and style Imperator Caesar M. Aurelius Divi Antonini Magni f. Divi Severi Pii n. Antoninus Pius Felix Augustus which, (less the filiation), was identical to that of Caracalla (or 'Antoninus the Great', as he seems to have become in Elagabalus' new style) and whose natural son he was claiming to be in order to strengthen his claim to supreme power.[227] On recognition by the senate three months later, when he was granted the tribunician and proconsular power (back-dated to 16 May) and recognised – ironically as it turned out – as *Pontifex Maximus*; the senate also added *Pater Patriae*. In 220, he added the titles *Sacerdos Amplissimus Dei Invicti Solis Elagabali* – High Priest of the Unconquerable sun god Ela-Gabal.[228] He was consul – suffect – in 218, and thereafter ordinary consul in 219, 220 and 222.

He married three (although possibly five) times; firstly, in late summer 219, to Julia Cornelia Paula, thereafter styled Augusta.[229] She was described by Herodian as 'most noble'[230] but her family connections are difficult to delineate, especially as she was endowed with three rather common names. Her brother or father was probably the jurist Julius Paullus,[231] although the *Historia Augusta* claims he served as a senior civil servant under Severus and was appointed Praetorian Prefect by Severus Alexander, by which most commentators assume the history actually meant Elagabalus, which would make more sense.[232] This connection would not make Julia 'most noble', however, so perhaps the connection was a descent from Julius Paulus, a

---

227 ILS 467 (without filiation) & ILS 469 (with).
228 ILS 473
229 PIR² I660
230 Herodian, *op. cit.,* 5, 6.1
231 PIR² I453
232 V. Pesc. Nigr. 7, 4

praetor exiled under Nero[233] whose daughter was called Julia Agrippina, honoured at Antioch in Pisidia (near Yalova, Turkey) and bearing a *cognomen* probably relating to the Judaean ruler M. Julius Agrippa.[234] This might be seen as putting Elagabalus' first wife and his own family in the same ancestral circle of eastern potentates and make them distantly related. They had, however, divorced by the end of 220.

Secondly and illegally, he married late in 220 (or early in 221) the Vestal Virgin Julia Aquillia Severa, thenceforth also Augusta.[235] It was illegal because Vestals were sacred and not allowed to marry or have relations with men. Again, her family are not explicitly identified in the ancient sources. Probably her father or brother was M. Julius Aquillius Tertullus, an early 3rd-century aedile.[236] Whether he was indeed the parent, it is certainly thought that her brother was T. Jul[ius] Clatius Severus, suffect consul at about this period or a little later.[237] Their descent was almost certainly from C. Julius Severus, suffect consul in 139, and his wife Claudia Aquillia, and thus again a representative of the old client kings of the east; in the case of Julius Severus, of Attalus, King of Asia.[238] Julia could, therefore, have been another distant kinswoman of the boy emperor. They were divorced within a very few months.

He married thirdly in July 221 [Claudia] Annia Faustina, again thenceforth styled Augusta. She was a daughter of Ti. Claudius Severus Proculus consul in 200, himself a son of Cn. Claudius Severus by Annia Aurelia Galeria Faustina, fifth child of Marcus Aurelius. The bride's illustrious descent was clearly intended to bolster the emperor's flagging prestige, but he quickly tired of her and had divorced her before the end of the year, returning to Aquillia Severa. There was no known issue by any of these women.

Acceptance of the new ruler by the senate, sight unseen, and the ratification of his status was swift, despite misgivings engendered by the cruelty of Caracalla. The new emperor's supporters must have been extremely sure of his acceptance throughout the empire, for to dally nearly a year in the east and then to spend an inordinately long time travelling to Rome ceremonially accompanied in state by a large black stone might, in any other context, seem a recipe for disaster.

On arrival, the stone was installed in a new Palatine temple, and its high priest's only diversion from self-indulgence and cruelty lay in his daily morning devotions and sacrifices to it. The trend was to set Ela-gabal up as the centre of a monotheistic cult at the expense of Rome's traditional pantheon. This, of course, was never going to gain acceptance (if only they could have predicted the events of a century later!) and, almost as bad, involved massive public expenditure. Otherwise, licence ruled virtually unchecked, led by a narcissistic bisexual, transvestite and highly exhibitionist emperor.

---

233 PIR² I452
234 Reigned King of N. Judaea 53-92, d. 93; PIR² I132
235 PIR² I648
236 PIR² I172
237 PIR² I268
238 PIR² I573

Appointments of men from obscure backgrounds, on whom Julia Maesa – who, with her daughter, Julia Soaemias, Elagabalus' mother – directed imperial policy, could rely, caused much offence and derision. The army was never quite happy, although the Syrian princesses' competence and the sheer youth of the Emperor kept the inevitable crisis at bay for three and a half years against all the odds. Nevertheless, there had been four attempted rebellions within a year or so of Macrinus' murder, three in his native Syria, involving the imperial claimants Verus II, Taurinus, Gellius Maximus (I) and Seleucus (qqv).

Two policies were tried to give the boy-emperor some respectability. One, of course, was to marry him off suitably, which thanks to the emperor's capricious nature, was a complete failure. The second and last-ditch policy was to adopt an acceptable heir, on the assumption that he would never produce one of his own. The surviving son of Julia Maesa's younger sister, Julia Avita Mammaea, 13-year-old Alexianus, was therefore named Caesar late in 221, taking the name Severus Alexander. This merely resulted in loss of face for the emperor and repeated attempts to have Alexander killed, reviving still raw memories of the Caracalla-Geta conflicts. In the end, open support for Alexander amongst the praetorians resulted in Elagabalus throwing a tantrum in front of them and the guardsmen summarily killing him on 11 March 222.

Elagabalus was the second emperor to follow Caracalla and adopt the style 'Pius Felix Augustus' in his titulature. It was revived again by Gordian III, although Aemilianus was the first emperor to use it consistently on coins.

ETRUSCUS
251, May – 1st June

Etruscus was the elder son of Decius, whom his father made *nobilissumus caesar* and *princeps iuventutis* in the early summer of 250 clearly designating him his heir. He was consul with his father to open the year 251.[239] He was born c. 233/234 and was unmarried on his designation. That year the continuing Balkan campaign had suffered mixed fortunes, news of which seems to have prompted a rash of imperial claimants. The response in propaganda terms, and in riposte to a military success against the German Carpi, was that Decius raised Etruscus to the rank of co-emperor as Imperator Caesar Q. Herennius Etruscus Messius Decius Augustus, at which time he seems to have received the tribunician and proconsular power from the senate, and they proceeded to the theatre of operations in an attempt to conclude matters.[240] In the end, the campaigning came unstuck; a trap laid by the Emperor with his general Gallus to crush Gothic leader Kniva as he returned to cross the Danube went completely awry and both father and son fell in battle at Abrittus (Razgrad, Bulgaria) in lesser Scythia on the far north-eastern edge of the Empire, not far inland from the Black Sea coast, between 27 May and 1 June 251. Etruscus, it seems, was in fact killed in action an hour or two before his father.[241]

---

239 ILS 516
240 *trib. pot., cos. des.,* ILS 519
241 JRS XCII (2007) & AE (2003) 1415.

EUGENIUS (I)
303

Eugenius was the commander of a unit of 500 infantrymen engaged upon harbour work at Seleucia (near present-day Baghdad, Iraq). He was, for some reason entirely lost to recorded history, proclaimed emperor by his men. He subsequently advanced on the provincial capital, Antioch, but was defeated by the local commander and presumably killed in battle or dispatched immediately thereafter. The year is thought to have been 303.[242] He issued no coins, and nothing is known either of his origins or his family.

EUGENIUS (II)
392, 22nd August – 394, 6th September

This Western puppet emperor's unwelcome existence was made even worse in the eyes of Theodosius I for his having proclaimed religious tolerance in the western empire. He was raised up by a disaffected commander-in-chief who lasted no longer than his master. Arbogastes, the *magister militum* of Theodosius I, realized, once he had arranged the demise of Valentinian II in May 392, that he could never rule on his own account, and the hostile reaction to events in the west at Constantinople made it clear that he needed to raise a pliant candidate as emperor in order to legitimize his rule. In August he selected a man of senatorial rank, the *magister scrinii* (head of the civil service) Eugenius, to assume the role.

Eugenius' place of origin is unknown, although he had originally been a teacher of rhetoric. He had subsequently risen high enough to become a *vir clarissimus* by 385 under Magnus Maximus and attained his final bureaucratic post in 390.[243]

On elevation, Eugenius styled himself Dominus Noster Flavius Eugenius Pius Felix Augustus.[244] He received the tribunician and proconsular power, probably from the senate itself, and served an immediate suffect consulship, recognized in the west but not in the east. Apart from being middle-aged, nothing is known about him, except that he had a wife (presumably never recognized as Augusta) and children who were spared after his demise.

Eugenius adopted a policy of toleration towards paganism and, as the creature of an Arian, a blind eye was turned there, too. The temples were all re-opened and he became popular with the majority of the senatorial aristocracy who were still pagan, all of which hardened Theodosius against the old cults that asserted themselves after he had regained control of the west. Theodosius, in a repeat of the events that led to the demise of Masgnus Maximus six years before, was obliged to move west to deal with this upstart, but this time the final clash was far more destructive and damaging, Arbogastes being eventually defeated at the battle of the Frigidus (probably

---

242 PLRE I Eugenius 1.
243 PLRE I Eugenius 6
244 ILS7

the Vipava, Slovenia). After the battle, the captured usurper was summarily executed at the feet of the Emperor. Arbogastes escaped but was hunted down and killed the next day. As with Magnus Maximus, the empress and her children were spared, mainly on this occasion through the intercession of St Ambrose, Bishop of Mediolanum (Milan).

FAUSTINUS
274

It would appear that after the Battle of Châlons-sur-Marne, a second revolt flared up, but was probably short-lived and quickly crushed. This may have been the context in which the shadowy Faustinus flourished. We know absolutely nothing about him; we can only guess that he was governor of Belgica, the suggestion is Drinkwater's resting on reasonably reliable reports of further Gallic unrest after the deposition of Tetricus. Having tried to overthrow Tetricus before his final battle, he may have escaped and attempted to keep the Gallic realm in being by declaring himself Emperor. The lack of coins would merely confirm the fact that his time in the sun was brief.[245]

FIRMUS (I)
272

Firmus was supposedly a friend of Zenobia, a Seleucan merchant. Following the Syrian empress's defeat and capture by Aurelian, Firmus is said (only by the *Historia Augusta*, it should be noted) to have seized Egypt in 272 in an attempt to reinstate her *imperium*, but he was quickly defeated and killed by forces loyal to Aurelian. The story, uncorroborated elsewhere, may well be fiction.[246]

FIRMUS (II)
372/3, December/January – 375

He was an usurper in Africa, who constituted a serious threat but who was eventually crushed by the *comes* Theodosius, probably with help from his son, the future emperor of that name and, quite possibly his comrade-in-arms Magnus Maximus, too.

The son and heir of Nubel, King of the Moorish people in Mauretania, Firmus was a thoroughly Romanised member of a large and influential local tribe. His family claimed descent from C. Julius Juba (or a sibling) son of C. Julius Ptolemaeus, King of Numidia 23-39, himself the son of C. Julius Juba II, King of Numidia and Mauretania 25BC-23 and his first wife, Cleopatra Selene, daughter of Cleopatra VII of Egypt and Mark Antony.

---

245 Drinkwater (1987) 43, 91, cf. Zonaras 12, 27.11

246 PLRE I Firmus 1,cf. HA *Try. Trig.* 3, 1; *V. Aurel.* 32, 1-3 & *V. Probi* 24, 7 (born in Seleucia).

Juba II was a descendant of the famous Numidian King Massinissa who died in 146BC.[247]

He fell out with the *comes* of Africa, Romanus, who was corrupt and consequently went to considerable lengths to deny Firmus a hearing at court. In the end, the Moor's restraint collapsed and with the backing of several allied peoples and two important military units, he declared himself emperor late in 372 or early 373, being acknowledged in the surrounding provinces, too.[248]

He retained control well into 375, when the elder Theodosius, fresh from sorting out problems of a similar nature in Britain, arrived at the head of reinforcements, refused to treat with him and, after a series of sanguinary encounters, defeated him, following which Firmus committed suicide. He seems to have issued no coins, probably because his area of influence did not include a city with a mint.

FLORIANUS
276, June/July – August/September

M. Annius Florianus was the alleged half-brother of the emperor Tacitus, who opportunely succeeded his kinsman whilst on campaign and who, according to the historian Eutropius, 'did nothing worth remembering' before being killed by his own men in a revolt.[249]

Florianus is unlikely to have been the half-brother of Tacitus. That he was appointed Pretorian Prefect to the emperor seems, on the other hand, entirely convincing, if unconfirmed in the sources. With the assassination of the old emperor at Tyana (Kemerhisar, Turkey), whether he was complicit in it or not, Florianus was acclaimed as his successor.

Florianus' brief 88-day reign as emperor was to take place entirely on campaign in the east, as far as we can tell. He was, however, quickly recognised by the senate in Rome and was formally styled Imperator Caesar M. Annius Florianus Pius Felix Invictus Augustus and recognised as *pontifex maximus*.[250] He was also no doubt granted the tribunician power and proconsular *imperium* renewable in the usual way. The *Historia Augusta*, inevitably, claims he had many children.[251]

Having succeeded and been acknowledged by the senate, still the ultimate validating authority, Florianus moved against the Heruli once more with the intention of finally driving them beyond the boundaries (*limes*) of the empire and ensuring that they caused no further trouble. This was all going well when news reached the emperor that the commander of his forces in the east, M. Aurelius Probus (qv), the successor in that post of Tacitus' relative, Maximinus, had himself been acclaimed emperor by his men following a

---

247 Walsh, P.G., *Massinissa* in. *JRS* LV (1965) 149–160
248 PLRE I Firmus 3
249 Eutrop. 9, 16
250 ILS 592; pontifical style and trib. pot. I: ILS 593. PIR² A649/PLRE I. Florianus 6
251 HA *V. Taciti* 16.3-4

successful campaign against some turbulent allies of Persia and probably also as a result of the disaffection caused by Maximinus. Probus was quickly acknowledged throughout the eastern provinces, including Egypt, challenging the authority of Florianus. Consequently, he was forced to place a subordinate in command of a holding operation against the Heruli and march to Syria with the bulk of his forces with the intention of snuffing the rebellion out. Probus, who commanded a much smaller force, cleverly declined to be brought to battle and by raids and skirmishing managed to demoralise the emperor's army, which tactic subsequently led to a revolt that led to Florianus being killed by his own men at Tarsus in Cilicia (Turkey), probably to avoid a bloody conflict. He was the third emperor to die within a space of 12 months, and this hiatus undid much of the good work done by Aurelian in re-unifying the Empire.

GAETULICUS

39

Cn. Cornelius Lentulus Gaetulicus may have been merely a plotter, or even an alleged plotter, rather than a full-blooded usurper. He was a victim of Caligula, probably with his friend M. Aemilius Lepidus, who was married to the emperor's sister Drusilla. Our ancient sources rather fail us when it comes to unravelling what went on, or even the main sequence of events.

The prime movers appear to have been Lepidus and Gaetulicus, who – thanks originally to the patronage of the deplorable Sejanus – had governed Upper Germany for an entire decade from 29, a most unusual happenstance.[252] A member of a then numerous ancient patrician family, his father Cossus Cornelius Lentulus had been consul in 1, and in 6 had earned the hereditable *agnomen* of Gaetulicus in recognition of his defeat of the Gaetuli in Africa – the last non-imperial person ever to have been accorded this honour.[253] He belonged to a cadet branch of the patrician Cornelii Lentuli, which descended from L. Cornelius Lentulus Caudinus, consul in 275 who, in turn, is presumed to have been a descendant of an early Republican grandee living in 395 called L Cornelius Cossus.

Gaetulicus was probably born around 8BC and held the praetorship in AD23, following this with the ordinary consulship in 26 with C. Calvisius Sabinus, who may have been his brother-in-law and who had also been, slightly earlier, a casualty of Caligula's malevolence. He married Apronia Caesiana, daughter of L. Apronius, suffect consul in AD8. As governor of Upper Germany, Gaetulicus succeeded his elder brother Cossus, and his father-in-law L. Apronius was also then governing Lower Germany, making for a cosy family coterie. Such was Gaetulicus' calm manner of command, he was immensely popular with his four legions, not to mention with Apronius' four in Lower Germany, He was about the only member of Sejanus' faction to survive his fall, allegedly because he told Tiberius that he had only co-operated with the malevolent Pretorian Prefect

---

252 PIC² C1390
253 Op. cit. C 1340

because Tiberius had advised him to, an explanation which the old emperor seemed happy to accept. In 39, two new legions were being raised in Germany in preparation for Caligula's projected invasion of Britain, so Gaetulicus, more or less idolised by the eight legions manning the Rhine frontier, would have been in a very strong position to mount a *coup*, especially one co-ordinated with Lepidus in Rome. Yet the idea of the two men as working together is only hinted at by Suetonius, who mentions the *Lepidi et Gaetulici coniuratio*: nowhere else is the link specifically made and his statement is supported only by circumstantial evidence.

Yet, somewhere along the line, some kind of intelligence had reached Caligula's circle, and in a lightning dash to Germany, dragging Lepidus along in his entourage, both Lepidus and Gaetulicus were arrested and summarily executed.[254]

GALBA (I)
68, 9th June 68 – 69, 15th January

Galba was a stern old patrician who raised the standard of revolt against Nero, triggering the Year of the Four Emperors and, whilst his intentions were good, his lack of charisma, tight control of the state's finances and emphasis on discipline told fatally against him in the turbulence following his succession and arrival in Rome.

Galba was the first emperor from outside the Julio-Claudian dynasty; the first to be raised by the army, of which, as governor of Hispania Tarraconensis (southern Spain), he was a relatively senior commander. Although from outside the charmed – and very deadly – circle of the imperial dynasty, Galba was in fact distantly related, although this was no doubt but one element in his decision to put himself forward. At that time, such a connection would still have meant a lot; not for nothing was the name of Caesar endlessly adopted by the dictator's successors. Furthermore, we know that Galba was very proud of his ancient lineage. He had also been adopted into a junior branch[255] of the family of Augustus' Empress, Livia (who thought highly of him), which would have acted as a reinforcing factor.[256]

Ser. Sulpicius C. f. C n. Ani. Galba was born into the old patrician family of the Sulpicii on 24 December 3BC (other evidence suggests two years earlier) near Tarracina, son of C. Sulpicius Galba and Mummia Achaïca, a lady of distinguished consular ancestry but whose family had, subsequent to the two triumphs of L. Mummius as a result of victories in Spain (153BC) and against the Achaean League (146), fallen into obscurity.[257] As a youth, Galba was adopted as her son by his stepmother, Livia Ocellina, becoming L. Livius Ocella Ser. Sulpicius Galba, the first recorded example of an increasing

---

254 Barrett, A. A. *Caligula: The Corruption of Power* (London 1989) 101-113; Syme AA 179-180, Suet. *Caligula* 8; Tac, *Ann*. VI. 30.

255 Suetonius, *Galba* 4, 1.

256 *Ibid*. 3, 4

257 DNP 11. 8

fashion, especially common in the second century AD, of combining two entire names in one rather than the more usual formula of adding one's birth *nomen* to one's new name adjectivally, which in Galba's case would have come out as L. Livius Ocella Sulpicianus. In this instance, he certainly wished to keep his more presitigous birth name to the fore.[258] He married Aemilia Lepida in AD20.[259] She was a daughter of M. Aemilius Lepidus, consul in 11, himself a grandson of Lepidus the Triumvir, and through his mother descended from both Sulla and Pompey.

Galba's career in the senate was combined with a military life, which was consistently successful, aided by the patronage of the Empress Livia along with that of Tiberius, Caligula and Claudius. He was consul in 33 and went on to hold provincial commands in Upper Germany, where he enforced discipline after the apparent revolt against Caligula by Gaetulicus, in Africa and in southern Spain, where he was in charge from 60.

The events leading up to his *pronunciamento* began with the revolt of the Gallic aristocrat C. Julius Vindex (qv) at Vesontio (Besançon) in Gaul in May 68, which gave him his cue. Although Vindex was crushed at Lugdunum by Verginius Rufus, the governor of Germany, who subsequently declined his soldiers' offer of the purple (and lived), Galba had quietly gathered the support of his opposite numbers in five provinces, making the whole declaration look rather more carefully planned in advance than might first have appeared. His attempt was greatly facilitated by the declaration in his favour of the Praetorian Prefect C. Nymphidius Sabinus (qv).

Galba was actually proclaimed Emperor by his troops at Carthago Nova (Cartagena), Spain, on 3 April, but until 9 June, when Nero died, he has to be viewed only as an usurper. Thereafter, he assumed the imperial style Ser. Galba Imperator Caesar Augustus. Once again, like Claudius, he assumed the Julio-Claudian names of Imperator, Caesar and Augustus and indeed, from this time on, they were to become a *sine qua non* of imperial titulature. He was consul for the second time, suffect, in succession to Nero, in the same year and consul (for the third time) at the start of 69. Galba finally arrived in Rome in October, where the senate had voted him tribunician and proconsular powers and acknowledged him as *pontifex maximus*.

He thereupon set about being an old-fashioned disciplinarian. This included a certain amount of killing, but opinion was more poisoned against him by his haughty demeanour and the poor quality of his advisors, one an odious ex-slave, Icelus, granted equestrian status by Galba. The public purse being virtually bankrupt through Nero's profligacy, his first task was to claw back enough money to ease the burdens of government. Hence his calling in of all gifts made by Nero and his refusal of a donative to the Praetorians: 'I levy soldiers, not buy them,' he (rashly) declared. Furthermore, some of his supporters, whom he had been obliged to reward with positions in the government, turned out to be incompetent, greedy and unpopular.

---

258 Ocellina was apparently beautiful and wealthy, too: Suetonius, *Galba*, 3, 4. It would seem that the adoption was testamentary and that he retained his patrician status.

259 Syme (1986) 130

Nor was he devoid of rivals apart from Vindex, who had hardly risen above the status of rebel, for Macer (qv) had risen in rebellion in April 68 in Africa. He was apparently encouraged by a rather louche *femme fatale* and former lover of Nero's called Calvia Crispinilla, to reject Galba and use the corn supply from Africa which he controlled as a lever

to promote his own interests.[260] Galba reacted quickly, instructing the local procurator – the senior equestrian officer in a province – to kill the presumptuous legate. The procurator, Trebonius Garutianus, complied in October.[261] In the meantime, Macer, despite his praetorian rank, lack of powerful connections or potent familial alliances, had managed to issue coins in his own name as 'propraetor of Africa', suggesting a self-appointed elevation in status.

Galba's *coup* had not gone down well in Germany either, and for a variety of reasons. As a result, on 2 January AD69, Aulus Vitellius was acclaimed emperor there, suddenly impressing upon Galba that his position was by no means secure. On 10 January, under the threat of this mobilisation against him, the emperor felt it wise to adopt as heir a younger, more charismatic man (and also, being Galba, a very noble one), choosing L. Calpurnius Piso Frugi Licinianus, whom he consequently adopted as his son and successor, not only passing over his perfectly eligible nephew, Cornelius Dolabella – as it turned out, fortuitously, for Dolabella survived the upheavals and went on to a consulship under the Emperor Domitian – but also Otho, who, as governor of Lusitania when Galba was acclaimed, had supported him from the outset and had built up debt on the promise (widely believed) that he would be the old man's successor. As a consequence, and unsurprisingly, both Galbas were assassinated at the instigation of Otho in Rome five days later on 15 January, Galba an hour or two before his heir.

GALBA (II) see PISO

GALERIUS
305, 1st April – 311, 30th April

With Constantius I, Galerius was one of the first pair of caesars appointed by Diocletian and Maximian under the new tetrarchic system and is remembered chiefly for conducting the last great purge against Christians in his (eastern) half of the empire. Galerius was apparently called C. Galerius Maximinus *signo* Armentarius before being called upon to assume the role of Caesar. Thereupon he assumed Diocletian's *nomen* and Maximian's *cognomen* to become Nobilissimus et Fortissimus (as Joseph Addison observed, 'Modesty is not only an ornament, but also a guard to virtue') Caesar C. Galerius Valerius Maximianus, the latter name being the one he always seems to have borne officially, even though he was universally referred to as Galerius, both by contemporaries and all later chroniclers, in the same way that nobody referred to either Caracalla or Elagabalus as Antoninus.

He was born c. 254 at Romulianum near Serdica in Dacia – the name having been that of his mother, bestowed upon the region (*pagus*) by Galerius when

---

260 Tacitus. *Histories*, 7, 3.1
261 *Op. cit.*, 7.1

emperor in her honour;[262] it is now Gamzigrad, Serbia – and he was originally said to have been a herdsman. Although his mother's name (Romula) is known, his father's is lost to us. He served in the army under Aurelian and Probus. On being made Caesar, he was obliged to divorce his first wife (name unknown and by whom he had had a daughter, Valeria Maximilla) and marry Diocletian's daughter Valeria. As Augustus from 305, he was endowed with the tribunician and proconsular powers and the duplicated office of *pontifex maximus*. His style then became Imperator Caesar Galerius Aurelius Valerius Maximianus Pius Felix Invictus Augustus.[263] He also adopted the son of his sister, Maximin Daia, as his *caesar*. Thanks to fairly constant campaigning in the Balkans and the east, he had bestowed upon him the triumphal epithets of Germanicus Maximus II, Sarmaticus Maximus, Persicus Maximius, Britannicus Maximus, Carpicus Maximus, Armeniacus Maximus, Medicus Maximus, Adiabenicus Maximus; amongst which Britannicus Maximus looks highly dubious, as Britain was nowhere within his sphere of influence, what had he achieved to deserve it? He also held eight consulships, in 294, 297, 300, 302, 305, 306, 308 and 311.[264] He died of what appears to have been a particularly horrible affliction, perhaps bowel cancer or a particular form of gangrene, at Nicomedia (Izmit, Turkey) on 30 April 311. His reign was most notable to Christian writers for the vigour with which he persecuted Christians, although he is said to have repented on his death bed. He was succeeded by Maximin Daia.

GALLIENUS (I)
253, 29th August – 268, September

Gallienus was the last of the old-style *principes*, drawn from the ranks of the senatorial aristocracy. He succeeded his father, whose background this was. His sole reign perhaps marks the nadir of the original empire and the period in which the chaos of multiple barbarian incursions was combined with a vicious circle of continual attempts at supreme power instigated by various hard-pressed generals striving to hold the line, leading in turn to high inflation and instability, a situation only gradually remedied by the succession of Illyrian soldier emperors who succeeded him from his death in 268. Yet, amidst the chaos, compounded by the universal loss of face suffered by Rome with the capture and ignominious demise of Valerian, it was Gallienus who, by sheer doggedness, competence and administrative reforms, set the foundations for the recovery.

Shortly after his accession and faced with the instability following the rapid turnover of short-lived emperors combined with trouble on the Danubian frontier, Valerian appointed his 35-year-old son Gallienus – a general of proven competence – as co-emperor and, in the face of mounting

---

262 PLRE I Maximianus 9; FS1804; Syme (1971) 212, 226. Title as Caesar: ILS 630, 633, 635
263 ILS653
264 ILS642

crises in both the northern frontiers and the east, the empire was divided between them, although not formally, in 256.

P. Licinius Egnatius Gallienus was born c. 218, was probably quaestor c. 246/7, aedile or peoples' tribune c. 248/9 and praetor c. 250/251. Gallienus was in Rome when his father replaced Aemilian and the senate, in late August 253, appointed him *nobilissimus caesar*. Within four days his father had raised him to the rank of co-augustus as Imperator Caesar P. Licinius Egnatius Gallienus Pius Felix Augustus, adding Invictus soon afterwards and preceding it with Magnus after 260.[265] He was also joint *pontifex maximus* with his father, receiving from the senate all the usual powers. He is one of the first emperors to be formally styled *Dominus Noster* before his *cognomen* in lieu of Imperator Caesar, a tradition continued for all his children. He was consul in 255, 257, 260, 261, 263, 265, 266 and in 267. He was acclaimed *imperator* on accession and for the third time in 257, for the sixth time in 263 and no fewer than twelve times by 265. He had added the *cognomen* Germanicus by 257,[266] and Dacicus Maximus c. 264.[267] He married around 243 Cornelia Salonina Chrysogone, who from 253 was styled Augusta.[268] She was the daughter of P. Cornelius Saecularis, consul for the second time in 260, whose wife was probably Saloni[n]a, daughter of the senator M. Salonius Longinus Marcellus.[269]

On appointment, Gallienus was sent out to restore the situation on the Danube and Rhine frontiers, which he did with some success, earning both emperors the additional style Germanicus Maximus in 257. As if that wasn't enough, whilst Gallienus was occupied in Dacia in 256-257, a confederation of Frankish tribes managed to breach the Rhine frontier in more than one area and embark on an unparalleled rampage through western Europe as far as the Straits of Gibraltar, looting and burning en route. The Franks were eventually rounded up and persuaded to return back across the Rhine, but almost immediately that was done and the Rhine defences strengthened, the Alemanni broke out of Raetia and invaded Italy. Rapid reaction on Gallienus's part enabled him to win a crushing victory outside Mediolanum (Milan) and the intrusive barbarians were re-settled.

In Pannonia in 258 Ingenuus assumed the purple but was defeated and killed by Gallienus and his 2i/c, Aureolus at Mursa (on the River Drava, Croatia) in January 259, the fleeing usurper being killed soon afterwards. Yet within a year, the Pannonian troops replaced him with Regalianus, governor of Upper Pannonia, but *his* grab for power gave the Roxolani of Sarmatia (the north-western littoral of the Black Sea) the chance to overrun the province, Gallienus being busy in northern Italy throwing back the Alemanni at the time. Consequently, the soldiers, bottled up in Carnuntum (Bad-Deutsch Altenburg, Austria) by the Roxolani and other disaffected

---

265 ILS 536, 538
266 ILS 541
267 ILS 552
268 PIR² C1499
269 CIL. IX. 2592

elements, eventually deposed Regalianus and killed him. At this juncture, or a little before, the Emperor made his son Saloninus *caesar*.

With the capture of his father by Persian king Sharpur, a serious situation became desperate. In the west, Gallienus had considerable success on the Rhine and against the Carpi in the areas on the northern and western edges of Dacia, but had to deal with an usurper in the Balkans, Ingenuus, who seems to have clung on to power there for well over two years. Worse, his attention to the Rhine frontier – or the subsequent drop in attention to it in favour of the middle Danube – caused a further usurpation in Gaul in the person of Postumus who eventually presided over a breakaway Gallic empire which endured for some 15 years.

In the east a whole sequence of imperial claimants arose, all attempting to step in and halt the slide whilst at the same time grasping at a heaven-sent opportunity to obtain supreme power: Macrianus, Quietus, Regalianus and Aemilianus II. In most cases, the military situation was too fragile for the usurper to attempt to patch up a treaty and head for Rome and recognition; indeed, in many cases the situation was too fluid even for donatives to be paid or booty to be taken and claimants were cut down as quickly by their officers as they had been acclaimed in the first place. The only hope for men like this was to try and carve out a polity for themselves like Postumus or Zenobia and hope to come to terms or gain further advantage later.

In reality, 260 was the darkest single year in all Roman history prior to the fifth century. Yet Gallienus' military and organising abilities, not to mention energy, kept things on an even keel despite further barbarian incursions, like those of the Persians into Syria, and constant reports of usurpers. Yet he was, we are told, extraordinarily unpopular with almost all levels of Roman society. Nevertheless, by the time he eventually succumbed to the assassin's knife in 268, he had reigned for fifteen years and turned the tide. He would appear in retrospect to have been the victim of much adverse criticism because his re-organisation of the way the empire was administered was almost entirely at the expense of the senate, blocking its members' traditional career paths (*cursus honorum*).

All this Balkan activity meant that Gallienus' C-in-C Rhine had to be reliable and loyal, especially as the Caesar Saloninus had been installed at Colonia Agrippina as a figurehead ruler, in the keeping of one of the Praetorian Prefects, Silvanus. In the fatal year of 260, Silvanus fell out with Postumus who proclaimed himself emperor following a crushing victory by the acting governor of Rhaetia over the Semnones that had placed much booty in his hands.[270] This provoked Silvanus into acclaiming Saloninus as co-Augustus with his father. A confrontation began which resulted later that autumn in the death of Saloninus and his mentor, and the triumph of Postumus. At this stage, Q. Julius Gallienus, believed to be the emperor's youngest son, seems to have been briefly proclaimed *Caesar* as well.

---

270 The victor was M. Simplicinius Genialis, who may have made a brief bid for the purple after falling out with Postumus and before being suppressed by Gallienus: Drinkwater (2007) 54-57

Gallienus, despite an eventual partial invasion of Gaul, was unable in the end to take effective remedial action (and was himself wounded in a siege) with the result that the western provinces of modern Germany, Belgium, Britain, France and Spain became part of a breakaway political entity which was to endure for fifteen years. Once recovered from his wounds, Gallienus found he had other fish to fry.

Meanwhile, in the east, the provinces were collapsing before increased Persian raids, but Fulvius Macrianus, who had been Valerian's right-hand man in the east, held the line at Samosata (Samsat, Turkey), having turned down the opportunity of rescuing the emperor, which was probably a wise, cautious decision. Valerian's other Praetorian prefect, Ballista, managed to inflict a signal defeat on the Persians at Corycus (Kizkalesi, Turkey) in Cilicia, following which Sharpur was forced to withdraw. Ballista clearly thought the situation needed an Augustus on the spot. Sensibly deciding that he was not the man for the job – contrary to the claim in the *Historia Augusta* – he persuaded Macrianus to accept the throne, but he demurred on grounds of advancing years and lameness, suggesting his sons, Macrianus the younger and Quietus, both middle-ranking officers, instead, and these potential usurpers seem to have acceded in September 260.[271] Macrianus, with his father, having set the east to rights, then set out for the Balkans – presumably en route for Rome – but they were defeated and killed there by Gallienus' man Aureolus. In the chaos that followed, the *Historia Augusta* claims that there also arose two other alleged usurpers, Piso in Mursa (on the River Drava, Croatia), followed by his supposed nemesis, Valens, but both may be safely discounted (qv).[272] Aureolus, however, was himself acclaimed, although the circumstances may have required exceptional methods for he was allegedly deposed, forgiven and reinstated by Gallienus.

Meanwhile, Odenathus, King of Palmyra, offered inducements by Gallienus, set to work to dispose of Quietus, whom he eventually bottled up in Emesa (Homs, Syria) where the citizens, fearing a devastating sack of the town, killed the young co-emperor. This left Odenathus free to deal with the Persians himself, which he did with some aplomb, although Egypt set up yet another usurper, Aemilian II. In 264, Gallienus had celebrated a triumph in honour of Odenathus's success against the Persians.

By 267, Odenathus was complete master of the east, having defeated the Persians at their capital Ctesiphon the year before, and in gratitude Gallienus awarded him the title of *Imperator* and Governor of the East, only for him to be cut down by an ambitious kinsman, Maeonius, who was swiftly despatched as a result.[273] Odenathus' widow Zenobia then declared herself her husband's successor in all his appointments and titles, something of which Gallienus did not approve but was unable to deal with at the time. It has recently become apparent that she later elevated her young son Vaballathus

---

271 *Tyr. Trig.* 18
272 *Ibid.*, 19-21, but note that a Piso did really exist then but was never an usurper: PIR²
P428, cf. C298; PLRE I Piso 1; Syme (1971) 270
273 *Op cit.* 17

as Augustus between August 267 and August 268, simultaneously granting herself the same rank.[274]

This was all because Gallienus was busy elsewhere, for in the winter of 268 a massive force of Goths invaded the Balkans, being joined by a large horde of Heruli, a Germanic tribe from north of the Black Sea. Gallienus rushed to meet them and defeated them at a significant battle at Naissus (Niš, Serbia) but not before they had sacked Athens.

These events presaged the endgame for Gallienus. Taking advantage of this very serious diversion, the pardoned Aureolus, left in northern Italy to ensure that Postumus was kept trapped in Gaul, changed his allegiance at first to Postumus, but in the end attempted to have himself acclaimed emperor yet again, at Mediolanum (Milan). Gallienus, with all his characteristic energy, mopped up in Greece and the Balkans and returned to defeat Aureolus at the battle of Pontirolo, forcing his wayward general to fall back on Milan, where the Emperor bottled him up. Then, just as he was about to administer the *coup de grâce*, he was himself killed, probably very early in September 268, by his own officers, a group of Danubian comrades-in-arms that he himself had actively promoted. They allegedly included the Praetorian Prefect Heraclianus, the generals Cecropius and Marcianus, and the future Emperors Aurelianus, Probus and Claudius II; the latter, although not present, was almost certainly involved. The Emperor's brother Valerianus was also killed and the Empress was despatched not long afterwards, as were any other close kin, the murders sanctioned and driven forward by the senate, vengeful after having been stripped of almost all power and influence. The *coup*, which ushered in more than a century of non-senatorial soldier-emperors of a very different kidney, was nothing if not thorough. Furthermore, it marked an important watershed in the evolution of the monarchy. Nevertheless, Gallienus was reluctantly deified by the senate at the insistence of his successor.

Gallienus' achievements were by no means negligible. In order to minimize disaffection in the east, he had lifted the persecution of Christians inaugurated by Decius and continued by Gallus and his father. He re-organised the army to provide a central mobile corps to be based in Mediolanum, so it could be deployed rapidly to potential trouble spots. This was mainly made up of armoured cavalry, and there was a move towards cavalry elsewhere, lessons having been learned from Sharpur's use of mounted forces as well as that by the Sarmatians. This unit was officered by professional soldiers of equestrian rank largely drawn from the Danubian provinces, hardened men of proven ability; there was no longer any place for young tribunes of senatorial family.

In order to block – or at least cut down on – usurpers, Gallienus removed senators' exclusive right to ranks like senior tribune (*tribunus laticlavius*) or legionary commander and gradually increased the number of imperial provinces governed by men of equestrian rank appointed by the emperor, who were styled *praesides* (singular *praeses*), a process initiated by Severus.[275]

---

274 Millar (1971) 16
275 Webster (1969) 116-117

He must have felt that men of lower rank would be less likely to grab at power like the average senior senator, keen to enhance the *dignitas* of his family. Furthermore, many senators had extensive *clientelae* (people obligated to them in various ways, not to mention dependants) and estates scattered throughout the empire. Such support could be crucial in determining the likelihood of a successful bid for the purple. In this, Gallienus was to be proved wrong, of course. The lesson to be learned – as Maximin or Philip could have told him – was that it was the army at a general's back that made an emperor, not his rank. Gallienus had taken control of the empire at its lowest ebb and this apparent enthusiast for poetry and philosophy managed, by energy, ability and single-mindedness, to set the state on the long road back to health. One suspects that he is a much-underrated ruler, the usual negative attitude to him having been coloured by the hatred for him shown by classical chroniclers, influenced by the rancour arising from the side-lining of the senate.

GALLIENUS (II)
260

In autumn 260, Q. Julius Gallienus, believed to be the Emperor Gallienus' youngest son, seems to have been briefly proclaimed *caesar*, recorded on two types of very rare retrospective coins and posthumously struck to commemorate him and his better attested sibling with divine honours: Divo Caes[aris] Gallieno and Divo Caes[aris] Q. Gallieno.[276] Although there is some doubt about the authenticity of at least one coin type, the person commemorated seems to have taken over from Saloninus as Gallienus' heir and thus to have been nominated *caesar* in around autumn 260, just about the time that Postumus' *coup* was being played out. This Gallienus might well have been extremely young and clearly died prematurely. Presumably, his full style at death was Nobilissimus Caesar Q. [Egnatius] Julius Gallienus, although he may have had other names that are omitted on coins. Whether he made it to the dizzy heights of augustus or not, it was Postumus who swiftly neutralised and presumably killed him.

GALLUS see TREBONIANUS GALLUS

GELLIUS MAXIMUS see *MAXIMUS* (I)

GEMELLUS
37, 16ᵗʰ *March – June*

Tiberius Germanicus Julius Caesar Gemellus was nominated heir to the emperor Tiberius with Caligula in 35, and he thus succeeded jointly to power on the old Emperor's death on 16 March. However, Caligula contrived to have him eliminated 'within days' of that event. Gemellus

---

276 RIC 2, RIC 1

was a son of Drusus, brother of the widely admired Germanicus and a grandson of Tiberius himself. He was born in 19, twin with his brother Nero (who outlived him by a few months, dying in 38) and named with Caligula by Tiberius as his co-heir in 35. In 37 both were given, *inter alia,* the title *princeps juventutis* – Prince of Youth – and Gemellus was adopted as his son by the emperor. He was forced to commit suicide later the same year, suspected of involvement in a plot against Caligula. He was unmarried.[277]

GENCERIS
c. 354/8

Genceris is named on a single variant of the coins of Carausius II noted above and may represent the name of a successor or colleague, assuming that either man actually existed. Neither are named in any other context, most notably in Ammianus Marcellinus. Their absence from his pages is the most telling argument against their existence, if not entirely conclusive.

The most recent overview of the subject is by Casey, who does not quite commit himself.[278] If they are accepted as authentic, then they may have flourished in the turmoil following the fall of Magnentius and Decentius or that of five years later; both dates accord with the approximate coin type.

GENIALIS
260

M. Simplicinius Genealis, quite probably a senator of Gallic origin, was acting governor of Rhaetia when he inflicted a crushing defeat on the invading Senones in summer 260. It is thought that he may have subsequently fallen out with Postumus and been briefly elevated by his troops to the purple but was quickly suppressed, not by Postumus but by Gallienus, and presumably killed.[279]

GERMANUS
602, 22nd November – 2nd December

Germanus was an ephemeral usurper whose bid for the throne was made as Maurice (qv) fell. Germanus, usually referred to as Germanus Postumus, was married to Charito, a daughter of Tiberius II and was the son of another Germanus, a patrician in 536 and a nephew of Justin I. He was named as *nobilissimus caesar* on his marriage on 5 August 582, but later dropped the style and appears to have retired from court. By Charito he had one, possibly two daughters, whose names are lost to us. One married Theodosius III, Maurice's eldest son, who died with him in December 602.[280]

---

277 Syme AA 311f
278 Casey (1994) 165-167.
279 Drinkwater (1987) 54-57
280 PLRE III Germanus 3, 11; Theodosius 13

Germanus returns to the pages of recorded history in November 602 in the unfolding events preceding the deposition of Maurice. On the 22nd, Germanus, apparently with the encouragement of the future Emperor Phocas, was declared emperor, but within a few days it had become obvious that Phocas had changed his mind and had decided to proclaim himself instead, and once again Germanus retired, apparently unscathed. It may be, however, that after a few years he had returned to plotting against Phocas, for it appears that he was executed either in 605 or 607. His other daughter (or conceivably the same daughter who later married Theodosius III), formed a liaison with future emperor Heraclius I (610-641) by whom she bore Iohannes *qui et* Athalaricus – the soubriquet no doubt echoing the name of a Gothic ancestor, bearing in mind that Germanus' mother, Matasuntha, was a daughter of an Amal mother and the Goth Flavius Eutharicus (consul in 519). Ioannes enjoyed a career at court after his father succeeded to the throne in 610 before being exiled in 637 for being involved in a conspiracy, after which he is not heard of again.[281]

GETA
210 c. 1st November – 211, 26th December

Geta was the spare to Caracalla the heir during the lifetime of their father Septimius Severus, but was both hated and resented by his elder brother, who had no intention of sharing power with anyone, let along his despised sibling, with the result that he had him killed as soon as possible after the old Emperor's death.

Geta was born on 7 March 189; he was made *caesar* on his brother Bassianus' elevation to the rank of (co-)augustus in 198 as P. Septimius L. f. Geta Caesar.[282] He does not appear to have had a formal *cursus honorum* in the senate, only becoming a notional member of that body through his appointment as consul in 205 at 16. He was consul again in 208. His *praenomen* changed from 'Publius' to 'Lucius' a very few years later, his style becoming L. Septimius Geta Nobilissimus Caesar,[283] Confusingly, it was changed back again before he was appointed co-emperor in 210.[284] It may be that as Caracalla had become 'Marcus' in 198, Geta was entitled to his father's *praenomen* in lieu. It has also been suggested that it was to avoid being mixed up with his kinsman P. Septimius Geta, who was consul in 203, but the dates are not really sufficiently congruent.[285]

It is thought that Severus' intention was only ever to be succeeded by one son, the elder, but the Empress Julia Domna was a powerful and demanding woman who favoured her younger son. In so doing (despite no doubt being mindful of her elder son's character) she undoubtedly signed Geta's death

---

281 PLRE III. Ioannes 260
282 ILS 439
283 ILS 427
284 ILS 433
285 Birley (1988) 218

warrant. It was entirely thanks to her, too, that he was eventually appointed co-Augustus at York. His style on appointment as emperor was P. Septimius Geta Nobilissimus Caesar Pius Augustus and it is from this period that emperors increasingly adopt 'Pius' into their nomenclature in an entirely formulaic manner, although with the Severans it merely acknowledged their alleged membership of the *familia* of Marcus Aurelius. The fact that Geta's style retained the term *caesar* does rather suggest that he was very definitely the junior partner.

Geta was also appointed *princeps iuventutis* (Prince of Youth) and, with his elevation as co-emperor in October or November 210 received the (divided) pontificate, tribunician and proconsular power. He was constantly at loggerheads with his elder brother and, despite having become something of a martyr through being killed by Caracalla, there seems every evidence that he would have been much better either as person or as a ruler, had the position been reversed; both were spoilt brats, far too heavily imbued with the values of their eastern potentate ancestors rather than with those sober Roman virtues embodied, at least to some extent, in their father.

After succeeding, the two did everything in opposition, making governance difficult, and causing the palace to be physically divided into two completely separate establishments. A scheme likewise to divide the empire between them was scotched by their mother, in whose arms Geta eventually expired, unmarried, during an official audience on 26 December 211, having been stabbed in front of her by Caracalla – an audience being about the only occasion they could be together and far enough from their bodyguards to enable an assassination to be carried out. He suffered a *damnatio memoriae* after his death, passed *force majeure* by the senate.

GLYCERIUS
473, 3rd March – 474, 19th June

Glycerius was an ineffective cypher of a ruler, plucked, like Eugenius II and Libius Severus, from the ranks of the bureaucracy to act as a front for a scheming barbarian *magister militum.*

The death of Olybrius left the usual power vacuum in the west and, notionally, the Empire was once again united under the Emperor Leo I, whose effective viceroy was the Burgundian opportunist Gundobad. Leo took his time deciding on his next move, before finally elevating his *comes domesticorum* (commander of the guard) to the purple at the beginning of March the following year. From subsequent events it seems likely that Glycerius had been appointed to that position by Olybrius sometime in the middle of 472, which conferred upon him the status of *vir illustris.*

We have little information as to his origin, bar the inference from subsequent events that his mother lived at Ticinum (Pavia), suggesting that may have been his home town as well. The assumption is that he was a senator (albeit probably a bureaucrat of recent creation), rather than a military man risen to the top through martial prowess. With the Western Empire in meltdown, the senate had, especially since the death of Valentinian III, become the only recruiting ground for competent administrators, governors and even generals, a reversion to its first-century role. After the west had finally collapsed, senators still formed the backbone of the bureaucracy and administration of the successive regimes of Kings Odovacer and Theodericus and then of the eastern emperor, just as their coevals in Gaul (largely separated by the collapse from much actual participation in the senate in Rome) formed the underpinning of the Frankish, Burgundian and Visigothic kingdoms' administrations for the next two centuries.

The new appointee – a puppet emperor if ever there was one – was proclaimed at Ravenna but may not have been recognised by the senate at Rome, for although his coins were minted at Ravenna and Mediolanum (Milan), none were minted at Rome. In other words, it is possible that he was not even acknowledged throughout Italy, let alone in the surviving Western Empire. He was formally styled Dominus Noster Glycerius Augustus Felix Perpetuus Augustus[286] and it seems likely that he was western consul for 474, although this does not show up on the *fasti*, probably because the eastern emperor refused to acknowledge his elevation.[287]

Six months after Glycerius' elevation, Leo I died, leaving as his successor his grandson, Leo II and with the latter's father Zeno as co-emperor, leaving the unacknowledged Glycerius theoretically senior Augustus in the whole Empire. His chief achievement was that faced in early 474 with an invasion of Ostrogoths under their king, Videmer II, he managed through diplomacy to divert them from a planned descent on Italy and to go to Gaul instead. This had the effect of uniting them with the Visigoths, but at the cost of further losses of territory directly controlled by the Empire in southern Gaul. The ineffectiveness of the emperor led to much unrest in Italy, including a riot at Ticinum in which a mob threatened to burn down the house of the Emperor's mother. Imperial reprisals were only diverted by the entreaties of the local bishop.

Gundobad's father now died, and Gundobad returned to Gaul to reclaim his patrimony as co-ruler of the Burgundian peoples, leaving Glycerius without any real support. Simultaneously, the Eastern Court sent, rather as they had sent Anthemius in 467 and Olybrius in 472, another general to reclaim the west. This was the patrician and *magister militum* Julius Nepos, who landed with an army at Portus near Ostia at the Tiber's mouth, in June 474. Glycerius appears to have travelled from Ravenna to Rome and offered to abdicate in order to re-unite the Empire, an offer which was accepted. He was, like Avitus, offered and accepted the see of Salona in Dalmatia (Solin, Croatia), which he still held six years later. Apart from the fact that his mother was living when he was elevated to the purple, we know nothing for certain of his family. Barnish, however, has suggested that he might have been connected with Licerius [= Glycerius], a contemporary, whose son seems to have married the sister of St Ennodius and whose grandson was the senator Fl. Firminus Licerius Lupicinus.[288]

---

286 Coin evidence.
287 PLRE II Glycerius
288 PLRE II Licerius & Lupicinus 3; Barnish (1988) 155 & n. 214

GORDIAN I
238, 22nd March – c. 13th (22nd) April

Gordian was a remarkably short-lived emperor, elevated to oppose the fearsome Maximin I, who founded a remarkably short-lived dynasty and was recognised by the senate, even though he was at the time – unbeknown to them – dead. The Gordians, father and son, would be relegated to the status of mere usurpers were it not for the fact that they not only minted coins in both their names, but managed to obtain recognition from the senate, too, albeit in all likelihood posthumously. Indeed, Gordian was granted the title Africanus by the senate, but he probably went to his grave ignorant of the honour.

The elevation of the pair to the purple was through an unlikely and at first rather 'provincial' set of circumstances. Because the financial exactions of Maximin were allegedly so harsh, these fell hardest on the simpler farming folk of the provinces. The officers responsible for extracting this tribute were the provincial procurators, and the officer *en poste* in the province of Africa Proconsularis managed, by using force – even killing people – and in defiance of the proconsul, to arouse the ire of the local population to the extent that the provincial élite, led by a local town councillor, one Mauricius, resolved to assassinate him.[289] This was done at Thrysdus (El Djem, Tunisia) whilst the procurator was supervising the payment of the levies on olive oil, attended by the farmers, greater landowners and their tenants.

Having burnt their boats and virtually guaranteed bloody reprisals from the Emperor, these turbulent locals resolved to offer the purple to their elderly proconsul, M. Antonius Gordianus. He at first attempted to refuse but soon realised what a difficult situation they were all in; after all, Gordian as governor of the province, had either to have the procurator's murderers killed and order further reprisals, or go along with them and trust to fortune. Being – all authorities agree – 80 (or in his 80th year) and a humane man, he felt he had nothing to lose and accepted the acclamation.

As it happens, his son was with him, serving as his father's legionary legate. This situation is attested a fair number of times in the early Empire, though usually the son was a junior senator. Here, however, presumably because the governor was unusually old, he had persuaded his son to do the honours, although he, too, was an ex-consul and certainly not ordinarily obliged to serve in a capacity usually reserved for ex-praetors.

As might be expected, the *Historia Augusta* makes extravagant claims for the antecedents of the Gordians. Gordian I was descended, on his father's side, it avers, from the Gracchi – the assassinated aristocratic peoples' tribunes for 133 and 122-121 BC – and from his mother's side of the family from Trajan (who was childless!). It goes on to assert that Gordian's father, grandfather and great-grandfather all held the consulship, as had his wife's father and grandfather, not to mention two of her great-great grandfathers.[290]

---

289 But note, named only in the *HA, Tres Gord.* VII, 4
290 *Tres. Gord.* II. 2

M. Antonius Gordianus Sempronianus Romanus[291] was born probably in Cappadocia in c 159, probably of a senatorial family and presumably served as quaestor c. 187 and *aedile* c. 189, establishing that he was not of a patrician family. Whilst serving in this office the *Historia Augusta* tells us that he gave twelve gladiatorial shows, one for each month, a colossally expensive undertaking, indicating (if true) the enormous wealth of the family.[292] He was *praetor* presumably c. 191-192, but the upheavals following the death of Commodus may have delayed the advancement of his career, for although the *Historia Augusta* claims he was consul with Caracalla[293], it must have been after 216 when he was still an ex-*praetor*, serving as legate of Lower Britain (Britannia Inferior).[294] He thereafter must have been suffect consul – perhaps c. 222 in the wake of the elevation of Alexander – becoming governor of Africa c. 237, which was the usual interval after the consulship for such a prestigious position.

He took his own life on 12/13 April on hearing of the defeat of his son, and they were both deified by the senate on 22 April 238, the date the news of his death reached Rome.

GORDIAN II
22ⁿᵈ March – c. 13ᵗʰ (22ⁿᵈ) April 238

Gordian II was the son of Gordian I, who was serving as his father's legionary legate in Africa at the time of his acclamation as Emperor in March 238. Both would be dead a month later.

M. Antonius Gordianus Sempronianus Romanus, later Gordian II,[295] was born c. 192 and probably served as quaestor on the recommendation of Elagabalus c. 220/221, going on to serve as urban *praetor* on the recommendation of his successor, probably in 226 or 228.[296] He was suffect consul under Severus Alexander, probably in 229, after which he would have governed a province. He then offered to serve as his father's legate in Africa from 237 and both were acclaimed Emperor in the circumstances outlined above on 22 March 238.[297] It would seem that the philosopher Philostratus dedicated his *Lives of the Sophists* to an Antonius Gordianus, whom modern scholarship considers must be the son, rather than Gordian *père*, for he also claims him as a descendant of the famous eastern senator, Herodes Atticus (born c. 102), which would be almost impossible for the father, bearing in

---

291 PIR² A833
292 V. *Tres. Gord.* 3. 5; for a discussion of his ancestry and the sources, see Craven (2017) 284-288
293 *Ibid.*, 4, 2
294 Birley (1981) 181-186
295 PIR² A834
296 HA, *Tres. Gord.* XVIII. 4-5. There is nothing inherently unconvincing about this part of the HA's account.
297 The consulship is confirmed by a milestone at Caesaraea Maritima; only the *Historia Augusta* attests him as consul before his elevation, which is an example of it containing nuggets of truth.

mind that the sources mainly agree that he was around 80 in 238. Hence, on his acclamation, Gordian I associated his son with him in his rule as co-Augustus, probably in the hope that should he die or need military action, he was there by his side to give aid.

Having accomplished all this, envoys were sent to the senate at Rome to announce their elevation, and the senate duly acknowledged them, declaring, with unusual boldness, Maximin to be a public enemy, thereby setting in motion a civil war. The senate ordered coins to be struck in the names of the two Augusti, confirming that either on acclamation or by decree of the senate, old Gordian had been awarded the additional *cognomen* of Africanus.

The son seems to have adopted the style Imperator Caesar M. Antonius Gordianus Sempronianus Romanus Africanus Pius Felix Augustus.[298] It is not known exactly when his envoys reached Rome, but around 1 April or the 2nd he had been granted, jointly with his father, the tribunician and proconsular power, and been acknowledged as *pontifex maximus*. The two were also granted the title *Patres Patriae,* all included on their coins.

Meanwhile, back in Africa, Gordian II, leading a motley crew of militiamen and hastily raised levies, was defeated in battle on 12 April 238 by the governor of Numidia, Capellianus, just outside Carthage, and lost his life in the action. On hearing the news, his father committed suicide, but both emperors were deified by the senate on 22 April 238, the date the news of his death reached Rome.

Gordian II appears to have married but we only know his wife's name from the *Historia Augusta*: Fabia Orestilla, which is credible enough.[299] The same source, never to be outshone by history, also claims that he had 22 concubines by whom he had at least 66 natural children.[300] These even included the future emperor Claudius II, according to the *Epitome*.[301] The *Historia* at least allowed him one legitimate son it fails to name, perhaps having run out of inspiration.[302] If a son indeed existed, he must have perished with his father and grandfather at the hands of Capellianus, who may well have eliminated the entire family after entering Carthage. Had any son survived, Gordian III would not have been chosen to succeed Balbinus and Pupienus Maximus.

Before the deputation to the senate could return to Africa, news came that acting on the orders of Maximinus, Capellianus had defeated Gordian II. Their joint rule had lasted an estimated 22 days. Capellianus crowned his victory with a particularly bloody mopping-up operation in Carthage. Officially, however, the reign lasted until news of their defeat and death reached the senate in Rome on or before 22 April.

Apart from their coming to power and their demise, nothing is known of their reign in between. How they planned to neutralise Maximin is difficult

---

298 ILS 493
299 HA *Tres. Gordiani*. II. 2
300 *Ibid*. 19.3
301 *Epitome* 34, 2
302 HA *Tres Gordiani*. VI. 3

to estimate; the odds were heavily stacked against their success. Blocking the grain supply would have been their only ploy, as Macer found in 69. Perhaps the subsequent successful defence of Italy by their successors, Maximus and Balbinus, gives a clue. It could have been done, but the fact that they were still in Africa nearly a month after their acclamation suggests that neither was imbued with the sort of dash that got Severus to Rome in 193, or Pupienus Maximus to confront Maximin in 238; their inaction seems with hindsight to define them as rabbits caught in headlights – but then, one was by the standards of the time exceedingly old and the other middle-aged.

GORDIAN III
238, 29th July – 244, 25th February

The nephew of Gordian II, Gordian III, was adopted by Maximus and Balbinus as their heir through pressure (essentially blackmail) from the Praetorian Guard and duly succeeded them after their demise in July 238, thus becoming the sixth emperor in one year. His youth meant that his largely successful reign was shaped by his kingmaker, the Pretorian Prefect and the emperor's new father-in-law, Timisitheus, until it was ended by a military disaster during a campaign against the newly arisen Persian empire.

During the rule of Balbinus and Pupienus Maximus, the Praetorian Guard made much of the young nephew of Gordian II as they became increasingly restive. As a consequence, the two new emperors acquiesced and jointly adopted the youth as Caesar or heir apparent. The intention was no doubt to groom him to take over when the two old men should die. His original style was probably (although no coin or inscription has survived to prove it) M. Antonius Gordianus Caesar, although it is not known if the joint adoption of the boy had led to any change in his nomenclature, as happened with previous imperial adoptions. If there was any change, it was no doubt rapidly dropped in the wake of the assassination of the two emperors on July 29.

Reliable sources for the reign of Gordian III are sparse, for Herodian's and Dio Cassius' accounts of the empire both end at this point. Unlike Elagabalus and Alexander, however, he was not, as far as is known, under the control of a manipulative mother; indeed, we hear virtually nothing of her. That she was a sister of Gordian II there is no doubt and possibly she was called Maecia Faustina as the *Historia Augusta* claims, although doubts creep in when one reads that she was a descendant of Marcus Aurelius, hence her *cognomen*: possible but probably window-dressing. In the same source we read that her husband was called Junius Balbus, a suffect consul prior to the momentous events of 238, and perhaps a son or nephew of C. Junius Balbus, an equestrian officer who served as deputy praefect of the vigils (assistant chief constable) at Rome under Severus.[303] Hence, the new emperor's name at birth was probably simply Junius Balbus, no doubt embellished with a few other names to reflect ancestry.

---

303 PIR² I 733, 734

Gordian's style as officially adopted was Imperator Caesar M. Antonius Gordianus Pius Felix Augustus and he was unanimously acclaimed by the senate, being given the tribunician and proconsular power and made *pontifex maximus*, probably on 29 or 30 July. He was also styled *invictus* and *pater patriae*.[304] The reign was marked by a well-intentioned administration, seemingly carried out in partnership with the senate. Gordian's good fortune, however, which is doubtless why the reign lasted as long as it did, lay in the fact that one of the Pretorian Prefects, C. Furius Sabinius Aquila Timisitheus – appointed in the aftermath of a crisis in Africa in 240 – effectively acted as Gordian's regent and, by a happy chance, appears to have been a thoroughly decent man equipped with highly competent administrative and military skills. In due course, in 241 Gordian married Sabinia Furia Tranquillina, his prefect's daughter, who received the style of Augusta but – probably due to the youth of both parties – there was no issue.

Until 240, there had been a period of consolidation, with a successful campaign fought in Lower Moesia, but in that year the crisis in Africa erupted. An imperial claimant, Sabinianus, also proconsul of Africa, attempted – for whatever pressing reason is quite unclear – to repeat the action of Gordian I two years previously. It may be that this man claimed descent from Marcus Aurelius, which may have prompted him to act on his own account. This time, however, it was the governor of Mauretania, rather than Numidia, who suppressed the trouble.

These events, however, might have been the spur behind a move made the same year by Shapur, crown prince of the newly instituted Sassanian Persian Empire. He seized the strategic border town of Hatra (al-Hadr, Iran). This was quickly followed by further aggressive moves on the part of the Persians, who no doubt perceived the Empire as potentially without decisive authority at the highest echelons and under the rule of a boy-emperor.

Timisitheus put in hand measures for a military expedition to the east in 241. As before, the reduction in manpower on the Danube and Rhine frontiers tended to have the knock-on effect of causing incursions in these sectors once such information reached the barbarians beyond. Thus, whilst gathering extra units from the Danube, Timisitheus conducted a pre-emptive campaign against the Goths. By 243, the expeditionary force was in Syria, which was soon cleared of Persian elements and not long afterwards the Persians were decisively defeated in Mesopotamia at the battle of Rhesaina (Ras al-Ayn, Syria), the Romans recovering control as far as Nisibis and Carrhae, where Crassus had been defeated nearly 300 years previously, and which Maximin I had given away in his haste to return to Rome after assassinating Alexander. Thus far, the operation had been a success. That this was in large part thanks to Timisitheus is made clear by events that followed his death – probably from disease – later in that year.

The new Praetorian Prefect was a Roman citizen of Arab extraction, M. Julius Philippus. Almost all the (much later) Roman sources aver that from this point the Persian campaign was wound down and measures were

---

304   FS 661; ILS 499-501; PIR² A835

taken to undermine the Emperor by disaffecting his troops. Philip, in the meantime, appears to have got himself appointed regent as well, perhaps a misguided decision by Gordian's mother. An acute – and allegedly artificial – lack of supplies and some military reverses seem to have led to a mutiny at Circesium (Buseira, Syria) on the banks of the Euphrates, in which the soldiers were asked to choose between the 19-year-old youth Gordian and the hoary commander, Philip, with the Emperor having to plead for his life. The *Historia Augusta* even claims that Philip was elevated to the purple as joint emperor with Gordian before the final *débâcle*. The young emperor's only advisor, according to the same source, was the other Prefect, whom the *Historia Augusta* dubiously names as Maecius Gordianus, otherwise quite unattested. In the event, we are told that the soldiers chose Philip and Gordian was peremptorily put to the sword, his widow being allowed to survive, although we know nothing further of her.[305]

It can be argued that much of this does not ring true. If Philip wanted the throne, one could imagine less complex (and risky) ways of bringing about Gordian's downfall. Furthermore, if the shortage of supplies was combined with 'military reverses', one cannot help feeling that Philip was more likely to get the blame than Gordian. A Persian source, however, claims that the Sassanians had won a crushing victory as the culmination of a counter-attack NW of Ctesiphon (Al-Mada'in, Syria) early in the February and that Gordian had been killed in battle:

> When at first we [Shapur] had become established in the [Persian] Empire, Gordian Caesar raised in all of the Roman Empire a force from the Goth and German realms and marched on Babylonia against the Empire of [Persia] and against us. On the border of Babylonia at Misikhe, a great frontal battle occurred. Gordian Caesar was killed and the Roman force was destroyed.

A bas relief rock carving depicting Shapur's triumph at Bishapur in the Shiraz region of Iran, long thought to depict the submission of Valerian, makes a similar point showing a Roman emperor who is surely Gordian III being trampled beneath the hooves of Shapur's steed with Philip kneeling before the Great King offering tribute, supposedly of 300,000 *denarii*. A fire altar dedicated to Ahura Mazda by one Abnun, dateable to this time, also seems to celebrate the same Persian victory.

This rings true, much more so than the conventional tale of usurpation and murder, despite the tendency for such claims by Sharpur to include elements of exaggeration. In either case, there appears to have been a propaganda war waged. Perhaps, in truth, the campaign was indecisive for both sides. It may be, too, that Philip engineered the emperor's death in battle – that was to happen at least one more time in the coming years – or it may have been a genuine disaster caused by Philip's inferior military talents, but in either case, the bizarre scene retailed by the *Historia Augusta* fails to convince. Furthermore, if there had been a defeat, it was probably felt imperative that it should be airbrushed from the

---

305 HA,. *Tres Gord.*, 30, 1-9

Relief of the triumph of Shapur I over Valerian (c. 241–272. Philip the Arab is thought to be the standing figure by some but is probably kneeling offering tribute. Gordian III is dead at the feet of Shapur's horse. (Courtesy Diego Delso, Wikimedia Commons)

official accounts so as not to undermine the new ruler's authority. Had Gordian's arms met with unqualified success, it is hardly likely that a mutiny would have occurred or that a triumphant Emperor would have been assassinated.

A death in battle or from disease would at least have explained the senate's ready acquiescence in Philip's succession; the small matter of the 300,000 *denarii* might also have had to have been explained. Indeed, quite apart from his having been a possible battle casualty, a death from poison giving symptoms resembling those of a disease would surely have been a far more credible way of disposing of the young ruler than the farcical events described by the *Historia Augusta*. Either way, Gordian's reputation survived, and Philip urged upon the senators the deification of his predecessor, to whom he had, apparently, erected a monument on the banks of the Euphrates. Nor is there any real hint in this reign that people looked upon Philip, unlike Maximin Thrax, as some sort of grim usurper.

GRATIAN (I)
367, 24th August – 383, 25th August

Gratian was of the first late Roman boy-emperors, whose need to rely on military strongmen to rule bedevilled the later history of the empire, especially in the west. He survived a decade as sole ruler in the west but was killed as a result of the rise of Magnus Maximus.

Gratian was the only son of emperor Valentinian I and his first wife Marina Severa, who was born on 18 April 359 when his father was serving at Sirmium (Sremska Mitrovica, Serbia), and named after his grandfather. He was made consul aged 6 in 366 with the style *nobilissimus puer* (most noble boy) and proclaimed co-emperor with his father on 24 August the year following, as a result of Valentinian falling seriously ill whilst campaigning against the Alemanni on the Rhine frontier. This caused a certain amount of apprehension amongst the general staff, but on recovering, the emperor told them that his son's ability to rule would flow from his nobility of character and sense of justice and that in any case, he would grow into the role of commander. It spoke volumes when, on the next campaign, Gratian was left behind with his tutor, the cultivated Gallic senator D. Magnus Ausonius, whom his former charge later made consul in 379.[306] Also in 374, he married the posthumous daughter of Constantius II, Flavia Maxima; she was 13, he 15. The union produced a son (whose name we do not know and who appears to have died in infancy) who died early in 383 and Gratian re-married Laeta (apparently a love match), but there was no further known issue.

Nobility of character aside, it turned out that he was not an obviously martial youth, more one with a tendency to piety. The Empire's two senates confirmed his elevation and he took the style Dominus Noster Flavius Gratianus Felix Semper Augustus, and he was presumably endowed with tribunician and proconsular powers, although whether the senate had any say in this by this date is debatable.[307] He was also made *pontifex maximus*, a role much more likely to have been conferred or at least acknowledged by the senate, still at this date predominantly pagan, but he renounced the title later in his reign, in 382.[308] The new co-emperor was consul for a second time in 371, and thereafter in 374, 377 and 380.

Gratian succeeded his father as ruler of the west in 375 and when his uncle was killed by the Goths three years later, he and his half-brother Valentinian II continued to divide the Empire between them. The disastrous events of the battle of Adrianople (Edirne, Turkey) in 378 and the chaos which ensued ultimately led to the appointment, by a military *coup* – disguised as a move initiated by Gratian personally – as eastern ruler of Theodosius, son of Valentinian I's efficient commander of the same name.

News of the defeat at Adrianople encouraged incursions in the west, which eventuated in the young emperor at least taking the field (as he had done as a child with his father) and he won a considerable victory (entirely down to his *magister militum*, the Frankish-born Merobaudes) over the most southerly tribe of Germans at Argentaria (Colmar, Alsace). It perhaps earned him the additional style of Germanicus Maximus, although it is not recorded, as these usages were beginning to fall into desuetude.[309]

---

306 PLE I Gratianus 2
307 ILS 778
308 FS1685. He was probably the last emperor to bear it, cf. FS pp. 61-65
309 Revived under Justinian I

Later, Gratian moved his court from Augusta Treverorum (Trier) to Mediolanum (Milan) and visited Rome regularly, which was not as welcome as it sounds, for the young man managed to combine a love of the arena and of his blond barbarian personal bodyguards with a renewed persecution of paganism, which resulted in the alienation of the resurgent senatorial aristocracy. Furthermore, his increasing reliance on barbarian officers and advisors combined with his naturally un-martial nature also alienated the army in the north-west, especially after his departure to Milan, and the outbreak of a fresh problem on the Rhine in 383 coincided with the appearance on the continent of Magnus Maximus, previously acclaimed emperor in Britain (possibly with his kinsman Theodosius' connivance). Faced with the choice, important elements of his army defected to the newcomer, forcing Gratian to flee south as far as Lugdunum (Lyon) where he was overtaken by Andragathius, Maximus' *magister militum*, who, treacherously and almost certainly exceeding his orders, had him killed on 25 August 383.

GRATIAN (II)
407, c. January – April

Gratian was an ephemeral usurper in Britain, elevated as a result of the panic resulting from the barbarian invasions on the continent, but deposed and killed before seemingly having had a chance to achieve anything.

The loss of his predecessor, the equally obscure Marcus (III), must have created a problem if the initial British usurper really had been *Comes Britanniarum*, as has been suggested. No doubt he appointed one of the officers on the strength in the British provinces as his replacement. Yet with his death or deposition, we are told, at least by one reasonably reliable source, the clique of officers who brought about his demise had allowed his successor to be chosen from amongst the civilian leaders of British provincial society. Perhaps Sozomen was right, and his name was everything; after all, for all his faults, had not the first Gratian defeated and virtually annihilated a mass of German tribesmen who had crossed the Rhine in 378?

As the first Gratian had then been only 19, the idea that this might have inspired the British *comitatenses*' choice of replacement for Marcus seems unconvincing. Either way, the new British usurper, raised to the purple in the weeks or days following the reception of the news of the barbarian invasion of Gaul, was called Gratian, and had reputedly been a decurion (town councillor) or other civic leader in Britain, from which we might reasonably suppose that he was of Roman-British stock and perhaps held sway in Londinium (London).[310]. As we have absolutely no other information, it may be that, as with other instances of 'regime change' – Carausius springs to mind – he may have been appointed to a senior post by Marcus, perhaps as a *comes*, possibly as a fiscal officer, like *comes sacrarum largitionum*, from which dizzy eminence he may have been encouraged, like Allectus just over a century before, to replace his benefactor.

---

310 PLRE II Gratianus 3

All we know beyond that is that he was in power for about four months before being deposed by the army. What could have been going on in Britain during that time? Again, no known coins were minted, and one might wonder why not, as London had a mint and precious metal was available. The reason no effort was made to cross the Channel and try to restore order may have been Gratian's un-military background, but one might legitimately doubt this. Zosimus claims that the British establishment was at first primarily concerned that the barbarians would turn upon them. Perhaps the new usurper launched a diplomatic offensive to try to find out from Ravenna what was going to be done to protect the island. It may be that, with no progress being made, the army became restive and disposed of Gratianus, nominating a candidate of their own instead. That man was Constantine III. The date was probably some time in April.

GUNTHARIS
545, December – 546, January

Guntharis was a Roman officer of Frankish descent, first coming to notice in 540 as a member of the personal guard of the patrician Solomon, commanding in Africa as Belisarius's successor against the Vandals. By his rapid action, the proconsul was saved from certain defeat whilst leading a pre-emptive strike against a group of rebellious Moors. Solomon was later killed at the Battle of Cillium (Kasserine, Tunisia) against Stotzas, due to the treacherous performance of Guntharis who had fled at the crucial moment. Nevertheless, he was later forgiven this lapse and in 545 made *magister militum* and *dux* of forces in Numidia under the patrician Sergius, who thereafter left Africa for the capital. Encouraged by the younger Stotzas (II, qv), Guntharis therefore plotted rebellion, persuading the Moors to attack Carthage, which led to his being recalled from Numidia by the new Commander Areobindus to assist with the City's defence. Guntharis acted treacherously throughout, hoping his commander would be killed in battle allowing him to seize power opportunely, but when this did not come about he allowed the Moors to overrun Carthage, in the process defeating Areobindus, who was soon afterwards murdered at his instigation.[311]

Having established himself in the Imperial palace at Carthage he planned to marry Praejecta, Areobindus's widow, sister of the future Emperor Justin II and niece of Justinian. Whether his nominal style as usurper was the expected Dominus Noster Guntharis Pater Patriae Augustus of the period or not is unknown, in the absence of coins. Procopius describes him as *basileus* (king/*tyrannus*) and both he and Stotzas II as *tyranni* (usurpers), both terms clearly indicating that they wore the purple.

Guntharis' first project was the reduction of the Moors in Byzacena in order to extend his rule over more of North Africa. He despatched a force under the command of an Armenian, Artabanes. After a perfunctory victory, Artabanes returned for reinforcements and arranged the assassination of the usurper

311 Conant (2012) 223-2243

during the banquet held on the evening prior to the despatch of the reinforced army. Although he subsequently gave a pledge of safety to Stotzas II, he was soon afterward sent to Constantinople, where he was killed.[312]

HADRIAN
117, 7th August – 138, 10th July

Hadrian is one of the best known of all Roman emperors, being a successful soldier, a sound administrator, a cultured man and of course the man who authorised the building of the eponymous wall across northern Britain. He was one of the four emperors of the golden age of Empire.

Whilst Trajan may be portrayed as a paragon of manly virtue and an ideal soldier-emperor, Hadrian was a much more complex man. Although he enjoyed a very successful military career, fostered by his predecessor and cousin once removed, he also had a strong predilection for intellectual pursuits and the liberal arts, and a keen appreciation of the chase. He fancied himself as a Hellenophile – his contemporaries referred to him as *graecinus* (greekling) – and also dabbled in poetry and architecture, to the extent of persecuting Apollodorus of Damascus, Trajan's architect, after he expressed a little professional criticism of the Emperor's lavish new self-designed villa complex at Tivoli.

Hadrian claimed in his autobiography, which is preserved only in fragments both in the *Historia Augusta* account of his reign and that of the much more reliable Cassius Dio, that his family hailed originally from Hadria (Atri, Abruzzo), hence his *cognomen*.[313] Nevertheless, the family had been settled at Italica in Spain since an ancestor had been settled there with many other ex-soldiers by P Cornelius Scipio in 206BC. By the end of the Republic, the Aelii of Italica had become one of the leading families of the province of Baetica, indicated by the fact that the first named member of the family, Marullinus, was a senator under the triumvirate, if not earlier; the census to qualify was after all a million sesterces, although in the triumviral interlude, odd promotions were not uncommon, as with Marullinus' fellow Baetican, L. Cornelius Balbus, adlected to the senate after Caesar's death and the first ever non-Italian consul, holding office in 40BC. Birley suggests that Marullinus was a prominent supporter of Caesar in a largely Pompey-supporting province and that he had been made a senator as a reward in 48.[314] Much of our knowledge of Hadrian does rely on the *Historia Augusta*, but in spite of the caveats given about this work it is generally accepted that the material relating to the Antonine emperors it provides is reasonably sound.

On Trajan's death, there was once again a slightly dubious succession. Whereas Trajan might be suspected of having engineered – albeit at a distance – his own adoption by Nerva, the matter was at least done and dusted in public. When Trajan died, however, there was some considerable doubt as to whether Hadrian had been adopted by his predecessor at all,

312 PLRE III Artabanes 2, Guntharis & Sergius 4
313 SHA I, 1
314 Birley (1997) 13

so rapid was his demise, this despite Hadrian's relative proximity, as his kinsman's right-hand man in his capacity of governor of Syria at the time. Not only that, but when he finally returned to Rome – having divested the Empire of Trajan's two new Eastern provinces on equivocal terms and diverted to the Balkans en route to quell a revolt there – four senior senators of consular rank had been put to death, allegedly for conspiracy.

The lengths to which Hadrian went to deny involvement in these unfortunate events suggested his guilt to many, which burdened his reputation ever after. He himself laid the blame squarely on the senate, for that body's acquiescence was a *sine qua non* of such proceedings, which were invariably brought under one of a group of existing laws. Under men such as Tiberius, Nero or Domitian, the senators were cowed by threats – subtly expressed or otherwise – into voting for a motion to have someone exiled or killed. However, in this case, the Emperor was absent and unable to threaten, unless he covertly contacted one of his allies in the senate.

Unfortunately, too few details have come down to us for a reliable judgement to be made. Worse, the real motive for the removal of this powerful and well-connected group remains obscure. The simplest explanation must be that they opposed Hadrian's accession, either because they thought him not the right man for the job or saw though the fraudulent adoption masterminded by the Empress and took a high-minded (and fatal) stance in favour of senatorial election of a successor.

That aside, Hadrian subsequently undertook to execute no senator without fair hearing and, like his predecessor, ruled effectively whilst paying elaborate lip-service to the constitutional niceties preserved by Augustus to maintain the illusion that the Republic still endured.

P. Aelius P. f. Serg. Hadrianus was born in Rome on 24 January AD76, son of P. Aelius Hadrianus Afer, who had been praetor in 77 and was probably a grandson of (Aelius) Marullinus, the senator under the triumvirate. His father's sister had a daughter, whose husband's brother, Cn. Domitius Lucanus, was distaff great-grandfather of the future Marcus Aurelius. On his father's death he was still a child and became the ward of Trajan and of the *eques* Acilius Attianus.[315] In 94, he became *decemvir stlitibus iudicandis* (one of a board of ten to adjudicate on minor lawsuits) along with two prestigious quasi-religious appointments, as *praefectus feriarum Latinarum* (a temporary stand-in for a magistrate – usually a consul – obliged to leave the City to attend an age-old festival of the Latin League) and *sevir turmae equitum* – leader of a squadron of horsemen at the annual ride-past of the members of the Equestrian Order. He was Military tribune of II Legion *Adiutrix* in 95-96 and then with V Legion *Macedonicus* 96-97; he entered the senate in AD101 as quaestor and a member of Trajan's personal staff and, probably the year before, he was made a priest of the most junior of the four great priestly colleges, a *Septemvir (VIIvir) Epulonum*. He is also recorded as having been a priest of the cult of the Deified Augustus – one of the *Sodales Augusti* – but it is not clear when.

---

315 ILS 308

As these were generally patricians it may have occurred later and certainly implies that Trajan had raised his family to patrician rank; this must have been after his tribunate, which he held in 102 following his return from the Emperor's Dacian HQ. He is also recorded as *curator actae senati* – keeper of the senate's records. He held the praetorship in 105 – exceptionally about 18 months earlier than the rules allowed, probably through his newly bestowed patrician standing, after which he governed Pannonia Inferior (107) and held a suffect consulship in 108. He was appointed governor of the pivotal province (in the context of Trajan's Parthian war) of Syria, and was still *en poste* when the Emperor died. His adoption papers arrived on 9 August 117 and he heard of Trajan's death two days later (four days after the actual event), when he was duly acclaimed.

On accession Hadrian was styled Imperator Caesar Traianus Hadrianus Augustus,[316] hailed as *imperator* for the first time, appointed *pontifex maximus* and voted the tribunician and proconsular power by the senate, renewed on 10 December each following year. Unusually, he was only acclaimed *imperator* once more in his life, in 135, after the suppression of the Jewish revolt. He took a second consulship – an ordinary one this time – in 118 and a third and final one in 119, the sparing use of such titles being a potent sign of his confidence in the security of his position, despite the rocky beginning. He took the additional title of *pater patriae* as late as 128. He married Vibia Sabina in 100. She died in 136 and they had no issue.[317]

Although by no means disposed towards warfare, despite twenty years' close association with Trajan, Hadrian managed to visit every province in the Empire to acquaint himself with their officials, people and idiosyncrasies. These visits included one to Britain which led to the construction of the wall. This attention to the administration of the provinces created much good will, also making it easier for him to formulate policy and appoint administrators appropriately. The day-to-day administration of the Empire, radically improved by Trajan, was further streamlined and perfected by his successor. Hadrian was also something of an aesthete, a lover of Greek culture and was bisexual, the unexpected and unexplained accidental death of his favourite Antinous in about 130 causing him extreme grief, which may well have coloured his conduct thereafter. He peppered the Empire with statues of the youth.

Having spent fifteen years avoiding armed conflict, Hadrian then provoked it when he decided to re-found Jerusalem, sacked and largely abandoned by Titus (qv) in 70, as Aelia Capitolina. This involved building what was effectively a new city, and it included the highly provocative erection of a new temple, to Jupiter Capitolinus, on the site of the temple built by Herod. This triggered a catastrophic revolt led by a charismatic rebel called Simon bar Kokhbar, which lasted perhaps more than three years, required the military presence of the Emperor himself and according to Cassius Dio cost over half a million Jewish lives in actual combat, many more from famine and disease.

---

316 ILS 310
317 ILS 323

His reign ended as it had begun, with the deaths of distinguished senators, Hadrian's elderly brother-in-law L. Julius Ursus Servianus and his grandson, a promising young senator rejoicing in no fewer than ten names but known as Cn. Pedanius Fuscus. The latter, who, after his grandfather, was Hadrian's nearest male heir (and thus had been raised in the expectation of succeeding to the principate) was at the centre of what appears to have been a badly organised plot in AD137 that was quickly identified and dealt with. Both were forced to commit suicide.

Once again, the succession was fraught, for Hadrian was the fifth emperor in a row without children. In 136, with what appeared to be a serious debilitating illness developing, he adopted L. Ceionius Commodus, consul in that year. His nomination was a surprise, for his qualifications were and are difficult to discern. Not a relative, he was the stepson of C. Avidius Nigrinus, the consul of 110 who was one of the four senior men executed whilst Hadrian had been travelling to Rome at his accession: was he trying to make amends? [318] Commodus was also married to Nigrinus's daughter. No other explanation, except for the supposition – supported only by artfully assembled circumstantial evidence – that Commodus was Hadrian's illegitimate son, seems to be convincing.[319]

The problem was that Ceionius turned out to be more desperately ill than his adoptive father. Having been assumed cured from a disease which involved coughing up blood, he was given tribunician and proconsular power and sent to the Danubian provinces with special powers. He returned at the end of 137 but died suddenly on New Year's Eve. By this time, Hadrian's wife was also dying (she was dead by March) and he himself was very ill. On 25 February 138 he therefore hastily adopted a new heir, the fifty-one-year-old senator T. Aurelius Fulvus Boionius Antoninus, whose consulship had been back in 120 and whose military experience was extremely limited. This was the future Emperor Antoninus Pius (qv).

To complicate matters, but to keep the succession settled for the following generation, he obliged Antoninus, who had no son, to adopt in his turn the five-year-old son of Ceionius Commodus, along with the intended husband of Antoninus' daughter, a man called M. Annius Verus – later respectively the Emperors Lucius Verus and Marcus Aurelius. Some Roman and most modern commentators have assumed with hindsight that Marcus was the intended long-term heir, but T. D. Barnes has argued convincingly that it was, in fact, Lucius.[320]

This settled the succession, as it turned out, until Marcus's death in 180: a remarkable happenstance, given the volatility imparted by the prospect of total power and the general dislike for Hadrian in his declining years, fuelled by his initial choice of heir and by the fate of Servianus and Fuscus – and others, hinted at but not named by one source.[321] He died after a painful

318 PIR² A1407
319 Syme (1958) 601 & n. 4
320 Barnes (1967) 65-79
321 Birley (1997) 289-295, 300

illness – allegedly wished upon him by the dying curse of Servianus – at Baiae (Baia) on 10 July. He was subsequently deified by a (reluctant) vote of the senate on a motion of his successor.

HANNIBALIANUS
337, 22nd May to 3rd September

Flavius Hannibalianus was one of the designated heirs and kinsmen of Constantine who was made King of Pontus to that end, but who was rapidly disposed of by the emperor's sons in 337. The younger brother of Dalmatius, he was the son of the elder Dalmatius and grandson of Constantius I Chorus by his second wife, Theodora.[322] He probably took his name from the empress Theodora's father, the Asian Afranius Hannibalianus, Diocletian's Pretorian Prefect and later consul in 292. With his brother, he was educated at Tolosa (Toulouse) under the rhetor Exuperius and then sent to court at Constantinople. Here he married Constantina, the elder daughter of Constantine I in 335 and on 18 September he was made *nobilissimus caesar* and king of the people of Pontus as *Rex Regorum*, the intention being that he should assume power there, after a projected campaign against Persia. Coins were minted for him in this role.

The campaign had not begun when Constantine died on 22 May 337, at which point, along with his brother Dalmatius (qv) and their three cousins of the half blood, the surviving sons of Constantine, all notionally and jointly succeeded to power. Soon realising that he and his brother were being sidelined by the Emperor's surviving sons, both were involved in a mutiny at Constantinople along with Julius Constantius, another cousin, ex-consul and patrician (but not actually a *caesar*). This was stifled by the late Emperor's last right-hand man, the Praetorian Prefect Ablabius,[323] who rapidly moved to eliminate them, achieving this on 3 September and leaving the field clear for the sons.[324]

Hannibalianus appears to have left a daughter, Constantia, believed to have married into the senatorial high aristocracy of the west; her daughter Rusticiana married the late 4th-century senator and inveterate letter writer, Q. Aurelius Symmachus.

HERACLIANUS
412, c. November – 413, 7th March

Heraclianus was senior military commander in Africa in 412 who tried to take advantage of the chaos in Italy which arose from the invasion of Alaric and his Goths, using the African corn supply to prepare the way for a bold attempt to invade Italy and dislodge the emperor Honorius.

---

322 PLRE Dalmatius 6, Hannibalianus 2
323 PLRE I. Ablabius 4. He was an upwardly mobile Cretan, who rose to the senate and a consulship in 331; his daughter became Queen of Armenia and his granddaughter was a sister-in-law of Theodosius I (qv).
324 PLRE Dalmatius 6 & 7

He had been appointed *comes* of Africa in 408 by a grateful Honorius, mainly, it would seem, as a reward for killing Stilicho with his own hands at Ravenna on 22 August that year. His behaviour towards Rome (which relied on the export of corn from his Diocese) left much to be desired, but he remained loyal to Honorius throughout the period of Alaric's sieges of Rome and the regime of his nominee as emperor, Attalus; he even sent him financial assistance. However, at the insistence of Alaric's Goths, Attalus rashly sent a replacement for him to Carthage called Constans, whom Heraclianus rapidly disposed of, leading to a delay in corn supplies that ultimately contributed to the deposition of Attalus. Heraclianus was rewarded with the consulship (west) for 413 for his belated loyalty to Honorius, but hardly had he been designated than he declared himself emperor (or at least went into a formal state of schism from the government in Ravenna), stopping all exports of food to Italy.

We do not know how he styled himself as there are no inscriptions, and he seems not to have issued any coins. He did collect a large fleet and sailed to Italy to depose Honorius, but on landing he was defeated in battle and as a result he abandoned his fleet and army and retired to Carthage in a single vessel, where he was murdered on 7 March 413. His consulship was annulled, his supporters persecuted and his property (which was not enormous) seized.[325] The only thing we know about his family is that he had a daughter who married Sabinus, his second-in-command, who ended up in exile.

HERENNIANUS (I)
267

A supposed Palmyrene usurper, Herennianus was, with Timolaus (qv) one of the younger sons of Odaenathus, husband of Zenobia by a previous wife. He was alleged to have been raised with his brother to the rank of emperor but killed with him in uncertain circumstances in 267, unattested outside *Historia Augusta*.[326] Palmyrene inscriptions, coins and seals seem to suggest that Odaenathus had a son, probably not by Zenobia, who was called Hairan II (Septimius Herennianus); there was also a Hairan I who was either an elder brother of Hairan II or a brother of Odaenathus. The matter is far from resolved, but in either case, although they may have briefly held power in Palmyra, there is no suggestion they were ever strictly speaking usurpers.[327]

HERENNIANUS (II)
280

An Herennianus is alleged by the *Historia Augusta* to have shared imperial power with his father, the usurper Proculus, whose primacy was ephemeral

---

325 PLRE II Heraclianus 3. Heraclianus (II) was a 7th-century member of the Heraclid dynasty and outside the scope of the present work.

326 HA *Tyr. Trig.* XXVII & XXVIII

327 PLRE I Herennianus 1; Southern (2010) 8-10, 80-81

by any measure. If he did exist and was *caesar* or augustus, he presumably died with his father at the hands of the Emperor Probus.[328]

HERODES/HERODIANUS
267

If this man is correctly the [L.] Septimius Herodianus who was Prince of Palmyra from 267 and son of Odaenathus by his first wife, he must be one and the same as Herennianus I, all three variants of the name being derived, it is assumed, from attempts to Latinise or render into Greek the Palmyrene name Hairan. The *Historia Augusta* claims that he was 'effeminate, wholly oriental and given over to Grecian luxury', despite which, he probably married a Tyria who would perhaps have been sister or daughter of Tyrius Septimius Azizus (a Palmyrene *v[ir] p[erfectissimus]* – an equestrian official – c 260/268) and possibly of Phoenician origin. Herodianus was killed with his father in unexplained circumstances in 267, but inevitably, the *Historia Augusta* claims that he was made co-emperor with his father, for which there is no corroborating evidence whatsoever.[329]

HONORIUS
393, 10th January – 423, 25th August

Honorius was the younger son of Theodosius I and the timorous and indecisive Emperor of the west for 28 years who presided over the beginnings of the collapse of the Western Empire. The Emperor was born on 9 September 384, and was thus a boy when he acceded to the imperial purple as the colleague of his father and elder brother. Indeed, the chief problem for the Theodosian dynasty is that, apart from its founder, each representative came to power as a child and had any of them even had the potential to rule as effectively as Theodosius had done, they never had the chance, day-to-day government being in the hands of senior, mainly barbarian, generals, court eunuchs and female relations. These advisors and hangers-on were unwilling to take the risk of allowing the young emperors to assert themselves or even acquire the necessary skills.

In being nominated as co-emperors as children, Honorius and his brother Arcadius in the east were following a trend started by Valentinian I in nominating as co-emperor his sons as children (Valentinian II and Gratian) a strategy that became more and more frequently followed throughout the fifth century. Increasingly, the emperor's role started to become ceremonial, like the oriental rulers of more recent times, whilst powerful court factions strove to control and execute policy. In the end, it opened the way for powerful generals to dominate the government and nominate children of the dynasty to reign and later, harmless bureaucrats (when there was no dynasty).[330] It fatally weakened the west, although imperial power recovered in the east, even after

---

328 HA *V. Firmi* 12.4; PIR² H 98; PLRE Herennianus 2
329 PLRE I Azizus I; Tyr. Trig. XVI
330 McEvoy (2013) 326-329

two successive child emperors. As it turned out in the case of Honorius, it is doubtful whether – with all the advice and training in the world – he would have emerged as an effective ruler in his own right.

Prior to his elevation Honorius was styled *nobilissimus puer* and, in 386 when aged 13 months was consul before being proclaimed Augustus on 10 January 393.[331] Flavius Honorius was styled in a somewhat *retardataire* style as Imp[erator] Caes[ar] D[ominus] N[oster] Honorius Perp[etuus] Aug[ustus], although in some cases his formal *nomen* Flavius was also inserted.[332] He served a dozen further consulships, in 394, 396, 398, 402, 404, 407, 409, 412, 415, 417, 418 and 422.

In 395, he married the elder daughter of Flavius Stilicho, the Vandal-born commander who had succeeded Arbogastes in the West. She died c. 407/8 and he then married her sister Thermantia in 408, but she divorced him after his acquiescence in the murder of her father, without whose outstanding skills as a military commander (he was *magister militum* in the west for an astounding thirteen and a half years, from 394 to 407) the west might have succumbed permanently to the waves of barbarians who began to surge across the western provinces following his downfall. Both marriages were childless, which of course was to produce further problems for the future.

In fact, the first six years of the sole reign were peaceful, thanks to the effective settlements made by the two emperors' father and his reputation, which to some extent lived on after him. However, in 401, the Goths who had been settled south of the Danube in Thrace after 378 acquired a new, young and ambitious king in Alaric, and began to move westwards, raiding northern Italy in that year. They were successfully repulsed by Stilicho. Nevertheless, the court moved from vulnerable Milan to impregnable Ravenna on the Adriatic, still in northern Italy, and remained there for much of the rest of its existence. In 405, the Goths tried again but Stilicho drove them out once more. The respite was brief, for on New Year's Eve 406 the Rhine froze over and the Alemanni, Vandals, Alans, Sueves and Burgundians, pressed in the east by advancing Huns, crossed in force and began to ravage Gaul, before entering Spain in 409. This time, unlike the incursion under Valerian, their aim was not plunder but settlement.

The commanders on the spot were overwhelmed (their names have not come down to us) and local concern led to the acclamation of Constantine III (later grudgingly recognised as co-ruler), his predecessors and successors, leading to yet another revival of the Gallic Empire, this time as a matter of survival. Stilicho was tied up with the breakdown of a treaty he had made earlier with Alaric, and the Goths again had to be ejected from Italy, but this time it was not so straightforward, and any military reserves were still thin on the ground, due to the appalling losses at the Battles of Adrianople and the Frigidus. As a consequence, understrength efforts to regain control of Gaul and the north west were ineffective. Meanwhile, Stilicho was keen to re-unite the Empire after the death of Arcadius in 408, planning on a regency for the latter Emperor's infant son. A group of Honorius' advisers suggested he was

---

331 The date is given as 23rd January in some sources, cf. PLRE I Honorius 3.
332 ILS793-795.

more interested on placing his own son Eucherius (a great-grandson of the *comes* Theodosius) on the throne instead, and he was arrested and executed by an officer called Heraclianus (qv) on 23 August 408.

All the while, Alaric, keen to be granted a semi-autonomous polity within the empire in return for honours, security and military aid, was pressing the senate (which he respected as having some kind of primacy which it had in practice long lost) and the Imperial government for a settlement, investing Rome threateningly, but not proceeding further. Three-way negotiations – with the senate and with Honorius – broke down and in the end he opted for setting up his own regime centred on Rome. Alaric managed to carry the senate and most of the people with him, outraged as they were at the lack of support they had received from Honorius' government, by now vainly engaged in trying to contain Constantine III and the barbarians he seemed only partially able to repel. Alaric elevated the Prefect of the City, Priscus Attalus, to the purple. Attalus thereupon made Alaric his *magister militum* and together they marched on Ravenna to depose Honorius. He was saved by an unexpectedly rapid response to an appeal for military reinforcements from the government of the infant Theodosius II in the east, resulting in the swift arrival of six legions at Ravenna. A stalemate followed and, in 409 the *comes* in Africa (and murderer of Stilicho) Heraclianus cut off the grain supply to Rome in a gesture of loyalty to Honorius. Alaric, furious, insisted on sending a detachment of his troops to Carthage to teach him a lesson, but Attalus, honourably but unwisely, refused to sanction a barbarian invasion of Africa, resulting in his immediate deposition and, from 24 to 26 August 410, the sack of the City, an act that had a much more profound effect on people's morale than distant problems for the Empire.

The sack lasted three days and was moderately restrained, especially by ancient standards. Once finished, Alaric took Galla Placidia, the half-sister of Honorius hostage, and retreated south, intending to cross to Sicily from whence he proposed to invade Africa and punish Heraclianus. This never happened, a storm prevented him from reaching Sicily and he then took fever en route, dying in September at Consentius (Cosenza) in modern Calabria.[333]

If anyone thought that Honorius would lose control of the west completely, the death of Alaric would prove them wrong. At the right moment a new *magister militum*, Constantius, was appointed and within a year had disposed of Constantine III, although the Gallic secession had another two years to run before it was finally put to rest, after six turbulent years. Unfortunately, 413 also saw the loyal Heraclianus declare himself independent and he sailed for Italy intent on overthrowing Honorius himself. This time the venture failed through lack of resolve, and thereafter an uneasy peace was preserved, aided by a treaty formally settling Alaric's Visigoths under Imperial suzerainty in Spain, thus bringing Gaul some kind of stability. Alaric's half-brother succeeded him, falling in love and marrying their long-term hostage, the princess Galla Placidia, but he died (along with their infant son) not long afterwards. His successor, Walia, returned Galla to her family, and in due course the *magister militum* Constantius (also a long-term admirer of the

---

333 PLRE II Alaricus 1

princess) married her. At her insistence he was briefly made co-emperor as Constantius III (a move rejected by the court in Constantinople) but after his death his widow, whose beauty and allure must have been considerable, discovered that the Emperor her brother had also fallen for her and was becoming a nuisance, so she moved to the east.

Not long afterwards, Honorius died of an illness on 26 August 423, leaving a power vacuum. This was promptly filled by a man, Iohannes who, like Eugenius (qv), was the head of the civil service. Although recognised by the senate, the east did not reciprocate and he lasted only some eighteen months before an army from the east arrived, deposed him and installed as emperor the young son of Constantius III (qv) and Galla Placidia, Valentinian III.

HOSTILIANUS
251, June – late November

Decius' surviving (younger) son was Hostilianus, who, as *nobilissimus caesar*, was, somewhat surprisingly, allowed to succeed his father by Decius' successor, Trebonianus Gallus. C. Valens Hostilianus Messius Q. Perperna was born about 236/238, his nomenclature marking a break with convention, with the actual surname (*nomen, or gentilicium*) coming after the *praenomen,* two *cognomina* and being succeeded by another *praenomen,* a pattern which became more common amongst the élite about a century later. The name Perperna also suggests an alliance with a late Republican noble family of Etruscan stock, hence, no doubt, his brother's name, Etruscus.

He was appointed *caesar* at the same time as his brother, being thereafter styled C. Valens Hostilianus Messius Quintus Nobilissimus Caesar, also as *princeps iuventutis.*[334] Shortly before Decius' final campaign, he may have been designated Augustus as Imperator Caesar C. Valens Hostilianus Messius Quintus Augustus and was certainly recognised by the senate in July or August 251 as soon as news reached them of his father's and brother's death, on which occasion he was granted the tribunician and proconsular power, renewable in the usual way. It is less clear whether he was also made *pontifex maximus*. On Gallus' arrival in Rome, he was duly confirmed as co-emperor and adopted by Gallus (we do not know what changes would have been made to his name as a result), but died, ostensibly of plague – not unlikely – by the end of November that same year.[335]

HOSTILIANUS see *SEVERUS HOSTILIANUS*

HYPATIUS
532, 18th – 23rd January

Hypatius was a reluctant grandee, dragged out of retirement during a major disturbance in Constantinople and acclaimed emperor, probably against his

---

334 ILS 516, cf. coins.
335 His new style might have been C. Vibius Hostilianus or something similar.

will, but who was swiftly captured and killed. Flavius Hypatius was one of the three closest relations of Anastasius I, being the son of the emperor's sister Caesaria and the senator Secundinus.[336] This had two consequences: first, that he was destined for a brilliant career, and second that he was always going to be vulnerable during transitions of power. His brother Pompeius and cousin Probus were also in the same position and enjoyed equally illustrious careers, thanks to their proximity to the purple, although Anastasius passed all three over for the succession as a result of all three failing the Emperor's somewhat capricious selection exercise.

Hypatius was born c. 475 and served against the Isaurian rebels in the 490s before holding the eastern consulship for 500, serving unsuccessfully thereafter as *magister militum* in 503 as co-commander against Persia, where his failure was ascribed to inexperience. He was replaced in 505. In 513 he was re-appointed to the same post but in Thrace, where he provoked troublesome would-be powerbroker Vitalianus by insulting his wife, which resulted in a second revolt by this mercurial ex-imperial general. He was then re-appointed and sent against the rebel he had provoked but was defeated and taken prisoner by him, held in confinement until 514. He was appointed *magister militum* in the east 516-518 and again from 520 to 525 (by which time he had been made patrician) but was relieved of office by Justin I, probably on trumped-up grounds. He was made *magister militum* in the east a third time in 527, concluding a successful treaty and serving for nearly two years until the prospect of further conflict caused the Emperor to replace this somewhat unmilitary prince with the *magister militum* Belisarius. By the time the bloody Nika riots against Justinian I had broken out in Constantinople, he was retired and living at his palace there. By his wife, Maria, he left a son Pompeius and a grandson Iohannes, who married Praeiecta, the sister of Justinian's kinsman and successor Justin II, thus binding his family firmly back into the Imperial circle.[337]

The Nika riots began on 13 January 532, and there is no suggestion that Hypatius was involved in it at that stage. However, as matters got increasingly desperate and it looked inevitable that Justinian would be deposed, the more influential senators and others, aided and abetted by the rioters, decided that Anastasius' nephew Probus would make an ideal candidate for the purple. He, however, was prudently absent, and the resentful mob burned his residence before moving on to acclaim his cousin Hypatius, another man who they felt would made an ideal interim ruler. On the 18th he was tracked down, taken to the Forum of Constantine, gowned in purple and crowned with a gold diadem and duly acclaimed emperor, being accepted as such throughout most of the city. About four days later, with the riot brutally crushed, order was restored and Hypatius and his brother Pompeius were arrested and brought before the Emperor, who was inclined to be merciful, being aware that Hypatius' elevation had been *force majeure*. Unfortunately, the conniving empress Theodora was implacable, and he was condemned to

336 PLRE II. Hypatius 6
337 PLRE III Iohannes 63, Pompeius 1

death, facing his end with courage. His body was afterwards thrown into the sea. Justinian is said to have raised a cenotaph to commemorate him when his corpse was washed up later.[338] No official style has survived and no coins were minted in those few chaotic days.

INGENUUS
258, July – 259, January

Ingenuus was an usurper in the Balkans whose brief prominence was quickly ended by Gallienus' leading trouble-shooter. Ingenuus was a provincial governor in Pannonia who was proclaimed at Sirmium (Sremska Mitrovica, Serbia) having rebelled in the summer of 258, thus before and not, as previously supposed, in the wake of the capture of Valerian by the Persians.[339] There is, however, much debate about the chronology of events on the Danubian frontier at the beginning of the sole rule of Gallienus.[340] A senator of consular rank, he was the governor of Pannonia when proclaimed emperor by the legions of Moesia. He was perhaps son or grandson of the C. Julius Ingenuus, a senatorial youth who was recorded as military tribune of *Legio* III *Italica* which was stationed in Noricum in the later 2nd century.[341]

He was defeated by Gallienus' general, Aureolus, at Mursa (on the River Drava, Croatia) early in 259 and was probably killed by his own supporters in subsequent flight, although suicide cannot be ruled out. His rebellion was continued by Regalianus, who may indeed have been responsible for despatching him in the first place.

IOHANNES
423, 20th November – 425, March 425

Iohannes was a bureaucrat elevated in the Western Empire following the death of Honorius without an obvious successor, and who lasted less than two years before being deposed by intervention from the eastern empire.

When Honorius died unexpectedly of dropsy (Oedema) on 15 August 423, there was a power vacuum in the west which was technically a reversion to a re-united empire, under the Eastern Emperor, Theodosius II. Indeed, it was at his court that the nearest heir in blood to the Western Empire was closeted with his mother: Constantius III's son Valentinian, Honorius' nephew. Bearing in mind the fragile stability achieved by Constantius in the west prior to his untimely death two years previously, his successor as *magister militum* Castinus clearly recognised the urgent need for an emperor in his part of the empire. Being a capable and ambitious man, he probably reckoned that a competent civilian of not too eminent a background might be ideal, leaving him to exercise power behind the throne, as with Eugenius almost three

---

338 Procopius BP. 1.24. 19-31, 42-56, 58
339 PIR² I 23; PLRE I. Ingenuus 1 which dates the rebellion to 260-261.
340 Barnes, T. D., in *Phoenix* 26 (1972) 160-161, supported by a consular date.
341 PIR² I 359

decades before. With hindsight, it might be that he would have been better advised to choose a man within the wide family circle of the Theodosian dynasty, for on that basis recognition of what he had done would be more likely to have been forthcoming from the court in Constantinople. As it is, he chose a senior civil servant of unimpeachable integrity called John (Iohannes).

At the time of his elevation, which occurred after an interregnum (or united rule) of three months, Iohannes was *primicerius notariorum* (head of the civil service).[342] He was not the last senior bureaucrat to be raised to the purple by an ambitious commander-in-chief. We know nothing of his family or background; he is not even credited with a wife, and it may be that the lack of family ties commended him to Castinus – no relations to over-promote nor children expecting honours and position, or likely to make future claims on the purple. Two late sources claim he was of barbarian stock, either Vandal or Goth, but this may well be the working out of prejudice against a man who, in the east at least, was regarded as an usurper.

The new western ruler was acclaimed at Rome (rather than Ravenna) on 20 November 423, the occasion being driven by Castinus, although discreetly enough to escape being blamed directly for it in the ancient sources. The fact that he was promoted and made consul (in the West, not recognised in the East) for 424 seem to speak for themselves, however. He was styled in the usual way as Dominus Noster Iohannes Pius Felix Augustus.[343] As he was in Rome, it seems likely that he was swiftly recognised by the senate and, if such were still applicable at this date, granted the tribunician and proconsular powers. He was designated for a further consulship (west) for 425, but when he assumed the *fasces* his tenure was not, again rather predictably, recognised by the eastern court. He then moved the court back to Ravenna and awaited the outcome of a delegation to Theodosius II requesting recognition. This was not forthcoming and was accompanied by the raising of the infant prince Placidus Valentinianus to the rank and style of *nobilissimus caesar*. Although not recognised in the east, Iohannes was unchallenged in the west, and it seems reasonable not to label him an usurper as such, having been chosen in the traditional way to succeed a deceased emperor. The lack of recognition though could only mean one thing, that an expeditionary force would soon be on its way from Constantinople to topple him.

Little is recorded of his 18-month reign, except that Castinus had previously fallen out with his colleague Bonifatius, who retired in sulkily to Africa, appointed *comes* by the dowager Empress Placidia, to whom he remained loyal. An expedition to dislodge him seems to have been unsuccessful but not a disaster as Castinus survived it, reputation intact. The Emperor showed tolerance to all Christian sects – Arian and Donatist included – which alienated the Catholic hierarchy in Rome. In Gaul, he appears to have caused offence by subjecting priests to the jurisdiction of secular courts.[344] One favour he did bestow upon the Empire was the appointment of a young officer called Aëtius as *cura palatii* (guard commander); it was an inspired choice.

---

342 PLRE II Ioannes 6
343 Coins, where his name is invariably spelt with the 'h'.
344 Matthews (Oxford, 1990) 379f

Procopius, the 6th-century historian, records that he was both gentle, sagacious and capable of valorous deeds.[345] This, however, did not avert the inevitable. An army from the east invaded, invested Ravenna, which appears to have been betrayed from within and which fell in March 425. Meanwhile, Aëtius had been sent north to hire 60,000 Hun mercenaries, but they arrived back in Italy days after the fall of Ravenna. He engaged with the eastern forces but a truce was arrived at, under the terms of which the Huns were paid off and Aëtius took command of Gaul as *comes* and *magister militum*.

Poor Iohannes, however, was captured and, after being taken to Aquileia, where Galla Placidia and her children were awaiting the outcome, was ritually humiliated before being executed, probably in April. The Empire then became re-united yet again under Theodosius II, whilst preparations were made for the installation of a new regime.

ILLUS
484–488

Illus was an Isaurian high offical and would-be kingmaker, specialising in usurpers, having raised no less than three to the purple before being finally undone, apprehended and executed in 488.

Flavius Illus was a close friend of emperor Zeno and his brother Trocundes was possibly an uncle of the emperor, if John Malalas is to be believed.[346] As *magister militum* he was suborned by the scheming empress Verina to support the usurpation of Basiliscus, and was sent by him to try and apprehend Zeno who had fled across Asia. However, the senate, having discovered what a disaster Basiliscus was, secretly turned to Illus and he managed to rescue the Emperor and returned with him to Constantinople to depose the usurper in 477. He was consul in 478 but in 479 he elevated Marcian II to the purple (for the third time) and again had the support of the duplicitous old empress dowager, Verina. Illus however – as with Basiliscus – had second thoughts about the aristocratic usurper's suitablility and Marcian was deposed in favour of Leontius (qv) instead, whom Illus and his brother proclaimed in Syria in 484 before allowing themselves to become trapped under siege in an Isaurian stronghold, Papyrius. They held out for three years before the entire enterprise was crushed in 488. Illus' status during the endgame may have been quasi-imperial, although Leontius remained his chosen candidate for the purple.

IOTAPIANUS
248, c. June – 249, Sept.

Iotapianus was an usurper at Antioch whose position was brought about as a result of the rigorous exaction of increased taxation from the citizens

---

345 Procopius, *De Bellis* III.3.6. Translated by H.B. Dewing, *Procopius* (Cambridge: Loeb Classical Library, 1979), vol. 2 p. 25
346 PLRE II Illus; Malalas 15.12

of the east by Philip the Arab's elder brother, C. Julius Priscus, the *rector Orientis*. This is not necessarily something that would lead the soldiers into mutiny, but his measures may well have included trimming the soldiers' perks, reducing their opportunities for booty or merely a cut in pay. The east may also have been feeling the effects of the serious military reverse in 244 (cf. Gordian III). It is presumed that Iotapianus was the proconsul of Syria at the time of his elevation, and the fact that he seems to have maintained his position for over a year without coming to Rome to claim legitimacy and to try matters with Philip suggests that he was moderately successful, or merely that the developing crisis in the Balkans was taking the heat off him.

The name Iotapianus clearly suggests that this usurper rejoiced in a descent, like Avidius Cassius, from the former Kings of Commagene, where princesses called Iotape were relatively common. He also boasted a descent from Alexander, although whether Alexander of Macedon or Severus Alexander was intended has been the subject of debate; neither had any (surviving) children, so descent from the family of one or the other rather than the individual was indicated. Furthermore, Alexander Severus was a contemporary.[347] On his coins, Iotapianus is called M. F[ ] Ru[ ] Iotapianus, which is usually expanded to read M. Fulvius Rufus Iotapianus although a better case might be made for his first *cognomen* to be expanded as Rusticus, the Fulvii Rustici being even then a prominent senatorial family elevated to patrician rank, whereas no other Fulvius Rufus is discoverable in the élite of this or any other period.[348] If this is accepted, then one can point to Brixia in Italy as the place of origin of the male line; presumably his Commagene ancestry came through marriage.

The connection with Alexander the Great could well have been through Mithridates I. Callinicus, King of Commagene from 96 to 70 BC. He had married Laodice Thea Philadelpha, daughter of Antiochus VIII Gryphus, King of Syria 125-96BC by Cleopatra Tryphaena, daughter of Ptolemaeus VII, King of Egypt 145-116 BC, grandson of Ptolemaeus V Epiphanes, fourth in descent from Ptolemaeus I, stepbrother of Alexander the Great. Thus, their posterity may have been descended from Alexander's stepbrother, in all probability Iotapianus' claim.

Iotapianus must have been suffect consul c. 235/237 prior to being appointed governor – as it would appear likely – of Syria and, as a probable patrician, he would perhaps have been born c. 202, become *quaestor* c. 228/230 and *praetor* 232/233. After imperial acclamation in around June 248, he took the style Imperator Caesar M. F[ulvius] R[usticus?] Iotapianus Augustus. He appears to have achieved some kind of victory subsequent to his elevation, placing the appropriate slogan on his coins and an inscription at Palmyra probably reflects that. He was probably killed by his own troops in late August or early September 249, and his head was subsequently

---

347 Aurelius Victor 29; Körner (2001) 277-282. Syme (1971) 202

348 Also on CIG 4483/IGR.III.1033, at Palmyra where his cognomen is expanded to 'Ru[ ]'

brought before Decius in Rome.[349] This suggests that Iotapianus' challenge was eventually successfully crushed, perhaps by his own disaffected men, only a short time before, probably whilst Philip was trying to deal with Decius. We know nothing of a wife nor of any children, nor does the name recur.

JOHN see IOHANNES

JOVIAN
363, 27th June – 364, 16th February

Jovian was a stop-gap emperor, chosen on campaign following the death of Julian the Apostate, who was obliged to make a humiliating peace with the Persians in tricky circumstances but died unexpectedly returning to Constantinople. Jovian was born in 331 at Singidunum (Belgrade, Serbia) so maintaining the tradition of Balkan emperors. His father was Varronianus, who was a tribune of the *Joviani*, one of the new military units founded by Maximian, and after which unit the boy was named. The father rose to become a distinguished *comes* of Constantius II and it is said that it was thanks to his reputation that Jovian was singled out to replace Julian. Varronianus died not long after his son's elevation to the purple, in late summer 363.[350]

The shock of Julian's death deep in enemy territory must have heartened the Persians and brought apprehension to the Roman staff officers. On the next day, the aged Saturninius Secundus *signo* Salutius, Pretorian Prefect of the east, was offered and declined the purple in his place and the army instead chose the 32-year-old Jovian, commander of the Imperial Guard (*scholae*), mainly on the strength of his father's reputation. Nevertheless, his election caused considerable surprise, Ammianus Marcellinus suggesting that he was wrongly identified with the homonymous head of the Civil Service (*primicerius notariorum*), whose name also had been canvassed (and who was executed after his namesake's elevation for suspicious behaviour). Jovian at the time of his elevation had only just been promoted to his position by Julian, prior to the Persian campaign, from a less senior position in the *domestici*.[351]

The new Augustus took the style of Dominus Noster Flavius Jovianus Victori ac Triumfatori Semper Augustus.[352] He sent an embassy ahead of his withdrawal from Persia to inform the authorities of his acclamation and received the recognition of the senate and therefore may safely be assumed to have been granted the tribunician and proconsular powers. Being a Christian, it is likely that he dispensed with holding the post of *pontifex maximus,* and reversed most but not all of Julian's pro-pagan enactments; he began to introduce penalties against paganism, too, whilst maintaining a theoretical

---

349 Aurelius Victor, *loc. cit.*; PIR² I49
350 PLRE I Varronianus 1
351 PLRE I Jovianus 3
352 ILS757

freedom of conscience.[353] He was ordinary consul with his young son, Flavius Varronianus for 364, and the latter was given the style *nobilissimus*, but not accorded the rank of *caesar*, probably out of regard for his tender years.

Trapped on the wrong side of the Tigris, Jovian had little choice but to make a disadvantageous and in fact humiliating peace with the Persians, which made him very unpopular, although he was only making the best of a bad situation into which Julian's unexpected demise had placed his forces. The army withdrew very slowly to Antioch before proceeding towards Constantinople. It was on this journey that the Emperor died, apparently of carbon monoxide poisoning as a result of a brazier having been put into his bedroom for warmth; none of the sources suggest that this was an assassination. The date was 16 February 364. He had two sons. The elder, Varronianus, was blinded by Jovian's successor Valentinian, to ensure he was not going to grow up as a threat. The Empress, who was probably called Charito, went into a fearful retirement with her remaining children, although she and one son appear to have been still alive in 380.

JOVINUS
411, July – 413, c. March

Jovinus was a Gallic nobleman of senatorial rank who stepped into the breach when Constantine III was killed and who unsuccessfully crossed swords with Alaric the Goth's half-brother Athaulf, resulting in the demise of the Gallic empire forged to deal with the barbarian incursion of 406/407.

Nothing is known of Jovinus' career prior to his elevation, although he was probably an appointment of Constantine III's as *magister militum* or *comes rei militaris* on the Rhine frontier. He had two brothers, Sebastianus (qv), with whom he briefly shared power, and Sallustius. There is a suggestion that they were descendants (presumably children or grandchildren) of the consul of 367, Flavius Iovinus, who had been appointed *magister equitum* by Julian in 361 and who appears to have been a Gaul of distinguished family. Another relative was the rhetor Consentius of Narbo (Narbonne) in the 440s, who married a woman whose name is lost to us who was a descendant of the consul of 367; she may thus have been a daughter of Jovinus or one of his brothers.

It was in Gaul, with Constantine III in trouble, that there was disaffection amongst the troops on the Rhine, this time comprising levies of Burgundians, Alans, Alamans and Franks that had been re-organised by Constantine after the crisis of 407. Probably they had not been paid, itself no doubt a symptom of the upheavals being experienced throughout the north-western provinces. In order to remedy the situation, Guntarius, the Burgundian leader, and Goar, his Alan opposite number, raised Jovinus to the purple at Mundiacum (Muntzen, near Tongres) in Germania Secunda. One of his other supporters was Athaulf, leader of the Visigoths, still resentful about his people's treatment in Italy by the government of Honorius following the death of Alaric. The Gallic nobility also supported Jovinus (he being of their

---

353 FS p. 689

number) and Decimius Rusticus, the Pretorian Prefect who had deserted Constantine III, now joined him. Rusticus may even have been a kinsman, which might explain his willingness to change horses in the middle of such a fast-flowing stream.

Jovinus styled himself D[ominus] N[oster] Iovinus P[ius] F[elix] Aug[ustus] although as with Constantine, Constans and Maximus, we know of no certain governmental structures in place in the continuing breakaway empire that might have validated styles or awarded consulships etc., but there almost certainly *was* such a body, composed of the senatorial nobility based in Gaul (and Spain to 410) and the military élite. After the demise of his rival at Arles, Jovinus appears to have got a grip on the situation, but his chief problem was with the contending barbarian chieftains upon whose co-operation he depended to keep his regime stable in Gaul. This was fine up to a point, but Athaulf, who had with him the Princess Galla Placidia, the daughter of Theodosius I, began to make demands over and above what Jovinus was prepared to accept, his imperial hostage being used as a bargaining chip. Furthermore, Athaulf had managed to dispose of Honorius' former general Sarus, who had defected to Jovinus, but who Athaulf destroyed along with his men in revenge for past encounters. Promoting Athaulf as his right-hand man would have undoubtedly put the noses of his other barbarian lieutenants, Goar and Guntarius, out of joint, so instead, he made his brother Sebastianus his co-ruler in 412, to demonstrate to the Visigoth that he already had a deputy and successor. As a consequence, early in 413, an enraged Athaulf secretly sent to Honorius and offered him the heads of both usurpers in return for a favourable settlement treaty with his people. This offer, needless to say, was readily accepted. Athaulf was thereupon as good as his word, returning to Gaul, killing the new Emperor Sebastianus and capturing his brother, sending him to Narbo. Here, Claudius Postumus Dardanus, Honorius' Pretorian Prefect of Gaul, who had been discreetly supporting Athaulf after his defection back to the cause of Honorius, had them executed, despatching their heads to Ravenna. Both grisly trophies were subsequently sent to Carthage to join those of Constantinus III, Constans II and that of the recently executed Heraclianus.[354]

These executions marked the end of the short-lived second Gallic empire after some seven years. Henceforth, Honorius was once again able to reign over an undivided west, even if his control over Britain, portions of Gaul and large parts of Spain was more titular than effective.

JULIAN (I) see DIDIUS JULIANUS

JULIAN (II)
283, May/June – 285, September

Julianus was a relatively long-surviving usurper, governing a breakaway mini-empire in Pannonia, who had stepped into the void left by the death of

---

354 PLRE II Jovinus 2 & Sebastianus 2

Carus and Numerianus. He was able to survive for over two years thanks to the chaos elsewhere in the west.

Julian's full name was M. Aur[elius] Julianus according to the coins he minted at Siscia (Sisak, Croatia) and he was probably another of that cadre of Illyrian-born officers who seem to have had a monopoly on the purple (and attempts at the purple) in the later third century and beyond. He styled himself Imperator Caesar M. Aurelius Julianus Pius Felix Augustus and the reverses of his coins bear the legend *Pannoniae Aug[ustus]* (Emperor of the Pannonian [provinces]) which seems to suggest that he viewed himself as ruler of a Pannonian empire along the lines of Postumus in Gaul and Zenobia in the east. Whilst we know that Carinus was obliged simultaneously to deal with another usurper also called Julianus (III), there are discrepancies concerning the place at which the usurper was killed and in his nomenclature. It seems sensible to fall in with a recent scholarly suggestion that there were *two* imperial claimants of this name who appeared in the wake of the deaths of Carus and Numerianus, and who were thus rivals of Carinus and of Diocletian.[355] It seems most likely that the first usurper was he who is mentioned by Zosimus as having seized power in Pannonia on the death of Carus in May or June 283.[356] He was probably Pretorian Prefect up to that point on a special command on the Danube.

Julian seems to have survived unmolested until Carinus set off to deal with Diocletian's bid for power in spring 285. Once his mission had been accomplished, the future tetrarch could deal with his break-way Pannonian provinces and Julian was defeated (and presumably killed) in Illyricum. We have no knowledge of any family.

JULIAN (III)
284, c. July – September

The 'other' Julianus was an usurper in Italy, who also rebelled against Carinus but who was more rapidly suppressed than his Pannonian namesake. Sabinus Julianus was *corrector* (junior provincial governor) in northern Italy and was thus a senator, too, for the minor provinces of Italy remained within the purlieu of the much-diminished powers of the senate even at that time. He was acclaimed by the troops there, presumably in summer 284, on receiving the news of the death of Numerianus. That there were troops in his province at all is surprising, as one of the reasons why the senate was left with the power of appointment over such provinces was that they contained no allocations of troops which their governors could use to back a coup. Possibly they were part of Carinus' imperial *comitatenses*, in the area temporarily.

Zosimus mentions this man first, in his account of the period, although analysis would suggest that he post-dated Julian (II) by up to a year.[357] He was subsequently and probably very rapidly defeated by Carinus, probably on his

---

355 PLRE I Julianus 24 & 38
356 Aurelius Victor, 39, 10 cf. PLRE 1 Julianus 38
357 Zosimus 1, 73.1 cf. PLRE 1 Julianus 24

way back to Rome to celebrate his triumph, at Verona without, it would appear, having had time to mint any coins. Nothing further is known about him.

JULIAN (IV) 'The Apostate'
360, February – 363, 26th June

Julian was a kinsman of Constantine the Great who was a competent general but who was most famous for trying to reverse the effects of the Edict of Milan and reimpose state-sponsored paganism.

Flavius Claudius Julianus was born in May or June 332 to Julius Constantius and Basilina, a noblewoman of unknown family, and an Arian (later orthodox) Christian, who died not long after his birth. He escaped being culled in the *putsch* of 3 September 337 thanks to his tender age. He enjoyed a lengthy education in rhetoric and philosophy, which convinced him that he was a traditional pagan. He also wrote extensively. He was made *nobilissimus caesar* on 6 November 355 and shortly afterwards married Helena, one of the sisters of his cousin Constantius II. His style thereafter became Julianus Nobilissimus Caesar and as such he served as consul in 356, 357 and 360.

In being sent by Constantius II to Gaul, Julian was being dealt a very poor hand by his cousin. Much of the western currency had been demonetised by a decree, partly to remove memories of the usurpers Magnentius and Decentius, but also to prevent Julian from being able to accumulate enough cash to make a donative to the troops on the German frontier with a view to making a claim on the purple. There had also been the usurpations of Carausius II – if we can accept the reality of it – and of Silvanus, which had left the troops demoralised (exacerbated by the lack of cash to pay them, needless to say). The border Germanic tribes were eager to make mischief. Julian was a far superior general to his cousin (who had been continually battering away at the Persians with mixed success since his accession) and soon brought the Rhine and related borders to order, gaining much popularity in the process, which only increased the unease and distrust of Constantius II. As a result, Julian' remit and powers were reduced, and consequently early in 360 he was acclaimed emperor by his troops at Lutetia Parisiorum (Paris).

Constantius II seems at first to have been prepared to recognise his junior colleague's acclamation. However, after a considerable delay he changed his mind and started out to suppress him, dying early on in the process at Mopsucrenae in Cilicia (Turkey) on 3 November the following year. This had the advantage of leaving Julian as sole emperor and of preventing a great deal of bloodshed.

The new emperor was styled Dominus Noster Flavius Claudius Julianus Pius Felix Augustus and by 361 he had been hailed as *imperator* seven times.[358] He reinstated the old Roman Pantheon, giving it the position it had enjoyed until 313 as the official state religion and deprived Christianity of its special status, taking on the role and title of *pontifex maximus*. This earned

---

358 ILS753; PLRE I Julianus 29

him the epithet 'The Apostate' from hostile Christian chroniclers. He was granted the tribunician and proconsular power by the senate and, like all his predecessors prior to Constantine the Great, was adlected into all the priestly colleges.[359] He served a fourth consulship in 363. He also reformed the civil service and administration generally, saving money and enabling him selectively to reduce taxes.

In March 363, he led a concentrated and well organised expedition to the east to force a final confrontation with the Persians, bearing in mind that for twenty-five years his predecessor had not really prevailed against them at all decisively. The Persians were accordingly defeated before Ctesiphon, their winter capital. The main Roman force then moved northwards to join up with reinforcements with the intention of making a final offensive and bringing the matter to a conclusion but became seriously bogged down by the terrain and adverse climate, putting them at a disadvantage for the first time. Furthermore, whilst en route, the Emperor was wounded, apparently in a skirmish. Julian's wound became infected and he died, probably from septicaemia, on 26 June. There were no children, or surviving children, and the House of Constantine – except for Constantia, the two-year-old daughter of Constantius II – was at an end after 57 years, though a new dynasty was about to emerge, later reinforcing its claim through the marriage of Valentinian's son Gratian (qv) to Constantia.

JULIUS CAESAR
48BC, 1st January – 44BC, 15th March 44

Julius Caesar is probably the most famous Roman of all, thanks to Shakespeare's tragedy and indeed the drama of his very public assassination. He was not quite the founder of the subsequent empire, although that long-lived institution owed much to him, especially in the preferred nomenclature of its heads of state. He was, in fact, the last of a line of Roman statesmen – Marius, Sulla, Catilina – who toyed with personal rule whilst failing to make it stick, constrained by the Roman myth of the evil of their ancient kings and an ingrained aversion to anything that even resembled kingship. Accounts of the emperors of Rome invariably begin with either Julius Caesar or his nephew and adopted son Octavian, later called Augustus. Both had emphatically made themselves sole ruler by a vote of the senate and through manipulating Republican magistracies by distorting them to suit their purposes.

Caius Julius Caesar belonged to a patrician family, but to a lesser branch of a relatively obscure one, long in eclipse. Nevertheless, in the first century BC being a patrician still counted. Patricians continued to strive to fill their share of magistracies and priesthoods and as a group they still retained a distinct but difficult to define *cachet*. Furthermore, Sulla's settlement had gone some way to re-entrench their privileges, but especially amongst the less successful patrician dynasties the desire to recapture the half-forgotten splendour and the *dignitas* of their distant forebears remained a sometimes

---

359 FS1676

perilous spur and an incentive to political recklessness, particularly notable in the near-contemporary careers of L. Sergius Catilina (whose political gamble failed ignominiously) and indeed Caesar (whose similar risk-taking succeeded triumphantly). Sir Ronald Syme considered the patricians to be 'loyal to tradition without being fettered by caste or principle. Either monarchy or democracy could be made to serve their ends to enhance person and family ... they were older than the state.'[360]

Casear's family, the Julii, like several patrician clans (*gentes*), claimed descent from mythological forebears who may well have been real people – Professor Wiseman's analysis of the mythology of Rome points to the weight of evidence, much of it circumstantial, in favour of at least some veracity in this.[361] In this case, the Julii claimed descent from Aeneas, Prince of Troy and the founder of a Trojan colony on the Italian mainland. Furthermore, through Aeneas' first marriage to Creusa, the daughter of Helen of Troy and King Priam, they could trace a descent from Dardanus son of Jupiter and Batea, granddaughter of Scamander. Rohl's hotly debated chronological revision of the ancient world would, if accepted, actually endow the myths with a plausibility that would justify this observation by Professor Cornell:

> It is likely enough that many of the stories preserved in the literary tradition were handed down by word of mouth in the fifth and fourth centuries, and that at least some of them were celebrated in drama and song. This is altogether much more probable than the alternative: that the stories were consciously invented after the practice of historical writing had been introduced at the end of the third century. As for the authenticity of the stories ... they should not be dismissed out of hand. There existed more than one means or oral transmission, and there can be no objection in principle to the suggestion that the traditional stories might be based on fact.[362]

Naturally all this is completely unprovable, especially as there are three unbridgeable gaps. From Aeneas' son Iullus/Ascanius there would appear to have been some twelve generations,[363] representing their period as members of the princely élite of the proto-Roman Italian kingdom of Alba Longa, until we reach Iullus Julius to whose son, Proculus Julius, the recently dead Romulus allegedly appeared in the guise of the god Quirinus in 716.[364] Such speculation notwithstanding, we have to remember that Livy, in relating all this – which conveniently placed the Julii amongst the most ancient of patrician families – was writing under the sway of their descendants, something likely to undermine the impartiality of the author.

From Proculus Julius there are a further five generations in the Julii missing before one arrives at N. Julius, whose existence is inferred from the filiation

---

360 Syme (1939) 69-70
361 Wiseman (2004) *passim*
362 Rohl (2007) 303-343, 463-487 (and see introduction *supra*); Cornell (1995) 12
363 Representing approximately 250-300 years.
364 Livy, I.16

given by later generations (on what basis is not clear) to his grandson, C. Julius Iullus, said to have been one of the consuls for 489BC.

The next Julius was the consul's nephew, Vopiscus Julius Iullus in 473, whose filiation establishes that he was the grandson of the previous Julian consul's father Lucius.[365] Note, too, that the *praenomen* Vopiscus (and the earlier one, Proculus) lies well outside the usual canon of sixteen or so common ones: it was a habit of ancient patrician families to cling to such unfamiliar *praenomina*, culled from the lost recesses of their family history, in the first century or so of the Republic, bearing in mind the caveat that there is little proof that the *fasti* from 509 to 367 bear much resemblance to what actually went on, having been, it is thought, retrospectively compiled from unknown evidence.

One might think that having recorded the first family consul (and thus provided at least a name from two centuries earlier) it might be possible to trace Caesar's descent thenceforth without too much trouble. In fact, there are further gaps, the first coming in the mid-fourth century BC – as with a number of otherwise well-attested patrician families – just about the very the time, as it happens, that the patricians had been obliged to share their power with plebeian families.[366]

Caesar's own ancestry is traceable only from the first to bear his cognomen, Sex. Julius Caesar, consul in 157BC. He was grandfather of Lucius, the consul of 90 and great-grandfather of another Lucius, the consul of 64, yet we still cannot positively confirm the precise detail of the Dictator's descent. The consul of 64 was proscribed by the second triumvirate in 43 and no more is heard of him. Very possibly he succumbed in the proscriptions. His sister was Mark Antony's mother.[367] Julius Caesar's poverty and obscurity, despite his patrician status was therefore because he was descended from a junior branch of a family of only middling political attainments.[368]

The future dictator was the only known son of a younger son of a younger son, so even within his own branch of the family, he was about as junior as one could get.

Caesar's full style was C. Julius C. f. C. n. Fab. Caesar. He was formally in power from the beginning of 48BC to 44. He was born in 100 and was famously assassinated on 15 March 44. His earliest office was quaestor in 68 followed by service in Hispania Citerior (Further Spain) and then by election as curule aedile in 65. He engineered election to the prestigious religious office (then reserved for patricians) of *pontifex maximus* in 63, was praetor in 62, followed by a successful military command in his old province in Spain that entitled him to a triumph, which he waived in order to stand for the consulship, to which he was elected for 59.

In that year, in response to a seemingly intractable constitutional crisis, Caesar became part of a quasi-constitutional alliance with Cn. Pompeius

365 All the dates in this entry are BC dates.
366 Munzer (1999) 27, 413
367 Syme, RR 64, 164, 192, 197
368 Syme (1939) 25

Julius Caesar,
restored marble bust,
after the antique.
(Private collection)

(Pompey) and M. Licinius Crassus, usually referred to as the First Triumvirate. They pushed a land reform bill in order to help set former soldiers up with adequate plots of land to which to retire and also instigated the recording of the proceedings of the *curia*. After his consulship, Caesar obtained a five-year term as commander of a large army in Gaul and Illyricum, renewed in 55. In 58 he twice defeated the Helvetii and also bested the Sueves, followed by victories over the Belgae and Nervii the following year, before campaigning beyond the Rhine for the first time in 56 and again in 53.

Meanwhile, the Triumvirate had come under strain, partly because of the inevitable potential jealousy amongst the triumvirs and partly due to unrest in Rome caused by a succession of poor harvests, which the people blamed on their agrarian reform of 59. The three therefore parleyed at Luca, renewing their alliance for a further five years and also renewed Caesar's command in Gaul. Here he survived a difficult siege at Aviracum and defeated the Avernian leader Vercingetorix twice in 52 at Gergovia and Alesia, by then with Mark Antony as his 2i/c. His conquest of Gaul (with two expeditions to Britain in 55 and 54BC) and the immense booty therefrom, ensured his popularity and primacy at home, but this alarmed the senate, which required him to return unarmed once his term of office ended in 51. Being suspicious of their motives, he felt unable to do this, and sent Antony back to propose a compromise, whereby both Caesar and Pompey's men would lay down their arms – a perfectly reasonable suggestion but which was rejected by the consuls at Pompey's instigation.

In the end, Caesar had little choice but to return to Rome with his army – entering Italy on 10 January 49 at the head of it illegally – effectively seizing power. Pompey's alliance with Caesar, always shaky, had essentially evaporated on the death of Crassus at the hands of the Parthians at the Battle of Carrhae in 53 and on Caesar's approach he allied himself with the conservative faction in the senate and rashly left the city without engrossing the treasury and was defeated at the battle of Pharsalus (Farsala, Thessaly, Greece) in 48. Caesar followed his opponents' supporters to Egypt, where he intervened in the civil war between Cleopatra and King Ptolemaeus, her brother, defeating the latter and forming his famous alliance with the victorious Queen. In 46 and 45, he was obliged to lead an army again against residual supporters of Pompey's faction, winning battles at Thapsus (Bakalta, Tunisia) against the Republican Metellus Scipio (leading to the suicide of Cato the younger at Utica) and against the sons of Pompey at Munda.

To maintain executive power, Caesar had a compliant senate vote him into office as *dictator* from 49 to 44, at first with reasonable conformity with the Republican constitution, for six-month periods (the limit for a dictatorship, conceived as an emergency magistracy), but for an unprecedented ten-year term in 46 and in perpetuity from January 44, thus effectively establishing a monarchy. He served again as consul in 48, 46, 45 and 44. His reform of the calendar was introduced from 1 January 45. Having eradicated all noticeable traces of opposition by spring 45, he was planning a campaign the following year against the Parthian empire, which had been trying to take territorial advantage of the upheavals that Rome had been experiencing.

Despite three marriages, Caesar died without surviving legitimate children, his only daughter, Julia (by his first wife, Cornelia who died in 69), having died in childbirth, probably in 54, her son by Pompey surviving for only a short time. He then married Pompeia in 67 but divorced her in 62, his third wife being Calpurnia, daughter of L. Calpurnius Piso Caesoninus (consul in 58) whom he married in 59. He did, however, leave a natural son, Ptolemaeus XV Caesarion, by Queen Cleopatra VII of Egypt, with whom he enjoyed a dalliance in 48-47, and quite probably when the Queen and her entourage came to Rome in 46, where they stayed until Caesar's death in 44. There is some uncertainty about poor Caesarion, for there is no mention of him in Caesar's will, and all subsequent accounts of him are later, which means there must remain some doubt that he really was Caesar's child.[369] Yet the sources all seem to accept this and the fact that he was liquidated by Octavian in 30, after his mother's suicide, goes a long way towards confirming it, although he had been designated joint ruler of Egypt by his mother, which would perhaps have made him just as vulnerable in Augustus' eyes.

Caesar, throughout his career, seems to have been maritally incontinent, hence the potential credibility of a first-century AD claim of an upper-class

---

369 Suetonius *Caes.* 52.2; Plutarch, *Caesar*, 49; most recently discussed in Goldsworthy (2006) 496-497.

Gaul to be descended from him. Unfortunately for him, being a Gaul rather negated any effect that this lofty descent might have endowed. There were also rumours that M. Junius Brutus, his co-assassin, was his natural son, Brutus' mother Servilia having been prominent amongst the dictator's paramours, and at about the right time. His descendants, however, failed to survive the Civil Wars, unlike those of P. Cornelius Dolabella, born either in 76/75 or 71BC, suffect consul in 44, also alleged by some to have been Caesar's son.[370]

JULIUS NEPOS
473, December – 9ᵗʰ May 480

Julius Nepos was one of the last emperors in the Western Empire, nominated by Leo I, who made valiant efforts to prevent the take-over of the Auvergne in Gaul by the Visigothic king Euric but was betrayed by his own *magister militum* and who exercised his remaining years ruling the northern Balkans from Dalmatia. When he was finally killed in 480, he was technically the last western emperor to remain in office, albeit in control of a vastly reduced polity.

Nepos was probably of western senatorial family, for his father had been a senior commander of Majorian in Gaul in 458/459, a man who was praised by Sidonius. His uncle Marcellinus had also been *magister militum*, his command extended by Majorian, Leo I and Anthemius at various times, but which was primarily based in Dalmatia, where he may have had estates. Julius Nepos appears to have inherited the authority of Marcellinus in Dalmatia and may have been appointed or merely recognised as *magister militum* (west) by Anthemius when his uncle was killed in 468; he was certainly holding such an appointment (but from the eastern emperor) when he descended on Italy in 474. He was also then patrician. He was nominated as new Western Emperor during the last illness of Leo I, probably in December 473; his commission was to take Italy and depose Glycerius, which, after a delay until the start of the next campaigning season, he duly did.

Having received the submission of Glycerius, Nepos was actually proclaimed emperor on 19 (some sources say 24) June 474. He was accepted and installed by the senate and was perhaps even granted the usual tribunician and proconsular powers, for the senate was a notable repository of arcane traditions and such a confirmation would have endowed its members with a taste of the authority that ancient body once enjoyed and which, since the time of Constantine, it had to an increasing extent managed to regain. Accordingly, he adopted the rather *recherché* style of Dominus Noster Julius Nepos Pater Patriae Augustus.[371] He may also have served a (western) consulship in 475, but his name does not appear on the *fasti*, and it may be that, as with Glycerius, such a move was not sanctioned by the Eastern court,

---

370 Syme RP III (1984) 1236-1250; if true of Brutus, an additional (and very personal) motive for tyrannicide.
371 ILS814; coins: D[ominus] Noster] Jul[ius] Nepos P[ius] F[elix] Aug[ustus].

although why that might have been, seeing that he was their man, is difficult to say. Possibly he served only a suffect consulship.

Once Italy had been secured, his main preoccupation was to try and prevent the Visigoths under their new, anti-Roman and anti-Catholic king, Euric, taking over the Auvergne, still part of the Empire. Ecdicius, one of the sons of the Emperor Avitus, a stalwart loyalist, was made patrician and *magister militum* and in 474 managed against fearsome odds to relieve Arelate (Arles) but was less successful the following year, not helped by the fact that although Nepos had some Eastern army units to support him, there were no military resources available to assist Ecdicius.[372] Nevertheless, Ecdicius was relieved of his responsibilities, and was replaced by Orestes. This man was yet another hardened soldier of Danubian stock, who had also once served as the secretary of Attila the Hun. Having been appointed patrician and *magister militum*, he acted unpredictably. Instead of marching to the relief of Arelate (Arles), which duly fell to the Visigoths, in order to neutralise the threat from Euric (which he thus failed to do), he turned his forces instead against Nepos in northern Italy and laid siege to Ravenna. Nepos, realising that he was the victim of a *coup*, on 28 August 475 wisely took ship with his entourage to Dalmatia, his power base. Here he was well-known and appreciated, and his intention was to regroup and recruit there prior to making an attempt to return to Italy to eject Orestes, who had proclaimed his young son Romulus emperor in Nepos' place.

This he signally failed to achieve, for the eastern court withdrew the support he would have required. Thus, for the following five years he ruled Dalmatia and those parts of neighbouring provinces where the writ of the Western Empire still ran – southern Pannonia south of the Sava, Histria and parts of Noricum. After the fall of Romulus, he tried once again to obtain the assistance of Zeno, the Eastern Emperor, to regain his position. This effort also failed, probably because Zeno was happier to accept a united Empire than have a western colleague who could only function with the allocation of scarce military resources. Thus Nepos, who had not abdicated, remained as a nominal, semi-acknowledged Western Emperor with only limited effective reach. Nevertheless, his mini-empire in the Balkans acted as a useful buffer state to help shield the Eastern Empire from problems from that quarter, whilst they dealt with the havoc being caused by the Ostrogoths in northern Pannonia and Dacia Ripensis. In 477, under his nominal rule, Masties (qv) made an attempt to usurp the purple in Numidia but was suppressed by the Vandal kingdom after a few months, depriving the west of yet another piece of territory.

This relatively stable state of affairs all came to an end on 9 May 480, when Nepos was assassinated at his palace at Salona (Solin) by two *comites* called Viator and Ovida (qv), allegedly put up to it by the exiled and resentful Glycerius, still serving as the local bishop. Ovida then continued Nepos' *imperium*, although whether as emperor or merely as a sort of warlord is

---

372 Table LXIV Brief Lives

unclear.[373] These events left only Syagrius as holding any form of imperial power in the Western Empire, the remains of which had fallen into the hands of the Hunnic adventurer Odovacer in 476, nominally under the suzerainty of Zeno.[374] A decade later, Clovis the Frank finished the job.

A temporal gulf distances Nepos from the Julii Nepotes who were senators in the mid to late second century and no connection is likely; nor is it certain that Julius was a *nomen* in the traditional sense. However, as he was apparently the heir to his uncle Marcellinus, who was an important power broker (if not warlord) in Dalmatia, it may well be that his own family were also from Salona or nearby. It may be that Ovida was some kind of relation, perhaps of Nepos' mother. We also know that his wife (of whom we hear nothing during his reign, implying she may have died before he took power) except that she was related to, very probably a niece of, the Empress Verina, the wife of Leo I and sister of that rather dim but persistent imperial claimant Basiliscus.

JUSTIN I
518, 10th July – 527, 1st August

Justin was the unlikely successor to Anastasius, who ruled competently with the increasing assistance of his nephew and eventual successor, Justinian I, settling some trying religious conflicts and presiding over a period of relative tranquillity.

Like his predecessor, Justin was getting on in years, about 67 on accession and entirely illiterate, having been born into Thracian peasant stock at Bederiana, near Naissus (Niš, Serbia) in the province of Dardania, part of the Diocese of Dacia Mediterranea. He and two companions are said by Procopius to have travelled to Constantinople to enlist in the army. He must have been endowed with considerable ability, for having been enrolled in the palace guard, he was soon commissioned and by the mid-490s had attained the rank of *comes rei militaris*, fighting as 2i/c to a succession of commanders in the Isaurian War, then in the Persian war of 503-504 and finally at the siege of Antioch in 504/505.

In 515 he was made Imperial Guard Commander, as which he transferred his military skills to naval warfare, helping to defeat Vitalinus at sea, routing part of his fleet. His appointment carried senatorial rank, which represented an impressive rise for a man who was obliged to use a stencil to sign his name. Nevertheless, the critical Procopius labelled him a donkey.[375] Just as the Emperor's family background was obscure and lowly, so was the Empress's. Of barbarian stock, Lupicina was sold into slavery and put into concubinage, but later freed and she subsequently married Justin. Yet she was very moral and upright, if a trifle unrefined, and had no interest in affairs of state. She did, however, see Theodora, the future wife of Justinian, for what

373 PLRE II Viator 1
374 PLRE II Odoacer
375 PLRE II Justinus 4

she was, and refused to approve their marriage. If the Emperor and Empress had any children, they died prior to Justin becoming emperor. Yet like Anastasius, the Imperial family was quite extensive, thanks to the emperor's two siblings marrying and having children. Unfortunately, we do not have the names of either, but Justinian was the son of his daughter and there were three sons born to the other sibling, whose gender is not known, but who was probably male. Justinian's sister's children triply married into the families of Anastasius and Olybrius, anchoring the new Imperial family to several earlier ones, thereby strengthening its perceived right to rule

The new Emperor was proclaimed within 24 hours of the death of Anastasius, and then only because of a slightly bizarre set of circumstances. The old Emperor had no idea whom to appoint as his heir, despite the existence of a number of entirely suitable candidates, including three nephews who, according to the *Anonymous Valesianus*, managed to eliminate themselves in various ways. The same source claims he next resolved to nominate as his successor the first person to enter his chamber the following morning. This happened to be the *comes excubitorum* Justinus. Under the reformed arrangements, he held the position of commander of the crack troops which comprised the Imperial Guard, as the *scholae*, who previously performed the role, were by this date reduced to being entirely ceremonial.

The Emperor died shortly after this modest stratagem had been played out, on 9 July. His chamberlain Amantius (a eunuch) put the *comes* Theocritus forward, but Justinus outmanoeuvred him and managed to stage-manage his own acclamation the following morning, with the result that Theocritus tried to set up a counter-coup, but this was quickly thwarted and the principals executed.

Justin's other potential rivals were the late emperor's three nephews, of whom Probus and Pompeius seemed to have no imperial ambitions and Hypatius, who without doubt did, was safely out of harm's way on the eastern frontier as *magister militum*. Justin moved quickly to make a donative to the troops of five *solidi* per man, paid for out of Anastasius' replete treasury.[376]

He was proclaimed in the style of Dominus Noster Justinus Pater Patriae Augustus by the senate and his Empress (by whom he had no surviving children), was given the additional name Euphemia and made Augusta.[377] He held the consulship for 519 with the Goth Eutharicus Cilliga as western colleague, a man whom he made his 'son at arms', suggesting that he acquiesced in his father-in-law Theodericus' designation of him as successor designate as ruler of the west. He held a second and final consulship in 524.[378]

The new Emperor moved swiftly to effect an ecclesiastical settlement and before the end of his first month Chalcedonian Orthodoxy was restored and the Monophysite faction side-lined. The was an essential move to free

---

376 Generally, these donatives were made on accession and when a consulship was held by the Emperor to mark a five- or ten-year anniversary, a tradition that was dropped by Justin: Burgess (2011) XIV *passim*

377 PLRE II Euphemia 5

378 Moorhead (1992) 201; Fl. Rufius Opilio, an aristocrat, was his western colleague.

Justin for a trial of strength with the disaffected but equally orthodox former *magister militum* Vitalianus, who was causing trouble in the Balkans, the more so because he considered he himself had a claim upon the purple. Justin prudently made his peace with him, confirmed him in office, made him patrician and designated him as consul for 520. He was then put to work to settle outstanding difficulties with the church in the west, which he managed to achieve successfully, albeit at the price of the *amour propre* of the eastern faction, a price the Emperor thought worth paying to achieve unity. Nevertheless, Vitalianus was always seen as a threat and was eventually murdered in the palace in July 520 along with two members of his staff, probably on the initiative of the Emperor's nephew, the future Emperor Justinian I, who had been the *eminence grise* behind the ecclesiastical accords. The ambitious nephew acted very competently as Justin's secretary of state, whilst at the same time ensuring his own place in the succession. As the reign went on, Justinian's influence was seen to be increasingly pre-eminent hence, no doubt, Procopius's donkey jibe.

After 520 and the elimination of Vitalianus, the emperor's nephew was virtually sole ruler of the empire, being made *magister militum* and patrician. He was later styled *nobilissimus* (most noble), a title normally coupled with that of *caesar* but here used separately for the first time to indicate someone on the brink of succession, or at least fitted for it, rather as the term *capax imperii* had been five centuries before. Probably after the Empress's death, which seems to have occurred early in 527, Justinian was at last made co-emperor and formally adopted as Justin's son, thus avoiding a succession crisis when the old Emperor finally expired aged 77 on 1 August.

JUSTIN II
565, 14ᵗʰ November – 578, 5ᵗʰ October

Justin II as Emperor conducted an imprudent policy towards the barbarians and Persians, persecuted the Monophysites, allowed the Lombards to invade Italy and created the exarchate of Italy to regularise newly imposed imperial rule over that part of the empire.

During the final years of the reign of Justinian I, his nephew Justinus was said to have been the virtual ruler of the Empire, just as Justinian himself had been during his uncle's regime in the 520s. The younger Justin had been born about 510, the son of one Dulcidius by Vigilantia, the daughter of Sabbatius who had married another Vigilantia, sister of Justin I. His only known office was the largely honorific one of *cura palatii* (Head of the Imperial household), which he had held from before 552, the year he was accorded the status of honorary consul. He spent the rest of the time troubleshooting for the Emperor: holding talks with Pope Vigilius, supervising the movement of peoples in the Balkans and twice suppressing factional violence at Constantinople. He had long been a friend of his cousin and namesake, Flavius Justinus, the Eastern consul in 540, to the extent that an understanding existed between them that whichever succeeded to the purple would give the other second place in the empire. In the event, the new

Emperor felt too insecure to let this happen and had his kinsman demoted and then killed.[379]

The succession went smoothly, and Justin II was crowned on the very day his uncle died. He was styled Dominus Noster Justinus Pater Patriae Augustus and acknowledged by the senate in the usual way. He held the ordinary consulship on his accession, for the following year and for an unprecedented third time in 568. He considered himself the embodiment of the old Roman virtues: courage, prudence, self-confidence and fortitude. He was arrogant enough to believe that these qualities could be applied to the governance of the empire, especially in his dealings with its enemies, and that he was the God-given instrument by which all might be achieved.

His first move was to halt the payment of tribute to the various groups and polities which ringed the limits of the empire, the distribution of which Justinian had used to funnel the aggression of these peoples into defending the frontiers from yet more determined enemies swarming and mingling beyond. The policy had long proved successful, but Justin was minded to stop it. This had the unfortunate effect of re-igniting the Persian War and turned the Tartarish Avars east of the Danube against the Empire too, with the knock-on effect that in 568 the Lombards moved west and entered Italy, just after it had finally been re-conquered and before any serious reconstruction of its devastated infrastructure could begin.

At about the same time the Emperor had appointed a formal governor of Italy, treating it more like one of the Dioceses set up under the system initiated by Diocletian, and styling this new viceroy *exarchus*, although the title was not recorded as such until 584. An official of similar rank also oversaw the control of Africa from that date. Narses, who had taken over the task of recovering the west from the *comes* Belisarius, was effectively the first Exarch of Italy. He was succeeded by Longinus who served until 575.[380] The settlement left by Narses envisaged the separation of powers, in that the old civil and judicial system in Italy was restored to be run by the western senatorial aristocracy and the military administration in the hands of *duces*, answerable to the exarch. As the Lombards swarmed in and settled, their leaders were recruited as nominal Roman *duces*, and the duchies that were to dominate Italy for almost a millennium and a half began to evolve, some firmly under the control of Lombard freebooters and some under the direct control of the Exarch. The Lombard kingdom itself was finally contained within northern and north-west Italy and survived until absorbed into the restored Western Empire of Charlemagne from 800. Nevertheless, it was under Justin II that a substantial amount of mainly coastal southern Spain was re-conquered for the Empire.

Meanwhile in 571 came a turning point. Justin II initiated a persecution of the Monophysites (amongst which he himself had been numbered in his younger days), which, although falling short of the creation of martyrs, led to a wholesale replacement of adherents in high office, a change which came

---

379 PLRE III Justinus 5
380 PLRE III Longinus 5

about at a time when anything of the sort was best avoided. Then following the defeat of the Romans by the Persian army at Dara in November 573, the Emperor began to lose his sanity, suffering fits of child-like behaviour contrasting with attempts at self-defenestration and extreme violence. The Empress Sophia (a niece of the Empress Theodora, Justinian's wife) therefore took upon herself the day-to-day administration of the Empire.

Finding this a severe burden, Sophia, in one of her husband's more lucid moments, persuaded him in 574 to adopt the *magister militum* Tiberius. He was made *nobilissimus caesar* and, at the end of September 578, promoted to the rank of co-Augustus as Tiberius II, about nine days before Justin died on 5 October. With Sophia Justin had two recorded children, Justus, who died young and Arabia, who married a patrician, Baduarius, Justin's *cura palatii*, who later served as *magister militum* against the Lombards, by whom he was killed in action.

JUSTINIAN I
527, 1st April – 565, 14th November

Justinian, nephew of Justin I, was one of the longest ruling emperors (at 37 years, less than Theodosius II but exceeding in length the reigns of Augustus, Honorius and Constantine) and, after narrowly being deposed as a result of a riot in 532, went on to recover imperial control over Africa and Italy, albeit at the cost of irreversible devastation, and whose virago of an Empress vitiated the effectiveness of his rule. He also codified Roman law and initiated the construction of the Church of the Holy Wisdom at Constantinople.

Justinian was the son of his predecessor's sister, whose name is lost to us. She married a man called Sabbatius, about whom nothing whatsoever is known.[381] As he was born in 483, before his brother-in-law had achieved even modest eminence, Sabbatius was probably of middling rank, although unlikely to have been in such a lowly station in life as that in which Justin had been born. He was probably dead well before his son became part of the Imperial family, otherwise we would have heard more of him, ties of blood in high office carrying such weight. The future Emperor was born at a fortress called Bederiana (now Bader) hard by Tauresium (Gradiste, Macedonia), suggesting his father may have been an army officer but not necessarily a native of the area (i.e. a Thracian). Justinian's full name, Flavius Petrus Sabbatius Justinianus, appears traditional (albeit that the *praenomen* is Christian and the Flavius was probably added as an imperial honorific) but may well have been amplified after the family's rise to eminence.

At the time of his uncle's elevation to the purple, Justinian was serving in the ceremonial *scholae*, having become one of their officers. Indeed, when Anastasius died, one of those proposed for the purple was the elderly and distinguished general Flavius Patricius (consul in 500), but he was unacceptable to Justin's men, the *excubitores*, from whom the old boy had

---

381 PLRE II Sabbatius

to be rescued by the quick thinking of Justinian, who was himself promptly put forward over his uncle, an honour from which he was quick to distance himself.

He was almost immediately thereafter made a *comes* and following the murder of Vitalianus in 520, which he appears to have masterminded, he became *magister militum* (effectively chief of the general staff) as well. This elevated him to the senate and the rank of *vir illustris*; he also held the consulship in 521 and the celebrations and games accompanying this were held with conspicuous generosity, which did his popularity no harm at all. He was also made patrician around this period and this raised him in rank to the relatively new style of *vir magnificus*. He was made *nobilissimus* and, after the death of the Empress, he married and was made co-Augustus with his uncle, who died four months later.[382]

His new bride, unlike his aunt, the Empress Euphemia, was to loom large in the affairs of state, which we know from the account of her by Procopius, who knew her. Born c. 495, she was originally from Cyprus and became an exotic dancer with a reputation for her erotic performances and louche lifestyle. In this she followed in the steps of her anonymous mother, who had married Acacius, keeper of the animals for the Green faction of the circus. She had two sisters and at least two children, a daughter and a son, Johannes, but by whom is lost to us. She had gone to Libya c. 518 as the mistress of the governor, Hecebolus, but they fell out and she returned home via Alexandria paying her way as an *horizontale*. On her arrival she turned to religion – and Monophysitism at that. She met Justinian and became his mistress. He persuaded his uncle to elevate her to the rank of *patricia*, and he married her once the disapproving Empress had died and Justin had had time to amend the long-established law against senators marrying actresses. They were certainly married by the time Justinian had become co-emperor in April 527. Thereafter, Theodora took an active role in government, attending the Imperial Council (*consistorium*), advising the Emperor and exercising the power to make or break, of life and death over his associates. She comes over as essentially insecure, her controlling nature deriving therefrom with all the capriciousness and mental *chiaroscuro* that comes with it. Indeed, if the hostile account of Procopius is to be believed, she was everything her husband was not. He was hard working, generally affable and fiscally careful, whilst she was extravagant, slothful, haughty and volatile.

Justinian was acclaimed by the senate and court as sole emperor on 1 August 527. His style was Dominus Noster Iustinianus Pater Patriae Augustus, later adding in 539 Alanicus and Vandalicus, having subdued the Alani and re-conquered Africa. Later still he added Alemannicus, Gepidus and Langobardicus.[383] He served a second consulship in 528 and two more in 533 and 534 before the institution was effectively abolished after the (western) consulship of Flavius Anicius Faustus Albinus Basilius Junior in

---

382 PLRE II Iustinianus 7
383 Barnwell (1992) 95

541.[384] Thereafter, all consulships were honorary, except for newly acceded emperors who usually held an ordinary consulship. Years were counted *post consule Basili* ('following the consulship of Basilius') I, II, etc., until Justinian's death.

Most commentators see four events (called pillars by Scott) marking out the reign: the codification of Roman law, the building of Hagia Sophia cathedral in Constantinople, the closing of Plato's Academy in Athens, and the re-conquest of the west. The chronicler John Malalas mentions all four, the latter briefly, but this aspect has been magnified by the historian Procopius's account which focuses on the *reconquista*.

The first major achievement of the reign was the thorough revision of the legal code, much more far reaching than that published under Theodosius II. It was carried out with remarkable speed in 528-529 by a committee chaired by the corrupt but efficient and remarkably able jurist Tribonianus, who was *quaestor sacri palatii* (Lord Chancellor or chief legal officer) 529-532 and 535-542, producing the *Digest* and the *Institutes*.[385] Despite Tribonianus's alleged paganism, the Emperor ensured that nothing in the finished work would be incompatible with Christian teaching.

There was also a thorough reform of the tax system, coupled with a centralisation of bureaucracy, done to improve revenue and to increase efficiency. This was masterminded by another major figure, but who was also perceived to be corrupt, John the Cappadocian.[386] As it turned out, there was to be much for the treasury to fund. There was also a crack-down on paganism (leading to the closure of the Athens academy) and other heresies (but not Monophysitism, *pace* the Empress) which was pursued with too much rigour, resulting in a major revolt in northern Palestine by the Samaritans, the suppression of which devastated much of the province. After five years of rule, there was much discontent, especially in the capital, exacerbated by laws limiting the privileges of the circus factions, which struck at the heart of the celebrity culture that the ever-popular circus imbued.

The third pillar arose as a consequence of another event consequent on the tax reforms (and other irritants). These accumulated grievances burst forth one day at the Hippodrome in Constantinople on 13 January 532, where a demonstration caused an over-reaction on the part of the authorities which spiralled out of control, with a vast mob chanting Níκα, Níκα (victory! victory!). This gave the name to the event (the Níka riot or riots) which rapidly broadened out into eight days of rioting, during which much of the city was destroyed by rampaging and resentful mobs (largely comprising peasant and city dwellers, alike dispossessed by the harshness of the new imperial tax regime) mainly by fire, and during which the nephew of Anastasius, Hypatius, was raised to the purple, largely against his will. The uprising (for such it had become) was only ended because the Empress persuaded her husband not to flee when he was minded so to do, and because

---

384 The previous year (540) had been the last with two consuls, east and west.
385 PLRE III Tribonianus 1
386 PLRE III Ioannes 11

two generals, Belisarius and Mundus, who were passing through the city on the way to new postings took charge of the counter *putsch*. In this they were aided by the grand chamberlain, the Armenian eunuch Narses, who took the initiative in bottling up a vast concourse of rioters in the hippodrome, which had become a sort of headquarters of the rioters, allowing the two generals systematically to butcher them all – allegedly between 20,000 and 50,000 people. Needless to say, the riot swiftly collapsed. Later, Hypatius and his brother Pompeius were arraigned before Justinian who was inclined to forgive them (they had been implicated largely against their will, after all). Theodora however, demurred and true to form demanded their execution, which followed immediately, the remains of the victims being thrown into the Golden Horn.

In rebuilding the shattered city, the Emperor spared no expense, and the major public buildings, churches and infrastructure were renewed on a more impressive scale, notably the spectacular and architecturally adventurous cathedral of St Sophia (Ἁγία Σοφία), designed (probably in advance of the riot) by Anthemius of Tralles and Isidorus of Miletus and still a building of international importance to this day, preserved by its conversion into a mosque in 1453 and secularisation as a museum in the 20th century by Mustafa Kemal Pasha (Atatürk).[387]

In mentioning Belisarius, it is worth noting that the early military business of the reign had been a campaign against Persia, led by him in his first command (replacing the absent imperial candidate of 528, Probus, a prince of the house of Anastasius), although he obtained only qualified success and was soon replaced. It was on returning from his second command that he came to be in Constantinople during the Nika riot, a happenstance that did no harm to his prospects, for the emperor chose him to lead a new expedition to Africa to attempt to dislodge the Vandal kingdom. This was the first step in the fourth pillar, the *reconquista*. If successful, this venture was to be the first in a series of planned campaigns envisaged by Justinian to recover the Western Empire. Belisarius was to turn out to be the greatest commander of his age or indeed of any other age of the Empire.

The Italian campaign was only launched after the death of King Theoderic in Italy who, it has to be remembered, was theoretically ruling a part of the Empire as the Emperor's appointee. He had been a made patrician and was a former *magister militum* who had finally received imperial recognition in 493. His death in 526 and that of his dissolute grandson Athalaric eight years later plunged the benevolent Ostrogothic regime into doubt concerning its continued loyalty to Constantinople. This was the opportunity which prompted the Emperor to commission Belisarius to take the peninsula back. Much of Belisarius's good work there was undone in the 540s by imperial incompetence and the accession of a capable Gothic King, Totila. Belisarius's second campaign from 544-549 was less successful due to lack of resources, and he was recalled after the death of Theodora, then his chief supporter.

---

387 It was re-commissioned as a mosque by President Erdogan of Turkey in 2021 in a drive against secularisation.

The situation was restored by the elderly eunuch Narses with John, the nephew of the former rival of Justin I, Vitalianus, who fought a series of effective campaigns from 552 to 556, albeit with a much larger army. The result was the restoration of Italy, a small part of Gaul (essentially the *Côte d'Azur*) and much of southern Spain, but at the cost of the dereliction of much of Italy, both countryside and cities, the weakening of its defences and the deleterious effect of a reformation of its governance by a sanction which established a viceroy (later called an exarch, qv. *sub* Justin II) at Ravenna. This last left the western senate at Rome, which had administered Italy with considerable competence since the reign of Valentinian III, completely by-passed in such a way that within three generations it had virtually ceased to exist and the ancient senatorial aristocracy was dispersed or impoverished (except for those families which had wisely migrated to the east).

The continuous conflict in Italy, perturbations in reclaimed Africa and constant warfare on the eastern borders with Persia were a severe drain upon the fisc, accelerated by an apocalyptic plague in the 540s (originating in north-east Africa) which killed millions (including the Empress) and seriously depleted the reserves of manpower upon which the empire could draw. That so much was achieved was, in the circumstances, little short of miraculous. Justinian associated his nephew Justin with his rule from around 562, entrusting him with several delicate tasks and clearly marking him out as his successor. The old Emperor died aged around 83 on 14 November 565 but left no issue by Theodora, but by at least two mistresses he seems to have been father of Iohannes (consul in 576) and Theodorus *qui et* Tzirus, who served as *magister militum* under Justin II, who himself duly succeeded on Justinian's death. (The rule of Justinian II, 685-711, lies outside the parameters of this book.)

LAELIANUS

269, January – March

Laelianus was a Gallic empire senatorial usurper on the Rhine frontier who was suppressed by rival usurper Postumus after a few months. At the beginning of 269, Laelianus, almost certainly Postumus' governor of Upper Germany, rebelled and proclaimed himself emperor. The catalyst may have been the re-annexation to the Empire of Postumus' Spanish provinces, assuming that this occurred so early in the year (or late in that preceding) and the accompanying loss of Postumus' prestige. The alternative cause might have been the refusal of Postumus to go to the aid of Aureolus the previous autumn, an occasion he might have used to take over the entire west.

In any case, [C.] Ulpius Cornelius Laelianus was cartainly a senator and a former suffect consul, either under Valerian or as an appointee of Postumus,[388] He was styled after his elevation Imperator Caesar Laelianus Pius Felix Augustus and was soon confronted by Postumus, defeated in battle and besieged at his capital, Moguntiacum (Mainz). The city was eventually

---

388 PLRE I. Laelianus 1; HA incorrectly calls him Lollianus (*Tr. Trig.* 5).

taken and Laelianus captured, although his subsequent fate is not recorded. He was probably killed along with Postumus, if not executed beforehand. The length of his reign is uncertain, but it was long enough to enable him to issue coins. Postumus probably wanted to see the onset of spring before moving against him. We can say nothing of this man's family. The *cognomen* occurs in a branch of the senatorial Pontii in the 2nd century, but thereafter the name is not met with until this man. *The Historia Augusta*, with its customary cavalier attitude to facts, calls him Lollianus and contributes not a single reliable fact about him.[389]

LEO I
457, 7th February – 474, 18th January

Leo I was a competent emperor who sought successfully to diminish the influence of Germanic levies and generals in the imperial army but whose delegated attempt to re-conquer the provinces of North Africa failed through the appointment of the bungling nephew of his Empress, Basiliscus. He also nominated two western emperors, to no particularly good effect.

When the emperor Marcian died in 457, the obvious successor was his son-in-law, the future Western Emperor Anthemius, who had been appointed *magister utriusque militum* (C-in-C) by his father-in-law when he became Emperor. Possibly his succession would have cramped the style of the other powerful general, Flavius Ardaburius Aspar. Leo did, however, retain him in office, which suggests that the two generals rubbed along well enough. Perhaps Anthemius was sensible enough to turn the idea of succeeding down. In fact, the *magister militum* Aspar acted quickly. As a man of Alan (German) descent, there was no possibility of his own accession to the purple being acceptable, so he was obliged to act in the manner of Ricimer, and rule through a nominee. Yet he chose not a malleable child but another seasoned soldier, Leo, who was proclaimed emperor eleven days after Marcian's death.

The new Emperor was born in 400 or 401 in Thrace of Bassian (Dacian) descent, although the names of his parents are lost. He was another Danubian general in the mould of the successors of Claudius II. Like his predecessor, Leo seems to have been an ex-tribune and at the time of his elevation was in command of a unit of auxiliary levies at Selymbria (Silivri, Turkey, a suburb of Constantinople) and also a *comes*. He was by then married to Aelia Verina, sister of the incompetent usurper Basiliscus (qv) and aunt by marriage, it is believed, of Julius Nepos (qv). They had a daughter, Aelia Ariadne, who married the future emperors Zeno and later Anastasius, and another, Leontia, whose second husband was the usurper Marcian II. There were also at least two sons, both of whom died very young.

Also like his predecessor, Leo was installed and crowned in the Cathedral at Constantinople by the Patriarch, whose position had been formalised and enhanced at the Council of Chalcedon. The new Emperor took the style

---

389 *Tyr. Trig. 5*, 1-8

Dominus Noster Leo Pius Felix Perpetuus Augustus.[390] He held his first consulship in 458 with Majorian as colleague, demonstrating his desire to make a rapprochement with the west and acknowledging the legitimacy of his western colleague. He held the consulship again in 462 (with Severus III), 466, 471 and 473, on the latter occasion alone. Although he had been raised up by Aspar, the new Emperor forbore to become his creature and sought to diminish the Germanic influence at court and in the army, on the whole with success. That this did not result in all-out conflict reflects on the realism of the patrician and the tact of the Emperor. He recruited Thracians to the Imperial Guard, henceforth called the *excubitores* (sentinels) replacing the largely decorative *scholae*, and he recruited Isaurians – a rough, half-savage people, who occupied the mountainous interior of southern Asia Minor – to replace the Germans in the élite units of the field army. One senior commander of these levies in particular, Tarasicodissa, was made *comes domesticorum* (guard commander), marrying the Emperor's daughter Ariadne in 467, at which time he was appointed *magister militum* in Thrace; this man was, of course, the future Emperor Zeno.

In 468, Leo set plans in motion for a new attempt to eliminate the African Vandal kingdom of Gaiseric. He installed the trusted and competent Anthemius as Western Emperor and recruited Marcellinus, the uncle of Julius Nepos, to assist. He then had a had a rush of blood to the head (or was browbeaten by the Empress) and entrusted the entire enterprise, mounted on a massive scale, to his brother-in-law Basiliscus, the heterodox sibling of Verina, who had made common cause against the Emperor's reforms with Aspar. Apart from such obvious *lèse majesté*, Basiliscus was a Roman of impeccable pedigree but plainly unsuited to command, being slow-witted and indolent; he also had eyes on the purple. The entire African episode was a disaster, resulting in obloquy for Basiliscus and odium for Aspar, who was accused of soft-pedalling the expedition to preserve his fellow Arian, the Vandal King. Yet, within two years, the Emperor's other daughter had been allowed to marry Aspar's younger son, the patrician Julius Patricius, who was soon afterwards declared *nobilissimus caesar* (effectively heir presumptive) and Basiliscus' life had been spared by the entreaties of his sister. Within months, in 471, Aspar's son Ardaburius was caught red-handed conspiring to suborn the Isaurians, and he and his father were killed; Patricius was stripped of his rank of Caesar but survived. This was followed by a final purge of Germanic elements at court and in the army.

In autumn 473, the emperor, now about 75, was fading, and he nominated the Empress's kinsman Julius Nepos to the throne of the west (which he delayed taking up until the following spring) but inexplicably passed over his closest confidant and son-in-law, the patrician and *magister militum* Tarasicodissa (now calling himself the more Greek Zeno) and named Zeno's son Leo, aged seven, his heir. He died on 18 January 474.

---

390 ILS810 & coins.

LEO II
473, December – 474, 17th November

Leo II was a child emperor whose only known act was to nominate his father Zeno as his co-ruler, probably at the prompting of his mother. Leo was born in 467 and was proclaimed *nobilissimus caesar* in October 473, being raised to co-emperor by his grandfather two months later, by-passing Zeno. He became sole ordinary consul for 474 on 1 January. On the death of the senior Augustus, Leo I on 18 January, he became sole emperor. He took the style Dominus Noster Flavius Leo [Junior] P[ius] F[elix] Aug[ustus].

On 9 February 474, prompted by his mother, he helped to crown his father co-emperor. Coins were struck with the legend DN Leo et Zeno PP Aug., but with the bust of Zeno on the obverse, although some issues were struck with Leo alone. He was still only 7 when he fell ill and died in November that year.[391] (The remaining emperors called Leo, starting with Leo III in 717, lie beyond the parameters of this book.)

LEO see BASILISCUS (II)

LEONTIUS (I)
484, 19th July – 488, September

The usurper enjoyed an unexpectedly long time in the highest office having been raised to the purple by the Isaurian *magister militum* Illus (qv) as his puppet with the connivance of the Empress Verina.

Leontius was an Isaurian military man, relatively young and well educated, who was described as handsome (although pock-marked), long haired, with a straight nose, good eyes and polite manners. In 484 or somewhat earlier he was appointed *magister militum* in Thrace. He was also made a patrician and an honorary consul, the latter an honorific which had largely superseded the holding of suffect consulships in the east from the time of Leo I, the first example recorded dating from 475.[392] Soon afterwards, he appears to have been commissioned to move east to suppress the revolt of Illus, Zeno's old friend, who had turned against him and who was at the time *magister militum* in the east. Illus had just elevated Marcian II to the purple (for the third time) and had the support of dowager Empress Verina. A parley was held, and the result was that Marcian was deposed in favour of Leontius.

The old Empress crowned Leontius at Tarsus on 19 July 484, after which they moved to Antioch and stayed in the city from 27 July to 8 August, when new coins were issued. His imperial style was Dominus Noster Leontius Perpetuus Augustus.[393] Illus and the new imperial claimant were subsequently worsted in a battle outside Antioch with the forces of Iohnnes

---

391 Coins; PLRE II Leo 7

392 PLRE II, 1246; Crawford (2019) 201

393 Coin evidence. Only three *solidi* from his issue are known; they are greatly outnumbered by fakes.

(John the Scythian), sent to suppress them by Zeno, and they withdrew to a near-impregnable fortress in the Isaurian uplands called Papyrius. There they were subsequently besieged for four years by the imperial forces. At some stage during the siege, the ex-Emperor Marcian II was able to leave and travel to Italy in the hope of obtaining help from Odoacer. This effort seems to have failed, after which we hear no more of him. After an act of betrayal ended the siege, Leontius, Illus, and the dowager Empress (and possibly the family of Marcian) were all captured and executed, Leontius' head being sent to Constantinople for public display.[394] (The reign of Leontius II, 695-706, lies beyond the parameters of this work.)

LEPIDUS see *GAETULICUS*

LIBIUS SEVERUS III
461, September – 465, 14th November

Libius Severus was a senatorial non-entity and creature of the western warlord Ricimer, whose reign was marked by fresh hostility from the Vandals of North Africa and whose elevation led to the creation of a breakaway imperial polity in Gaul, control over which the west never regained. He was elevated to the throne by Ricimer with the intention that he should reign as a figurehead whilst the barbarian *magister militum* ruled the western empire (he hoped) unhindered. The demise of Majorian had left the empire technically united under the emperor Leo I, with Ricimer firmly in charge in the west. Yet he seems to have realised that he could not govern effectively without either official recognition from the east or an emperor through whom he could exercise power.

The death of Majorian had as bad an effect on affairs in Gaul as the deposition of Avitus had five years earlier. The *comes* and *magister militum* there, a native grandee with impeccable senatorial roots, Aegidius (qv), refused to recognise Severus, Ricimer's next nominee and all but southern Gaul was thenceforth lost to what was, in effect, a third Gallic empire – one that was to outlast the main western imperial polity by six or arguably even ten years. Whilst there is debate as to whether Aegidius was an emperor or not, the fact was that he and his son controlled central and northern Gaul, latterly from Noviodunum (Soissons), for the next 25 years and noting the terminology used by contemporary commentators, they viewed themselves as of imperial standing. Indeed, Ricimer may have been conflicted about whom to put forward for the purple, for Aegidius's claim was impeccable, but he was probably rejected for the same reason as Majorian had met his fate – he was just too competent; another possibility was that the man we now believe to have been a younger son of Petronius Maximus, Anicius Olybrius, had married the younger daughter of Valentinian III. As her elder sister had been abducted from Rome and married by Gaiseric, the Vandal King was now a

---

394 PLRE II Leontius 17, cf. Kadellis (2015) 62-63

member of the former dynasty and brother-in-law of Olybrius. This would also have guaranteed the acquiescence of the eastern court. But in the end, Ricimer went for a cypher.

Libius Severus, possibly bore the *signum* (nickname) 'Serpentius', and was a senator of whose family we know nothing, except that they came from the Lucanian region of Italy. We have no information as to any career prior to his elevation.[395] There is no mention of wife or children. His *nomen* Libius is a late imperial mutation from the more resonant name of Livius, previously met with in an imperial context in Galba; few Livii are recorded in the senate after his time.

Flavius Libius Severianus Severus was proclaimed on 19 November, although his elevation might well have followed only about a month after the deposition of Majorian; it may be that the pattern followed the elevation of the latter. The new Emperor may have been acclaimed in September and an embassy sent to Constantinople to seek confirmation from Leo. When this was not forthcoming, he was given an official elevation and installation, with the usual endorsement by the senate, as recorded on 19 November. His style was Dominus Noster [Imperator] Libius Severus Perpetuus Augustus.[396] The new Emperor served as consul in 462 with Leo I, although as far as Leo was concerned there was no western consul.

The acclamation of Severus rekindled the ire of Gaiseric, who wished to see his brother-in-law Olybrius established as emperor of the West, so he renewed his harassment of the Italian mainland. Countering this was becoming increasingly difficult, especially as the loss of most of Gaul meant that a vast amount of potential tax revenue was not available to subsidise and increase the forces available. This must partly explain the lack of activity recorded for this reign, with the loss of control over most of Gaul, Africa, Spain and the north and north-west. Only Dalmatia, part of Illyria, Italy and Sicily and southern Gaul remained under direct control.

Severus died at Rome, after a life of religious rectitude, on 14 November 465, allegedly from drinking from a poisoned chalice at the instigation of Ricimer, but more probably, as Sidonius tells us, from natural causes. Murdering him, in the absence of the slightest motive, would not have been in the least advantageous.

LICINIUS I
11th November 308 – 324

Licinius was the surviving eastern tetrarch who emerged ruling that part of the empire from 308, who was obliged to endure an uneasy relationship of sixteen years' duration with his western colleague, Constantine the Great, and who refused to go quietly when brought to battle by Constantine on two occasions.

Licinius was from Dacia Ripensis and was reputedly of peasant stock. He was born c. 265 and made his career in the army, serving with Galerius,

---

395 PLRE II Severus 18
396 ILS 811 & coins.

with whom he had shared a tent on campaign and to whom in the long run he owed his position as Augustus. He had fought against the Persians in 296-297 as Galerius' second in command. He was later sent as a legate or envoy to Maxentius at Rome in the wake of the demise of Severus II but was never called upon be a Caesar in the tetrarchic system, being hurriedly appointed emperor in the wake of the crisis conference held under the chairmanship of Diocletian at Carnuntum (Bad Deutsch-Altenburg, Austria) in 308.

His original name is lost to us – it might have been Licinius Licinianus or similar, but with his elevation to the rank of augustus, he assumed the name and style Imperator Caesar C. Valerius Licinianus Licinius Pius Felix Invictus Augustus, He was granted the tribunician and proconsular power, made *pontifex maximus* and was consul in 309, 312, 313, 315, 318 and 321 (in the east only).[397] He was also later styled Sarmaticus Maximus and Germanicus Maximus.[398]

At first given sovereignty over the Balkan provinces only, in 313 he took inspiration from Constantine's elimination of Maxentius and moved against Maximin Daia in the east, quickly overcoming him and executing him (and his children). From 313 for eleven years he and Constantine divided the empire east-west between them, and he had, of course, married his colleague's sister in 313, by whom he had a son, Val[erius] Licinianus Licinius, born in summer 315 and often called Licinius II, although he was never augustus. The younger Licinius was consul at the tender age of four in 319 and again in 321 (latterly in the east only) and on 1 March 317 was declared Caesar along with Constantine's sons Crispus and Constantinus (later Constantine II).[399]

The co-operation between the two emperors was never particularly amicable, and in 315 Constantine provoked a breach by proposing his nephew Bassianus as Caesar in the west. Licinius refused, fearing that such a move might shut out his own son, with the result that Bassianus was killed on the pretext of his trying to foment revolt after his not being made Caesar.

In 316 Constantine invaded the Balkans, hoping to dispense with his colleague altogether. He carried all before him at the first encounter, leading Licinius to set up his commander Valens II as co-augustus in opposition to Constantine. A second battle, at Adrianople (Edirne, European Turkey), was indecisive, and the two had to come to terms at Serdica (Sofia, Bulgaria) on 1 March 317 when the three under-age Caesars were appointed and poor Valens, who had served his purpose, was killed. One result was that Licinius became less inimical to the Christians, a legacy of his association with Galerius. Yet he was still a pagan himself and a close friend of pagan philosophers and others within his sphere of influence, whilst his imperial colleague was actively promoting Christianity. Rightly suspicious of Constantine's motives, he suspected that Christians were acting as a fifth column inside the eastern polity and from c. 320 started purging them from his bureaucracy and army. He also suspected the bishops of disloyalty and began executing them. This

---

397 PLRE I Licinius 3
398 ILS678, 679
399 ILS680, 712

led to another open breach with Constantine, who met his opponent at the second battle of Adrianople on 3 July 324, defeating him soundly.

Licinius fled to Asia, and appointed the commander of his guard, Martinianus, his co-emperor. Constantine came after him again, crossing the Bosphorus and inflicting a second defeat on him at Chrysopolis (Üsküdar, Turkey) on 18 September 324. Within a week, Licinius and Martinianus surrendered to Constantine at Nicomedia (Ismir, Turkey). Licinius was spared, sent into exile at Thessalonica but killed anyway by the ever-fickle Constantine, being hanged in spring the following year. Later that year a similar fate befell Martinianus. Young Licinius was also spared, but in typical Constantinian fashion was executed later anyway in 326. An illegitimate son of Licinius, later legitimated, was also spared, but in 336 was reduced to servile status and sent to work in the women's quarters of an opulent residence at Carthage.[400]

LICINIUS II see LICINIUS I

LUCIUS VERUS
161, 7th March – 168, c. 1st February

Lucius Verus was the first emperor to rule jointly without serious problems, the son of Hadrian's first choice as ruler. His efforts were overshadowed by those of his kinsman and co-ruler Marcus Aurelius and he is forever linked to the destructive plague his campaign in the east brought into the empire.

Despite notionally Verus being the senior partner in their joint rule, Verus and Marcus Aurelius grew close and formed a genuine partnership. But Lucius ended up very much the junior element and this may have formed his character, for he turned out to be a something of a voluptuary and a man not noted for any particularly sterling qualities.

Yet, as events following his accession in 161 were to show, neither did he display any particularly evil tendencies either, and any inclination he might have had to plough a furrow that might have cut across any of Marcus' plans was deflected by the consideration – and on occasion, patience – which the latter constantly showed him.

L. Ceionius Commodus was born on 15 December 130 at Rome.[401] The Ceionii, from which family he descended, were of Etruscan stock, perhaps from the colony of Bononia (Bologna). The only Ceionius – an exceedingly rare name – to come to the notice of history prior to the man with whom Verus' pedigree begins is the otherwise anonymous Ceionius who was a *praefectus fabrum* (prefect of the camp, a military equestrian WO1) in AD9;[402] a bloodline is thus possible but unproven. The family had been raised to patrician rank by creation in 74. The name reappeared later (setting aside

---

400 PLRE Licinius 4. It was probably the safest place for the son of a fallen Augustus, with an eventual prospect of manumission.

401 PIR² C606; JRS LVII (1967) 65-79

402 Stech (1912) no. 241

the entirely fictional father of Clodius Albinus alleged by the HA)[403] in [M.] Nummius Ceionius Albinus (consul (ii) 263), who was probably descended from Verus' kinsman M. Ceionius Silvanus through the unrecorded marriage of a female descendant.[404] From them stemmed an extensive dynasty of Ceionii and Albini traceable into the 6th century.[405]

Verus' name changed on his father's adoption in 136, probably to L. Aelius Commodus but he was again adopted on 25 February 138 by Antoninus Pius, simultaneously with the latter's adoption by Hadrian, becoming L. Annius Aurelius Commodus.[406] He was given the *toga virilis* in 146, was *quaestor* 152 and consul in 154.

On accession, Marcus caused the senate to vote Lucius the titles Caesar and Augustus, and having himself taken the additional surname of Antoninus in consideration of his adoptive father, he bestowed the additional *agnomen* of Verus upon Lucius, and the pair were jointly acclaimed *imperator.* He was thenceforth given the formal style Imperator Caesar L. Aurelius Verus Augustus and served his second consulship in 161.[407] He was voted the annually renewable tribunician power and proconsular *imperium* on 7th March 161. The office of *pontifex maximus* was, however, deemed to be indivisible, and was granted to Marcus Aurelius rather than Verus – whether by agreement or by *fiat* is impossible to say. In 163, he married Marcus Aurelius' daughter Annia Aurelia Galeria Lucilla, later granted the style of Augusta, and they had a daughter and son, both of whom died young and their names are unknown.[408] Lucilla was to be exiled to Capri by Commodus for allegedly inspiring a conspiracy against him and was later killed.

Verus was nominated to lead an expedition in 162 to quell a potential conflict with Parthia over a client state in the buffer zone between the two empires: Armenia. The following year Armenia was re-taken and one of the commanders, the future usurper Avidius Cassius, went on to invade Parthia and capture the capital, Ctesiphon. The key to the entire campaign was that whilst Verus appears to have lazed around in Antioch enjoying himself (and a rather unsuitable courtesan called Panthea), he was being excellently served by his generals, who turned out to be able and loyal.

Thus, little real credit was accorded to Verus for winning the war, which was celebrated by a triumphal return to Rome in 166. Nevertheless, the Emperor's right was to celebrate a triumph, even if he had not been leading from the front. One is almost inclined to give Verus the credit for leaving the campaign to the professionals, who amply justified his faith in them. The only foolish thing was to be perceived to be luxuriating in the oriental

---

403   Ceionius Postumus, HA *V. Albini* 4, 5-6, also suggesting descent from the patrician Postumii Albini of the Republic.

404   PLRE I Albinus 9 & stemma 21 (p. 1141)

405   PLRE I stemma 13 (p. 1138)

406   ILS 357

407   ILS 366

408   Settipani allows the daughter to live to age 16 (182) marry the senator [Ti] Claudius Pompeianus Quintianus and have a son., L. Aurelius Commodus Pompeianus (consul 209): *op.cit.* 302

fleshpots whilst the fighting was actually going on. Yet he demonstrated another positive side to his character by inviting Marcus, his co-ruler, to share his triumph with him – as well he might. He was given the additional styles of Armeniacus in 164 and Parthicus Maximus in 165, both a year before Marcus.[409] He added Medicus in the year of his triumph, which was held on 12 October 166, the additional *agnomen* granted to celebrate suppression of a revolt amongst the Medes. By 167, *Pater Patriae* had also been added to his titles and a third consulship followed that year, with imperial acclamations in 163, 165, 166 and 167. Yet this successful campaign is widely believed to have been responsible for the importation of a particularly pernicious plague from Parthia, which weakened the empire at a crucial point.

No sooner had these festivities been concluded than an attack began on the Danube frontier, followed by a full-scale assault on the Empire in this quarter. In 168 both Emperors set off to deal with the situation, although they were not far along the way when news reached them that the trouble had been dealt with. Nevertheless, they pressed on, oversaw a re-ordering of the defences in the sector and then set off back to Rome. On the return journey Verus suffered a stroke, was carried on to Altinum (Altino near Venice) and died three days later, very late in January or early February AD168, his demise having very possibly been accelerated by the plague. He was subsequently deified by the senate.

Later, Marcus Aurelius wrote of him in his *Meditations* that he was a brother 'whose natural qualities were a standing challenge to my own self-discipline; at the same time as his deferential affection warmed my heart.'

MACER
68, April – October

Clodius Macer was a provincial commander who took it upon himself to oppose Nero in the turmoil following the *pronunciamento* of Galba, by whom he was eventually killed. Lucius Clodius Macer was praetorian legate (colonel) commanding the one legion stationed in Africa Proconsularis in the time of Nero. He revolted in April or May 68, cutting off the food supply of Rome, possibly at the instigation of Calvia Crispinilla – a vengeful *femme fatale* who had been a former mistress of Nero – which cannot have done much for the emperor's equanimity. Probably at first encouraged by Galba, Macer raised a legion, the Legio I Macriana Liberatrix, in addition to the Legio III Augusta that he already commanded, presumably raising suspicion that he harboured imperial ambitions and, once installed at Rome in October 68, Galba had him killed by his provincial procurator Trebonius Garutianus, probably aided by Papirus, a senior centurion.[410]

Although Macer did not directly assume an imperial style, he minted *denarii* at Carthage bearing his portrait and name along with the legend S[enatus] C[onsultum], suggesting senatorial approval for his actions, which

409 Barnes (1967) 71
410 Tacitus, *Histories*, i. 7, i. 73 & ii. 37; cf. Morgan (2006) 40, 43, 96, 258

he is unlikely to have received; certainly there is no attestation for such a thing. It harks back to a Republican tradition and style dormant since the Second Triumvirate. He also styled himself *liberator* and *propraetor Africae*, which suggests he was putting down markers as to his ambitions.[411]

As a legionary legate, Clodius was relatively junior, having only held the praetorship, nor is he known to have had any discernible family connections, least of all to the imperial house. Unless he was a scion of the family of L. Clodius Rufus (suffect consul in 7BC) and, say, a woman from the praetorian Mytilenian family of Pompeius Macer, he was probably the first of his family to enter the senate, which would leave him with even less leverage as events unfolded. Indeed, Tacitus called him a 'small-time tyrant', the term *tyrannus* being established short-hand for a usurper in his time. He cannot be seen as an overt would-be emperor, as evidenced by the lack of a laurel wreath on his coin portrait, but by issuing a coinage, raising troops and acting independently, he was everything but. Certainly, he was seen by Galba as such or he would not have gone to the trouble of having him liquidated. It may be that the SC on his coinage suggests that he aspired to restore the Republic in some way.

MACRIANUS (I)
260, 17th May – 261, April

Macrianus was the elder son of the man on the spot – also Macrianus – when Valerian made his undignified exit as a prisoner of the Persians in spring 260, who together with his younger son, Quietus, attempted to stabilise the military situation before establishing both sons as emperors in Valerian's place.

[T.] Fulvius Macrianus was Valerian's equestrian *procurator arcae et praepositus annonae* – his quartermaster general.[412] Few sources present Macrianus' refusal to attempt a rescue of the Emperor as an act of self-promoting treachery, as anyone reading the history of the previous forty years might have supposed. Indeed, things were so chaotic that the elevation of a responsible general on the spot to the purple was both inevitable and militarily desirable.

The elder Macrianus was hailed as emperor at the urging of the barbarian Pretorian Prefect Ballista[413] but declined on the grounds of age and infirmity – perhaps an unconvincing response, considering he had so recently been Valerianus' second in command in the campaign. Instead, he proposed his two sons, present as legionary legates, [P.] Fulvius Junius Macrianus and T. Fulvius Junius Quietus, who had been appointed as military tribunes by Valerian according to the *Historia Augusta* but in fact were probably by then senators of praetorian rank.[414] Stein adduces the descent of this family

---

411 RIC I. Clodius Macer 6, 15, 35 var. & 36
412 PIR² F549; PLRE I. Macrianus 2
413 An imperial claimant himself according to HA. *Tyr. Trig.* 18: a groundless supposition.
414 PIR² F546, 547; PLRE I. Macrianus 3, Quietus 2; *Op. cit., Tyr. Trig.* 12. 10

from an alliance in the mid second century between the Aurelii Galli and the Neratii Prisci, citing a number of pieces of circumstantial evidence.[415] If this could be better authenticated, it would give the two imperial claimants a connection with the 4th-century consular Neratii and through them to the Empress Justina, second wife of Valentinian I. Doubts obtrude, however, for the elder Macrianus was only an equestrian officer, albeit a very senior one, and thus is unlikely to have been able to boast a glittering array of consular ancestors, especially as there is nothing concrete to connect him with the man it is has been suggested might have been his father, L. Neratius L.[f. Gal.] Junius Mac[er], a senator and patron of Saepinum who had married a Fulvia Prisca.[416] His wife was probably of senatorial family and from the younger son's name, probably called Junia and thus conceivably a daughter or sister of Junius Macer.

The two sons were immediately recognised in the important provinces of Asia, Syria and Egypt and, with Gallienus under almost unsupportable pressure in the west, for a few months it looked as if the eastern part of the Empire was going to become a separate polity, presaging the formal division instigated under the Tetrarchs two generations later.

Macrianus set out for the Balkans with his father as C-in-C, probably with the object of gathering extra support and reaching Rome to legitimise his position with the senate. They no doubt banked on using the corn imports from Alexandria, which they controlled, to add leverage to their ambitions. Unfortunately for them, they arrived in Illyricum just as Gallienus' general Domitianus was mopping up after helping Aureolus depose Regalianus and were defeated by him in battle, both father and son being killed in action some time after 17 May 261.

MACRIANUS (II)

261, May

P. [or T.] Fulvius Junius Macrianus, son of the foregoing, was an ex-praetor and legate serving under his father, who was probably acclaimed on 17 May 260. He was styled Imperator Caesar Fulvius Macrianus Pius Felix Augustus but it is highly unlikely that he received any recognition from the senate.[417] We can thus say that he assumed the powers and chief priesthood, although he and his brother Quietus could have set up some kind of conciliar body or quasi-senate at Antioch, appointing themselves consuls and no doubt allowing various opulent local magnates to share suffect consulships too, putting their skills to use in administering the vast swathe of territory they now controlled. According to papyri found in Egypt, they entered into a second joint consulship on 17 May 261, confirming that Macrian was

---

415 PIR² IV (1966) p. 329

416 PIR² F565. *HA* tells us that the emperor's mother was a 'noblewoman': Tyr. Trig. 12.13, 1

417 Coins.

believed in Egypt to be then still living, although in fact he may have already met his fate; communications with the west were still disrupted at this time.[418]

Having stabilised the situation in Syria, it was then decided that both Macriani should go to Rome and establish the sons' rule throughout the Empire, Gallienus being as far as they knew struggling with the Alemanni on the Rhine and in any case damaged goods in the light of the fate that had encompassed his father in Persia. Quietus was left with Ballista to hold the east.

The alleged young and homonymous son of the younger Macrianus, is said by the author of the *Historia Augusta* to have been elevated to the purple in the Balkans whilst his father and grandfather were en route to the west, for which there is no evidence elsewhere, nor even for the young man's existence. The *Historia* alleged noble birth through his mother. He was apparently killed with his father on 17 May.

MACRINUS
217, 11th April – 218, 8th June

Macrinus had the dubious distinction of having been Rome's first emperor of equestrian rank, raised to the purple in the wake of the assassination of Caracalla, but whose efforts in stabilising his rule and ending the campaign against Parthia were thwarted by the Syrian faction of the Severan house, who quickly caused him to be overthrown and replaced by Elagabalus.

M. Opellius Macrinus[419] was a Numidian, born at Caesarea (Sharshal/ Cherchell) in Mauretania in 164, probably of equestrian parents. The fact that he was called Macrinus and his son Diadumenianus (Diadumenus in the *Historia Augusta* and some later sources) is a strange coincidence, bearing in mind that Nero had a freedman called Macrinus, alive in 64, whose father had been called Diadumenus.[420] Could there have been some remote line of distaff descent from him to the usurper? Although referred to as a 'Moor', he could have just as easily been of Roman colonising stock; the 'Moor' soubriquet seems to have been applied pejoratively in either case. Whilst the bearing of the names of the Neronian freedman and his father (above) may be coincidence, it is worth noting that the only previous Opellius with an élite appointment was a man of this name who served as a legionary legate under Mark Antony in Judaea around 35BC. Perhaps this man, having ended up on the losing side, rather than return to Rome and risk proscription by Octavianus after 31, went into exile in the train of the dynast's daughter by Cleopatra, who married Juba II of Numidia, later King of Western Mauretania, and settled there.

Macrinus trained as an advocate and his relatively undistinguished bureaucratic equestrian career flourished under the patronage of the African henchman of Severus, C. Fulvius Plautianus, whom he eventually succeeded

---

418 P. Oxy. 2710
419 FS 2579; ILS 461; PIR² O108
420 ILS 5798

as joint Commander of the Praetorian Guard around 212, having previously served as a procurator.[421] He is usually credited in the ancient sources with being prime mover of the plot to assassinate Caracalla, but the fact that it took three days to acclaim him after the murder suggests that those who engineered the emperor's death had not initially decided on a candidate to succeed him, or that it was a comparatively spontaneous act. Alternatively, the candidate upon whom they had first decided perhaps refused – possibly they had lighted on Macrinus' elderly and respected colleague as Praetorian Prefect, M. Oclatinius Adventus. It seems likely that the proscriptions of both Severus and his elder son had eliminated any credible candidates, any *capaces imperii*, from the ranks of the Severan kin or the governing élite in the senate. As it is, with hindsight, it might appear that Macrinus merely took advantage of a confused situation and had himself acclaimed, assuming the name Severus and bestowing that of Antoninus on his son, whom he associated with his rule by nominating him Caesar.

On his accession of 11 April 217, he styled himself Imperator M. Opellius Severus Macrinus Augustus, adding Pius Felix when he had been recognised by the senate (probably through relief at having seen the back of the murderous Caracalla), adlected into the Patriciate, given the senatorial rank of an ex-consul and declared *pater patriae,* probably in June.[422] They also granted him the tribunician and proconsular powers, nominally from his accession and renewable on 10 December each year. He was also recognised as supreme pontiff. He was ordinary consul for the year following, 218.

He married Nonia Celsa according to the *Historia Augusta*, but no coins were struck in her name, nor is any wife mentioned in any other source. If she existed at all, she may well have been dead prior to Macrinus' acclamation.[423] The name of her son suggested to Birley that she was in fact a daughter of the Puteolan *eques* Cn. Haius Diadumenianus, who had been procurator of both provinces of the emperor's native Mauretania about 202.[424] Birley speculated that her name therefore may have been Haia, not Nonia, unless her name *is* reported accurately by the *Historia Augusta*.[425] The only child of the union of whom we have knowledge is the son, Diadumenianus.

The reign began with some minor extirpation of difficult elements and by some administrative changes to bring trusted men into important posts. Macrinus allowed the late Emperor's mother Julia Domna to remain at Antioch and rather foolishly left her to her own devices, the sort of mistake the brutal Severus would never have made. He was aware, however, that she was seriously ill and must have assumed that she was no threat, although in reality she was conspiring actively, only starving herself to death when ordered to leave the Syrian capital when wind of her activities reached him.

---

421 Dio 78.11.1f

422 ILS 462, 463; HA, *V. Macr.* 7.1

423 *Ibid.*, *V. Diadumen.* 7.7

424 *Op. cit.* 191; PIR² H8. Her brother was a new senator of the same name, suffect consul by 202.

425 Birley (1988) 191-192

Even then, the ancient sources may have misunderstood, for she is thought to have had cancer, probably of the breast, and may have reached the stage of her affliction when she could no longer eat anyway. In either case, it suited the Severan party in the province very well to acquire a second martyr.

All might have gone well but for the fact that the delay in the Parthian campaign caused by Caracalla's self-indulgence in staying too long at Edessa, followed by the further delay caused by the succession, had allowed the Parthians, previously in disarray, to re-group. When the two sides met near Nisibis, the battle ostensibly ended in stalemate, although the subsequent truce concluded by Macrinus included the payment of a colossal subsidy to the Parthian king, which rather suggests that the emperor was at more of a disadvantage than might at first seem apparent. The 200,000,000 sesterces settlement and the fact that Roman arms were by no means triumphant, told heavily against Macrinus, as did his removal of some military privileges in the aftermath, probably as a punishment for the soldiers' failure to win a victory.

Consequently, a rebellion, without doubt fomented by the family of Julia Domna, broke out on 15-16 May 218, when the 14-year-old nephew of Caracalla, Varius Avitus, son of Domna's sister Julia Maesa, was brought from his native Emesa and smuggled into the camp of a nearby legion, where the officers and men acclaimed him, believing, it was said, that he was Caracalla's natural son.

Macrinus did not at first take this development too seriously, except that he proclaimed his son, Diadumenianus, already recognised as Caesar, as co-Augustus on that very same day, hoping thereby to win the propaganda war. Soon, however, Macrinus's forces began to suffer a stream of desertions, which a further donative failed to stem. The emperor thereupon fell back on Antioch to re-group. An engagement was fought with the rebels outside the city, in which Macrinus – to most people's surprise – was worsted, whereupon he retreated north in the hope of rallying support in Europe and sent his son east to Parthia. In the event, Macrinus did not make it across the Bosphorous, nor Diadumenianus across the Euphrates. The former was caught and killed allegedly on 8 June, although it could have been nearer the end of the month. There is an alternative tradition that has him surviving in hiding until October 218.[426] The 10-year-old Diadumenianus was captured and executed in late June.

MAEONIUS

267

Maeonius was an ephemeral supposed usurper in Syria following the end of the Palmyrene usurper Odenathus. The death of Odenathus and his elder sons appears to have been devised by a jealous cousin, named only in the *Historia Augusta* as Maeonius.[427] That work avers that in consequence he

---

426 Dio, LXXVIII, 39.1, cf. Herodian 5, 3.11 & 5, 5.8
427 Zonaras, 12, 24

promptly declared himself emperor.[428] If so, his reign was short, for there were no coins. The likelihood is that the cousin, whether called Maeonius or otherwise, may well have murdered the dynast and his son, but is quite unlikely to have made a bid for the imperial purple; after all, his victim had been careful to avoid just that. If the story is true, then it is possible that Maeonius was acting on behalf of the then-absent Zenobia, who indeed assumed power without delay. If that surmise is correct, then she probably despatched her hired assassin quickly to obviate any attempts at power on his own behalf. This pretender is best treated as a chimaera.

MAGNENTIUS
350, 18th January – 353, 10th August

Magnentius was an army commander who brought about the assassination of Constans I, but who spent the succeeding years fending off his brother Constantius II, having provoked thereby a ruinous civil war.

Fl[avius] Magnus Magnentius was a professional soldier who rose high in imperial service. The sources are united in calling him a barbarian (and attributing to him in consequence numerous negative attributes) but differ in whether he was the son of a German or a Briton. The latter might seem the more likely, and this tradition asserts that he was born at Ambianum (Amiens, Gaul) and that his mother was Frankish – hence perhaps the German supposition. He was probably born in 303. His earliest soldiering was done as a member of an infantry regiment (probably one of the old legions) on the north-west borders, but under Constantine I he advanced rapidly becoming a *protector* (officer in the Imperial Guard). At the time of his bid for supreme power he was *comes rei militaris*, imperial military advisor/commander with the *Ioviani* and *Herculani* (field army regiments constituted under the first Tetrarchs) under his command in Italy.[429]

On being proclaimed he styled himself Dominus Noster Magnus Magnentius Imperator Augustus Pius Felix, although this changed twice, to the much more traditional Imperator Caesar Magnus Magnentius Augustus and then the more pretentious Dominus Noster Magnentius Invicto Principi Victor et Triumfatus [*sic*] Semper Augustus.[430] Whether he managed to obtain recognition by the senate at Rome is doubtful, or Constantius II would surely have wreaked a terrible revenge upon its members, but it is claimed that this is precisely what Magnentius did after the failure of the revolt of Nepotianus.

He at first hoped that he would obtain recognition from Constantius II, especially as the latter was hard-pressed, and hence his adoption of the additional honorific name of Flavius. In this he failed. Furthermore, he had a reputation for brutality, and his usurpation caused consternation in Rome, where Nepotianus, the nephew of Constantine I, declared himself emperor in opposition that summer but lasted barely a month before one

---

428 HA *V. Gall.* 13,1 & *V. Tyr. Trig.*15, 55-6 & 17, 1-3
429 PLRE I Magnentius
430 ILS 743, 744 & 742

of Magnentius' marshals suppressed him. He then appointed Magnus Decentius, apparently his younger brother, *caesar* to hold the west whilst he moved against Constantius II.[431] He served as consul in 351 (recognised only in the west) and again in 353, which was only recognised in the Gallic Empire area. In September 351 he fought a bloody battle at Mursa (on the River Drava, Croatia), which was a Pyrrhic victory for the Eastern Emperor, for Magnentius, although defeated, remained in the field with some of his forces intact. He retreated to Gaul and once again recreated a form of Gallic empire, dormant since 340, and managed to retain it until the opening of the campaigning season of 353, when Constantius II came after him again, defeating him near Lugdunum (Lyons). He committed suicide on 10 August 353 to avoid being handed over to Constantius. He left a widow, a young lady of senatorial ancestry called Justina, who soon afterwards married the future Emperor Valentinian I (qv) and later encompassed the fall of Magnus Maximus (qv).

MAGNUS
235, late March – early April

Magnus was a rival claimant to Maximin I Thrax on the Rhine following the death of Alexander Severus, whose attempt to establish himself failed utterly. Magnus emerged as an usurper as the leader of an anti-Maximin faction in the Rhine army, a section of which – perhaps appalled by the fate of the young Alexander to whose family at least they were devoted – acclaimed him on hearing the news of the murder.[432]

He was apparently a patrician ex-consul but one who must have lacked conviction as a potential ruler, for he was refused recognition by the senate, although they may have been cowed by the fearsome reputation of Maximin or by the prospect of the new Emperor wreaking a dreadful revenge, as had Severus. They therefore officially deposed him – if we may trust the *Historia Augusta*.[433] We can, however, doubt this, as they were quick enough to recognise the two Gordians three years later. His identity is fairly clear, for a senator C. Petronius Magnus who appears on a list of patrons of the City of Canusium in 223 seems at a later date to have had his name erased, something only a *damnatio memoriae* could explain. He was praetor between 211 and 217, but the date of his suffect consulship is not clear. As an ex-consul in 235, it might have been held c. 218/223.[434] Unfortunately, there were several families of senatorial Petronii at this – as most – dates, and no evidence has yet emerged to link Magnus with any of them.[435] Furthermore, the *cognomen* is fairly common. There was another Magnus, a patrician

---

431 PLRE I Decentius 3
432 Herodian 7, 1. 4-8 ; PIR² M100
433 *V. Max.* 10. 1-6
434 ILS 6121, cf. PIR² P286
435 A descent from T. Pactumeius Magnus (suffect consul 183) seems possible, cf. PIR² P27, 28 & 29

suffect consul in the following generation who could have been a son, and of course, the family of Petronius Maximus and Olybrius is peppered with people called Magnus. In any case, Magnus' attempt failed miserably and he was executed by Maximin.

MAGNUS MAXIMUS
380/383 – 388, 28th July

Often dismissed as an usurper, Magnus Maximus seems to have engineered a far-reaching settlement to secure the frontiers of Britain before ruling the western empire (less Italy and North Africa) efficiently but going down to defeat against Theodosius I after having taken control of the whole of the west and deposing Valentinian II.[436]

In a largely unchallenged and universally acknowledged reign of over five years, his legitimacy was as strong as most other rulers of the era. He certainly started out as an usurper and from Britain, too, as had Constantine I, whom he probably regarded as having set a wholly valid precedent.

His date of birth is not known, but having a young family, it may reasonably be assumed that he must have been born around 340/346, in Hispania Gallaeca (Galicia, Spain). His recorded kinship with Theodosius, although not specified, was probably reasonably close, as he had served with him under his father in Britain in 367-369, when it has been suggested that he was the officer who suppressed the rebel or usurper Valentinus, although this remains unproven. They almost certainly served together again in the war against the African rebel Firmus a few years later, co-operating with the claimant's loyal brother, Gildo. Here he may have been the officer who settled the tribal groupings on the southern border of Africa as semi-independent principalities under the supervision of a prefect, an apparently successful arrangement which was praised by St Jerome a generation later.

He then more or less disappears from the record until 378, when he was present in the aftermath of the defeat and death of Valens at Adrianople. Gratian seems to have made him *comes rei militaris* in Britain (C-in-C armed forces) probably on the recommendation or insistence of Theodosius I, the island by then divided into four, perhaps by then five provinces. Once *en poste*, he appears to have inflicted a heavy defeat on the Picts and the Scots in northern Britain, but thanks to a re-calibration of the Chronicle of 452, seems to have lost little time in being acclaimed emperor, possibly even before his defeat of the raiders, probably in 380 rather than on the previously accepted date of 383. It seems clear from the emperor's legendary, British and post-Roman, insular legacy that he almost certainly was the person who re-settled the frontier tribes of Britain (even including some Irish elements) defensively and semi-autonomously, in the same way as had been done, probably under his auspices, in Africa a decade earlier. He set their leaders up as semi-independent princes – client states, in the north, west and south-west. If we can accept this, then he was the man who laid the foundations for the

---

436 Craven (2023) *passim*

continuation of the independence of the British frontier zones, long after central control of Britain had collapsed in the fifth century, hence explaining the ubiquity of his name in post-Roman insular sources.

In spring 383, by this time as Emperor and following an incursion across the Rhine of Alemanni under Fraomar, he crossed to the Continent and deposed Gratian after a confrontation near Lutetia Parisiorum (Paris) after which Andragathius had the young Emperor brutally killed, probably against Maximus' wishes and complicating future relations with Theodosius.[437]

Having deposed Gratian he established himself at Augusta Treverorum (Trier). He appears to have undergone baptism prior to his elevation, telling Pope Siricius that he had gone 'from the font to the throne'. The assertion that he wholly or partially denuded the Britain of troops is unlikely to be strictly true, although he would have crossed with sufficient forces to confront the Emperor and these troops would have been mobile units (*comitatenses*), freed for the task by his frontier settlement.

Maximus styled himself Imperator Caesar Dominus Noster Magnus Maximus Pius Felix Augustus. At this point, Maximus sent an embassy to Theodosius who, although apparently discomfited by the murder of his western colleague, was busy with Persian perturbations on his eastern frontier and was either pleased or obliged to accept his old comrade-in-arms's *de facto* position. For his part Maximus, in a deal brokered by St Ambrose, senatorial former provincial governor and strong-minded Bishop of Milan, agreed to respect the realm of Valentinian II in Italy and the Balkans. Circumstantial evidence suggests that although he did not control Italy, he obtained some degree of recognition from the senate, by which, in later decades, his memory appears to have been held in considerable respect.

Despite the accord which secured him recognition, both sides took precautions against a push south by Maximus: Valentinian's *magister militum* Bauto fortified the Alpine passes against a surprise attack, whilst Maximus for his part set out his stall by naming his young son Flavius Victor as co-augustus, probably in 384.[438] The two adopted the style Dominus Noster Magnus Maximus et Flavius Victor Invictis et Perpetuis Augusti.[439] The older man seems also to have adopted the *agnomen* Britannicus.[440] No doubt they accepted the tribunician and proconsular powers, probably from a provincial council-cum-senate, but there is no suggestion that the position of *pontifex maximus* was conferred or assumed, for Maximus was a zealous Christian and moved against the variant set of beliefs being advocated by the Spanish bishop Priscillianus, being the first Christian Emperor to condemn a Christian (Priscillianus himself) for heresy. He was consul (in the West only) in 384 and again in 388.

---

437 PLRE I Andragathius 3
438 He is called Magnius Victor Maximus [*sic*] on some coins, and the name Flavius was probably assumed on his elevation to Augustus. The mainly hostile contemporary sources call him a child, but his coin portraits seem to show a youth in his early teens: PLRE I Victor 14
439 ILS788; PRE I Maximus 39
440 Birley *loc.cit.*

Magnus Maximus,
gold solidus of c. 384
showing the Emperor
wearing a diadem.
The legend reads:
D[ominus] N[oster]
Mag[nus][Maximus
[P[ius] F[elix]
Aug[ustus] (Private
collection, Germany)

The rule of Maximus is nowadays accepted to have been successful. The Alemanni were put in their place and his good relations with several barbarian leaders ensured peace, during which the economy prospered, and he also remitted taxation to some extent and built up good relationships with the senatorial nobility within his *imperium*. He also streamlined the provincial administration. Ancient authors were critical, but by no means uniformly so, Orosius and Sulpicius Severus giving us a much more favourable picture of him, unlike the senator Pacatus' toadying panegyric, declaimed in front of Theodosius in 389, in which he went out of his way to blacken Maximus' reputation and deny his kinship with the dynasty; it is a pity Symmachus' panegyric on Maximus delivered the year before has not survived; it might well have given us the other side of the picture, albeit, no doubt, well burnished.[441]

The end of his reign was caused (not unsurprisingly) by ambition, spurred by religious orthodoxy. In 387 he invaded Italy, the *casus belli* being the eradication of Arianism in the Empire, in the person of dowager Empress Justina. He took Milan, forcing Justina and her son to Aquileia from whence they fled to Theodosius in the east. Maximus was now in control of nearly all of the western part of the empire. He had his position confirmed by the senate at Rome which he visited in person, extended his reforming government to his new Dioceses. For his part, Theodosius seemed at first likely to accept his cousin's *status quo*, but the exiled empress Justina, playing on human nature following the death of Theodosius' wife, pushed her daughter Aelia Galla

---

441 Quoted in Haarer (2014) 167

forward and, once the emperor had fallen in love with her, demanded that he act against Maximus in return for agreeing to allow them to marry.

Consequently, it was not until June 388 that he made his move into the Balkans, countered by his adversary. The outcome was that the Western ruler was worsted in two out of three battles and was captured at Aquileia. The defeated Emperor had some reasonable hope of having his life spared by Theodosius, who enjoyed a reputation for clemency and, when confronted by the Eastern Emperor, emphasised the point that he had sought and obtained his acquiescence in his position and had only moved into Italy in the interests of orthodoxy and the good of the empire. Whatever Theodosius had decided to do, however, was forestalled by his officers who, taking no chances, took Maximus and executed him shortly afterwards at the third milestone from Aquileia.

We hear little of Maximus' Empress (called Helena in most insular legendary sources)[442] although Sulpicius Severus, without naming her, describes her as a pious woman who waited silently upon St Martin whilst her husband entertained him to supper. Maximus also had a mother living (not named, nor, it would seem, made Augusta) and daughters. Not only are they mentioned by St Ambrose (but again, unfortunately not by name) as being entrusted to a relation of Theodosius after the death of Maximus, but one was apparently cured by St Illidius 3rd Bishop of Augustonemetum (Clermont) before 385.[443] Indeed, the suggestion that she, or another daughter, made a glittering senatorial marriage, perhaps to Anicius Probinus, is to some extent confirmed by the Byzantine historian Procopius, who claimed that Petronius Maximus was a descendant of Magnus Maximus.[444]

MAJORIAN
457, 1st April – 461, 2nd August

Majorian was a competent successor of Avitus, who made considerable progress in reforming the administration of the west and in reclaiming much of Spain and Gaul for the empire but whose failure to neutralise the aggression of the Vandals in Africa led to his death at the hands of his barbarian *magister militum*, Ricimer.

Following the deposition of Avitus on 17 October 456, the Empire was technically once more united under the Eastern Emperor Marcian. Majorian and his *magister militum* Ricimer were thereafter effectively Marcianus' viceroys in the west, but crucially, Ricimer was the senior partner as *magister militum*, whereas his colleague was merely *comes domesticorum* – commander of an Imperial Guard without an emperor to protect. Nevertheless, it would appear that they were content to exercise full powers under the eastern court for the duration of that autumn and winter. However, in February 457, Ricimer laid down office and accepted the title of patrician from Marcian

---

442 But one insular source calls her Keindreich, an approximate British/Old Welsh equivalent of Latin Speciosa (or Formosa).

443 Quoted in Morris (1972) 419.n 2

444 Proc, *HB* 1, 4.16

and Majorian succeeded him as *magister militum*. It may be that being subordinate to Constantinople cramped their style and restricted what they felt they needed to do to protect the west and, if possible, to restore it, especially following the Vandal raid on Rome of spring 455. Therefore, on 1 April, Majorian assumed the purple at Columellae, near Ravenna, although for some reason he was not formally acclaimed in Ravenna itself until 28 December and in between times used his military rank, probably because he was reluctant to assume the supreme office. It is possible that the formal installation had to await recognition by the eastern court.

The new Emperor, Flavius Julius Valerius Maiorianus, was of Roman stock and was relatively young, having been born c. 415. Little is known about his family, except that Sidonius Apollinaris tells us that his maternal grandfather, also Maiorianus, had been *magister utriusque militum* in Illyricum under Theodosius I, meeting with considerable success against the various swarming and mingling tribal upheavals of the Danubian littoral.[445] It may be that the elder Maiorianus was a Gaul or had been recruited from Theodosius' Spanish friends or family circle like (or by) Magnus Maximus. Nor do his two other names (bearing in mind that the *praenomen* Flavius was by this date more of an honorific than a real name) give us any real clue, both being remarkably common, even at this period. We hear nothing of a wife, nor of any children. Indeed, he may have been unmarried or widowed, for at one stage he was canvassed as a possible husband for Placidia, the elder daughter of Valentinian III, itself a possible reason for his apparent retirement prior to the murder of Aëtius.

Majorian had enjoyed a career in the army under Aëtius, seeing action against the Visigoths and the Franks in the 440s, but by the time of his old commander's murder he had retired to the country, probably in Gaul; Sidonius claimed that the jealousy of Aëtius's wife had brought about his retirement. He was made *comes domesticorum* by Valentinian III after Aëtius's murder and was considered a possible successor when the Emperor was killed. Instead, Petronius Maximus confirmed him in his post, as did Avitus. On 28 February he succeeded Ricimer as *magister militum*.[446] Shortly afterwards, he won a victory over a substantial incursion into Italy of Alamanni from Rhaetia.

As Emperor he adopted the style Dominus Noster Julius Maiorianus Perpetuus Augusutus[447] and was acknowledged by the senate and no doubt granted by them those powers that were traditional and which he would have exercised with or without their sanction, although he was theoretically one of their number. He was acknowledged by the eastern court sometime between April and December 457, most probably the latter. He was western ordinary consul for 458. His elevation led to considerable discontent in Gaul, where the deposition of their man Avitus caused much resentment. According to Sidonius, this led Marcellus (qv) to make a bid for the purple, although details of it are

---

445 PLRE I Maiorianus
446 PLRE II Maiorianus
447 ILS810

entirely lacking in the sources.[448] No more is heard of this and it is to be assumed that it fizzled out without serious repercussions. Certainly, Majorian was obliged to assert himself in southern Gaul before being able to find acceptance.

It is often said that Ricimer ruled the west through a series of puppet emperors, but the reality was somewhat more complex. Majorian was no puppet. He was a military man of proven success, a member of an established senatorial family, and virtually the equal of his friend and brother-in-arms Ricimer. The difference was that Ricimer had the ultimate hold over the largely barbarian-recruited army through his own family connections, and when the chips were down it was likely that Ricimer's will would prevail. Yet Majorian was faced with a declining population throughout the west, and the crushing burden of taxation to support the army was leading, amongst other things, to younger sons being forced into the church to save the expense of raising them, further restricting the number of people who could marry and raise children. He passed a number of laws to deal with this, remitted taxation and issued a decree against the dismantling of historic buildings in Rome on the pretext that the stone was required for public works. This must be the first piece of official conservation legislation ever passed in Western Europe, and was highly enlightened if, in all probability, largely ignored.[449]

The most pressing military problem was still the Vandal occupation of Africa and the economic problems it posed to Italy. The emperor recruited the *comes* of Illyricum, Marcellinus (in reality a semi-independent dynast by this time), to clear Sicily of Vandals, which was successfully accomplished. He meanwhile entered Spain and reclaimed much of the peninsula before preparing an expeditionary force to invade Africa via Mauretania from Carthago Nova (Cartagena). This was done with the full co-operation of the somewhat chastened Visigoths and demonstrated that although the Western Empire no longer enjoyed *direct* control over all its provinces, it was successfully operating a form of federal empire or temporary commonwealth of associated and theoretically subject polities, of which Visigothic Spain was one. However, the Vandal king Gaiseric struck a pre-emptive blow, managing to neutralise this existential threat by destroying part of the fleet before it could set sail and by laying waste much of Mauretania, so that it would not be able to sustain an invading army. This bought the Vandal kingdom a breathing space of some 70 years before the Eastern Empire was able successfully to dislodge the Vandals after nearly a century in possession.

Nothing daunted, the Emperor turned his attention to Gaul. Although there was still chaos and areas where the Empire's writ hardly ran – Cologne had been finally lost in 457, during the interregnum – Majorian clearly

---

448 Sidonius Apollinaris, *Letters* I. 11, 6. The Marcellus must have been the Praetorian Prefect of Gaul c. 441-443: PLRE II Marcellus 2 and not the Illyrian Marcellinus.

449 In times of crisis, the practice was to demolish all or part of a building to remove the bronze cramps which anchored the marble facing slabs or structural ashlar blocks together to melt down; the bronze fixings could by re-cycled as weapons and the marble ground down to make lime. The last recorded instance was that undertaken by the Eastern Emperor Constans III in the 660s which led to the collapse of many buildings: Llewellyn (1993) 157-158

expected to be able to restore matters even at this late stage, and Hugh Elton has set out to show how that aim was not necessarily the chimaera that one might suppose.[450]

Indeed, Majorian had all the natural ability and qualities the imperial office required at this time and could have pulled things back, at least in Gaul, were it not for his patrician, Ricimer. It seems to have occurred to the patrician that his imperial colleague was too independent-minded and competent for the barbarian to be able to pursue his own agenda, which centred on aggrandising himself and, if possible, loosening the hold the Visigoths had on his own people, the Sueves, in Spain. With the excuse of the failure of the Vandal expedition as his cue, Ricimer intercepted and deposed the Emperor on 2 August 461 and five days later had his former friend and comrade-in-arms put to death.

MARCELLINUS – see MARCELLUS (II)

MARCELLUS (I)
366, 27th May – early June

Marcellus was a short-lived usurper, self-promoted to the purple on the death of his kinsman Procopius, but who failed to survive. Procopius had been captured and executed on 27 May 366. Marcellus, a cousin, whom Procopius had appointed *protector,* on hearing that the usurper was dead, had himself proclaimed in lieu. He was soon caught by the Emperor's forces and also killed, probably early in June. We do not know the details of the relationship between the two, however, and Marcellus had had no time, it would seem, to issue any coins.[451]

MARCELLUS (II)
457, October

Marcellus was an unsuccessful possible usurper, or at least rebel, who sought, it would seem, to take advantage of the deposition of Avitus to maintain Gallic control of the western empire. Simultaneous with the deposition of Avitus and in the months of theoretical direct rule from Constantinople, we have a laconic reference in a letter of Sidonius Apollinaris (a kinsman and one of Avitus' numerous Gallic appointments) to a 'Marcellan conspiracy' He actually wrote '...de cupessendo diademate coniuration Marcellana',[452] which seems a clear suggestion that some other Gallic notable called Marcellus was put up as an imperial claimant, probably in place of Avitus. Yet no coins were issued, and nothing else is known, so it must be assumed that the bid ended very rapidly in failure. The identity of Marcellus is

---

450 Elton (1992) 167-178
451 PLRE I Marcellus 5
452 Sidonius Apollinaris, *ep.* I, 11 6

quite unclear; the best MS does not, it is now agreed, read Marcellinus, as previously accepted, which would have implied that the *magister militum* of Dalmatia was somehow involved, on the face of it highly unlikely.[453] There were a number of Gallic aristocrats around at this period of that name, and only the Marcellus who was praetorian Prefect of Gaul c. 441-443 stands out as a possible candidate, yet we have no evidence that he was still even living fifteen years later. The entire episode is a mystery.

MARCIAN (I)
450, 25th August – 457, 27th January 457

Marcian was the Emperor who persuaded Attila the Hun to move to the west, kept the eastern empire out of wars, re-stocked the treasury, remitted taxes and went some way to dealing with the Monophysite heresy.

As soon as news broke of the death of Theodosius II, there was an hiatus. Conventional wisdom would expect power to pass to the husband of the Emperor's heiress, Valentinian III. This would have re-united the empire, which was not thought desirable by Theodosius' sister, Aelia Pulcheria, nor did she have a high opinion of her western kinsman. She herself was in fact the heiress on the spot, but the Empire was not yet ready for an Empress in her own right; that had to await the accession of Irene three hundred and fifty years later. Again, as when Arcadius had died, the east was in capable hands, for the Augusta's chief support was Flavius Ardaburius Aspar (consul 434). In fact, the late Emperor had allegedly named (or been made to name) the 58-year-old retired colonel (*ex tribunus*) Marcian as his successor when on his deathbed, but his being named was not enough. Pulcheria agreed with the choice, grasped the initiative and early in August married him, although the arrangement included the preservation of the 51-year-old Augusta's chastity. This, however, probably presented the 59-year-old Emperor with little difficulty.

Flavius Valerius Marcianus was born the son of a military man in Illyria – still clearly a breeding ground for military emperors – in 392.[454] He followed his father into the army, enrolling at Philippopolis (Plovdiv, Bulgaria) and was commanding a unit of his own as a tribune by the time he went on campaign against Persia, some time before 420. On his return he was transferred to the *domestici* (Imperial Guards) under the command of Aspar and his father Ardaburius, serving 15 years, including in the fruitless campaign against Vandal king Gaiseric 431-434, when he was captured by the Vandals and met the king. Thereafter he entered the (eastern) senate. He had already been married (his wife had presumably died) and by her had a daughter living but no son.

Marcian I was crowned by the Patriarch of Constantinople, with his new wife seated in full splendour beside him: the first religious coronation of a

---

453 MacGeorge (2002) 64-65
454 He may have been Thracian rather than Illyrian; there is also uncertainty about his *nomen* Valerius: PLRE II Marcianus 8

Roman emperor, for previously the ceremony had been carried out in front of the assembled court in the palace or, with decreasing frequency, in the senate at Rome. The new Emperor took the style of Dominus Noster Flavius Marcianus Pius Felix Augustus and held his first and only consulship in 451.[455] His reign is notable because several problems were resolved, first amongst them being the refusal to pay tribute to the Huns and their subsequent removal to the west. The emperor is often accused of isolationism, of abandoning the west to its fate, but recent opinion has revised this position and it is thought that he gave covert assistance to the campaign by Aëtius against Attila who was considering attacking the Eastern Empire again when he died in 453. By this time, the Emperor had forged alliances with the Ostrogoths, whom he settled as federates south of the Danube to act as a buffer should the Hunnic leader resume hostilities. He also took measures to re-populate and rebuild the cities destroyed by the 447 Hun rampage. He left the east in good political and financial health. With the Hun tribute no longer an issue, the Emperor was able to cut the property tax, which endeared the senate to him, confine the holding of the ruinously expensive praetorship to the sons of *illustres* only (who should have been able afford the required lavish games), ended the sale of government posts and remitted all old (mainly tax) debts, which helped a wider spectrum. Assets also piled up through the lack of military expenditure on campaigns; the decision to stay out of the tumult following the assassination of Valentinian III was a canny one. Essentially, the Emperor was lucky as well as wise.

Discord in the church was making itself felt at the start of the reign, which was settled by Marcian calling the Council of Chalcedon in 451. This established orthodoxy of doctrine, making a modest compromise concerning the nature of Christ to keep the majority of Monophysite Christians within the church. In the short term there was unrest, mainly because the Emperor was so uncompromisingly Christian, but under his successor this died down, although Monophysitism managed to survive and make its influence felt for at least another century and a half.

The Emperor made no provision for a successor, however, and died on 27 January 457, leaving the Empire theoretically united under Avitus, although his daughter and sole heiress had just married the future western ruler Anthemius, who might have been considered as a likely contender for power. In the end Leo I was chosen.

MARCIAN (II)

479, December
480, c. March – May
484, c. April – June

Marcian was an imperial prince whose three attempts at gaining the throne of the east all failed dismally, the last fatally. Flavius Marcianus was one of the sons of the Western Emperor Anthemius, by the daughter of Marcian I,

---

455 ILS824

after whom he was named. Anthemius was the great-grandson of the usurper Procopius (365-366) and had married Aelia Marcia Euphemia, the daughter and heiress of emperor Marcian I (qv). There were three other sons and a daughter, Alypia, married to the western military strong man, Ricimer. Born c. 444, Marcian was consul with Zeno (before he became emperor) in 469 and for a second time, nominated by his father as Western Emperor, in 472 but, confusingly, as eastern consul. The year before, Leo I had made him *magister militum* at court and patrician on his marriage to his daughter Leontia, then about 14. He survived his father's destruction and his elder brother's death by remaining at Constantinople, where he supported the revolt of Basiliscus but, like most people, turned against him later.[456] Marcian was probably twice married and had a son, Procopius, by his first union and daughters with Leontia.

Marcian was the only usurping emperor to have survived two attempts at supreme power (which one might have thought would have instilled an inclination to caution) in order to have a third. His first came about in late 479, when he raised the standard of revolt aginst Zeno, hoping to exploit a wave of unpopularity against him in the capital and fuelled by resentment of Zeno's treatment of Verina, Empress of Leo I. In any case, he argued, was he himself not only the son of an Emperor but also married to a woman who was *porphyrogenita* – born in the purple – unlike the Empress Ariadne, who had been born *before* her father Leo's accession? These, of course, were not exactly copper-bottomed arguments by any estimation. Nevertheless, probably in the December he gathered a motley force of barbarian and Roman troops, supported by three senior commanders and by his brothers, the patricians Procopius Anthemius and Romulus.

The Emperor's Guard was under the command of the patrician Illus, who was unexpectedly defeated and retired across the Bosphorus. The operation was thus a complete success as far as it had gone, but at the crucial moment hesitation and poor management caused his support to slip away and after a few days he was captured by Illus and sent to Caesarea in Cappadocia, where he was ordained as a priest. It is just possible that he was designated as eastern consul for 480, and had the distinction reversed by Zeno, for there was no eastern consul for that year.[457] Of his brothers, Romulus escaped to Rome, where no more is heard of him, but Procopius Anthemius escaped to Thrace where he was sheltered by the Gothic *magister militum* Theoderic Strabo, nephew of the wife of Aspar, after which he joined his brother in Rome. After the accession of Anastasius he returned to Constantinople and held the eastern consulship in 515; his son also had a distinguished career, but neither was rash enough to revive the family's imperial aspirations.

Not so Marcian, however. His second tilt at power began after a few months, in spring 480. He managed to escape from Caesarea and gathered together another mixed force, this time of farmers, peasants, retired veterans

---

456 PLRE II Marcianus 17
457 Nor for that following, although Trocundus was rewarded for his efforts with the eastern consulship for 482.

and chancers. Declaring himself once again emperor, he entered Galatia and laid seige to Ancyra (Ankora, Turkey) but, after some time the defending forces under the Isaurian Illus's brother, the picturesquely named Fl. Appalius Illus Trocundes, managed to drive him off. After a few weeks he cornered him and accepted his surrender. Zeno, perhaps worried that a harsh punishment might lead to more unrest, exiled him and his wife to his native Isauria, where he was imprisoned in a fortress called Papyrius.

Marcian's third ill-fated attempt to emulate his father arose when the patrician and *magister utriusque militum* Illus was virtually in full control of Zeno's government from 479. The patrician's popularity alarmed his fellow Isaurian, the Emperor. Furthermore, the latter had fallen out with the Empress Ariadne over the treatment of the dowager Empress Verina. In 483, Illus was dismissed and his property confiscated and early in the following year, understandably, he rebelled. His first move was to consolidate his position in Isauria, proclaim Marcian emperor yet again and make overtures to Odoacer, ruler of Italy, the Persians and the Armenians for help. Alarmed, Zeno despatched the *magister militum* in Thrace, Leontius (another Isaurian), with an army to put the rebellion down, but on reaching Illus Leontius was persuaded to join him in opposing the Emperor. At this juncture, Marcian was for a third (and final) time deposed in favour of Leontius (qv), and with Leontius, Illus, his wife (the ex-empress Leontia), ended up under protracted siege at Papyrius, from whence he was despatched to Italy with an embassy to accelerate any help Odoacer might feel inclined to provide. After that, we hear no more of him. Possibly he settled in Italy (where he may well have had property) and resumed a normal existence there. Leontia, who had remained behind during all this, survived to re-marry Patricius, who had been eastern consul in 459 and left further issue.[458] Leontius' court and its adherents were all slaughtered in 488 when the fortress finally fell.

At no time did Marcian II ever issue coinage, and as a result we are ignorant of the manner in which he was styled, although Dominus Noster Flavius Marcianus Pius Felix Augustus seems most likely.

MARCUS (I) AURELIUS
161, 7th March – 180, 17th March

Marcus Aurelius was the epitome of the successful and enlightened Roman Emperor, a published philosopher who was the first to rule with a co-emperor without dissension, who strengthened the empire despite an outbreak of plague and survived an attempted usurpation, but had the misfortune to have left a son and heir entirely unfit to step into his shoes.

The Emperor Marcus was groomed for eventual succession from a very tender age, when he was adopted by Antoninus Pius as part of Hadrian's

---

458 She had issue with Marcian, details of whom are lost, in addition to Marcian having left a son by his first marriage, Procopius, whose homonymous probable grandson was governor of the Islands in the middle of the sixth century: PLRE Procopius 5; JRS CII (2012)

somewhat convoluted 'heir and a spare' succession settlement. That he could go through the entire lengthy reign of his adoptive father without taking violent measures to hasten his accession speaks much for the relationship between the two men, and for Marcus' temperament. All the sources agree that the relationship was harmonious, making an instructive contrast to the truculence, resentment and mistrust which existed between Tiberius and Augustus during the only earlier comparably lengthy imperial apprenticeship.

Marcus's male line of descent, the Annii Veri, came from Ucubi (Espejo), in the Spanish province of Baetica and it has been suggested by Sir Ronald Syme that prior to their migration there, Lanuvium (Lanuvio) might have been their town of origin.[459] In 48BC, Annius Scapula, an equestrian of undoubted Italian ancestry and 'of the highest rank and influence in that province' was executed for being involved in a pro-Pompeian plot to murder Caesar's governor there, Q. Cassius Longinus, a cousin of the conspirator. If not a direct ancestor, he was quite probably related to the Veri.

There are three other possible kinsfolk who have been identified. One was M. Annius Afrinus, suffect consul c. 67, in the era of Nero; the family increasingly used Marcus as a *praenomen* even when there was more than one brother, preferring to change the *cognomen* of each instead, so Afrinus could even have been a brother of the first Verus and a kinsman of Hadrian, his exceedingly unusual *cognomen* being closely cognate with, and a diminutive of Afer, Hadrian's father's name.[460] Such a connection would explain a great deal about Hadrian's second and final succession settlement.[461] The name Cornificia, which emerges in the family with Marcus's sister, may further suggest that the lost generations of this provincial family were closer to events in the capital than the surviving evidence might suggest, perhaps marriage with a granddaughter of L. Cornificius, consul in 33BC, also from Lanuvium, although he had otherwise no recorded descendants.[462] Finally, another first-century possible kinsman, also of equestrian rank, could have been Annius Faustus, an unpleasant *delator* in the last years of Nero who was condemned by the senate in the reign of Galba. His name recurs in that of the suffect consul of 121, suggested as a possible brother of M. Annius Verus, consul (iii) 126.[463] Both would therefore pre-date the alliance with Rupilia Faustina, whose extra name indicates a descent from the first-century BC *optimate* dictator, L. Cornelius Sulla, and was passed on to two empresses. Thus if the two Annii Fausti are indeed kinsmen, the occurrence of the *cognomen* is more likely to have been a coincidence rather than an indication of an even earlier alliance with the posterity of the triumvirs.

The other aggravation with which Marcus was saddled and which must have become provocatively manifest on his accession, was his younger adoptive brother, Lucius Verus, whose character was the antithesis of that

---

459 *Ancient Society* 13/14 (1982-83) 260 f.
460 Syme (1958) II. 792
461 Attested, but without specific details in Dio LXIX. 21.2
462 PIR² C1503; Wiseman (1971) 139
463 Settipani (2000) 299.

of the tolerant, philosophical, sport-loving Marcus, being venal, louche and indolent. Again, Marcus' astonishing capacity for tact, restraint and tolerance continued to be tested for the seven and a half years of their joint rule. It was the first occasion in Roman history in which two Augusti of equal rank had successfully taken and retained power. This very fact set a precedent for numerous further occasions from the 3rd century; it doubtless encouraged imitators, although more often than not with chaotic and often bloody results.

The success of the arrangement was predicated upon the fact that Antoninus Pius had always ensured Marcus had primacy over his adoptive brother, which suited the temperaments, it would appear, of all three. Furthermore, Marcus may have succeeded to the arrangement in the hope – soon proved a vain one – that by sharing power and responsibility, he might have time to pursue his study of philosophy.

The new ruler was born M. Annius Catilius Severus Verus, a patrician, at Rome on 26 April 121, son of M. Annius Verus (consul in 140) and he was the adopted son of his paternal grandfather from the death of his father in 124/125. In 127 was enrolled in the Equestrian Order by Hadrian, who apparently held him in high esteem, even in childhood, calling him 'Verissimus'.[464] According to the *Historia Augusta* he was 'named after his step-[great]-grandfather on his mother's side', which would suggest that his full name at birth was L. Catilius Severus [M.] Annius Verus, or similar.[465] This Severus, consul for the second time in 120, was called in full L. Catilius Severus Julianus Claudius Reginus.[466] The adoption by his grandfather may have later led to the dropping of Catilius Severus' name. In 136, Hadrian betrothed him to Ceionia Fabia, daughter of the man about to be the Emperor's chosen successor, L. Ceionius Commodus, and when that choice was made shortly afterwards, he clearly became the heir presumptive. This arrangement, of course, failed to survive Ceionius Commodus's death on 1 January 138, but on 25 February 138 Marcus was for a third time adopted, on this occasion by Hadrian's adopted successor, Antoninus Pius, taking the full style of M. Aelius Imp. Titi Aeli Hadriani Antonini f. Pap. Aurelius Verus, but the much simpler M. Aelius Aurelius Verus was most commonly used.[467]

He was appointed quaestor under age, also in 138, and in the year following was granted the name – or title, as it was rapidly establishing itself – of Caesar, changing his style to Aurelius Caesar Augusti Pii f. This would appear to be the first occasion on which an emperor or future emperor bore a style of nomenclature which had no *praenomen*, not even the honorific 'Imperator' first used by Augustus.

In 139 he held his first consulship, holding a second in 145, two years before receiving the tribunician power on 10 December 147. After Antoninus' accession, the betrothal to Ceionia Fabia was broken off and he

---

464 Dio LXI. 29.2. *Verus* = true; *Verissimus* = truest.
465 *V. Marci Aurelii* 2.3
466 PIR², C558
467 CIL.III.7060; ILS 354

was instead betrothed in 139 and married in April or May 145 to Antoninus' only daughter Annia Galeria Faustina (junior), who was raised to the rank of Augusta in 147 on the birth of her first child.[468]

On his accession, 7 March 161, Marcus Aurelius was hailed as *imperator* for the first time, made *pontifex maximus*, granted proconsular power and was styled Imperator Caesar Marcus Aurelius Antoninus Augustus, to which he added – reluctantly but at the insistence of the senate in 166 – *Pater Patriae*. Various additional honorific names to mark triumphal campaigns were added to the Armeniacus of 165 thereafter: Medicus and Parthicus Maximus in 166,[469] Germanicus in 172 and Sarmaticus in 175. He enjoyed a further nine imperial acclamations.

Calamities at home and a crisis on the eastern frontier left both new emperors with their hands full, Marcus dealing with the former whilst despatching Lucius off to the east to deal with Armenia. Possibly, Marcus thought that to be in charge of so important a venture would afford Lucius the opportunity to prove himself a capable ruler and soldier. Verus' return in 166 was accompanied by abundant booty and a magnificent triumph was celebrated, shared by both emperors. Unfortunately, Verus also brought back a serious infection, which played havoc with the City's population, not sparing the ruling élite and over the succeeding years it decimated the potential manpower of the empire, with the result that it was ever after short of home-grown recruits for the army. It may well have been this plague which impelled a group of Teutonic tribes to threaten the northern frontier in 167. A first irruption of these was successfully dealt with, but a second in 168 alarmingly reached northern Italy and both Emperors were obliged to set out to deal with the situation. Once again, order was eventually restored. The Emperors then settled the dispositions and appointments on the frontier before returning, Verus unexpectedly dying en route.

Thereafter, Marcus was able to govern alone until 177 when he felt obliged to associate his surviving son, Commodus, to power. This must have been an even bigger disappointment than having to cope with Lucius, for it was obvious from a very young age that the boy was deranged to some extent, showing signs of extreme cruelty, mood-swings, fantasising and extreme self-indulgence: all Lucius' faults with some of Nero's and Caligula's thrown in.

In between times, though, Marcus reigned in as exemplary a fashion as had his adoptive father, although he was obliged to return to the German and Danubian frontiers for over four years to campaign against further rebellious tribes, the Marcomanni and Quadi. This was eventually entirely successful, and had he not died when he did, plans were afoot to create a new province to the north-east to encompass Germany between Rhine and Elbe, a scheme unfortunately abandoned by his un-martial successor.

All this was despite the most successful general of Lucius' eastern campaign and governor of Syria, C. Avidius Cassius, mounting a full-scale usurpation in 175, which was put down without too much disruption. Again,

---

468 PIR² A716
469 ILS 366

great clemency was shown to the usurper's surviving family and throughout his reign, Marcus' relations with the senate were entirely deferential and designed to work as a partnership.

The last part of the reign was taken up with further campaigns on the north-eastern frontier before Marcus, who had long been in declining health, died near Sirmium (Sremska Mitrovica, Serbia) whilst on campaign on 17 March 180, leaving a large family, a desperately unstable son and heir and his *Meditations,* a work of Stoic philosophy reflecting on the contradictions between the ideal and the realities of humane governance. He was immediately voted divine honours by the senate.

The only one of the Emperor's sons to survive childhood was Commodus, who married but had no children. His next and youngest brother M. Aurelius Annius Verus was made next heir and given the title Caesar in AD166 aged just four, perhaps because Commodus was then ill, or merely as a precaution. He too died young, probably from the plague, in 169. All the daughters bar the eldest lived to maturity and married and most left descendants, some of whom survived the various proscriptions pursued by later rulers aimed at eliminating possible rivals, begun by Septimius Severus and continued sporadically by some of his successors.

MARCUS (II)
?249

A usurper called Marcus is mentioned by Zonaras as having been acclaimed by the senate in the reign of Philip but is spurious and a case of the author giving Philip's *praenomen* a life of its own.[470] A claimant called Severus Hostilianus (qv) is equally specious.[471]

MARCUS (III)
406, Autumn – 407, January

A man called Marcus is named in several sources as an ephemeral military usurper in Britain, whose acclamation and brief reign marked the beginning of the Gallic imperial secession of 407.

The reduction of troops on the Rhine frontier and a demand from Stilicho to the authorities in Britain to contribute detachments to reinforce his efforts against the eastern imperial government seem to have led to the acclamation of a Marcus in Britain. Birley said that it was 'reasonable to suppose' that he was one of the three senior Roman commanders in Britain: either the *Comes Britanniarum* (Count of the Britains), *Comes Litoris Saxonici* (Count of the Saxon Shore) or the *Dux Britanniarum* (C-in-C Britain) and points out that Sheppard Frere considered that he was in fact holder of the first of these positions.[472] One ancient source says of the third in the sequence of three

---

470 Zonaras XII, 18, cf. PIR² M271
471 Körner (2001) 391-393
472 Birley (1981) 342 & n. 2; cf. PLRE II Marcus 2

usurpers that followed this rebellion, that 'They appear to have chosen Constantine thinking that, as he had this name, he would firmly master the imperial power, since it was for a reason such as this that they appear to have chosen the others for usurpation as well.'[473]

This would suggest that this particular *comes* (if *comes* he was) reminded them of Marcus Aurelius, then doubtless still well remembered as a doughty defeater of barbarian attacks. Somehow, one cannot seriously consider the experienced senior military establishment in Britain (or anywhere else in the empire) would be so naive as to be swayed by any such considerations. He was surely chosen on merit for whatever qualities he might be able to bring to bear on their concerns in the crisis.

His acclamation is thought, on critical evaluation of the somewhat challenging evidence, to have occurred in 406 and not 407, possibly in the autumn, when unrest on the frontier first became apparent in military circles in the west. He did not last very long, 'because he did not agree with the soldiers' character' and was deposed and presumably assassinated. The chronology of this sequence of British acclamations suggests that he must have been disposed of some time in January 407.[474] Nothing whatever is known about this man's origin or family. By this date the name was most likely a *cognomen* rather than a *praenomen*.[475] If any coins were minted, they failed to survive.

MARCUS (IV)
476, c. October – 477, August

Marcus was elevated in desperation by the bungling serial usurper Basiliscus, but he reigned only nominally. He was the only named child of Basiliscus and his wife Zenonis and was proclaimed *caesar* on his father's acclamation as usurping emperor in autumn 476. His father's consequent and rapid loss of support was the spur to his elevation in the hope, no doubt, of bolstering his popularity. He was deposed with his father and died of starvation shortly afterwards.

MARIUS
March – June 269

Marius usurped rule in the breakaway Gallic empire, founded by the man he disposed of, Postumus, but failed to consolidate his regime. Following the capture of Moguntiacum, Postumus refused to allow his forces to sack the city, which caused sufficient resentment amongst the troops, ever eager to be rewarded with plunder, for an officer called M. Aurelius Marius to lead a revolt which ended in the murder of the Emperor, the sack of the city and the elevation of the instigator, who then removed to Augusta Treveriorum (Trier).

---

473 *Op. cit.* 343, quoting Sozomen.
474 *Ibid.*, 344, & n. 15
475 Cf. PLRE I Marcus 2, 3 & 4. A 'citizen of the Island of Britain' according to Orosius *Adv. Pagan.* vii. 40, 4

Marius' name suggests descent from a family granted citizenship by Marcus Aurelius, a member of his family, by Severus after 195 or most likely by Caracalla. The *Historia Augusta* claims that he was astonishingly low-born and a former blacksmith.[476] The other related sources, Aurelius Victor and Eutropius, label him as of common origin or a tradesman.[477] One suspects that, obscure though his family background may have been, he would have been chosen by the military for a good reason – probably because he was an officer and, as one source declares, *strenuus* – energetic. The same sources only credit him with a reign of between one and three days, but from the coins he issued and their quantity he probably lasted three or four months before being killed by his troops and, after a two-day *interregnum*, being replaced by Victorinus.[478]

As emperor, Marius used the style Imperator Caesar M. Aur[elius] Marius Pius Felix Augustus.[479] He is known to have held the tribunician power (presumably by grant of the anti-senate established by Postumus), but no coin records a consulship. Coin portraits show a man with close cropped hair and much in the mode of the Illyrian soldier emperors like Claudius II and his successors. Indeed, it is perfectly possible that he *was* from Ilyricum. No concrete information has survived concerning his family.

MARTINIANUS
324, July – 18th September

Martinianus was a stop-gap junior tetrarch appointed by Licinius to replace his predecessor, who had been killed in action, before suffering final defeat with his senior partner three months later.

Although neither Valens (IV) nor Martinianus received recognition from the senate or in the west at all, least of all from Constantine, they do not really count as usurpers, having been raised up and dispensed with (albeit in a cavalier fashion) by a legitimate tetrarch in the person of Licinius I. Before his elevation, Martinianus bore the entirely new office of chief minister, (*magister officiorum*) which was to become commonplace in the following years. His imperial style was Imperator Caesar Mar[   ] Martinianus Pius Felix Augustus although one issue of *follis* places an 'S' between C[aesar] and his name, thought by some to suggest 'Sextus'; it is more likely to have been a blundered die.[480]

He was appointed under virtually identical circumstances to Valens, following the defeat of Licinius at the second battle of Adrianopolis on 3 July 324, and surrendered to Constantine after his defeat at Chrysopolis

---

476 *Tyr. Trig.* 8. 1
477 Aur. Victor, 33, 9; Eutropius 9, 9. 2
478 Drinkwater (1987) 177-178
479 Coin evidence.
480 His *nomen* was probably either Marius, Marcius or Martius – perhaps the last, which then generated his *cognomen*.

on 18 September and is thought to have died the following year.[481] Nothing is known of any family.

MASTIES
c. 477 – 516

Masties was a Numidian military strong man who proclaimed himself emperor after the deposition of Western Emperor Romulus, and who lived to enjoy his enhanced status, more or less unmolested, to a very great age.

After it became clear that there were to be no further western emperors, the *dux* (leader) of the Romans and Moors in Numidia proclaimed himself emperor instead and according to his monumental inscription, datable to 516, he maintained himself as *imperator annis XL* (emperor 40 years) and had been *dux* for 67 years! He came from Arris (Arris Batne, Algeria) and must thus have been born c. 425, being appointed *dux* not before 449 (when Numidia was still under the sway of the western empire) which was probably an acknowledgement by the governor of his position as ruler of the Moors on the death of his predecessor. His self-proclaimed elevation to the purple, after the example of Aegidius, may have been made in conjunction with a revolt against the Vandals which began in the Aurès mountains in 477, resulting in his gaining control of an independent political entity. Nothing further is known of this man nor of his family, except that the Vandals, who wasted the province in 468, seem to have left him to his own devices, and that he died in 516.[482]

MAURICE [TIBERIUS]
582, 13th August – 602, 27th November

Maurice was an able emperor who defeated the Persians twice, formalised the way the empire's provinces in the west were to be governed, re-ordered provincial boundaries throughout the empire and improved administration with the aim of putting the empire's finances back onto a sound footing after the profligacy of Tiberius II. Partly as a result of these fiscal strictures, his reign ended tragically in a brutal military *coup* which also led to the slaughter of many of the ruling élite.

Emperor Mauricius was the son of Paulus and was born at Arabissus in Cappadocia (Afşin, formerly Yarpuzin, Turkey) in 539. It is said that Paulus, his father, was descended from a family originally from Rome itself, which is not impossible, given the steady drift of senators and their families to Constantinople in the mid to late fifth century. The source, Evagrius, does not claim that they were particularly aristocratic, and in view of the intensity of Roman settlement in the general area of Asia Minor over the previous 600 or so years, the claim is feasible.[483] His mother's name

---

481 PLRE I Martinianus 2
482 PLRE II Masties; Conant (2012) 278, 280, 287, 293
483 Evagrius, *Ecclesiastical History* v. 19

is unknown, but one Damiana, daughter of Iannina, shared a niece with Maurice, suggesting that she may have been herself a first cousin through the mother of the emperor.[484]

The young Mauricius embarked upon a bureaucratic career and the Emperor Tiberius in due course made him commander of the *excubitores* (Imperial Guard) with the rank of *comes*. Later, he was appointed *magister militum* in the east, by which time he was styled *vir illustris* and made a patrician. His task was to continue the war against Persia, which he did with considerable success, invading that empire twice, taking much booty and concluding in 581 with a favourable treaty. He returned in triumph to Constantinople in 582 and was probably named as Tiberius' heir (as *nobilissimus caesar*) on the strength of his success. The date was 5 August, and the Emperor was already dying. Maurice was also betrothed to Constantina, the Emperor's daughter.

He was proclaimed Augustus on 13 August, the day before Tiberius died, taking the additional name of Tiberius at the old Emperor's request, and is sometimes consequently known as Maurice Tiberius, but, as there were to be another two Emperors called Tiberius (one an imperial claimant in Sicily and another who reigned at Constantinople from 698-705), it is less confusing to use the style of Maurice alone.[485] With Constantia, Maurice had six sons and three, possibly four, daughters.

Maurice succeeded Tiberius on 14 August, taking the style of Dominus Noster Tiberius Perpetuus Augustus and holding the ordinary consulship for 583.[486] The Empress was duly appointed Augusta at some date before May 585.[487] In 587 he associated his four-year-old eldest son Theodosius with the purple by making him official heir with the title *nobilissimus caesar* before promoting him, aged about six, to co-Augustus. He was the first Emperor since Theodosius II to have been born to a ruling emperor: he was thus *porphyrogenitus* – 'purple-born'.

The first success enjoyed by the new emperor was the ending of the very draining war with Persia. A civil war there enabled him to support one contender, Chosroes II, and once established, the King agreed an extremely favourable settlement with the Empire in 591. Maurice also formalised the exarchate of Ravenna to govern Italy, Sicily and other dependencies in the face of the Lombardic incursions there and established a second exarch at Carthage to control Africa, in response to increasingly frequent Moorish attacks. These were essentially the old Praetorian Prefectures revived under a new name. He also re-ordered the provincial boundaries, taking into account more recent changes on the ground and making the empire somewhat easier to administer.

A serious problem was the legacy of the fiscal profligacy of Tiberius II, which resulted in Maurice being obliged to retrench, leading to pay

---

484 She was the mother of Athenogenes, Bishop of Petra: PLRE III Damiane (*sic*)
485 Even so there was a claimant in Rome 643-644, also called Mauricius (II).
486 PLRE III Mauricius 4
487 PLRE III Constantina 1

reductions for the army, with the consequence that a mutiny had to be suppressed in 588.

The army was being particularly tested in the Balkans due to incursions of the Avars. Under Tiberius, Sirmium (Sremska Mitrovika, Serbia) had fallen and the immense agricultural and social disruption caused by the uncontrolled movement of these Slavic barbarians into settled communities had a deleterious effect on the economy of the Empire and tied down large military units, which made heavy inroads upon the exchequer.

Maurice also fell out with Pope Gregory the Great, a member of one of the great western senatorial dynasties, who had objected to the Patriarch of Constantinople unilaterally adopting the title 'ecumenical'. Instead of placating the Pope as had happened on previous occasions, he supported his patriarch, thus causing a breach at a time when unity was of the essence. The dissension was eventually patched up, and it was a straw in the wind presaging events more than four centuries later. He appears, too, to have been the only eastern emperor to have recognised that governing the west was not best left to eastern exarchs and Pretorian Prefects and at one stage, late in his reign, he proposed sending one of his sons, presumably the second, Tiberius, then aged about 17, to Rome as western emperor, although in the end nothing came of this plan as Maurice's deposition and death supervened.[488]

Yet it was his attempts to replenish the treasury which led to Maurice's undoing. He refused to ransom some 12,000 prisoners taken by the Avars in 599, the result being that the barbarians called his bluff and slaughtered the lot. The consequent decision to refuse to allow part of the army on the Danube to return south of the river for the winter of 602-603 caused a mutiny, for the men, after a season's hard fighting, had acquired much booty and without a return to base would have been unable to sell it in the city markets at home. And of course it would have deprived them of their wives, families and friends. This placed the C-in-C in the area, Petrus, the Emperor's brother, in a difficult situation, but he was firm and as a result a middle ranking officer with a previous record for general disrespect called Phocas was raised up as the leader of a revolt.

Petrus rushed back to Constantinople to warn his brother and to present the mutineers' demands, which included that Maurice should abdicate in favour of Theodosius or, failing him, his father-in-law, Germanus (qv). The inevitable result was that both, who were away hunting, were recalled and accused of treason. This news leaked out and rioting instigated by the circus factions began, with the Greens baying for the Emperor's blood. On 22 November, Maurice and his family decided to leave the city, and Theodosius was sent on to obtain help from Chosroes II. Meanwhile, Germanus had been in sanctuary, and with the Emperor gone, he made a bid for the purple himself, but this failed dismally, for the same reason that the attempt by Maurice failed: the Green circus faction refused to support him and instead opened the gate to an armed military delegation led by Phocas

---

488 Theophylactus Simocatta, *Historia* 8.11.9-10; Salzman (2021) 333 n. 141

which had just reached the capital. The following day, Phocas had himself crowned in a suburban church and on 24 November entered the City proper and obtained the recognition of the senate, made a donative to the army and raised his wife Leontia to the rank of Augusta.

The same day a detachment of the guard was sent to eliminate Maurice and his family, prompted by shouts of 'Remember, Mauricius is not dead,' during Phocas' inauguration. It was recorded that he died on 27 November, unresisting and with great dignity. Such was the detestable character of his successor, he was being widely mourned within weeks. Needless to say, Theodosius soon met a similar fate.

MAXENTIUS
306, 28ᵗʰ October – 312, 28ᵗʰ October

As with Constantine, Maxentius was the son of a Tetrarch, by-passed by the cumbrous machinery of Diocletian's supposedly foolproof system of inheritance, and was thus prompted to take matters into his own hands, eventually unsuccessfully.

M. Valerius Maxentius was born c. 287, son of the future tetrarch Maximian. After Maximian's elevation, his father's new status had given Maxentius senatorial rank. He lived at Rome, had a house on the Via Labicana and in 305 was married to Valeria Maximilla, the daughter of his father's successor, Galerius, who bore him two sons, one called Romulus and another whose name we do not know.[489] He was only 19 when proclaimed emperor.

He seized power in Rome as a consequence of Galerius revoking the tax privileges of the city. His style then changed to Imperator Caesar C. (but still sometimes Marcus) Aurelius Valerius Maxentius Pius Felix Invictus Augustus, and was granted the proconsular *imperium* and tribunician power as well as being declared *pontifex maximus*, which meant four holding this office at this juncture, rather making a mockery of the state's chief priesthood.[490] In view of the youth of Maxentius, it would seem that however disappointed he may have been about being passed over as one of the new Caesars in 305, only a man of the stature and maturity of his father could have masterminded his acclamation in the autumn following the elevation of Constantine, who had been in the same situation, but who was a decade or more older and quicker off the mark. His first move was to be acclaimed as *imperator caesar* – the usual prefix for emperors since Augustus, but it was only when Galerius refused to recognise him that he added *augustus* in April 307.

He saw off an attempt by Severus II to eliminate him and he controlled Italy, Sicily, Corsica, Sardinia, Africa Proconsularis and those African provinces to the west of it, although he did have to contend with the imperial claimant Alexander (II) there. Soon, to boost his authority, his father came out of retirement and brokered an alliance with Constantine. After his

---

489 ILS667
490 ILS670

son's final elevation to the rank of Augustus, the old tetrarch attempted to replace him completely but was thwarted and fled to the court of his new ally, committing suicide in 310 after a failed attempt to re-enter the fray in late 309. Once Galerius and Severus II had died, the way was open for Constantine to move against Maxentius, who, on being heavily defeated at the battle of the Milvian Bridge outside Rome, was drowned in the rout. It was the sixth anniversary of his coming to power; he was still only 25. He served as consul in 308, 309, 310 and 312. His younger son is thought to have either survived or died with him; Romulus, probably his designated heir, seems to have died before him, probably of natural causes.

MAXIMIAN (I)
286, 1ˢᵗ April – 305, 1ˢᵗ May
308, May – November
309–310, January

Maximian was a less competent companion-in-arms of Diocletian, with whom he co-founded the Tetrarchy, and who ruled the western half of the Empire with moderate success but was unable to handle the prospect of having to retire, which led to all sorts of trouble.

As with his older comrade, we do not know what the rest of the new Emperor's names were before he assumed the imperial style of Aurelius Valerius Maximianus Nobilissimus Caesar, on his appointment as Diocletian's junior colleague.[491] He clearly adopted two names exactly as borne by his colleague (probably acknowledging a notional, if not formal, adoption of the one by the other) and they also co-ordinated their birthdays, presumably the younger man's being brought into line with Diocletian's. As Augustus, his style was modified to Imperator Caesar M. Aurelius Valerius Maximianus Pius Felix Invictus Augustus, and he was acknowledged as *pater patriae*.[492] The office of *pontifex maximus* was again divided, being also bestowed upon him, and he was granted the tribunician and proconsular powers enjoyed by his senior colleague.

Maximian was born near Sirmium (Sremska Mitrovica, Serbia), marking him out as yet another Illyrian, probably in c. 243/245. Syme suggests that he may have been a relative of the emperor Tacitus.[493] He appears to have served with Diocletian under Aurelian and Probus, although it is not clear what position he held prior to his elevation. Conceivably, he had been appointed Pretorian Prefect by Diocletian after his successful *coup* against Aper on the death of Numerianus. Both Emperors retreated from the monotheistic worship of Sol (the Sun God) much favoured by most of their Illyrian predecessors and revived the ancient religion of the empire. To reinforce this they allowed themselves divine *signa*, Maximian taking that of Herculius.

The two Augusti went on to campaign remorselessly, Maximian in the west, accumulating imperial salutations and triumphal *agnomina* in

---

491 *Ibid.*
492 PLRE I Maximianus 8
493 Syme ((1971) 247

profusion. Each one earned – Sarmaticus Maximus, for example – was borne by both emperors, although only one of them would have actually earned it. Maximian had internal problems to unravel as well, for a serious outbreak of brigandage manifested itself in Gaul, led by a vagabond called Amandus (qv) who had the temerity to declare himself emperor before he could be suppressed. At virtually the same time, in 286, Carausius also rebelled and, like Postumus, stayed put, although his sway eventually included large parts of the northern Gallic coast for a while, including the naval base at Boulogne. Maximian, being busy with the problems posed by suppressing Amandus and fighting on the Rhine frontier, was obliged to leave him be until things quietened down. Maximian was consul in 287, 288, 290, 293, 297, 299, 303, 304, and 307. In the west he appointed his Pretorian Prefect Constantius as Caesar, who married Galerius' daughter Galeria Valeria.

Thereafter, imperial control began to be asserted in earnest, despite a tribal rising in Africa and the continuing problem posed by Carausius and his successor Allectus, who was eventually dealt with very effectively by Constantius, the western Caesar, who recaptured the Gallic possessions of the breakaway empire in 293 and then in 297 invaded Britain and eliminated Allectus.

The consequences of the retirement of the two Augusti in 305 were entirely foreseeable. The two men appointed to rule in their place, Galerius and Constantius I, were chosen for their loyalty and competence. In turn, the retiring emperors, rather than the newly elevated ones, chose the two Caesars, and ignored their *protégés'* sons (who were not only fully adult and, as it turned out, competent) but elevated two other old comrades-in-arms Severus (II) and Maximin II Daia, and again, alliances were cemented by marriage. Thus, the sons of Maximian and Constantius were passed over in favour of two cronies of Galerius and Diocletian, but thanks to the tortuous series of dynastic marriages, they were nevertheless bound tightly into the nexus of the tetrarchic Imperial family. It was inevitable that at some time or another one of both of the two who had been passed over would make a bid for power.[494]

In 306, Galerius, short of revenue, was rash enough to remove the privileged tax-free status of Rome, causing an outcry exploited by Maxentius to seize power, threatening the position of Severus, Galerius' *caesar*. He then appointed his supposedly retired father as his colleague. They both then recognised Constantine as Augustus but had too few troops at their disposal to achieve very much against Severus, who in due course was ordered by Galerius to crush the uprising. He advanced on Rome, where his troops unexpectedly deserted to Maximian (a move doubtless lubricated by the promise of a donative – retired emperors were hardly likely to be hard up) and Severus was captured, forced to abdicate and later killed. To cement all this, Fausta, sister of Maxentius, was duly obliged to marry Constantine.

An attempt to wrest power in the west away from Maxentius failed almost as dismally as that of Severus. Yet, in spring 308, Maximian decided to stop

---

494 The entire idea of the Tetrarchy being a formal quasi-constitutional arrangement has been challenged by Leadbetter (2009) *passim*.

playing second fiddle to his son and had himself acclaimed senior western Augustus, but this ploy failed completely and he was forced to flee to his son-in-law, Constantine. He then prevailed upon Galerius to fetch Diocletian out of retirement in an attempt to resolve the issue. The result was more of an arrangement on paper: Galerius remained Augustus in the east and appointed another old crony, Licinius, to replace Severus in the west with Constantine as his Caesar and Maximin Daia as eastern Caesar. This left Maxentius still in control of Italy and Africa as unofficial Augustus and Constantine, whilst officially Caesar, had already been acclaimed as Augustus two years before. Needless to say, this left uncertainty into which an usurper called Alexander (II) arose in Africa to challenge Maxentius and it took nearly two years to dislodge him. Even as Alexander was being neutralised, Maximian seized his chance whilst Constantine was conducting a spring campaign against the Franks and escaped south to Arelate (Arles) where for the third time he was proclaimed Augustus. On hearing that his son-in-law was coming after him, however, he moved south to Massilia (Marseilles), where the citizens had no intention of being involved in a siege and turned the old man over to Constantine. It was given out not long afterwards that he had committed suicide by hanging in late 309 or early 310. Maxentius, in a gesture of filial piety, had him deified by the senate.

MAXIMIAN (II) see GALERIUS

MAXIMIN I THRAX
235, 21st March – 238, 24 June

Maximin was the first of the third-century soldier-emperors, and one whose alleged uncouth brutality and disregard for the delicate balance required between *princeps*, senate and administrative class led to a failed rebellion in Africa and his unexpected downfall at the hands of a pair of elderly senators.

It is extraordinary that Maximin, usually known additionally as 'Thrax' (The Thracian) was the first emperor to have risen to the purple from the ranks of the army and the first successfully to govern the empire without once visiting its capital. He was the second (following Macrinus) to succeed as a non-senator and was not even a member of the equestrian order.

The *Historia Augusta* claims that he was an exceedingly large man with an innate confidence in his own ability and a military talent that his superiors had recognised by promoting him swiftly, being at the time of his elevation Prefect of the Recruits (*praefectus tironum*).[495] This appointment, if true, would in fact suggest that he was less of a battle-hardened general and more a military bureaucrat.

C. Julius Verus Maximinus was born in 172 or 173, allegedly in a village near Oescus (near Pleven, Bulgaria), a part of the area of *Colonia Trebelliana* in Lower Moesia, an ethnically Thracian part of the province attached to the latter by Domitian in 86.[496] Contemporary references to him

---

495 Haegemans (2010) 52-56
496 PIR² I619; his age is given by Zonaras, XII, 16

as a barbarian or *semibarbarus* may reflect this, although he was said to have been a Roman citizen prior to joining up and it should be remembered that his father was also said to be of Gothic descent. From his *nomen*, some antecedent must have been enfranchised by one of the first three emperors or by a subsequent senatorial Julius. In fact, Syme points out that most of this is fiction in any case, driven by a bad press. He considers him to have been a person of Roman descent – as the traditional form of his name might suggest – long settled in the Lower Moesian area.[497] He is really the precursor of the great run of Illyrian emperors that dominated the second half of the century and beyond, up to the death of Licinius I. The barbarian parents ascribed to him by the *Historia Augusta* were furnished with the names of Micca and [H]abiba, the mother allegedly an Alan woman, and are also considered to be entirely fictitious. No other relations are known in any source.

He is alleged to have started life as a shepherd boy but because of his prodigious size and strength was recruited into the army under Septimius Severus. In fact, he almost certainly enlisted in an entirely conventional manner when of age. By sheer ability, he rose to the rank of prefect and then later, legate of the *Legio* II Traiana, in Egypt, from whence senatorial officers were barred by an edict of Augustus. In Severus Alexander's eastern campaign, he served as prefect of Mesopotamia. As Prefect of Recruits in 235, he would seem to have suffered a demotion of sorts; perhaps it was just that, and it rankled, which might explain his willingness to lead the revolt which ended with the deposition and murder of Alexander.

Following his *coup*, Maximin was given an imperial acclamation and was hailed as Augustus on 21 March 235, Alexander being killed the next day.[498] His style as Augustus was Imperator Caesar C. Julius Verus Maximinus Pius Felix Invictus Augustus and it may be that the Verus element was adopted on his elevation, being appropriated from the family of Marcus Aurelius, just as Severus had similarly re-invented himself as an Antonine.[499] His elevation was confirmed by the senate on 25 March 235, which body also recognised him as *Pontifex Maximus* and granted him the tribunician and proconsular power, renewable on 10 December, before which date he had received a second imperial acclamation.[500] In 236 he began the year as ordinary consul, assumed the additional style of Germanicus Maximus and associated his son as heir; thereafter he received two more imperial acclamations. In 237 he was further styled Dacicus Maximus and Sarmaticus Maximus and was hailed as *imperator* for the fifth and sixth times.[501] His wife, Caecilia Paulina, almost certainly predeceased him, probably prior to his elevation to the purple.[502] She always appears

---

497 Syme (1971) 186
498 See note above about the insecure nature of this date.
499 ILS 490
500 CIL.VI. 2001, 2009
501 ILS 488
502 ILS 492; PIR² C91; they married c. 213.

on coins with Divine honours, probably voted her by the senate at the Emperor's request.

The reign having begun with the reluctant recognition by the senate, a body that he seems to have despised, ending any pretence that the senate might determine policy or support the *princeps*. Nevertheless, he seems to have left in place the policies and personnel of his predecessor's regime, and mounted an immediate punitive expedition across the Rhine to deal with the Germanic tribes (specifically the Alemanni), which was successfully achieved despite two attempts to overthrow him, by the usurpers Magnus and later Quartinus, the former involving a group of senators and their military contemporaries and the latter arising from an attempt to destroy Maximin's Rhine pontoon bridge, leaving the Emperor on the far side with little support, on the assumption that the barbarians would do the rest before Maximin could organise any resistance. Both attempts failed dismally and, in their wake (perhaps understandably), the cruelty of the new Emperor in dealing with these conspiracies became more marked. Furthermore, the Alemanni at this time constituted very little threat and there is the consequent suspicion that the new Emperor had chosen to attack them to earn easy honours to bolster his authority in Rome. Nevertheless, having dealt with these Germans Maximin then turned his attention to the Danube frontier, also apparently in turmoil, with Barbarians taking advantage of the troop reductions occasioned by Alexander's eastern campaign. Here he defeated the Dacians and Sarmatians 236-237, gaining more honours.

Both these campaigns were, however, costly and the exactions required by the imperial fisc to cover the ever-increasing military expenditure were much resented in civilian circles, especially at Rome, where the aristocracy's attitude to the emperor was one of socially grounded distaste combined with resentment at not only being fleeced but also comprehensively by-passed. The fisc being unable to supply sufficient funds, the Emperor resorted first to extortion and confiscations, which only served to increase tensions with the governing élite. His second resort was to antagonise the lower echelons of society. He cut back on several of the benefactions traditionally handed out to the Roman masses, like the *annona* (corn dole). He also further debased the coinage, which increased inflation.

His son Maximus, serving as a military tribune in the army elsewhere, was summoned to the Emperor's side and given the name and title of *caesar* probably in 236, thus designating him his heir. The *Historia Augusta* also has the young *caesar* betrothed to Julia Fadilla, an alleged descendant of Antoninus Pius.[503] If this unlikely match is accepted, it would show Maximin repeating the strategy of both Julia Mamaea and Julia Soaemias in trying to ally a prince perceived to be well outside the loop of the mainstream

---

503 *V. Due Max.* 27, 6

governing class with a matron from the highest echelons of the senatorial aristocracy, preferably – as here – with previous imperial connections.[504]

The son, C. Julius Verus Maximus, was born c. 214/215, serving as military tribune under his father in Egypt and made heir with the style C. Julius Verus Maximus Nobilissimus Caesar, to which the senate (in all probability) added *Princeps Iuventutis*. He was hailed at least once as *imperator* and bore all the same victory epithets as his father: Germanicus Maximus, Dacicus Maximus and Sarmaticus Maximus. He was co-opted – presumably *in absentia* and in one case supernumerically – into two priestly colleges. Despite somewhat unreliable evidence, he seems not to have become co-Augustus with his father.[505]

In the event, Maximin's exactions and confiscations pushed the élite too far, and one rather footling incident set off the rebellion (and rapid suppression) of the two Gordiani and then the senate's nomination of the joint emperors Balbinus and Maximus, resulting in the Emperor and his son hurrying towards Rome with an army, determined to extirpate these impertinent aristocrats. Both father and son had been declared public enemies (*hostes publici*) by the senate on 1 or 2 April 238, but they were effectively sole rulers again from 12/13 April – when the co-emperors Gordian I and II died – to 22 April when the senate appointed Balbinus and Maximus. Maximin and Maximus Caesar were killed by their own troops on or about 24 June under siege at Aquileia, leaving no known issue.[506] It is this final débâcle that encourages one to wonder about the real quality of Maximin's abilities as a general, in that he was so rapidly defeated by what was, in essence, a bunch of part-timers led by elderly amateurs.

MAXIMIN II DAIA
310, 1ˢᵗ May – 313, July/August

Maximin Daia was a low-ranking military non-entity raised to be Caesar by Galerius, who later promoted him to the rank of augustus and whose demise was the result of in-fighting amongst the tetrarchs. Described as a semi-barbarian of low birth and originally called just Daia, Maximin II was born on 20 November 270 and seems originally to have been an infantryman, then a member of the *protectores* and later a tribune, prior to his coming to wider notice. He was appointed *caesar* in 308 by his maternal uncle Galerius and in the process adopted the names Galerius Valerius Maximinus Nobilissimus Caesar, or C. Valerius Galerius Maximinus *signo* Iovius. He was also made *princeps iuventutis*. He was raised to the rank of augustus in the wake of the elevation of Licinius in 310, again at the behest of Galerius. He was given the proconsular and tribunician power, made *pontifex maximus* and was consul in 307, 311 and 313.[507] He was given responsibility for the east, and as augustus he kept it, with Licinius squeezed between him, Constantine I

---

504 She was actually a cousin three times removed from Pius (PIR² I 668) being great-great-granddaughter of P. Julius Lupus (*ibid.*, I 389) second husband of that Emperor's mother, Arria Fadilla.

505 PIR I620

506 Herodian 8, 5

507 This last consulship appears to have been suffect.

and Maxentius. He also continued the persecution of the Christians initiated by Galerius, although with reduced intensity. But once Constantine had eliminated Maxentius, Licinius was emboldened to do likewise with Maximin, defeating and killing him (and presumably his children) in summer 313.[508]

Licinius was married with a son born in 305 and a daughter born the previous year. As his wife was never recognised as Augusta (which is presumably why her name is lost to us) she may have died relatively young, perhaps in childbirth.

MAXIMIN (III)
539

Maximinus was an officer of the bodyguard of Theodorus, *magister militum* in Africa in 537. He planned a revolt but the emperor's kinsman Germanus, in order to neutralise the threat he posed and in some way to assuage his ambition, appointed him commander of his own bodyguard. He nevertheless persisted in his plans, but having made a *pronunciamento* the mutiny was promptly put down and its leader, described by Procopius as a *tyrannus* and therefore a definite usurper, was brought before Germanus, condemned and executed at Carthage in 539.[509]

MAXIMUS (I)
218, March/April – 219

Maximus apparently made a bid for power in Coele Syria following the elevation of Elagabalus. [(L.) Gellius] Maximus was the son of a doctor – presumably of equestrian rank – called L. Gellius Maximus, of a family long settled in Pisidian Antioch. He was legate of the IVth (Scythian) Legion, but his reign was fairly short and he was killed in 219. He is mentioned as 'Gellius', under Diadumenianus in the *Historia Augusta*.[510] Nothing further is known of the family.

MAXIMUS (II) see PUPIENUS MAXIMUS

MAXIMUS (III) see MAGNUS MAXIMUS

MAXIMUS (IV)
409, c. June – 411, September
419, c. July – 421, February

Maximus was a puppet emperor twice elevated to the throne in Spain during two separate periods of turmoil in the Diocese, on both occasions at the instigation of a warlord.

---

508 PLRE I Maximinus 12
509 PLRE III Maximinus 1; Conant (2012) 216
510 Dio, 79. 7, 1-2; HA *V. Diadumenian.* 9, 1 cf. 8, 4-9; PIR² G130 cf. G123, G131

Having decided to make a break with Constantine III, his *magister militum* Gerontius for some reason decided not to have himself acclaimed, possibly because his reputation for severe discipline meant that the move would not be wholly popular amongst his troops. He therefore chose his *domesticus* and dependent, Maximus, as emperor at Tarraco (Tarragona), probably in early summer 409. From a modest coinage of silver *siliquae* minted at Barcino (Barcelona) c. 410 his style was D[ominus] N[oster] Maximus P[ius] F[elix] Aug[ustus].

Maximus is described as a 'dependent' of Gerontius (meaning close relative) and is considered to be most probably his son. The only reason to doubt it is that if Gerontius was held responsible by the Roman population of Spain for allowing the barbarians in, why would they have let his son live after he had taken his own life? The answer may lie in the gratitude of the Vandals, amongst whom Maximus seems to have lived for the eight years between his reigns and who elevated him to the purple a second time when showing defiance to a Roman administration which they felt had not dealt fairly with them. Added to this, there is the suggestion, albeit embedded in the later and untrustworthy Welsh genealogies, that Gerontius and Constantine III were also close kin.[511]

Having broken with Constantine, Gerontius's first task, originally assigned to him by Constans II as Caesar, had been to overcome a pro-Honorius uprising amongst the local élite in the Spanish province of Gallaecia led by a group of the Emperor's relations, Theodosiolus, Didymus, Lagodius and Verianus. The uprising was quickly quashed. The first two were captured. Lagodius and Verianus escaped to Constantinople. Once Constans had returned to Gaul for the second time and Maximus had been installed, Gerontius felt able to pursue a more aggressive policy. He settled the Barbarians that were already in Spain and greatly enlarged his forces with them before going to war against Constantine.

It would appear from all the evidence that the new imperial claimant was mainly a figurehead, with Gerontius, a first-class commander, making all the running: arranging treaties with the Vandals in Spain, conspiring to dethrone Constantine III, besieging Viennensis and killing Constans II. Had Maximus been the prime mover in these, he would without doubt have been killed when the army mutinied. As it was, when Honorius' forces arrived at Arelate where Gerontius had been engaged in eliminating Constans, Gerontius and Maximus were obliged to retreat and return to Spain. This loss of face (and the opportunity to plunder) led to their army turning on their British general, with the result that Gerontius killed his wife Nunechia and then himself. Maximus seems to have survived, in some sources as Emperor, until some time in 412, before going to ground. He is said to have lived quietly on a Spanish estate (presumably in Gallaecia) amongst the very Vandals whom the local grandees had accused Gerontius of introducing into their Diocese.

In July 419, however, we find a Maximus appearing in Spain as an usurper. It is not absolutely certain that this is the same man as Maximus IV but the circumstantial evidence strongly supports it.[512] This time, he was empurpled by

---

511 Craven (2023) 238-239
512 PLRE II Maximus 4 & Maximus 7

the ruler of the Vandals, Gunderic, whose people had been forcibly moved after a confrontation with the Sueves, both peoples having been settled by Gerontius in Gallaecia. Gundericus's people were moved to Baetica, another Spanish province, and the Gothic auxiliaries who had policed the move withdrew west of the Pyrenees. Thus, in about July 419, Maximus was trotted out and restored as emperor whilst the *vicarius* of the entire Diocese was expelled. Nevertheless, the *comes Hispaniarum*, Asterius, fresh from dealing with the Sueves, seems to have been able to deal with the usurper before the arrival of the Western government's *magister militum per Gallias* (C-in-C Gaul) Castinus, sent to do the work. Asterius took the ever-useful Gothic auxiliaries with him and fought a series of running battles, in which Maximus was captured, probably in February 421. Castinus then took over, being made a patrician as a reward.[513] Initially successful, Castinus, by refusing to compromise, later suffered a crushing defeat that sealed the future of Roman Spain forever and allowed the Vandals to settle where they had triumphed (hence modern Andalusia).[514] Maximus was sent back to Italy, where he was slaughtered in the arena as part of the Emperor's thirtieth anniversary games on 10 January 423.

MAXIMUS (V) see PETRONIUS MAXIMUS

MAXIMUS CAESAR see MAXIMIN I

MEMOR
262, c. April?

Memor is mentioned by Zosimus as an usurper in Egypt at the same time as Antoninus (V) and Aureolus.[515] The most likely context for him is that he was a senior official of Aemilianus (II) and made an attempt to continue his regime. He was swiftly captured and killed, probably within weeks of Aemilianus' overthrow. He may never have actually become established as an usurper before his demise. His career and family are totally obscure.

MERIADES see *CYRIADES*

NEPOS see JULIUS NEPOS

NEPOTIANUS
350, 3rd – 30th June

At Rome, the assassination of Constans and the acclamation of Magnentius was received very badly and what appears to have been a clique of senatorial grandees thought that, with a grandson of Constantius I amongst their

---

513 Kulikowski (2000) 123 ff
514 Livermore (1971) 85
515 Zosimus 1, 38; PLRE I. Memor 1

number, there might be a chance of dislodging the usurper, or at least keeping him pinned down until Constantius II could intervene. Their candidate was Flavius Julius Popillius Nepotianus Constantinus, whose father Virius Nepotianus, consul in 336, had married Constantius' daughter Eutropia. He had probably survived the counter-coup killings at Constantinople on 3 September 337 either because he was in Rome or due to his extreme youth, as he was probably born c. 328/333.

The self-appointed avenger of the House of Constantine entered Rome (having probably been acclaimed at his suburban villa) at the head of an armed force composed mainly of gladiators, and was recognised by the senate on 3 June 350, thus legitimizing his rule. He cannot, despite his ephemeral rule, really be regarded as an usurper, having been recognized by the senate and having tried to stand up to a murderous usurper. The senate, to which he belonged by birth – the first such emperor since Gallienus almost a century before – no doubt accorded him the annually renewable proconsular and tribunician power. There appear to be no lapidary inscriptions to him surviving, but coin evidence provides him with two main imperial styles: Fl[avius] Pop[illius] Nepotianus Augustus and Fl[aviu]s Nep[otianus] Constantinus Augustus.[516] One shows him, most unusually for the time, bare headed, the other laureate. These suggest that he assumed the *agnomen* Constantinus subsequent to his elevation in order to bolster his claim to legitimacy. The lack of a depiction of a diadem or radiate crown along with the use of a contemporary prefix, like *dominus noster*, might also suggest that his senatorial sponsors saw themselves as asserting a long-departed influence and reverting to a more traditional style of principate. He also issued coins in the name of Constantius II and, in one account, made his son Nigrinianus *caesar*.

After attempting to resist, the Prefect of the City, Fabius Titianus, a supporter of Magnentius, fled, leaving the new ruler to establish his position. But Magnentius quickly dealt with the situation by sending a force under his *magister officiorum*, Marcellinus. In the ensuing rather one-sided encounter on 30 June the hapless augustus was killed, his head put on a lance and paraded around the city *pour encourager les autres*. His mother, Eutropia. possibly a prime mover in the matter, was also killed the day afterwards, along with his son, various other members of the Constantinian family in the capital and a large number of other people involved, most of them senators.

NERO
54, 13th October – 68, 9th June

Nero was the last member of the Julio-Claudian dynasty, and a ruler who, even before his demise, was mired in infamy, held up by Christians as a monster and in popular memory as a callous spoilt brat; recent attempts to rehabilitate his reputation by emphasising his love of art, architecture and culture have been only partly successful.

---

516 PLRE I Nepotianus 5

L. Domitius Cn. f. L. n. Ahenobarbus was born at Antium on 15 December AD37, a member of the ancient plebeian nobility by descent, son of Cn. Domitius Ahenobarbus (consul in 32) and Julia Agrippina, but who was also a grandson of Mark Antony. His mother was a great granddaughter of Augustus, and a daughter of the successful marshal and heir presumptive of Tiberius, Germanicus. The blood of Lepidus and Cato also flowed through Nero's veins. He was adopted by the Emperor Claudius in AD49 as Nero Claudius Caesar Drusus Germanicus, making him a patrician. He was brought up from the age of three by women, chief amongst them his ruthlessly ambitious mother Agrippina (junior). He was eleven when he suddenly found himself in the Imperial family and barely twelve before he was adopted by his stepfather, with all the pressures, both covert and public, his new position inevitably attracted, leaving him little chance of a normal childhood even by aristocratic Roman standards.

He succeeded Claudius in October 54 jointly with his adoptive brother Britannicus, Claudius' only son. He was styled Nero Claudius Caesar Augustus Germanicus, adding the office of *Pontifex Maximus* and the title *Pater Patriae* ('father of his country') after Britannicus' convenient death in February, 55. He was the first emperor never to have been a senator prior to his accession, and although granted the tribunician power by the senate on 4 December following his accession, he did not hold a consulship until 55, following it with others in 57, 58, 60 and 68. He was hailed as *imperator* on his accession – now a formality, having nothing to do with success on the battlefield – and thirteen times subsequently.

Despite the highly suspicious demise of Claudius, followed by the appallingly public and still highly questionable death of his half-brother, his reign started well. Holland, perhaps rightly, goes as far as to remove from Nero the motive for conniving or acquiescing in the death of Britannicus.[517] He maintains that he was a young aesthete with literary, thespian, poetic and sporting pretensions, with no particular desire to become the hag-ridden ruler of most of the known world – he just wanted to be free. This argument fails to take into account the social obloquy likely to be attracted to a senator of patrician rank indulging such tastes publicly. As it turned out, only by wielding supreme power was the young emperor able to indulge his exhibitionist love of the performing arts. Yet it may be doubted that his reputation would have stood up to scrutiny had he occupied a private station in life.

Nevertheless, Nero's predilections, especially as he got older, were much appreciated in the Hellenised east. Under the guidance of his tutor L. Annaeus Seneca the younger and the Pretorian Prefect Sex. Afranius Burrus, appointed in 51, the first few years were tranquil and successful ones, although Nero did tend to make unsuitable political decisions against advice. Yet the tensions with the senate experienced under Claudius were largely avoided and even after the untidy killing of Agrippina in 59, Nero was still able to rule fairly sensibly.

---

517 *Op. cit.* (2000) 81-82

Yet from AD60-61 he began to show signs of instability and appalling self-indulgence – the behaviour of a spoiled brat suddenly freed from control. In this case, the constraints were removed by the execution of his mother (in 59), the poisoning of Burrus (in 62) and the retirement not long afterwards of Seneca who, in 65, pre-emptively took his own life over alleged implication in a conspiracy.

Despite acceptance in the eastern provinces, aided by the triumphant progress of the brilliant general Cn. Domitius Corbulo (no relation), there was much discontent, especially in the west. Provincial government underwent a number of convulsions caused by maladministration or complacency, culminating in Boudicca's British revolt in 61 and various other perturbations.[518] The excessively bloody reaction to the apparently serious conspiracy of C. Calpurnius Piso, the famous fire at Rome and the public extravagance and boorishness of the emperor all conspired eventually to spark revolt. This manifested itself in Gaul in 68, under the local aristocrat C. Julius Vindex (qv), who tried to involve the support of the long-serving governor of Hispania Tarraconensis, Galba. The latter hung back until Vindex had been dealt with by neighbouring governor Verginius Rufus but, with the unexpected backing of the praetorians under Nymphidius Sabinus (qv), he raised the standard of revolt and Nero, seeing that his position was hopeless, took his own life outside Rome on 9 June 68, allegedly uttering the famous words *qualis artifex me decessit* – 'what an artist dies in me!'

He left behind him no obvious heir – he had had most of his surviving relatives, even quite distant ones, murdered – and the universal realisation that the army, not the senate, would in future be the final arbiter of the succession. To reach that conclusion, three more emperors were to die and thousands killed in civil conflict: a heavy price to pay to learn what is to us, with hindsight, obvious.

In 53 Nero married Claudia Octavia, his half-sister as the daughter of Claudius and Messallina, whom he divorced as barren in 62 and who was killed in exile on Pandateria later that year on the bizarre charge of being adulterously pregnant. His second wife, who had been his mistress for some time previously and whom he married twelve days after divorcing Octavia, was the outstandingly beautiful (Ollia) Poppaea Sabina. Nero forced her compliant second husband – his contemporary, drinking partner and future emperor, M. Salvius Otho – to agree to a divorce. She was already pregnant by Nero at the time with their daughter, Claudia who lived only three and a half months; he took her death very badly indeed. Poppaea miscarried in 65 and died of internal haemorrhaging, although malicious rumour put it about that he had kicked her to death after she scolded him for coming home late from chariot racing. This seems unlikely. She was later deified by the senate. In 66 he married for a third time Statilia Messallina (he was her fifth husband) by whom he had no further issue. She survived him and was wooed by Otho in 69. She long outlived them all.

---

518 The more Celticised version of the queen's name, Boudicca, is more favoured these days, although Boadicaea is what the Romans called her.

NERVA
96, 18ᵗʰ September 96 – 98, 27ᵗʰ January

Nerva was an elderly stop-gap emperor, put in place by those who had contrived the end of Domitian to hold the fort whilst Trajan was manoeuvred into position to succeed him.

The Emperor Nerva is, in historical terms, something of an appendage to the Flavian era, being an acknowledged temporary measure, acclaimed to ensure that the political vacuum created by the assassination of Domitian was adequately filled whilst the true inheritor of the Flavians, Trajan, marshalled his forces and in due time effected a smooth takeover, ushering in the next era, wherein once again there was something of a partnership – however illusory – between *princeps* and senate, between the ruler and the ruling class. Nerva acted as a bridge between the two.[519] The choice by those privy to the assassination of Domitian – not their first – of the elderly senator Nerva is not an obvious one to modern eyes, except insofar as the old fellow (he was actually only 61, albeit in indifferent health) was childless and his family was virtually extinct and thus unlikely to produce any claimant to his position on his death; although Dio says he did have relatives then living, one of whom might well have been, as Syme surmises, Ser[gius] Octavius Laenas, suffect consul in the significant year of 97.[520] The new ruler himself appears to have been without enemies, which also helped. The choice, moreover, was the senate's, which was good news as far as the ruling élite were concerned, but less so for the army and general populace, who had less animus toward Domitian – after all, neither element was likely to lose any sleep over the regular executions by the emperor of kinsmen or senators.

The Cocceii were from Narnia (Narni) in Umbria and seem not to have been of senatorial rank until the Triumvirate, although the brothers Lucius (a legate in 41 and 37BC) and M. Cocceius Nerva, consul in 36BC, were probably adlected into the senate by Julius Caesar.[521] That the suffect consul of 39, C. Cocceius Balbus – also doubtless a Caesarian appointment – was a relative is not in much doubt.[522] Balbus was made a patrician by Octavian in 30 and that enhancement in status appears to have also applied to the Cocceii Nervae, suggesting that they were three brothers. Unfortunately, the surviving *fasti* (consular lists) fail to endow either M. Nerva or C. Balbus – both supporters of Mark Antony – with a filiation, depriving us of the chance of drawing any further conclusions about their ancestry. Both M. Nerva and Balbus were hailed as *imperator* following feats of military prowess. Genealogically, Nerva belonged to the previous era, in that he was the brother-in-law of the emperor Otho and that his maternal aunt was the daughter of Tiberius' granddaughter Julia. As, however, he adopted Trajan in his own lifetime rather than by testamentary bequest, he stands at the

519 Syme (1958) 1-12; Syme AA, 220, 223
520 Dio LXXVIII. 4. 1; Syme (1958) II. 627
521 Wiseman (1971) Nos. 125 & n. 126; PIR² C1223-1224; Syme (1986) 48 & n. 106, 221 f., cf. Syme (1939) 200, 267
522 Wiseman, *op. cit.* no. 124; PIR² C1214

beginning of this fresh sequence of rulers, a regular uninterrupted succession down to 192. It can be seen as an era of continued and fruitful co-operation between emperor and senate in governing; it is also generally considered to have been the Empire's high point. By the end of the following dynasty, the Severans, the cracks were beginning to show.

M. Cocceius [M.f. M. n. Pap.] Nerva was born a patrician on 8 November 35 at Narnia (Narni), north of Rome. He entered the senate with election as quaestor in about 62 and was rewarded by Nero, extraordinarily, with triumphal ornaments and two statues for his aid in exposing the plot of C. Piso in 65, perhaps suggesting that he was inclined to cultivate the ruler of the day.[523] He served as praetor in 66 but missed a consulship in his earliest qualifying year (*suo anno*) of 68; perhaps Nero had gone cold on him by then. Nevertheless, he was accorded the honour of being Vespasian's colleague as consul in 71, going on to a second consulship in 90; he was also a respected figure to Domitian, as with Nero, which suggests that the story that he had once seduced the young Domitian was spurious. There is no record of him as provincial administrator, general or even, like his father and grandfather, jurist, only a reputation as a minor poet and intellectual. He was also cautious, self-effacing when things got tricky, and safe. His sister married Emperor Otho's brother Titianus. The suggestion that another (unrecorded) sister married Vespasian's elder brother Sabinus is speculative.[524]

On being acclaimed emperor, Nerva was hailed as *imperator* and took the style Imperator Nerva Caesar Augustus to which a relieved senate added, within a few days, *Pater Patriae, Pontifex Maximus,* the proconsular *imperium* and the tribunician power. He served his third consulship in 97 and another in 98, receiving a second imperial acclamation in October 97, when the *agnomen* Germanicus was added to his imperial style, no doubt reflecting an unrecorded success of Roman arms in that part of the Empire, the upper province of which was then, significantly, under the governorship of M. Ulpius Traianus – the future emperor Trajan.

Nerva's reign was touch-and-go during its first year, however, culminating in a mutiny of the Praetorian Guard in the early autumn of 97, an event that often betokened the immediate demise of the incumbent emperor. The prefect Casperius Aelianus, at the head of a strong detachment of his men, locked Nerva in the palace and demanded the release into their custody of two of the six men responsible for the murder of Domitian, the only emperor to have increased their pay since Claudius. Nerva stood up to them and the men were seized and summarily killed anyway. That the elderly Emperor was in declining health and was childless probably saved his life. Nonetheless, his authority was entirely vitiated, a fact he appreciated well enough to realize that the designation of an heir likely to be effective and popular with the army was required with immediate effect.

He chose as successor the man who had been involved in the suppression of the insurrection of L. Antonius Saturninus (qv) in 89, M. Ulpius Traianus,

---

523 Tacitus, *Annals* 15, 71
524 Settipani (2000) 273

a highly competent general and almost certainly a nephew by marriage of the popular and fondly remembered Emperor Titus, a factor which contributed much to the selection of a man from a family relatively new to senatorial rank. At the end of October 97, Nerva formally adopted Trajan, who thenceforth was styled Caesar Nervae f. Nerva Traianus Germanicus.

The question remains as to what extent Trajan manipulated the adoption himself, how much the running was made by his allies in Rome and how much was due to unbiased good advice offered to Nerva. As Trajan was away in Upper Germany throughout the reign, it is difficult to see his involvement being a particularly important factor. Nerva died three months or so after Trajan's adoption, on 27 January 98, and the new Emperor succeeded with what appears to have been a complete lack of problems, despite not even being in the capital.

NIGER see PESCENNIUS NIGER

NIGRINIANUS (I)
(?282/4)

An inscription recorded at Rome reading *Divus Nigrinianus nepos Cari* ('The divine Nigrinianus, grandson of Carus') and a coin type bearing his portrait with a similar inscription (reverse *consecratio*) clearly relating to the family of Carus, suggests that Carinus, Numerianus or their sister Paulina left a son who may have lived on into the reign of Diocletian.[525] It is not known (but doubtful) whether he was made *nobilissimus caesar* or augustus. The most likely suggestion is that he was son of Numerianus, whose murdering father-in-law Diocletian had neutralised shortly after Numerian was found to have died. It may be that Nigrinianus survived the *coup* but died whilst still young and that, as a pious gesture, the new Emperor persuaded the senate to deify the boy. Some scholars have suggested he was the son of Carinus who might have been deified before the collapse of the dynasty, but the omission of the parents' names suggests the hand of Diocletian. There is no evidence for the names 'M. Aurelius' preceding Nigrinianus as some sources suggest.

NIGRINIANUS (II)
350, June – 1ˢᵗ July

Popillius Nepotianus Nigrinianus was the son of Constantine's senatorial nephew, Nepotianus, who briefly seized power against the usurper Magnentius from 3 to 30 June 350. He was, according to one source, made *nobilissimus caesar* but was killed the day after the elimination of his father when the attempt failed on 1 July 350.[526]

---

525 CIL VI 31380; PLRE I Nigrinianus 1; RIC 471, 472 & 474
526 Craven (2020) 428 & Table LII

NUMERIANUS
283, May – 284 November

Numerianus was the younger son of Carus, whom he succeeded whilst on campaign, who was murdered by his father's Pretorian Prefect. Numerianus was born c. 253 and was styled *nobilissimus caesar* from his father's accession in September 282, but from his accession on his father's death he was styled Imperator Caesar M. Aurelius Numerius Numerianus Pius Felix Invictus Augustus. He was left in command of the army fighting the Persians when his father unexpectedly died in August 28 and was able to mop up and arrange treaties after his accession, the Persian campaign having essentially been successfully completed prior to his father's death. He then withdrew the army to Syria, where the Emperor had to nurse his eye, which had developed a serious infection after sustaining what was probably a minor wound in the fighting in Mesopotamia en route to Persia.

After a while, as the army moved slowly back to Rome, Numerianus was obliged to travel in a closed litter, and by the time they had reached Sirmium (Sremska Mitrovika, Serbia), he had obviously died, for in the heat, a distinctive stench was emanating from the litter. Either he had been carried off by his infection or had been opportunistically murdered by his scheming father-in-law, the Pretorian Prefect Aper, who was certainly widely suspected of murdering the young man. Whatever the truth, a kangaroo court of senior officers put him on trial, but he hardly had time to be heard before, on 20 November, the troops acclaimed Diocles, then commander of the household mounted guard (*protectores domestici*), as emperor. Diocles moved swiftly to have Aper disposed of. A dispassionate eye might indeed discern the hand of Diocles, who now became emperor and re-named himself Diocletianus, in the entire sequence of events, the death of Carus as well as that of Numerianus and Aper – who, after all, was a member of the Imperial family – the latter framed and conveniently disposed of. By Aper's daughter, Flavia Aprilla, he is thought to have been the father of Nigrinianus (I).

ODAENATHUS
266–267

[L.] Septimius Odaenathus II was Prince of Palmyra 261-267, having been adlected into the Roman senate with the rank of ex-praetor, about 250/1. He was exarch of Palmyra with his father 251-267 and suffect consul c. 252/257. He was killed with his eldest son (or possibly sons, cf. *sub* Herodes/Herodian, Herennianus and Timolaus) in 267, probably at Emesa. The *Historia Augusta* claims that he was acclaimed Augustus but was killed shortly afterwards by Maeonius (qv), for which there is no evidence.[527]

---

527 Southern (2010) 78-81

OLYBRIUS
472, April – 2nd November

Olybrius was a Western Emperor imposed from Constantinople who died of natural causes just when he had obtained control over the shambles that was then the western empire. He is also important as a member of a quasi-imperial dynasty with huge influence both in Rome and Constantinople.

Anicius Olybrius was recognised as a leading member of the senate before he was forced to leave Rome on the fall of the man some scholars suspect was his father, Petronius Maximus, in 455.[528] He had inherited his name from Q. Clodius Hermogenianus Olybrius (consul in 379) who married an Anician family heiress, Anicia Juliana and whose own daughter and heiress married the great administrator of Valentinian I's reign, Sex. Claudius Petronius Probus, himself thought in some circles to have been a distaff great-grandson of the emperor Probus. Through his Anician forebears, he was also descended from L. Sergius Paullus, consul for the second time in 168, and descended from the L. Sergius Paullus who was consul early in Claudius' reign.[529] He was in all probability also a great-grandson of Magnus Maximus too; his family could hardly have been more grand or better qualified, by the standards of the time, to become emperor. By his first wife he had two sons, Olybrius, Pretorian Prefect of Italy in 503 and Eugenius, finance minister to King Theoderic. His second wife, Placidia, younger daughter of Valentinian III, bore him two further daughters, Anicia Juliana and Magna, whose posterity included a great granddaughter who married the brother of Emperor Justin II.[530]

Unlike his predecessor Anthemius, Olybrius was not an experienced soldier nor even, like his probable father, a distinguished administrator, but through marriage to Placidia, he was a member of the Theodosian dynasty and brother-in-law to Gaiseric, Vandal King of Africa, who had ceaselessly promoted his cause as his desired candidate as western emperor from the time of the fall of Majorian in 461, probably in the knowledge that Olybrius would not launch any attempt at an African *reconquista* against his own brother-in-law. Olybrius was made eastern consul in 464 (there was no western consul that year, just two eastern ones, but the fact that Olybrius was really a western senator probably justified it) and was made a patrician. Leo I sent him to Rome to make peace between Ricimer and Anthemius and having done that he was supposed to go on to Carthage to sign an accord with Gaiseric, too. Instead, he got caught up in events in Italy, finding himself entering Rome as Emperor on 11 July 472, probably having been acclaimed by the western *magister militum* Ricimer *in absentia* in April, whilst Anthemius was still alive.[531] He was almost certainly designated as

---

528 If not Petronius Maximus' son, he must, from his name, have been a very close relation.

529 ILS5926, *Acts* 13.7. They were also raised to patrician status by c. 150: Syme, RP III 1 325

530 Juliana married Areobindus (consul 506); Magna married Paullus (consul 496) brother of Anastasius (qv).

531 Salzman (2021) 208-209

western consul for 473 (with Leo as eastern colleague) but he died before the beginning of that year and the western consulship became vacant.

It is not known what sort of reception the new Emperor received from his fellow senators, but no doubt it was favourable as he was one of their own, and they installed him and accorded him the powers required. He took the style Dominus Noster Anicius Olybrius Pius Felix Augustus.[532] He had established himself when first elevated by minting coins at Mediolanum (Milan), but what precisely he did during the long siege of Rome is not known. It is likely that he was present during at least part of it. Once installed, his only recorded act was to confer the title of patrician upon young Gundobad, the son of Ricimer's sister. Gundobad's Burgundians at this time formed the backbone of the army and this guaranteed the soldiers' loyalty. Thus, when the Emperor died from natural causes on 2 November, it was Gundobad who held all the cards. He was succeeded after an interval of four months by Glycerius.

OTHO
69, 15th January – 16th April

Otho was the second ruler in the notorious Year of the Four Emperors, who seems rapidly to have transformed himself from drinking companion of Nero and rake into one who emerges from the enterprise he undertook as decent and loyal. Galba appointed Vitellius to govern Lower Germany in December 68, but Vitellius was already intriguing to replace the aged martinet. Meanwhile, Nero's former companion Otho had been a keen supporter of Galba and was another of his appointees during his bid for the purple. Otho was on the spot later when it became clear that the Praetorian Guard were sufficiently disaffected as to be prepared to depose Galba. By that time, the younger man had come to feel disaffected in that he had been passed over in favour of Galba's nominee as heir, Piso. His *coup* was entirely separate from anything Vitellius was hatching in Germany. Otho became emperor on 15 January 69.

M. Salvius Otho was born on 28 April 32, the younger son of L. Salvius Otho Titianus, who was the first consul of what was previously a relatively obscure senatorial family.[533] Suetonius tells us that Otho's grandfather was the first member in the senate and whose own father had been an equestrian married to a 'peasant' girl, conceivably of unfree stock.[534] However, M. Otho, as peoples' tribune in the tumultuous year of 43, must have been a very close kinsman, if not the future Emperor's great-grandfather. The senate was heavily purged after the inauguration of the Second Triumvirate, and M. Otho could well have been one of those recently ennobled (or even of more ancient, if obscure stock) sent packing back into the ranks of the equestrian order. If so, to retire during the Civil Wars to the family's native

---

532 Coin evidence.
533 FS 2975; PIR² S43
534 Suetonius *Otho* 1, 1-2

Otho: an 18th-century grand tour bas relief, with the Emperor's nomen misspelt *Silvius*. (Bamfords Ltd.)

Ferentium (Ferento) would have been a logical, prudent move. Otho's father was given patrician rank by Claudius in 48. Whilst the family appear to have originated in Ferentum, there were senatorial Salvii under the later Republic, a *prefectus Sociorum* in 168 and a *praetor* of 74; they might well have been kin.

Otho entered the senate with a quaestorship in 58, having already become a member of the priestly Arval Brethren, probably through the especial favour of Nero. He was sent to govern Lusitania from whence he returned to Rome as a leading lieutenant of Galba. He married c. AD56, as her second husband, Poppaea Sabina (qv Nero), by whom he had no children by the time he was sent to Lusitania by Nero, whose mistress she already was and whose wife she promptly became. Although he was actively seeking a second wife after his accession, he never had a chance to re-marry and died just short of his 37th birthday without issue.

Having been acclaimed emperor he held a suffect consulship. He adopted the imperial style Imperator M. Otho Caesar Augustus and was probably invested with the tribunician power following his announcement to the senate on the evening of 15 January that he had accepted the purple; if not, it would have followed within days. He became *Pontifex Maximus* from 9 March, the date of his departure from Rome to face Vitellius.

Thus, although he obtained the extremely reluctant support of the senate and most of the provinces, he never really had time to consolidate his position, for Vitellius had begun to move against him almost from day one of his principate. His restoration of Nero's statues – ordered to be pulled down by Galba – was no doubt a bid to win the support of all those who never lost their affection for the last of the Julio-Claudians. He also attempted to ally himself with Vitellius, dangling before him the prospect of joint power, even proposing marriage to the governor of Germany's daughter, although in the process he was obliged to soft-pedal the overtures he had been making to Nero's dowager empress, Statilia Messallina.

Despite deploying what limited forces he had to prevent Vitellius crossing the Po, aid from the Balkans was too slow in reaching him and he was defeated at the first battle of Cremona on 14 April. He considered matters for a day or so and then, to spare the Empire further civil strife – or so he thought – took his own life on the 16th at nearby Brixellum (Brescello). Vitellius thus succeeded to the empire by a third successive violent *coup*. Tacitus, usually a harsh critic, notes that Otho's personal conduct as Emperor – unlike his profligate days as Nero's soul-mate – was both exemplary and praiseworthy. He was popular in death in a way he could only have dreamt of in life.

OVIDA
480, 9th May – 482, December

With Viator, Ovida was a *comes* of Julius Nepos (to whom he was conceivably related) who decided with his colleague to do away with his master and who personally took over in his stead, ruling Dalmatia and a considerable surrounding area, and lasting until overthrown by Odoacer in December 482.[535] Whether he styled himself Augustus and was thus a full-blooded usurper, or merely gave himself some honorific like *magister militum* is not clear. On precedent and circumstantial evidence, the former would seem the more convincing. No coins are known, however, although this is not wholly surprising. Julius Nepos had claimed to be emperor of the west even when confined by events to Dalmatia and presumably, Ovida maintained a similar illusion, otherwise one might doubt whether Odoacer would have bothered to depose him.

PACATIANUS
248, c. 22nd April – c. July

Pacatianus was a general serving on the Danube who was proclaimed, probably in desperate circumstances, in the reign of Philip the Arab, but whose attempt at power failed to develop and who was probably killed by the very men who had in the first place acclaimed him.

The rise of the usurper Pacatianus on the Danube frontier, presumably again in (probably Upper) Moesia, may be related to the swift rise and fall of Sponsianus, unless both were elevated at about the same time in adjoining provinces in response to the same crisis, perhaps a military defeat. The removal of troops from the Danubian frontier to wage war against the Persians by Timisitheus seems to have come at a time when the barbarian peoples beyond were coming under pressure and the resulting perceived weakness of the Empire's defences seems to have encouraged these tribes to test them. That they probably found them wanting might seem evident from

---

535 PLRE II Ovida

the sequence of usurpers in the era and the subsequent defeat of the emperor Decius in 251. Pacatianus attempting to challenge Philip as a primary aim would seem unlikely, especially in view of a coin type he issued bearing the legend *Victoria Augg.* ('the victory of the emperors'). The doubling of the last consonant indicates two emperors reigning together in supposed harmony, or at least Pacatianus claiming that he was doing so; either he anticipated coming to an arrangement with Philip or he actually did.[536] In which case, his uprising must have occurred prior to Philip II being made Augustus – or the news had yet to reach him. Probably he merely anticipated coming to an arrangement.

Ti. Claudius Marinus Pacatianus[537] was son of [Ti.] Claudius Solemnis, suffect consul (presumably fairly late in life) c. 230. His mother may or may not have brought the name Pacat[ian]us into the family. As we do not know the name of the usurper's grandfather, we cannot tell if he was Marinus, Pacatianus or something else entirely. Pacatianus himself must have served as a suffect consul before c. 246/247, when he was presumably appointed governor of Lower or more probably Upper Moesia. Assuming his career was normal and that his family were not patrician, he would have been born c. 205, *quaestor* c. 233/234, *aedile* or people's tribune 235/236 and *praetor* c. 240, after which he would have served as commander of a legion or been governor of a lesser province. He was imperially acclaimed on or just after 22 April 248, adopting the imperial style Imperator Ti. Claudius Marinus Pacatianus Pius Felix Augustus[538] and he was killed in July or possibly August the same year. No wife is known, nor any issue, but one should note Claudius Julius Pacat[ia]nus, a senator who governed Campania at some unknown period in the later 4th or earlier 5th centuries.[539]

Pacatianus' rebellion provided an opportunity for a renewed Gothic incursion which lasted nearly three years, causing the utmost chaos on the Danube and accounting for the lives of the emperor Decius and his elder son, as well as that of the usurper Priscus. All this may have been the reason that he was apparently killed by his own men in the late summer of 248. The senate, ignorant of his demise, later condemned him as a public enemy.

PERTINAX

193, 1st January – 28th March

Pertinax was a venerable old soldier who was called upon to fill the vacuum created by the assassination of Commodus, but who failed to assert himself sufficiently to avert a descent into tumult. No one could say that the conspirators who seized their chance in murdering Commodus had really evolved any consequent plan if they succeeded, so the Pretorian Prefect

---

536 The third alternative was that the mintmaster used an extant reverse die for Philip I and Philip II.

537 PIR² C390; Körner (2001) 282-288

538 Coin evidence. The 'Pius Felix' seems to have been added after an interval.

539 PLRE II. Pacatianus 2; ILS 6505. The names are by no means uncommon, however.

Laetus and the Imperial freedman Eclectus, the Emperor's *cubicularius* (chamberlain), having pulled off their *coup* on New Year's night 192, had to act extremely quickly to avoid civil war.

Quite why they chose the first-generation senator, freedman's son and former general Pertinax is unclear, except that he had a track record of being a steadying influence. Yet there were several kinsmen and sons-in-law of Marcus Aurelius still then living and in Rome whom they could have chosen, one or two quite possibly better choices. Indeed, one of them, Claudius Pompeianus, actually proposed the 66-year-old retired general Pertinax to the assembled senators, supported by M.' Acilius Glabrio, another kinsman of the Antonine dynasty. Glabrio, a scion of the Republican nobility, had himself been proposed as Emperor by Pertinax prior to the general's acceptance of the purple for himself, but had wisely demurred. In consequence, he left descendants traceable into the sixth century.

P. Helvius Pertinax was born on 1 August 126 at his mother's villa in the Appenines at Alba Pompeia (Alba). At first, from c. 147, he worked as a teacher, but in 161 he became dissatisfied with the low pay – nothing changes – and joined the army. Although an equestrian, he was rapidly commissioned and enjoyed a quite remarkable career which, in view of his lack of powerful patrons, has to reflect exceedingly well on his abilities as both a soldier and an administrator. He was next appointed prefect of a cohort of Gauls in Syria, going on to become tribune of *legio* VI Victrix stationed at York. His natural aptitude and leadership qualities underpinned his rise and he was given a command in Moesia on the Danubian frontier where he quickly covered himself in glory. Thereafter he served as *procurator alimentorum* (quartermaster) and *praefectus classis* (fleet commander) in Germany.

He was made a senator aroud 170 by being adlected on the Emperor's nomination, either amongst the tribunes of the people or the aediles. He served as praetor in 171/172, thereafter commanding a legion in Pannonia Superior, where he achieved a notable victory beyond the frontier of the province. He was nominated suffect consul in 175, in which office his colleague was, ironically, his successor as emperor, Didius Julianus, after which he governed successively the Moesias, Dacia and Syria, being *en poste* at the latter when Commodus succeeded. On his return, he was encouraged to retire but was recalled in 185 to be entrusted by Commodus with the suppression of a mutiny in the army of Britain, after which he governed Africa.[540] He was appointed prefect of the City of Rome (PUR) in 189, in which office he was still serving when offered the purple. He had served as ordinary consul in AD192, an honour that usually accompanied the successful tenure of the urban prefecture. He was never given patrician status and was thus the first fully recognised emperor unquestionably not to have been of this status.

Pertinax was perceived as a safe pair of hands and his house was conveniently placed for the conspirators to reach under cover of darkness.

---

540 PIR² H73; cf. Birley (1981) 377f., where he suggests that the HA biography is, on the whole, truthful.

The backing of the Praetorian Guard was, however, crucial, and their loyalty was quickly bought by a donative of HS12,000 per man, a move wisely endorsed by the new Emperor who, although thought to be strict and prudent, was reluctant to make the same mistake as Galba. This sordid but necessary preliminary over, the newly acclaimed Emperor, soldiers and people marched to the senate house, where he was duly acclaimed.

On 1 January 193, he assumed the consulship (his third) which Commodus had expected to take up, was appointed *pater patriae*, given the tribunician and proconsular powers. He was also named *princeps senatus* (president of the senate) and assumed the style Imperator Caesar P. Helvius Pertinax Augustus.[541] His wife, Flavia Titiana, was made Augusta on her husband's elevation.[542] She was a daughter of T. Flavius Claudius Sulpicianus, whom Pertinax appointed PUR in his own stead. Sulpicianus was later to make a bid for the purple himself in the famous 'auction' of 28 March 193 (qv *sub* Didus Julianus) being relieved of office in consequence but spared in the aftermath. The new imperial couple had two children living: a son, P. Helvius Pertinax the younger who added Caesar to his name, was appointed *princeps iuventutis* and lived to serve as consul in 212, and a sister who married the senator M. Nummius Senecio Albinus.

The main problem to be faced was the near bankruptcy of the treasury, not through poor administration but by the colossal cost of Commodus's vanities, in spite of the seizure of the property of numerous liquidated senators. This Pertinax rashly blamed on the Imperial freedmen rather than on Commodus himself, the memory of whom, like that of so many tyrants, was still cherished by the Roman mob, isolated by their anonymity from his murderous caprice.

The situation was, in fact, much as it had been on the assassination of Nero, therefore, and Pertinax began to make all the same mistakes, being too strict and trying to introduce all the reforms that he rightly saw as being urgently needed rather too quickly, thus alienating most elements of the governing élite, especially the Praetorian Guard, who were the real power-brokers. Indeed, early in March the praetorians tried to stage a *coup* whilst Pertinax was out of town, although quite why they chose the patrician consul Q. Sosius Pompeius Falco is unclear; possibly they reckoned he was good for a hefty donative should the *coup* succeed. However, it didn't really get off the ground and Falco was pardoned; the matter had not got far enough even to qualify him as an usurper.

The Praetorians tried again at the end of the month. On 28 March a detachment of some 300 guardsmen burst into the Imperial Palace and meeting little resistance burst in on the Emperor who, despite being urged to flee, thought he could outface his attackers. Whilst reasoning with them and trying to explain his policies, one hothead, perhaps seeing that the old general was beginning to be heeded, rushed forward and ran him through with his sword, shouting, 'The soldiers have sent you this,' at which the remainder

---

541 ILS 407, 408, 409

542 PIR² F444

lost their grip and Pertinax died under a welter of blows. He was deified by the senate on 1 June 193, confirmed by an elaborate ceremony some ten days later, his cult to be supervised by the *sodales* (priests) of the cult of the Antonine Emperors, of which Pertinax junior was appointed *flamen* by Septimius Severus.[543]

PESCENNIUS NIGER
193, April 193 – 194, c. 1st May

Niger was one of three ambitious generals who, on hearing of the death of Pertinax, vied to become emperor and who, whilst failing to reach Rome, held out in a polity of his own in the east until snuffed out by a vengeful rival, Septimius Severus. C. Pescennius Niger should really rate as an usurper rather than a canonical emperor, for his elevation was never recognised by the senate. Yet he issued a fairly prolific coinage and is usually included in the official canon of emperors.

The episode of the murder of Pertinax and of Didius Julianus' assumption of power, once news of it had reached the provinces and more especially the armed provinces, produced outrage amongst their governors and legionary legates. Many of the former were contemporaries and perhaps even friends of the participants, but few can have failed to have been appalled by the events of 28 March 193. In the event, three senatorial governors were, or had themselves, proclaimed emperor, and a repeat of the events of 68-69 seemed about to unfold.

C. Pescennius Niger was born c. 135/140, and although his father's name is unclear, his grandfather had allegedly been a minor official at Aquinum (Aquino), whence the family came – but the author of the *Historia Augusta* immediately qualifies this information with '...this fact is even now considered doubtful'.[544] We are not vouchsafed this man's name, either. Pescennius Niger had a brother, Publius, a member of the arval brethren and hence a senator, who may have left descendants. Niger began his career as a centurion in the army and by dint of talent and success appears to have reached a senior equestrian command, distinguishing himself in Dacia early in the 180s alongside Clodius Albinus. This might suggest that by this time he had been adlected into the senate, but this is not necessarily so; he could have been one of Albinus's prefectorial commanders. Nevertheless, he must have been adlected sometime in that decade, for he rose to a suffect consulship in c. 189/190, going on to govern Syria, where he was still *en poste* when he heard of Pertinax's murder.[545] His wife's name is unknown, but the *Historia Augusta* claims there were two sons.

---

543 PIR² H74

544 A Republican *triumvir capitalis* (and thus a potential senator) C. Pescennius in 129 and L.Pescennius T. f., who made a dedication at Firmum at about the same period are recorded; one of them or a kinsman may well have enfranchised Niger's family. The *Historia Augusta* calls his father Annius Fuscus.

545 This and the command in Dacia are attested by Dio 72. 8 & 74. 6

Both Septimius Severus and Pescennius Niger were proclaimed at about the same time – immediately news came through to them at the very beginning of April – Niger in Syria and Severus in Upper Pannonia. Niger was proclaimed by his legions at Antioch (he could command ten overall) but seems to have thereafter made no move. Indeed, he is said to have been a rather negative sort of person, 'remarkable for nothing, good or bad',[546] which is strange, for his proclamation was widely supported by rioting in Rome.

He took the style Imperator Caesar C. Pescennius Niger Justus Augustus,[547] 'Justus' being a post-acclamatory assumption, presumably in order to set the tone for his rule. He must have achieved some kind of recognition from the senate, to whom he apparently sent numerous messages, for he assumed a second consulship either on acclamation or at the beginning of 194 – he is *co[n]s[ul] II* on three separate types of coin – but the consulship was, if recognised at Rome at the time, a suffect one, for the ordinary consuls for that year were Severus and Albinus. Likewise, his coin types make no mention of the pontificate, nor of the proconsular and tribunician power.

By the time Severus, whose province was much closer to the capital and who acted with commendable celerity once he had been acclaimed, was in control of the capital, Niger's proclamations and messages to the senate were being intercepted. By the end of June, the claimant's children were being sought to be placed under house arrest, whilst those of Asellius Aemilianus – Niger's chief henchman in Rome, despite being a kinsman of Severus' then ally, Clodius Albinus – were seized.

Niger set up HQ at Byzantium and began to strike coins (albeit from rather crudely engraved dies) but was besieged there by an army under L. Marius Maximus, later a notable historian, to whose aid Severus had despatched his ally L. Fabius Chilo, before even having arrived in Rome. Chilo had suffered a reverse by July, but nevertheless Niger's success caused the senate, under pressure from Severus, to declare him a public enemy. Undeterred, Niger remained confident and was soon calling himself a 'new Alexander', despite being put on the defensive by the proximity of Marius Maximus and the imminent arrival of Severus himself. Not long afterwards, when Severus, had arrived, Niger made an offer to share the Empire with him, which was summarily rejected, although as a counter-offer Severus declared that he was prepared to spare his rival's life if he were to surrender and go into exile. This offer may have been refused on the basis that Severus was unlikely to honour it and indeed, his later treatment of opponents reinforces such a view. It may be, too, that Niger saw that remaining in control of the east and consolidating his position might be a better medium-term policy, rather anticipating the sort of division of the Empire made by Valerian and Gallienus, later by the Tetrarchs and permanently by Theodosius I.

By October, Niger's lieutenant Aemilianus had been defeated and killed and by the beginning of 194 Severus' general Ti. Claudius Candidus had won a last-minute victory over Niger at Nicaea, news of which caused Egypt

---

546 Dio 74f
547 Coin evidence.

to defect to Severus. After two more months of cat-and-mouse, a final battle was fought by this 'New Alexander' on the river Issus – the site of one of Alexander the Great's most momentous victories – in which his forces were routed and he fled to Antioch intending to make for Parthia, but he was caught and killed in late April or early May. The last resistance was over by the 21st. Thereafter, Severus's only rival was Albinus.

Severus returned to Rome and conducted a bloody purge of senators who had been disloyal in various ways. In the *Historia Augusta's* list of these unfortunates, some of the names are attested (though largely considered spurious); it includes a gaggle of Pescennii.[548]

PETRONIUS MAXIMUS (V)
455, 17ᵗʰ March – 31ˢᵗ May

Maximus was a senatorial nobleman of the highest distinction who became emperor in the wake of the murder of Valentinian III, in which act he may well have been complicit, but whose espousal of the widowed empress led the Vandal ruler Gaiseric to raid Italy and sack Rome, during which the new emperor was killed by the mob for his inability to defend them.

Petronius Maximus was the first member an old senatorial family to accede to the purple, other than as an usurper, since the elevation 202 years before of Valerian and Gallienus in 253; although no ancient source tells us precisely who his parents were. However, modern scholarship has pieced together a pedigree which is taken as accepted as virtually certain, even without direct attestation.

His father is believed to have been Anicius Probinus (consul in 395) son of a distinguished administrator, Sex. Petronius Probus, and he may have been descended from the emperors Probus and Magnus Maximus (qv).[549] He was a member of the powerful Anician family through Anicia, first wife of Petronius Probianus, consul in 322. It is possible to trace a descent from the probably senatorial father of Q. Anicius Q. f. Faustus, a suffect consul in 198 who was given patrician status by Septimius Severus.[550] In his turn, his forebear may have been Q. Anicius Faustus, a *duumvir* (town councillor) of Italian colonial origin at Uzappa (Ab'd el-Melek), in Africa living early in the second century, making Anicius Faustus a fellow African and therefore admirable, as far as Severus was concerned.[551]

Maximus was born c. 396 and was praetor in 411 (when he was about 15, the magistracy having become notional by this stage and merely a platform for the recipient's family to give lavish games). At 18 he was appointed *tribunus et notarius* (a prestigious civil service sinecure) followed by the responsible post of *comes sacrarum largitionum* (keeper of the privy purse)

---

548 HA *V. Sev.* 13.3
549 *Historia Augusta* V. Probi 24, 3 (viewed cynically by Syme (1968) 11); the latter on the testimony of Procopius, cf. Mommaerts & Kelly (1992) 111-120
550 PIR² A595
551 ILS1263

c. 416-419 and the prefecture of the city (PUR) 420-421 (one was normally in office for eighteen months). He was PUR for a second time later, probably in the 430s, when he undertook repairs to the basilica of St Peter. In the early 430s he served as Pretorian Prefect (of which part of the west is not clear) and held his first consulship in 433 with the Eastern Emperor Theodosius II as colleague. Then, from 439 to 441, he was again Pretorian Prefect, this time of Italy. In 443 he held a second consulship (west) during which and for the two years following, he undertook the construction of a new forum at Rome on the *Mons Caelius*. By 445 he had been created a patrician and *vir illustris*. His career, for a senator especially, was notably distinguished, but it seems to have given him imperial ambitions and having, it was said, engendered the fall of Aëtius, his only rival, he was in a position to dictate the succession to the childless Valentinian.

The story from the fall of Aëtius to the death of Maximus has all the elements of tragic opera. Following the death of the general at the hands of the emperor himself, Maximus lobbied hard to be appointed *magister militum* in his place (a first for a senatorial aristocrat) along with a third consulship, but the emperor refused and instead appointed the Gaul Majorian. According to John of Antioch, Maximus then used the rape of his wife (whom he names as Lucina, but who is not elsewhere attested[552]) by the Emperor as a motive for the assassination, the deed being accomplished very publicly by two officers, thought to be in Maximus' pay, in the *Campus Martius* on 16 March 455.[553]

Following the murder, Maximus moved to make a donative to the army and neutralise the ambitions of Majorian, being acclaimed the following day. He immediately set about consolidating his dynastic position by marrying the Empress Eudoxia (apparently against her will) and also marrying his son Palladius to the late Emperor's daughter, widowed by the fall of her father-in-law Aëtius, which appears to have brought his son Gaudentius to ruin, too. It seems likely that his younger son and the future emperor Olybrius (the relationship is nowhere attested but is increasingly accepted) had by this time already married the younger princess, Placidia.[554]

Maximus took the style Dominus Noster Petronius Maximus Pius Felix Augustus, and as a leading member of the senate would undoubtedly have had himself voted the usual powers and probably was declared consul designate for the year following, although this is not directly attested. His eldest son, Palladius, was made *nobilissimus caesar* at approximately the same time. Although he was unable to obtain recognition from the eastern court (it might have been forthcoming if events had turned out differently), he was acknowledged in the west.

He appointed his probable ex-brother-in-law, the Gallic senator Avitus, as *magister militum* and despatched him to Gaul to conclude a treaty with the

---

552 She must have died or been divorced by the time of Maximus's accession, however and is more likely to have been called Palladia and to have been a sister of Avitus, thus explaining the name Palladius for one of his sons.

553 PLRE II Maximus 22

554 The chronicler Hydatius only says Palladius was married to a daughter of Valentinian III; Conant *inter alia* favours Eudocia: *op. cit.* (2012) 27

Visigoths and to bring a detachment of them to strengthen the armed forces at the new emperor's disposal. To this end, the Emperor seems to have minted an unusual amount of gold coin both at Rome and Ravenna, undoubtedly to pay the Gothic auxiliaries and the donative to the troops already on hand. There are no known base metal or silver coins from this reign.

His reluctant Empress, in emulation of her sister-in-law's appeal to Attila, apparently called upon the Vandal King Gaiseric to come to her aid. He was only too pleased to do so, and arrived in Italy before Avitus had returned with the Visigothic reinforcements. Maximus had insufficient troops at his immediate disposal to defend the city and decreed its evacuation. Understandably, the prospect of being present in a major sack by the feared barbarians turned the population against him, and he was killed on 22 or the 31 May, apparently torn limb from limb and his remains hurled into the Tiber. It is assumed that Palladius died with him.[555] Gaiseric entered the city two days later and looted it, although a full sack was avoided thanks to the intercession, yet again, of Pope Leo.

PETRUS
506

A curt entry in a western chronicle informs us that one Petrus had attempted to hold Dertosa (Tortosa) in Spain against the Goths and had been killed by them. The name suggests he was a member of the local Roman élite and the description of him as *tyrannus* is the normal term for an usurper. Whether he set himself up as a potential western emperor or merely as a local one with the hope of resisting Gothic expansion and consolidation, is not known.[556]

PHILIP I
244, 25th February – 249, 26th August

Philip was the second of the third-century succession of military emperors who followed Gordian III, who made peace with the Persians, celebrated the millenium of Rome, lost control and fell victim to the man he had sent to suppress a revolt in the Balkans.

Whether Philip the Arab – so-called from his origin – was guilty of treachery in having Gordian III deposed and killed, or whether the Persians were correct in claiming that the young Emperor died in battle, he acceded with something under a cloud of suspicion, exacerbated by the disadvantageous way the war against Sharpur was broken off.

This involved a payment of half a million *sestertii* – not that much, bearing in mind that the qualification for the senate was twice that – and with an annual grant thereafter. But Philip could not afford to be dilatory in returning to Rome, as Niger had been after 193: that way lay ruin – hence the treaty.

---

555 PLRE II Palladius 10

556 PLRE II Petrus 25 cf. Barnwell (1992) 69. *Tyrannus* is the normal Latin shorthand in the later empire to describe unsuccessful rival emperors, cf. Vortigern and the 6th-century African rebels.

It left the Romans with Lesser Armenia and Mesopotamia, so there was some small advantage there to help save face. In addition, he appointed his brother-in-law Severianus as governor of ever-troublesome Upper and Lower Moesia and left his brother Priscus behind in the east as governor of Mesopotamia, later appointing him Praetorian Prefect and 'ruler of the east', a most unusual title, but one that presaged the division of the Empire under the Tetrarchs half a century later.

M. Julius Philippus[557] was born in Trachonitis (Al-Lajat, Syria) c. 204, almost certainly the younger brother of Priscus. He was probably a senior army NCO, rising to deputy Pretorian Prefect under his brother from 242 or 243. He was promoted to full Pretorian Prefect by Gordian III late in 243, no doubt on the advice of Priscus, as Timisitheus' replacement. He was acclaimed emperor either as a result of plotting or in the aftermath of a severe military setback, on 25 February 244.

Philip's family came from the southern edge of Syria, east of the Jordan. His native village, of which his family were chiefs, was later incorporated by the emperor as a city called Philippopolis (today's Shabba). The fact that the family name was Julius indicates that they had received full citizenship before Caracalla's enfranchisement of the whole empire. As petty Arabian princes, their citizenship might indeed have gone back considerably further, possibly even to the earlier first century. We do not know the details of the Emperor's ancestry beyond his father, however.

On arrival in Rome, Philip made his peace with the senate, obtained divine honours for his predecessor and gave him a lavish state funeral. He adopted the style Imperator Caesar M. Julius Philippus Pius Felix Invictus Augustus.[558] The senate confirmed him in office with the grant of the tribunician and proconsular powers[559] and made him *Pontifex Maximus*.[560] Shortly thereafter, the senate further granted him the style Persicus Maximus, suggesting the Emperor put a good deal of positive spin on his exploits since the death of Gordian. He was consul in 245, acclaimed Germanicus Maximus in 246 and Carpicus Maximus in 247, when he held a second consulship and soon afterwards raised his son Philip to the rank of co-Augustus. He was married to a lady of senatorial rank, Marcia Otacilia Severa, created Augusta in 244.[561] At Rome itself, his reign was marked by a number of impressive public works and lavish games to mark the thousandth anniversary of the founding of the city in 248.

The Danube frontier seems to have been a continuing problem and in 245, the Emperor set out for Dacia, for his brother-in-law's efforts to stem the tide in the adjacent Moesias had proved ineffectual. He seems to have gained a complete victory over the Carpi in Dacia. The grant of the title by the senate in 247 of Germanicus Maximus alongside Carpicus Maximus suggests that

---

557 PIR² I 461; see also Körner (2001) *passim*
558 ILS 507; Körner (2001) 42-49
559 Inscription quoted in JRS XCII (2007) 216
560 ILS 506
561 ILS 507

he then went on to deal with the Quadi, a troublesome German tribe settled a little further north and west along the river.

Yet, even while the capital was indulging in an orgy of games, feasting and donatives in 248, the Danube (and probably the Rhine) frontiers were still giving trouble. Three imperial claimants appeared in quick succession. Two, Silbannacus on the Rhine and Sponsianus[562] on the Danube are only names (although both managed to issue some very scarce coins, only recently recognised as genuine) but their actions should probably be seen in the light of some desperate crisis on the frontiers rather than as a deliberate effort to remove Philippus. Indeed, one may have been acclaimed to deal with the other. Sponsianus (qv) certainly had this effect in Moesia, for another usurper, Pacatianus (qv) seems to have put himself forward in order to neutralise him. Underlying all this may have been resentment amongst the provincial governors and legates – all at this period mainly senators – over the appointment over their heads of Philip's kinsman Severianus to both Moesias, perhaps intensified by incompetence on Severianus's part. This in its turn could well have persuaded Pacatianus at least to have in his sights the removal of Philippus, although his coin inscriptions suggest a (temporary) accommodation between them, unless such a development was wishful thinking on Pacatianus' part. He was soon assassinated by elements of his own forces. Any overbearing behaviour by Severianus gains more credence when one turns to the activities of the Emperor's brother Priscus in the east. His incompetence and the perceived injustice of his exactions in the region caused an uprising under the locally credible pretender Iotapianus, who not only claimed descent from Alexander the Great but kinship with Alexander Severus.

Faced with what had begun to look like military disintegration, Philip began to suffer what could have been a nervous breakdown. Instead of the immediate military response one might have expected, he chose to go to the senate and offer to abdicate, a suggestion which was received in stony silence, one senator correctly suggesting that the usurpers would soon be killed by their own men, no doubt citing the recent examples of Silbannacus and Sponsianus. This, indeed, is precisely what happened, first to Pacatianus and then, probably the following year, to Iotapianus, who from his coin inscriptions may have scored a victory – presumably fairly minor – over the Persians.

In the end, Philip appointed a senator with Danubian connections, Decius, as supreme commander (*dux*) of Moesia and Pannonia – effectively replacing Severianus – which put him in command a very powerful army. In the event, Decius secured the Danube frontier once again by the end of 248 and it remained quiet until somewhat later, when the Goths, Carpi *et al* perceived further unrest on the Roman side of the frontier and took their opportunities. The only trouble was that some unknown event caused Decius' army to proclaim him emperor in mid-June 249. Philip rejected an offered

---

562 Sponsianus has recently been suggested as one of the usurpers who arose on the defeat of Valerian.

arrangement through distrust of Decius. Although weakened, we are told, by old age and some (unknown) infirmity, he gathered a considerable force – presumably from Gaul or Africa – and set out north to confront the claimant, by this time en route to Rome to consolidate his position. If the ancient author called the Chronographer of 354 is to be believed in his estimate of the reign as 5 years, 5 months and 29 days, Philip was killed in the subsequent battle near Verona around 26 August 249.

The Christian writer Eusebius claims – as repeated by St Jerome in *Chronici Canones* – that Philip was the first Christian emperor, a declaration not accepted by modern scholars. Nevertheless, we have the testimony of his contemporary, Bishop Dionysius of Alexandria, that he showed such remarkable tolerance towards Christians and that the Empress intervened to save the life of St Babylas, Bishop of Antioch.[563] Of course, if he *had* been a Christian, his position would have been by no means as secure as that of Constantine I in 313 and he would have practised his beliefs discreetly. Yet no contemporary gossip picked it up and Eusebius was surely influenced by the contrast with his successor, Decius, who instituted a savage persecution. Yet it may be argued that this might have been done in reaction to Philip's perceived Christianity, or tolerance of it; the persecution, in either case, probably incorporated an element of finding a scapegoat for the upheavals of the Empire, which were having an impact on all levels of society

PHILIP II
247 May – 249, 9th September

Philip the Arab's son, M. Julius Severus Philippus,[564] was born in 237 or 238, declared Caesar in spring 244 as Nobilissimus Caesar M. Julius Severus Philippus and styled *princeps iuventutis*.[565] In 247, he was made co-emperor and invested with the same powers as his father, including the chief pontificate as Imperator Caesar M. Julius Severus Philippus Augustus.[566] He was also consul with his father and again in 248. Philip II, having reigned as sole emperor for about two weeks, was sought out and killed by a returning detachment of disgruntled Praetorian Guards at their camp in Rome early in September 249; his mother the Empress is thought by some sources to have survived.

PISO (I)
69, 10th – 15th January

Piso, hurriedly adopted son and heir of Galba, died with his adoptive father, having achieved only discord through his appointment as heir over the heads of at least two others. Galba's *coup* had not gone down well in

---

563 Discussed in Körner (2001) 260-273
564 PIR² I462
565 ILS 512
566 ILS 511, 513

Germany, for a variety of reasons. Therefore, on 2 January AD69, Aulus Vitellius was acclaimed emperor there, suddenly impressing upon Galba that his position was by no means secure.

On January, under the threat of this mobilisation against him, the Emperor felt it wise to adopt as heir a younger, more charismatic man (and also, being Galba, a very noble one) choosing L. Calpurnius Piso Frugi Licinianus, whom he consequently adopted as his son and successor, not only passing over his perfectly eligible nephew, Otho who, as governor of Lusitania when Galba was acclaimed, had supported him from the outset and had built up debt on the promise (widely believed) that he would be the old man's successor.

Like the Emperor's late wife, Aemilia Lepida, Piso was a descendant of the triumvirs Crassus and Pompeius – the former's grandson having been adopted by M. [Calpurnius] Piso Frugi. Galba's new heir was the son of the triumvir's great-grandson, the distinguished consular M. Licinus Crassus Frugi, consul in 27, whose family were raised to patrician status by Claudius in 47.

As the Emperor's legal son, Piso seems, from a fragmentary inscription, to have taken the style [Ser. Sulpicius Gal]ba C[aesar Licinianus] presumably becoming Galba instead of Piso, and so strictly speaking, Galba II. Both were assassinated at the instigation of Otho five days later, on 15 January, Piso surviving an hour or two longer than his adoptive parent.

PISO (II)
260

Piso was an usurper of dubious authenticity, alleged to have been a member of the distinguished Republican family of the Calpurnii Pisones. He was, according to the *Historia Augusta*, supposed to have made an attempt at supreme power, having been sent by Macrianus en route west, to eliminate the equally unattested usurper Valens, following the capture in the east of Valerian. Piso withdrew into Thessaly and was acclaimed emperor, allegedly adopting the style Piso Thessalicus, which would ordinarily celebrate the winning of a victory. Thereafter, he is alleged to have been killed by his troops but was deified by the senate, which also proposed a gilded statue of him be made. He is nowhere else attested, nor are any members of the Calpurnii Pisones reliably recorded as having survived into this era. Piso is widely thought to have been invented to make up numbers for the 'Thirty Tyrants'.[567]

POEMENIUS
353

Poemenius was *dux* in Trier in 353, probably appointed by Magnentius, but changing his allegiance he closed the city to Decentius on his retreat from the Rhine after a defeat by the Franks. He is thought by some authorities

---

567 HA *Tyr. Trig.* XXI. Cf. XIX 2 & *V. Gall.* II2-4

on numismatic evidence to have become thereby an usurper, although this is generally considered relatively unlikely.[568] Later, he was tortured and killed in September 355 for having supported Silvanus' usurpation.

POSTUMUS (I)
260, August – 269, March

Postumus was the first emperor of the breakaway Gallic Empire, who took advantage of the chaos reigning in the east and in Germany to establish a viable polity in north-west Europe. Postumus[569] was the governor of either upper or lower Germany – he is described using anachronistic terminology – and was acclaimed emperor in May or very early August 260.[570] Having Saloninus (qv), the son and titular heir of Gallienus, within his sphere of influence at Colonia Agrippina (Cologne) and with one of the Pretorian Prefects, Silvanus, acting as the young prince's minder, a major falling out was inevitable, and Silvanus and his charge died, whilst Postumus was recognised as emperor by all the provinces of north-west Europe.[571]

M. Cassianius Latinius Postumus may himself have been of Batavian or Gallic stock; his *nomen,* created from the adjectival form of Cassius, is certainly reminiscent of Gallic family names from this period. The 'Latinius' element might well have been senatorial Italian (the *Historia Augusta* claims his father was also called Postumus[572]) and perhaps derived from his mother. It may be, therefore, that he was at least a second-generation senator and, if indeed Gallic, something of a rarity at this period. A Gallic ancestry might also help to explain his remarkable success.

He had served as suffect consul before 258, so had been born around 210 and would therefore have entered the senate in c. 232/4. He became emperor as Imperator Caesar D[ominus] N[oster] M. Cassianius Latinius Postumus Pius Felix Augustus,[573] had himself recognised locally as *Pontifex Maximus* and obtained a grant from his *consilium* of proconsular and tribunician powers, renewable, it would seem from coin evidence, on 10 December yearly, adhering to tradition. He appointed yearly consuls and he himself held further consulships, in 261, 262, 266 and 269. He was thus able to govern his provinces in the traditional way through senatorial ex-magistrates, although the exact detail is lost to us. By the beginning of 269 he had been consul five times, had held the *tribunicia potestatis* ten times and been granted the style of *Pater Patriae.*

It transpired that the new ruler was cannier than most usurpers, deciding to stay where he was and to consolidate those provinces that had supported his

---

568 Amm. Marc. 15, 6; Kent (1959) 105-108

569 PIR² C467; PLRE I. Postumus 2

570 *Dux* and *praeses* by the HA: *Tyr. Trig.* III. 9

571 Drinkwater (1987) 26-27

572 HA *Tyr Trig.* 3-4; it makes Postumus a 'tribune' in 257.

573 Full names, ILS 560-562; CIL.II. 4943 etc.; on coins it is abbreviated to his *cognomen* only.

cause. Gallienus meanwhile, being beset by would-be successors elsewhere, decided for a time to let him be, possibly even recognising him, enabling him to retrench further. In 265, after Postumus had managed to re-consolidate the Rhine frontier, Gallienus at last attempted to re-take his Gallic provinces, but after a good start, he was wounded during a siege and withdrew, albeit in good order.

When Aureolus seized power in Milan, Postumus refused to come to his aid, presumably because Gallienus' general had led the campaign to unseat him in 265. This failure to grasp what must have appeared as a golden opportunity to seize the whole Western Empire might have represented a loss of prestige which perhaps led to his death, early in the following year, at the hands of a group of his officers, following the suppression of the usurper Laelianus. He was killed probably in March 269, ushering in a Gallic Year of the Four Emperors.

Nothing is known of his wife and only the *Historia Augusta* mentions any offspring, a son, also Postumus, allegedly made Caesar and later Augustus.[574] No other source has any of this and it may safely be ignored. It would appear that Victorinus was the emperor's intended successor, which would suggest that there was no son, son-in-law or brother who could have filled this role.

POSTUMUS (II) see POSTUMUS (I)

POSTUMUS see also AGRIPPA POSTUMUS

PRISCUS (I)
185

Priscus was an unidentified governor of Britain who sometime in 184 was offered the throne by his disaffected legionaries. He wisely refused but was later removed from his post by Commodus' Pretorian Prefect Perennis, along with most other legionary commanders, and replaced by men of equestrian status. If this man can be identified with the Caunius Priscus who was effectively governor of Numidia in 186 and indeed with an unplaced Priscus who was suffect consul in about 190, then he clearly lived to tell the tale. A relieved Commodus assumed the additional style of Britannicus Maximus as a result.[575]

PRISCUS (II)
259, c. November – December

T. Julius Priscus was governor (*agens vice praesidis*, usually abbreviated to *praeses* – a governor of equestrian rank) of Macedonia and Thrace, where Philip had founded another city named after himself. There is a strong

---

574 HA *Tyr. Trig.* 4.1; cf. PIR² C467; PLRE I. Postumus 1
575 Dio 77.9.2a, HA *Commodus*, 8.4; discussed in Birley (1981) 260-262

possibility that he was the cousin of Philip II. During his governorship, to which he could have been appointed under his uncle's regime and, because of the chaotic situation at his fall, had not been removed, had to defend this Philippopolis (today Plovdiv, Bulgaria) from an attack by Goths under their king, Kniva, in winter 250/251, mainly as a result of Decius inflicting an insufficiently decisive defeat upon them further north. Being in no way seriously impaired, Kniva had moved south to invest Philippopolis.[576] Priscus' position became critical and his troops mutinous. As a desperate last throw of the dice, he declared himself emperor around November 250 and used the authority he was thus perceived to have acquired to make terms with the Gothic King. Somehow, however, it all went completely wrong, and the Goths sacked Philippopolis anyway. Priscus was probably killed, although whether by his own men or the Goths is unknown. In July, he was posthumously declared a public enemy by the senate, ignorant of his death. His *praenomen* is wrongly given by Aurelius Victor as Lucius.

Were he really a nephew of Philip I, one might have thought one or more of the sources would have mentioned it, but they are so fragmentary and inadequate that this is not necessarily a bar. Indeed, kinship with the late emperor might have encouraged him to adopt this unlikely and desperate solution to a siege which was not going his way.

PROBUS
276, July/August – 282, September

Probus was, with Aurelian, one of the strongest and most efficient of the third century soldier emperors and the one whose memory seems to have been revered. Probus was the successor of the somewhat ephemeral, if generally acknowledged, Emperors Tacitus and Florianus and, like Aurelian, managed to stop the rot once he had secured his position, and earned unalloyed adulation from senatorial historians as something of a paragon, a man of virtue, gracious nature and fairness. The reasons for this are complex and not wholly agreed upon, although it is clear that he was regarded as just as fine a commander as Aurelian, who was the more abrasive character and noted for his short fuse.[577] That the two Augusti had once been comrades-in-arms seems highly likely and both may have been part of the group of Illyrian officers involved in the demise of Gallienus only eight years before. Probus was acclaimed in Syria, probably as soon as news of the death of Tacitus and the elevation of Florianus had reached him. His early weeks seem to have overlapped most of the latter's reign. Unfortunately for so important a figure, most of what we know of Probus derives from the notoriously unreliable *Historia Augusta*.

M. Aurelius Probus was born at Sirmium (Sremska Mitrovika, Serbia) on 19 August 232, according to a number of sources, including the *Historia*

---

576 PIR² I489; Aurelius Victor, 29; Polemius Silvius, 39-40 who dates it all to 251; Zosimus 1, 23.1
577 Eutropius 9, 17

Augusta.[578] Aurelius Victor names the father of Probus as Dalmatius and the *Historia Augusta* credits him with kinship with Claudius II and with posterity, who settled at Verona and 'were destined to become leaders of the senate'.[579] A convincing case has been made for the existence of a daughter by Mommaerts and Kelley, who strongly suspect that the widespread aristocratic use of the name Probus amongst a tightly knit group of families in the fourth and fifth century west (especially Gaul) and in the seventh century in Constantinople, was due to this daughter having made a glittering marriage to the future consul of 314, Petronius Annianus.[580] If this is accepted, then the bloodline unites a whole group of more or less short-lived emperors and in fact might explain why they aspired to the purple at all. This postulation has not gone unchallenged, especially concerning connections with the Anician family.[581] It should be noted that a variety of sources, from the *Historia Augusta* and (much) later, endow the emperor with other, unattested kin: Maximus for a father, a son, Domitius (mentioned in late hagiographies), a brother, Domitius, another, Calocerus, Bishop of Byzantium, two distaff nephews, [H]adrianus and Demetrius (military martyrs according to Nicephorus) and a half-sister, Claudia.[582]

He may have borne the *signum* Equitius, for this name appears as his *nomen* in Aurelius Victor and on one issue of coins, causing slight confusion, most easily thus explained.[583] His pre-imperial career is only given in the *Historia Augusta*, which claims, perfectly plausibly, that he served as a tribune under Valerian on the Danubian frontier and also under Gallienus, miraculously managing to preserve both life and career through the various usurpers and barbarian incursions of those years. Later, he is said to have served in Egypt under Aurelian before being appointed to succeed Maximin as *dux* or governor in the east.[584]

Despite their recognition of Florianus as Tacitus' successor, the senate was quick to recognise his successor, too; papyri confirm his recognised elevation as pre-dating 29 August 276. Once the news of Florianus' demise had reached them, he was recognised as *pontifex maximus* and granted the tribunician power (to be renewed annually) and proconsular *imperium*; he also assumed a suffect consulship. He was ordinary consul in 278, 279, 281 and 282. His regnal style was Imperator Caesar M. Aurelius Probus Pius Felix Invictus Augustus.[585] He was also officially recognised as *Pater Patriae*.

The following year, following his settling of the problem of the marauding Heruli – which had put paid to the careers of his two predecessors – he was granted the *agnomen* Gothicus.[586] He is said by the *Historia Augusta* to

---

578 PLRE I Probus 3
579 HA *V. Probi* 24, 1-3
580 Mommaerts & Kelley (1992) 111-121
581 Eg. Cameron, A., *Anician Myths* in JRS CII (2012) 133-171
582 Nicephorus *Historia Ecclesiastica* i. 773; *Acta Sanctorum*; HA, *loc.cit.*
583 *op. cit.* 36,2; the coins were minted at Ticinum.
584 HA *V. Probi* 3, 5; 4, 2; 5, 1, 6-7 & 9, 5
585 ILS596
586 ILS594

have continued Tacitus' reform of the senatorial *cursus*. Two years later, he was able to add 'Maximus' to Gothicus and amplify his style to Germanicus Maximus, earned following two years hard pounding in clearing various Germanic peoples from Gaul and the Rhenish provinces, where they had taken advantage of the chaos of 276 by breaking through and causing unparallelled and widespread destruction, for which service his reputation in Gaul during the century following remained remarkably high, out of gratitude. He also re-consolidated the Rhine frontier. In 279, he moved to the lower Danube, inflicting a defeat upon the Getae before moving on to Asia minor where a large band of outlaws (*bagaudae*) under an Isaurian called Lydius was causing similar destruction to that suffered by the citizens of the Gallic provinces. Lydius was killed after a fairly lengthy siege of his fortified hideout before Probus was then obliged to deal with further Persian incursions into Syria, which the troubles with the outlaws had precipitated. This latter campaign we know only implicitly because in 279 he assumed the additional style of Persicus Maximus. After that, he was obliged to move swiftly on to Egypt to deal with a similar outbreak caused by Nubian people called the Blemmyae, following which he had some of the marshes bordering the Nile reclaimed (a similar project had been initiated by him on the lower Danube) and he ordered numerous new bridges to be built and began restoring temples there as well.[587]

He then returned to Rome and might have considered the firefighting part of his reign finished, leaving him scope to get on with economic and infrastructure consolidation; unlike Aurelian, he realised that ending the continuing military crises required more than a round of police actions and counter-attacks. He had already, in Gaul, begun the task of rebuilding and is credited with widespread initiation of viticulture there, as well as in the provinces of the lower Danube, to help rebuild the economy of these areas. Unfortunately, it was probably at this stage, in 280, he was obliged to deal with a pair of imperial claimants, Bonosus and Proculus at Colonia Agrippina (Cologne) in Germany, who were generating sufficient momentum as to threaten a new Gallic empire. In the chaos engendered by their suppression, another claimant popped up, who also had to be dealt with, but this did not require the Emperor's personal presence.

Even as all this was happening in the north-west, Syria was once again the hub of a new revolt by its supreme commander, a Moor called Saturninus (qv). This man was murdered by his own officers after a few months, which enabled Probus to return to Rome in 281 and celebrate an impressive triumph over the Germans, whom he had also had to deal with once more, in the wake of the revolt at Cologne. In 282 (when he was consul for the 5th time and held the tribunician power for the 7th) he again set out for the east, to repair any damage caused by the revolt of Saturninus, and also with the intention of dealing a hammer-blow to the turbulent Persians. En route, he

---

587 We rely on the (probably fictitious) epitaph from his alleged tomb near Sirmium described by the *Historia Augusta* (*V. Probi* 21) for most of this information, although much of it is plausible and some is borne out by archaeology.

sent one of his Pretorian Prefects to the upper Danube to ensure order there. However, early in September, this man, Carus, was acclaimed by his troops, and Probus was obliged to turn back to deal with him. Unfortunately, years of draining marshes and undertaking public works under strict military discipline, thus depriving them of the opportunity for plunder, had left the army (or at least the Praetorian Guard) disenchanted and his advance party threw their lot in with Carus. When news of this reached the main army, it encouraged the men to turn on their Emperor, especially as he had paused at his birthplace to get the troops to repair a reservoir and ditches damaged by winter rains. Whilst it may have been a mere mutiny rather than a revolt linked to Carus' acclamation, the result was the same: the soldiers chased him to a signal tower not far from the city and slaughtered him there. The date of this is very uncertain; all we can say is that he died between 28 August and 31 December 282, thanks to Alexandrian coins issued for his 8th year. If the story of his burial in a large tumulus nearby can be accepted, it is likely that he was held in somewhat higher esteem by his fellow provincials than by his men and that they decided to commemorate him in this way. He was subsequently deified by the senate.[588]

PROBUS see also HYPATIUS

PROCOPIUS
365, 28ᵗʰ September – 366, 27ᵗʰ May

Procopius was an obscure member of the House of Constantine who unsuccessfully attempted to supplant the incompetent Valens in the eastern empire against a promise of succession allegedly made to him by Julian the Apostate (qv)

Julian is said to have acknowledged Procopius as a kinsman and at some stage to have promised him the succession, should he die without issue. Both matters are retailed by Ammianus Marcellinus, so there would seem no reason to doubt them, although his kinship is not exactly known; probably it was through his mother.[589]

He was born in Cilicia around 326 of noble family and brought up at Corycus (Kız Kalesi, Turkey). His wife was Artemisia – presumably the Constantinian connection – by whom he had a family, from whom descended the future Emperor Anthemius, although she was reduced to poverty in the wake of the fall of her husband. In 358, Constantius II appointed him *tribunus et notarius* (senior civil servant) and sent him on an embassy with Jovian's father-in-law Lucillianus to Persia. Subsequently, he reached a high position in the service and Julian, presumably out of familial solidarity, made him *comes* and appointed him to command a military unit on the eastern frontier.

588 CIL I² 255
589 PLRE I Procopius 4, quoting Amm. Marc. 23, 3.2 etc. (and repeated by other writers).

After the accession of Jovian, he voluntarily relinquished his claim to the succession and was given the task of organising the funeral of his predecessor at Tarsus, after which he retired with his family to his estates. Valentinian and Valens considered him a threat, so he fled to the Chersonese (Crimea). Eventually, he seems to have decided that as he was a marked man in any case, he might as well make a bid to fulfil Julian's promise to him after all, and he returned to Constantinople. Here, with the support of some of the senate and two resting military units, he was proclaimed Dominus Noster Procopius Pius Felix Augustus on 28 September. The population supported him because he promised to relieve the crushing taxation the new emperors had imposed to pay for the military campaigns of Julian and Jovian, and his kinship with the House of Constantine must also have been a powerful spur to many. He was also backed by 3,000 Goths who were bound by treaty to the heirs of Constantine. Troops assembled by a worried Valens in Asia also went over to him and the Eastern Emperor seriously considered abdication. Although his resolve was stiffened by his *magister equitum* Lupicinus (the same who later bungled the transfer of the Goths across the Danube), Procopius made all the running militarily until the non-arrival of Egyptian corn supplies that he had promised (without necessarily being able to deliver), caused his support to slip, coupled with the necessary re-imposition of heavy taxation. Valens also achieved the upper hand in a propaganda war, and by the spring managed to win two victories over his opponent, the second despite serious defections. The unfortunate usurper was captured and executed on 27 May 366.

PROCULUS
280

Proculus was one of the more obscure later third-century usurpers, apparently concurrent with Bonosus in Germany. At some stage in the reign of Probus, two Rhine commanders had themselves proclaimed emperor, most probably in spring 280. Bonosus was commander of the army on the Rhine and the acclamation took place at Colonia Agrippina (Cologne). Quite how Proculus fitted in is obscure. The two may have commanded the armies in the two Germanies and thought to make their bid jointly. To confuse matters, Aurelius Victor omits Proculus entirely, although he is mentioned by Eutropius.[590] Most of our information comes from the *Historia Augusta* and is not to be relied upon. Proculus, it declares, came from Albingaunum (Albenga, Liguria) and was of noble family, although later on he is said to have had Frankish blood.[591] The two were quickly suppressed and killed by Probus, so probably their reign lasted a month or six weeks or so; there was apparently no time for any coins of Bonosus to be minted, but there has long been known a billon *antoninianus* of Proculus and, being unique, much suspicion fell upon its authenticity.

590 *Op. cit.* 9, 17
591 PLRE I Proculus 1

However, in 2012 a metal detector found another, unfortunately not part of a group or hoard, apparently from the same die, suggesting that Proculus did indeed mint coins.[592]

Predictably, the *Historia Augusta* provides both these imperial claimants with families. Proculus was, it claims, married to Vituriga (*alias* Samso) and they were parents of Herennianus, related to one Maecianus and the family continued at Albingaunum.[593] Herennianus was apparently made *caesar*, according to *Historia Augusta*, but this is entirely uncorroborated.

PUPIENUS MAXIMUS (II)
22nd April – 29th July 238

Pupienus Maximus was one of a pair of co-rulers nominated by the senate to protect Rome from an avenging Maximin Thrax after news of the fall of the Gordians had reached the capital, who achieved what they set out to do but fell victim to the mob in the aftermath.

News of the demise of the two Gordians seems not to have reached Rome until 21 or 22 April, Maximin (qv) again being sole unchallenged ruler during that time, albeit outlawed by the senate. However, on 22 April, the senate, no doubt in a febrile and apprehensive state, met to deal with the crisis, bearing in mind that the cruel emperor was likely to exact a terrible revenge on their number for their condemnation of him and enthusiastic support for the Gordians. Indeed, as soon as news came that the Gordians had raised the standard of revolt, the senate appointed a panel of twenty ex-consuls (*vigintiviri*) to make arrangements for the eventuality of the Thracian invading Italy.

The senate deified the two late emperors and nominated the two senior presiding consulars of the *vigintiviri* as joint emperors: M. Clodius Pupienus Maximus and D. Caelius Balbinus Calvinus, henceforth the emperors Maximus and Balbinus. Despite being informed by the *Historia Augusta* that Maximus was a distinguished ex-general of undistinguished family,[594] scholarly analysis suggests that, like Balbinus, both were upper-class patricians, Maximus indeed having been a successful if rather strict general. Being a senior member of the committee, he was, of course, advanced in years.

M. Clodius Pupienus Maximus was born c. 175. Zonaras gives his age as 74 on accession, but the evidence seems not to bear this out. Herodian tells us Maximus was of patrician rank, which would have given him an accelerated career; his son's career tells us that *he* was certainly patrician.[595] The *Historia Augusta* claims Maximus was also 'adopted as a son' by an unattested Pescennia Marcellina, which is uncorroborated.[596]

---

592 *Daily Mail* 16/11/2012

593 PLRE I Herennianus 2 & Vituriga; HA *V. Firmi* 8 *et al.*, 12, 4, 7 & 13, 5. PIR² H 98

594 V. *Max. et Balb.* 2. 7, cf. PIR² C1179

595 ILS 1185; PIR² C1179; XII, 17; Settipani rather daringly adduces his descent from the ancient Republican patrician Claudii Pulchres: *op. cit.* 118-128 and pedigree p. 123

596 HA, *V. Max. et Balb.* 5. 7

There are many clues as to Maximus' origin, but few firm facts. The tale the *Historia* peddles that he was the son of a blacksmith is pure fiction. The Pupieni appear to have come from Volterrae (Volterra) of Etruscan origin. His wife's name is nowhere supplied by ancient sources, but from the first appearance amongst his children of certain names, we are on pretty firm ground in supposing her to be a Sextia and probably the daughter of T. Sextius Lateranus, consul in 197 and he the grandson of T. Sextius Africanus, consul in 112 and a member of an old senatorial family going back to one of Caesar's adherents, T. Sextius, who acquired his *cognomen* Africanus from a notable proconsulate of Africa 44-40 BC.[597] The fact that she was not named in any of the accounts of the events of 238 and that no coins were struck in her name strongly suggests that she was dead before her husband's elevation. Their daughter's name suggests that the Sextii had contracted a fairly recent marriage with the Cornelii Cethegi – a relatively obscure but ancient patrician family from the Republic still managing to survive in the later 2nd century.[598] As regards Maximus' male ascendancy, it is only possible to push back one or possibly two generations, but it is tempting to see a Statilia M[axim]a and her husband, a mid 2nd-century senator whose *nomen* began [.] Pu[   ] as the emperor's grandparents, with the woman supplying him with his *cognomen* Maximus. There is also a freedman of a person called L. Clodius Pup[ienus] whose status is unknown, nor date closely assignable, but who could be the same man or a close relation.[599] On the distaff side, the name Clodius, originally the plebeian version of the patrician Claudius, looks as though it might have come via the emperor's mother, whom we only know as Prima, from the *Historia Augusta* and unconfirmed elsewhere. The Pulcher element, borne by a son, usually associated with the very grand Claudii of the Republic, was perhaps nothing to do with any Clodian ancestry that may have been enjoyed by Prima, but as her name is questionable in any case, it may have commemorated a distant descent via heiresses from the Claudii/Clodii Pulchres. Either way, whilst such a connection is perfectly plausible, it seems to have escaped record.[600]

The most interesting aspect is that not only did this emperor have issue, but that they and three generations afterwards bore elements of his name, which is rare. The use of the *signum* Gennadius by probable descendant M. Ulpius Pupienus Silvanus seems to point to further continuity of the family, even down to the to the early 7th century.

Maximus was suffect consul in c. 215/217. He thereafter governed either Upper or Lower Germany, followed by Asia, before becoming ordinary consul in 234, following this with the office of Prefect of the City, in which

---

597 Wiseman (1971) No. 102; *Classical Quarterly* (1964) 130-131; they were possibly a junior branch Republican family of consular rank, the Sextii Calvini: Syme (1987) 176.

598 They may have been a branch of the Cornelii Lentuli which revived the *cognomen* as they demonstrably had that of Scipio, both in the late 1st century BC. The name Cethegus survived into the 6th century amongst the Roman aristocracy.

599 Syme (1971) 174-175 quoting CIL.IX.5765 at Ricina.

600 Syme *loc.cit.*

he was remembered, according to the *Historia Augusta*, as being severe, if not harsh, but by Herodian as having exercised the office without bias.[601]

Once appointed, it became clear that neither the urban plebs nor the Praetorian Guard were too keen on being presented with a pair of ageing patricians as joint rulers, especially as the Guard had not been consulted. Consequently, the former rioted and the latter failed to make any effort to control them. In the end, it was made clear that the two new Augusti should share their rule with the nephew of Gordian II, who appeared to enjoy some popularity, was exceedingly rich – enabling the Emperors to pay a donative to calm febrile expectations – and who was thenceforth adopted jointly by them before the end of April and nominated *nobilissimus caesar*.

This done, Maximus proceeded to head north to Aquileia, to defend Italy and, it was hoped, stop Maximin from advancing any further, whilst Balbinus remained in charge in Rome. In the event, despite his rather motley collection of forces, Maximus was successful, the vengeful Thracian emperor was killed and Italy was saved from potential pillage.

Maximus came back to an ovation (*ovatio* – only one stage down from a triumph) but trouble at Rome with discontent and unrest, meant that he was greeted with a diminished respect. The stage was thus set for the two to fall out. This they duly did, despite the increasingly insistent evidence of their coin issues that they were working in harmony. What clinched it was the deployment of Maximus' personal German guards to protect the Emperors from a praetorian-led mob that had turned ugly at the conclusion of the Capitoline Games. Balbinus had opposed their deployment, assuming it was a ploy to get rid of him. Whilst the two Emperors were arguing about this, on 29 July 238, the praetorians entered the palace, dragged both of them out and killed them, proclaiming the youthful *caesar* Gordian III as emperor in their place.

QUARTINUS
235/236

Quartinus was an usurper in distant Mesopotamia who was pushed into rebellion against Maximin by the mutiny of an obscure unit. Quartinus, apparently an ex-consul, attempted to seize power in 235 or 236, encouraged by a mutiny amongst the Osrhoenian auxiliaries, formerly fanatically dedicated to Alexander Severus.[602] The *Historia Augusta* claims he was a former tribune of a Moorish auxiliary unit, cashiered by Maximin, which hardly sits easily with his status as a former consul.[603] His revolt was put down after six months by an officer called Macedo, a man subsequently

---

601 Syme (1971) 171; Herodian 7, 10. 4, but who later agreed that he *had* been severe (*ibid.* 7, 10. 6). For the approximate year, Mennen (2011) 260

602 There is confusion about the exact date, but it probably happened much later than Magnus' rebellion and could have lasted up to six months.

603 *Tyr. Trig.* 32, 1-2

executed by Maximin for bringing only the usurper's head to him![604] If his supposed period in power was accurate, it is legitimate to enquire why this man issued no coins in his own name.

Herodian calls him Quartinus, the *Historia Augusta*, Titus, from which it is perhaps possible to identify him as T. Fulvius Quartinus. If so, it is conceivable that he was a brother or half-brother of P. Fulvius Macrianus[605] the father of the later usurpers Macrianus and Quietus. Quartinus is said by the *Historia Augusta* to have been married to a Calpurnia, descended from the illustrious Calpurnii Pisones of the Republic, last securely recorded a century before.[606] Were this snippet corroborated elsewhere, it might fit neatly with the later (alleged) usurper Piso II, but as it is likely that he, too, was fictitious, the matter can safely be discounted. There is no hint of any issue.

QUIETUS
260, c. 17th May – 261, November

Quietus was the younger son of a commander, elevated in the field on the defeat and capture of Valerian, but whose attempt to establish himself and his brother failed ignominiously after a promising start (cf. Macrianus).

With his elder brother and father on the way to Rome, T. Fulvius Junius Quietus remained to consolidate the east, especially as Ballista had inflicted an unexpected defeat on Persian ruler Sharpur and driven him back across the Euphrates.[607] As the younger brother, he looks suitably youthful on his coins. He was probably acclaimed, like his brother, on 17 May 260, and styled Imperator Caesar Fulvius Quietus Pius Felix Augustus, with the same powers as his brother, including an immediate consulship.[608] Once his elder brother and co-Augustus had been eliminated by Gallienus in 261, the Emperor managed to persuade the astonishingly loyal Prince of Palmyra, Odenathus, to field a force to overthrow Quietus. Odenathus, thus appointed Palmyrene supreme commander in the east, was eventually able to surprise Quietus at Emesa and the young usurper was killed by the citizens of the city, who were reluctant to endure the privations of a siege and the inevitable reprisals that the City's fall would entail.[609]

According to the *Historia Augusta*, he married and had issue, amongst whom was the mother of Cornelius Macer, a senator allegedly *floruit* c. 300/315, but who is completely unattested elsewhere and therefore quite probably fictitious.[610]

---

604 Herodian, VII, 1, 9-10 portrays him as a treacherous advisor. Perhaps a son of [?C.] Ofilius Valerius Macedo, suffect consul before 198 and in 204 a *XVvir sacri faciundis* [FS 2567, cf. ILS 5050A & 5934] HA *V. Due Max.* 11. 2-4; *TT.* 32, 6

605 PLRE I. Macrianus 2

606 *Tyr. Trig.* 32. 5

607 PIR² F547; PLRE, I. Quietus 1

608 Coins.

609 The dates of these proceedings are to some extent confirmed by an Egyptian papyrus from Oxyrhincus, no. 2710, cf. Zonaras, 12. 24 & HA, *V. Gall.* III.4

610 *op. cit.*, 14. 5 & 3, 5

QUINTILLUS
270, September – October

Quintillus was the brother of Claudius II, hastily acclaimed emperor on news of the latter's death, but without doubt not through his choice, a fact that may have contributed to his rapid eclipse.

M. Aurelius Quintillus was in command of troops in Italy at the time of the death of Claudius; the fact that his command was a relatively unimportant one rather supports the supposition that he was in no way regarded by Claudius II as a possible successor. It is possible that he was born in 229, for his age at death is recorded as 41 in one very late source.[611] Had Claudius been murdered, it is far more likely that a successor would have been proclaimed on the spot at Sirmium and some ancient sources aver that he nominated Aurelian.[612] But such was the euphoria created by Claudius' victories that Quintillus was acclaimed by the army at Aquileia on news of his death and received immediate recognition from the senate in the style of Imperator Caesar M. Aurelius Claudius Quintillus Augustus; although at first, for instance on his *aureus* issues, the name Claudius is absent, and one suspects that he was born plain old M. Aurelius Quintillus, adding his brother's name after a fairly short interval to emphasise the continuity.

Eutropius remarked that his elevation was with the agreement of the soldiers and that he was also a man of 'singular moderation and grace', if anything, superior to his brother. Yet following his formal installation by the senate, he lasted only seventeen days, although this has long been suggested as an error for a longer period, maybe 77, for a number of coin issues were produced, more than would have been required merely to pay the soldiers a donative. Perhaps it was not enough. (It was Aurelianus who held the fate of the empire in his hands.) Quintillus died at Aquileia, although whether killed by his disaffected soldiers or by suicide is disputed, several versions having come down to us. The *Historia Augusta* claims he left two sons.[613]

REGALIANUS
260, August – 261, March

Regalianus was an usurper, left to hold the Danube by Gallienus, who was elevated by his men to the purple but in due course suffered a military reverse, which led to him being killed by those who had elevated him.

When Sir Ronald Syme reviewed the emperors from the Danubian provinces – loosely Illyricum[614] – he seems to have overlooked Regalianus.[615] Almost our only information about Regalianus comes, inevitably, from the *Historia Augusta*, and is thus unreliable. It includes the fact that Dacia is claimed as his

---

611 Banchich & Lane (2009) 122
612 Zonaras 12, 26
613 Eutropius, 9, 12; HA *V. Claud. loc.cit.*
614 Syme RP III (1984) 892-898
615 PIR² C2. HA *Tyr. Trig.* 24 wrongly calls him Trebellianus.

place of origin,[616] and Sir Ronald elsewhere concurs.[617] We are also told he was commander – *dux* – in Illyricum but that he was acclaimed in Moesia. In fact, as his wife was a member of a grand senatorial family it seems far more likely that he was the senatorial governor of Moesia Inferior or Superior.

What we do know is that Gallienus, in the wake of the rebellion of Ingenuus, had re-organised the Danubian defences but whilst doing so had to hurry back to Italy to deal with an influx of Alemanni, a Germanic people, leaving Regalianus there to complete his measures. This was just as well, for a tribe called the Roxolani, recently re-settled by Gallienus inside the Empire in this sector, rebelled and attacked the forces of Regalianus, who fell back on Carnuntum (Bad Duetsch-Altenburg, Austria). He only became an usurper in around August 260 by the acclamation of his troops. When acclaimed, he took the style Imperator Caesar P. C[assius] Regalianus [(?)Pius Felix] Augustus. We might speculate as to whether he arrogated to himself the pontificate and the powers usually bestowed by the senate; in all probability he did, but the senate were never rash enough to recognise him.

Regalianus was in fact unlikely to have been of Dacian stock, claimed for him by the *Historia Augusta*, which averred that he was kin to Decebalus, the King of Dacia, removed at great cost by Trajan 105-107. On his coins he is merely 'P. C. Regalianus', where the C was long thought to strand for Cornelius, but a diploma of Severan date discovered relatively recently introduces us to a hitherto unknown suffect consul, C. Cassius Regallianus, who may well have been this claimant's father. Hence the 'C' in this case may reasonably be taken for Cassius. However, thanks to his desire to strike coins depicting his wife, Sulpicia Dryantilla (styled Augusta), a Lycian from a senatorial family, we can see that he was well connected.[618] The Empress was also a descendant of the sister of the later 2nd-century usurper Avidius Cassius. Regalianus would have been born c. 215, have entered the senate and eventually served as suffect consul at some date prior to 259 before being appointed governor of one of the Moesias.

Once acclaimed under siege, Regalianus held out for several months, managing to last long enough to issue coins, most (but not all) of which have as part of their reverse legend the formula 'AUGG.' suggesting that he was, at least temporarily, recognised by Gallienus, or considered that he was. With the situation in Carnuntum desperate and no obvious way out of their predicament, his men probably killed him in desperation, in the late winter or early spring of 261.

ROMANUS
470

Romanus was *magister officiorum* in the west and had been made patrician by 470, probably by Anthemius. However, later that year, Cassiodorus reports

---

616 *Tyr. Trig.* 10, 1-17
617 Syme (1971) 211
618 DNP 1096

that he was somehow involved in a conspiracy against the Emperor, possibly engineered by his friend Ricimer, which resulted in his being proclaimed emperor himself. However, the matter was swiftly put down and the hapless pretender arrested and put to death.

We know nothing of his earlier life nor of his family background. There were no coins issued in his name of course, so we can only guess at the style he employed as Augustus.[619] As a result of his brief rise and fall, Ricimer himself rose in revolt, but after some threatening manoeuvrings a reconciliation was effected with Anthemius, which lasted until 472.

ROMULUS AUGUSTUS
475, 31ˢᵗ October – 476, 4ᵗʰ September

The last generally recognised Emperor of the Western Empire, Romulus, who ruled for nearly a year in succession to Julius Nepos, was elevated, like so many of his immediate predecessors, by a military strong man – in this case his father.

Julius Nepos was driven out of Ravenna on 28 August 475, but the new Patrician, Orestes, did not do anything about replacing him for two months. During that time, as on several previous occasions, the empire was re-united, at least notionally. As a native-born Roman rather than a barbarian, it is strange that Orestes did not himself don the purple, but it may be that he appreciated how devalued the currency of the western throne had become. Or it may be that he was hoping for recognition of his position from Eastern Emperor Zeno but, if so, it was not forthcoming. Consequently, he decided to elevate his young son (thought to have been about 14) to the imperial dignity on 31 October 475.

The young ruler was Orestes' son by the daughter of a *comes* called Romulus, after whom he was named. Orestes was the son of an army officer called Tatulus, Young Romulus, whose other given name was Augustus (hence his universally adopted nickname Augustulus, 'little Augustus') seems to have had a brother living called Herculanus. Orestes himself had a brother, Paulus, whom he appointed a *comes* the same year. According to his contemporary, St Ennodius, the family of Romulus were descended from the Valerii Messalae, whom he calls the Corvini.[620] P. J. Barnish has thus suggested that the family was 'perhaps intermarried with the Corvini', by which it is presumed the Valerii are meant, which would give them very grand senatorial connections going right back to the dawn of the Republic.[621] The only obvious concatenation of a Valerius of this family and a Romulus is via a presumed union between a sister of Flavius Pisidius Romulus (city prefect in 406) and the senator Valerius Hermonius Maximus, whose father

619 PLRE II Romanus 4. His bid for power was also reported by John of Antioch and the much later Lombard historian Paul the Deacon. Later emperors called Romanus fall outside the scope of this volume.

620 Ennodius, ep. I 9, 4

621 Barnish (1988) 127

Valerius Poplicola, praetor in 375, may be considered a descendant of the old patrician Valerii, or at least one so identified.[622] Pisidius Romulus was probably the grandson of Flavius Romulus, consul in 343, but there seems to be no clear evidence to connect him with the *comes* Romulus of 440.[623]

The teenage Emperor took the style Dominus Noster Romulus Augustus Pius Felix Augustus. It is not clear if the senate was involved at any stage, but probably it acknowledged the new Emperor and voted him the empty powers tradition dictated. Orestes' actions in installing his son would have been taken with confidence, for he had diverted from attacking Euric in Gaul to depose Nepos and he probably thought that, with luck, he might be able to start a dynasty.

Romulus was probably nominated as consul for 476 by the senate in Rome, but this would have been rejected by the eastern court, which only acknowledged its own, the Empress Verina's brother Basiliscus, but in fact, the latter's consulship was annulled when he attempted a *coup*, and another of Verina's relations, Armatus, served the year out and there is no mention in the *fasti* of Romulus.

Orestes managed to negotiate a reasonably favourable peace accord with Gaiseric in Africa that allowed Italy to recover economically, with grain shipments restored at last, although the price to be paid was much higher than when the province had been under direct imperial control. The one concession seems to have been that the Vandals were to continue to hold their enclave of Lilybaeum on the far western tip of Sicily, which was merely a recognition of a *de facto* state of affairs. This treaty, however, encouraged the barbarian levies serving in Italy as Orestes' army – mainly Heruli, Scirians and Torcilingi – to make demands for land in Italy on which to settle. Orestes then miscalculated, thinking that this was a negotiating ploy, especially as he was most disinclined to concede anything like as much as this in the heartland of the Western Empire. The troops' leader was the Hun soldier of fortune, Odoacer. He was married to a niece of the Empress Verina and therefore closely related to Nepos. His motive for what he did next might even have been notionally on behalf of his imperial kinsman, still nominally ruling in Dalmatia, although there is not enough evidence to be sure.

He had served under Ricimer against Anthemius and had subsequently been made an officer of the *domestici* (the Imperial Guard), before serving in an unknown but very senior capacity under Orestes. He told his men that if they made him their king, he would guarantee their land allocation and, on 23 August 476, they duly acclaimed him king, although quite of what is unclear, although he was effectively King of Italy – or King *in* Italy.

He then led his army to face Orestes at Ticinum (Pavia), drove him out, sacked the city and cornered and captured him at Placentia (Piacenza) on 28 August, Orestes being put to death. The Hun leader finally took Ravenna and captured the imperial court on September 4, Orestes' brother and deputy, Paulus, being killed. He spared young Romulus, however, on account of his

---

622 PLRE I Maximus 37, Poplicola 1, 2, cf. II. 1 & Romulus 5
623 PLRE I Romulus 1, 2

youth, granted him a pension and packed him off to live in Campania in the villa built by L. Licinius Lucullus in the 60s BC.[624] He and his mother were recorded as still alive and enjoying the pension Odoacer had settled upon them (renewed by Ostrogothic King, Theoderic) in 511. In his comfortable retirement, Romulus may have married Barbar[i]a, sister of the western senatorial grandee Rufius Magnus Faustus Avienus (consul in 502) and thus been father of Rufius Gennadius Probus Orestes (consul in 530).[625]

SABINIANUS
240

Sabinianus was proconsul of Africa in 240, implying that he was a fairly senior senator and an ex-consul (he should have held office around 225/228), but only a suffect one, as his name does not identifiably appear on the *fasti* – the official list of ordinary consuls by which each year was named. There is very little authentic information about him, except that his imperial acclamation took place at Carthage in 240 and that his rebellion was suppressed by the loyal governor of Mauretania by the end of that year.[626] The reason that the troops needed to overcome Sabinianus had to be summoned from Mauretania was that the military situation was in some turmoil in the aftermath of the Gordians' rebellion and its brutal suppression; and because the senate, on behalf of Gordian III, had cashiered the units that Capellianus, the man who dispatched the Gordians, had commanded in April 238. Probably Sabinianus was the governor sent out to Africa by the senate to replace Gordianus I.

It is not clear who this man actually was; the leading contenders are M. [Triarius Rufinus] Asinius Sabinianus (suffect consul c. 225) or C. Vettius Gratus Sabinianus (consul 221). Neither really fit: the first appears to have been governing Asia in c. 238/239 or 239/240, which eliminates him.[627] The family of the second went from strength to strength after 240, which would hardly have been the case had he been an usurper.[628] Possibly, this Sabinianus was a descendant of M. Annius Libo, suffect consul in 160/161 and a member of the family of Marcus Aurelius. He seems to have married the daughter of a surviving member of the Flavian Imperial house, producing M. Annius Sabinus Libo, a senator living c. 190 and M. Annius Flavius Libo (consul in 204).[629] Whilst we cannot prove that the family *cognomen* mutated from Sabinus to Sabinianus, kinship to two past (and well regarded) emperors might seem a likely spur to taking a tilt at the purple in 240, even if the claimant's motivation seems obscure.

---

624 PLRE II Romulus 4; Paulus 23

625 PLRE II Avienus 2, PLRE III Orestes. Note that Pope Severinus (May-August 640) was son of an Avienus, and thus perhaps a descendant of the consul of 502 and quite possibly of Romulus.

626 HA. *V. Gord.*. 23, 4; Zosimus I, 17, 1; PIR² S18

627 PIR² T 343

628 PIR² V 330 = V 331; Mennen (2011) 127-128

629 As convincingly proposed by Birley (1987) 243

SABINUS
68, June/July

C. Nymphidius Sabinus, after service as a junior equestrian officer, was appointed praetorian prefect by the emperor Nero in 65 and on the Emperor's fall in 68, he persuaded the Guard to support the Emperor Galba. However, he swiftly became disillusioned with Galba and made a futile and failed attempt to claim the imperial purple for himself. He was quickly turned on by the praetorians and rapidly dispatched, presumably unmarried and childless.[630]

Sabinus was the son of Nymphidia, daughter of C. Julius Callistus, a freedman of the Emperor Caligula who became a trusted member of his staff and was later a senior civil servant (a *libellis*) under Claudius.[631] Her husband was a man called Asiaticus – not the 35 suffect consul married to the sister of Caligula's empress Lollia Paulina – but Sabinus claimed that his father was none other than Caligula himself, hence the basis for his unexpected and fleeting bid for supreme power, the memory of Caligula being still green amongst the praetorians.

SALONINUS
260 c. July – November

Saloninus was the long-time heir apparent of Gallienus, who was only proclaimed Augustus by the usurper Silvanus, but perished with his mentor in the chaos from which emerged the so-called Gallic empire.

Whilst beset with usurpers and barbarian incursions, the emperor Gallienus made his son Saloninus Caesar. P. Licinius Cornelius Saloninus Valerianus, who was born c. 245/6, in 258/259 *nobilissimus caesar* and *princeps iuventutis* in place of his elder brother.[632] Although called Augustus on Alexandrian coins minted some time between 258 and 260, he only appears to have been formally declared emperor at Colonia Agrippina (Cologne) after the outbreak of the revolt of Postumus. All this Balkan activity meant that Gallienus' C-in-C Rhine had to be 100% reliable and loyal, especially as the *caesar* Saloninus had been installed at Colonia Agrippina as a figurehead, under the keeping of one of the Praetorian Prefects, Silvanus. Unfortunately, in the fatal year of 260, Silvanus fell out with Postumus, who proclaimed himself emperor following a crushing victory by Genialis (qv), the acting governor of Rhaetia over the Semnones, which had placed much booty in his hands. This provoked Silvanus into acclaiming Saloninus as co-Augustus, notionally with his father Gallienus. A confrontation began which resulted later that autumn in the death of Saloninus and his mentor, followed by the triumph of Postumus. It is doubtful if Saloninus' elevation ever received recognition by the senate in his lifetime and thus he probably received no vote

---

630 Plutarch, *Galba* ix.1
631 PIR² I229
632 PIR² L183; ILS 539, 558, 559

of the usual powers and titles. He was styled Imperator [Caesar P. Licinius Cornelius] Salon[inus] Valerianus Augustus. He was unmarried and was subsequently recognised and granted divine honours by the senate.

SALUTIUS
363, 26ᵗʰ June & 364, 16ᵗʰ February

Salutius was Pretorian Prefect of the east under Julian the Apostate, serving with him on this campaign against the Persians. On Julian's death on 26 June, a meeting of his senior officers decided to offer the throne to him, but he refused on grounds of old age, and on behalf of his son, also under threat of this dubious honour. Jovian was elected instead, and Salutius stayed in service whilst Jovian continued the campaign, dying on 16 February the following year. Some sources allege that Salutius was again offered the throne, but again refused, although the most reliable source, Ammianus Marcellinus, fails to mention it, so possibly it never happened.

Saturninus Secundus Salutius, a Gaul, had a long career, serving as *praeses* of Aquitania and after some increasingly senior bureaucratic posts, governed Africa before being appointed Pretorian Prefect by Julian in 361. With one brief hiatus, he served four emperors loyally, retiring with the rank of patrician in 367.[633]

SATURNINUS (I)
89, 1ˢᵗ – 25ᵗʰ January

Saturninus was the governor of Upper Germany who mysteriously rebelled briefly against Domitian at the beginning of 89 and was swiftly suppressed by the governor of the neighbouring province. The would-be usurper L. Antonius Saturninus was probably a member of a knightly family of Roman origin long settled in Tarraco (Tarragona) in the province of Further Spain. Little is known of his antecedents, nor do we know the name of his wife. Syme suggests his father is probably to be identified with a cultic high priest and retired magistrate of Tarraco, L. Antonius L. f. Gal. Saturninus. He was adlected into the senate by Vespasian, either in 69 or as a result of his censorship in 74, with praetorian rank, going on immediately to govern Macedonia 74/76 followed by Judaea in 78/81, after which he was suffect consul.

He was appointed governor of Upper Germany either in 87 or 88 and was acclaimed at Moguntiacum (now Mainz), Lower Germany, on 1 January 89 at the head of a military revolt, being defeated in battle 25 days later by A. Bucius Lappius Maximus, the governor of Lower Germany; the mopping up was done by M. Ulpius Traianus (junior), the future emperor Trajan. Saturninus was either killed in the fighting or took his own life subsequently. He seems to have issued no coins.

633 PLRE I Salutius 3; *Amm. Marc.* xxv. 5. 3

Some commentators have linked the shadowy affair of the execution of the governor of Britain, Sallustius Lucullus – put forward rather daringly but perhaps not wholly convincingly by Dr Miles Russell as having been the son of the British (Catuvellaunian) prince Adminius.[634] It seems that Lucullus was put to death for having the temerity to name a new type of spear after himself and not the emperor.

Was the real reason resentment on Lucullus' part (or on the part of his officers) in having to withdraw from the successful part-conquest of Scotland achieved by Agricola, himself later disgraced? And was Saturninus' bid a closely related event? These are murky waters and, as so often with unsuccessful usurpers, little light seems to penetrate to allow the true course of events and real underlying motives to be discerned with our present state of knowledge.

The reasons behind the revolt are extremely difficult to fathom, nor does there seem to be much evidence that Saturninus was actually acclaimed emperor; he had few qualifications for the purple – he was no kinsman of a triumvir. He was a man with no following in the circles likely to matter; although it is worth noting that Sir Ronald Syme did consider him a full-blooded usurper and not just a rebel.[635] It is impossible to even hazard a guess as to whether he jumped, was pushed into revolt, or was the victim of circumstance.

One source claims that he was a 'disgusting and scandalous fellow' and not to be trusted with money, lent some credence by his seizure of his legions' pay chest, although that might be viewed as a sensible precaution by anyone attempting a military *coup* in the provinces.

We know of no family, although an Antonia L. f. Saturnina was recorded in the late 2nd century to have married the senator C. Arrius Pacatus and might conceivably have been a descendant.

SATURNINUS (II)
260/268

Saturninus was characterised as the 'best of Generals' who the *Historia Augusta* claims seized power sometime in Gallienus' reign but does not specify exactly where, so doubt must be cast on his existence. He was apparently killed by his own men shortly after assuming power.[636]

SATURNINUS (III)
280, c. December – 281, March

This man was a high-ranking usurper in Syria against Probus who, like so many such aspiring emperors before him, was eliminated by his own officers

---

634 *Current Archaeology* 204 (5/2006) 630-635; author's argument against, letter, *op. cit.*, 205 (7/2006)

635 Syme (1958) I. xi

636 HA *Tyr. Trig.* XXIII . 1-4, cf. *V. Firmi et al* XI.1; PLRE I Saturninus 1

in less than four months. Saturninus was allegedly an old comrade in arms of Aurelian that the Emperor appointed either to govern Syria or to be C-in-C of forces on the eastern frontier (*dux limitis orientis*). He subsequently became an usurper by military acclamation in the east, and was acknowledged throughout the region, minting coins at Alexandria.

He seems to have been killed at Apamaea (Qalaat al-Madiq, Syria) in Syria by his own officers before Probus could divert from other problems and deal with him. Zonaras identifies him as an African (whether 'Moor' is accurate is anybody's guess).[637] His coins tell us that his *nomen* was Julius, which leads PLRE I to suspect that he may be identifiable with C. Julius Sallustius Saturninus Fortunatianus.[638] This man is known from an inscription in Africa (confirming Zonaras) and had been pro-praetorian legate (and thus a senator) in Numidia under Gallienus, commanding that Emperor's third Augustan legion.

He was probably one of the last such office holders before this and other military posts were closed to senators. He had also been suffect consul, c. 260. His inscription also tells us that after his stint in Numidia he had been *comes* (military courtier) of an emperor who is not named, but could be any, from Gallienus to – as the *Historia Augusta* suggests – Aurelian. The same source contains much about this man, mainly patently fictitious, although part of it relates to his not being permitted to enter Egypt, which, as the man we suspect of being this usurper was a senator, would probably reflect the truth, rather than his having been of modest background and trained as a rhetorician as the *Historia* claims.[639] His imperial style was Imp[erator] C[aesar] Jul[ius] Saturninus Aug[ustus], as on his coins.

For once the *Historia Augusta* fails to endow him with any family but, if he can be identified with Fortunatianus, then we are able to say something about his background. He was probably a grandson or great-grandson of Sallustius Saturninus, who served as a procurator under Septimius Severus, possibly by the distaff.

Alternatively, he might have descended from T. Julius T. f. Fab. Saturninus, another procurator, who served in Germany under Marcus Aurelius and whose probable brother, C. Julius Saturninus, was suffect consul in about the same period.[640] He was certainly married to Vergilia Florentina. It is suspected that C. Julius Fortunatianus, a late third century *vir egregius* (equestrian) may have been his son and we know that this Fortunatianus in his turn also had a son called C. Mevius Silius Crescens Fortunatianus who was a *clarissimus puer* (boy of senatorial rank).[641]

---

637 PLRE I Saturninus 12; Zonaras 12, 29

638 *op. cit.*, Fortunatianus 6 cf. PIR² I540/546

639 HA V. *Firmi et al*, 7, 3 & 9, 2-4. The Saturninus of HA *Tyr. Trig.* 23 is entirely fictional.

640 PIR² I548, 547

641 PIR² I319

SCRIBONIANUS see CAMILLUS

SEBASTIANUS
412, c. October – 413, c. March

Sebastianus was a Gallic usurper with his brother Jovinus in continuation of the regime initiated by Constantine III. Jovinus was the prime mover in this second grasp at power against Honorius and he made Sebastianus his co-ruler in 412. Sebastian's style was, as was now the norm, D[ominus] N[oster] Sebastianus P[ius] F[elix] Aug[ustus]. He was soon enough betrayed with his brother, and killed by Athualf in spring 413, when Honorius' government was able to re-establish some form of control in Gaul.

SELEUCUS
?231

Seleucus was a mysterious usurper somewhere in the east, whose identity remains in doubt and whose activities are shrouded in mystery. He occurs only in two late sources[642] and seems otherwise to be unknown. It is possible he could have been the general who led a rebellious legion from Egypt to join Alexander Severus in 232. If so, he would have been of equestrian rank, Egypt having been barred to senators since the time of Actium. If not, then he may be identified with [C.(?)] Jul[ius] Ant[onius] Seleucus[643] under Elagabalus, who was pro-praetorian legate in Lower Moesia and after that – promisingly for this identification – consular legate in Coele Syria at just this date. He is thus also possibly to be identified with the contemporary Antonius Seleucus, styled *v[ir]. c[larissimus], consularis noster.*[644]

The name suggests a descent from Seleucus IV Philopator, King of Syria 187-175BC via the Egyptian royal house and either the children of M. Antonius and Cleopatra or the descendants of C. Julius Antiochus Epiphanes, last King of Commagene (AD38-72). There were a number of members of mediatised royal houses in the second-century senate, and such connections might indeed impel a man to aspire to the purple, following the successful example of Elagabalus and Alexander, bearing in mind that the Royal House of Emesa was probably regarded as somewhat less illustrious than those of Syria and Commagene. [...] Jul[ius] Ant[onius] Seleucus was suffect consul in the early 3rd century and was probably of the family of the Julii Maiores, descended in the female line from the daughter of Mark Antony. If this identification can be accepted, then the Commagenian connection would be through the female line. The only other senatorial candidate might be M. Flavius Vitellius Seleucus, consul in 221; if he usurped, as a former ordinary consul, it is unlikely that a writer like Herodian would have omitted to mention it.[645]

---

642 Polemius Silvius *Laterculus*, II. 30-31 & *Chronica Minora*, 520-523
643 PIR² I 154, where the identification with this imperial claimant is doubted; cf. Syme (1971) 159
644 Gilliam, J. F., in *American Journal of Philology* LXXIX (1958) 231 f.
645 Syme, *loc.cit*, n. 6

SEPTIMIUS SEVERUS (I)
193, 9th April – 211, 4th February

Severus was the brutally successful soldier/emperor who broke the deadlock of the post-Didius Julianus outbreak of imperial declaratons, steadied the ship, moved the role of *princeps* further towards the autocracy that eventually found expression in the Tetrarchy and whose dynasty was effectively the last before the beginning of the third-century turmoil of threatened frontiers, economic failure and constant rebellions by elements of the army.

L. Septimius Severus was born on 11 April 145 of native Punic, rather than indigenous, stock from Lepcis Magna (Khoms, Libya) in Africa, a scion of a well-to-do family that was part of the local aristocracy and was thoroughly inter-married with brides from families of Roman settlers. The family would appear to have acquired full citizenship in the earlier Flavian era, perhaps enfranchised by Septimius Flaccus, legate of *Legio III Augusta* stationed at Lepcis in that period – assuming, that is, the name is not an error for 'Suellius'.[646]

Severus was a soldier of exceptional ability, and a man apparently utterly convinced of his own destiny.[647] He is thought to have served on the Board of Twenty in 164, as quaestor in 169 and again in Sardinia in 170-1. He served as legionary legate to his cousin C. Septimius Severus during his pro-consulship of Africa in 173-74, serving immediately thereafter as people's tribune. He married in 173 or 174 a Lepcis woman of Roman descent, Paccia Marciana, who died c. 184/186.[648] There may have been two daughters of the marriage if the *Historia Augusta* is to be believed, but they are not attested elsewhere, despite being allegedly provided with husbands and dowries in 193.[649] He was praetor in 177 and thereafter a legionary legate of *Legio IV Scythica* in Syria under the future emperor Pertinax, but both were dismissed by Commondus in 182.

Severus' career went into eclipse until he was recalled to govern Gallia Lugdunensis in 184. In the summer of 187 he re-married, his bride being Julia Domna, daughter of Julius Bassianus, a member of the ruling family of Emesa and high priest of the local cult there, and by her he had two sons. He went on to govern Sicily in 189 and in 190 he was one of the unprecedented 24 suffect consuls appointed. In summer 191, he was appointed governor of Upper Pannonia, where he was acclaimed emperor on 9 April 193 and received his first imperial acclamation.

It has been suggested that Severus was lined up as a sort of imperial long-stop when Pertinax was elevated to the purple, in case anything went wrong. His appointment to Upper Pannonia in summer 191, effectively by Pretorian Prefect Aemilius Laetus (a fellow African), after having been left idle following his consulship, is instructive; his was the nearest army to Italy.

---

646 Birley (1988) 219

647 FS 3036; PIR² S346

648 ILS 440

649 *Op. cit.*, V. *Sev.* 8.1; of course, if they existed, they could have died in infancy.

Was the murder of Commodus and elevation of Pertinax (or some worthy brother-in-law of the Emperor) already being planned by Laetus and his brother Pudens, with a medium-term maturation date? Did the conspirators foresee Pertinax (or another mature contender) as a holding candidate, like Nerva, prior to putting in their own man and fellow African?

The fact that Pertinax had to face down two alleged plots prior to his own murder – those of Maternus and Falco, neither of which progressed far enough even to qualify as imperial acclamations – may, as we have seen, have put Severus on the alert. Even if Laetus had *not* told him he was their preferred candidate (it would have been safer not to, after all), his own astrologically propelled ambitions might well have been sufficient for him to be fully motivated to seize the main chance.

When the crunch came and the news of Pertinax's murder reached him, it is not clear whether Severus proclaimed himself emperor before he heard about the elevation of Pescennius Niger or not; the news soon reached him, and hence his neutralising of Clodius Albinus in Britain by associating him in power as *caesar*. He made all the right decisions thereafter. He marched swiftly on Rome, stayed aloof once news reached him of the death of Julianus – psychologically very astute – before neutralising the Praetorian Guard, taking them by surprise by sacking the entire corps and then entering the city and restoring order with brutal thoroughness, applying sufficient tact to avoid further rioting by supporters of Niger. He formed a fresh Praetorian Guard from provincial soldiers drawn from his loyal legions and permitted soldiers to marry for the first time.

He then received an imperial acclamation – his second – and having contrived an elaborate ceremony for the deification of Pertinax, whose name he took, initially styled himself Imperator Caesar L. Septimius Severus Pertinax Augustus. On 9 June 193 he was voted the tribunician and proconsular powers (although as proconsul of an armed province he already had the latter for the short term) and the pontificate.[650]

He also assumed the (suffect) consulship, his second. He was voted the style Father of his Country (*pater patriae*). Only then did he set out for the east to deal with Niger, whose entourage and supporters in Rome he had extirpated ruthlessly: a warning, if any were needed, to those in Rome who might have been inclined to switch their allegiance to Albinus. Following this, he waged a brilliantly successful campaign deep into Parthia as further retribution for the Parthian King's support of Niger, looting Ctesiphon, restoring the recaptured Trajanic province of Mesopotamia, attempting to capture Hatra and making a visit to Egypt.

It was during this campaign that he declared himself to be a son of Marcus Aurelius and made his son Bassianus *nobilissimus caesar*, thus throwing down the gauntlet to Albinus. As Severus returned slowly west in 196, Albinus set about trying to consolidate a power base from which to match him in the inevitable clash. He should have advanced on Rome as soon as he heard of his rival's dynastic declaration in 195, only that could have given

---

650 ILS 413

him the advantage he needed, commanding far fewer legions. Even so, the final battle was an extremely close-run thing.

On his return, Severus cowed the senate much as Sulla had done at the end of the Social War, and proscribed 67 senators, of whom 29 were killed. The amount of property seized caused him to appoint a new procurator to deal with it all. He debased the coinage to pay the army, their first (notional) rise for over a century; even Albinus's coinage was of a better standard. This marked the first of many debasements that happened with increasing frequency over the next ninety or so years. Severus received two more imperial acclamations during the year following, four in 195, another after Albinus' defeat in 197 and another two later that year, adding a British one in 207, twelve in all. In 194 he was ordinary consul and in the summer of the following year re-styled himself Imperator Caesar L. Septimius Divi Marci Pii f. Divi Commodi fra[ter] Severus Pius Pertinax Augustus Arabicus Adiabenicus – the latter pair of honorifics being added to mark his wresting of those provinces back from the Parthians. At the same time he re-named his elder son Bassianus 'Antoninus' and declaring him *nobilissimus caesar*. Just as his attempt to link himself to the name of Pertinax had been useful in his initial efforts to legitimise his position, now he was keen to associate himself with the preceding dynasty to which he in fact had marital links, via the Petronii Mamertini and the brothers L. and M. Flavius Aper. The link, one that was well known amongst the senatorial élite, was something he clearly felt he could draw upon and enhance in order to give his regime an additional perceived underpinning of legitimacy. So confident was he that he felt able to call himself Commodus' adoptive brother, no doubt as a sop to the people, who had much less cause to hate the late tyrant than the senate, whose numbers he had so assiduously diminished. Henceforth, Severus was another son of the Divine Marcus, and his own elder son could stand confidently as heir bearing the late and well-beloved Emperor's name, too. In 198, after his second eastern campaign, he added Parthicus Maximus to his titles and in 209 or 210 Britannicus Maximus.

By the time he returned from the east in 202, his elder son Bassianus, now M. Antonius Antoninus but known to history as Caracalla, had been declared co-Augustus, but his arranged marriage to the daughter of Severus' boyhood friend and closest advisor, C. Fulvius Plautianus – commander of the Praetorian Guard with extra powers, which he seems to have misused extensively – was much resented. In 205, Plautianus was killed, either for plotting to seize the Empire for himself, or because Caracalla had 'set him up' in revenge for having had to marry the daughter whom he hated. She herself was sent into exile and was killed as soon as her ex-husband succeeded as sole Emperor.

In 208, Severus set out for Britain, taking both his sons – for long irreconcilably at loggerheads – with him. The province had suffered a barbarian insurrection and internal tribal rebellion during the period when Albinus, the governor, was pursuing his imperial ambitions in Gaul, and the emperor's intention seems to have been to settle the island once and for all – to carry on where Cn. Julius Agricola had left off 125 years before.

The younger son, Geta (qv), was left in charge of civil administration whilst Caracalla and his father campaigned north of the wall, meeting with a considerable degree of success, although Severus' increasing frailty combined with Caracalla's indifference to the aims of the war made them less effective than intended.

They retired to Eboracum (York) for the close season 210-211, where Severus finally breathed his last on 4 February. Caracalla, for his part, having decided that he had curried sufficient favour with the army, immediately declared that enough had been done in settling the north – an ironic echo of Commodus breaking off the Marcomannic War in 180 – and the two brothers returned in haste to Rome with their father's ashes. On arrival the senate decreed his deification – a move that no doubt stuck in the craw of many senators, resentful at Severus' brutality and lack of respect for the institution that they represented, from which he had come and which, after all, effectively produced the élite that governed the empire for him.

Whilst he restored stability to the empire, his cruelty and single-mindedness finally ended the deferential diarchy which had existed between *princeps*/emperor and the senate under the long summer of the Antonines. The disturbances which followed from the assassination of Commodus were far more prolonged at almost four years than anything that had followed the death of Nero. Yet it was a mere *apéritif* for the chaotic years to come from the mid-3rd century. Nevertheless, as a war-leader – whether against rivals or foreign enemies – his arms met with unparalleled success, never to be seriously repeated. He had left a legacy of stability and good government unaffected by the rivalry and cruelty of the court.

SEPTIMIUS
271

Septimius usurped the purple in Dalmatia early in the reign of Aurelian. He was killed by his own men not long after his elevation.[651] There are no other clues as to his identity and no known coins.

SERVATUS
?378/379

Servatus was named with a number of other usurpers by Polemius Silvius and is the only one not readily identifiable.[652] Polemius wrote: '...Honorius, under whom Gratianus and Constantinus, and Attalus twice, Maximus and Servatus, Marcus, Magnus and Maximus, Jovinus, Sebastianus, and Victor were usurpers.'

Either he appeared under Honorius c. 395-423, which is what Polemius implies (bracketing him with Gerontius' man, Maximus) , or – bearing in mind the slightly garbled list – perhaps c. 378 and thus the reason for

---

651 Aurelius Victor 35, 3, Zosimus 1, 49. 2; PLRE I. Septimius 1
652 PLRE II Servatus 1; Polemius Silvius, *Laterculus* 78-79, quoted in Birley (2005) 455

the appointment of Magnus Maximus to Britain: an otherwise unrecorded attempt at the purple, perhaps impelled by worried troops in face of a barbarian incursion (which Maximus is well known for having suppressed).[653] Yet nothing specifically connects this man with Britain, although the list certainly implies the west is meant.

SEVERUS ALEXANDER (I)
222, 11th March – 235, 22nd March[654]

The not unexpected demise of Elagabalus at the hands of the Praetorian Guard propelled his young cousin, the Caesar Alexander, to power. With him came his mother, Julia Mamaea. Unlike her unfortunate sister, Julia Soaemias, Mamaea was able to control her son, and he turned out to be a relatively normal youth, although perceived as being inordinately under his mother's thumb. Not only that, but behind Mamaea was her own mother, Septimius Severus' sister-in-law, Julia Maesa, and for almost two years these two powerful and strong-willed matrons ruled the empire effectively as joint Augustae in Alexander's name. When he reached the age of maturity and failed to free himself from their influence, matters began to drift out of his control.

[M.] Gessius Alexianus Bassianus was born on 1 October 208, or more probably 209, at Arca Caesaraea (Arqa, Lebanon).[655] He appears to have come to Rome in 219 in the train of Elagabalus with his mother. He was adopted by Elagabalus in late autumn 221 as his heir, being granted the name and style M. Aurelius Alexander Nobilissimus Caesar, adding *imperi et sacerdotis princeps iuventutis* ('power-endowed and priestly prince of youth').[656] He was consul for the first time as colleague of his cousin in 222. He was acclaimed by the praetorians on 11 March 222 and took the style Imperator Caesar M. Aurelius Severus Alexander Pius Felix Augustus.[657] He was given an imperial acclamation on 13 March and the same day was recognised by the senate and granted the proconsular and tribunician power; he was also recognised as *pontifex maximus*; later he was granted the title of *pater patriae*. In 226 he was consul again and received a second imperial acclamation; he was acclaimed *imperator* another eight times between 226 and 235, the precise dates unclear. He held his third and final consulship in 229. He celebrated a triumph in September 233 on his return from Mesopotamia, the *Historia Augusta* claiming that he added Persicus Maximus to his name, but as this appears neither on coins nor inscriptions, it must be considered dubious.

He married in October or November 225 Gneia Seia Herennia Sallustia Barbia Orba Orbiana, the daughter of the senator L. Seius [(?) Sallustius

---

653 Craven (2023) 56 n.32, 106-107
654 The date is not certain. The HA opts for 22 March, but modern analysis of the evidence suggests about ten days earlier.
655 PIR² A1610; he was only 12 in 221: Herodian 5, 7, 4
656 ILS 474
657 ILS 479

Herennius Macrinianus], being accorded the title of augusta whilst her father became L. Seius Caesar.[658] His identity is elusive, although he was probably a descendant of P. Seius Fuscianus, consul for the second time in 188, childhood friend of Marcus Aurelius and a patrician by creation. Yet a note of caution needs to be sounded, for Syme urges us 'not to entirely discard' the *Historia Augusta's* name for him – Macrinus – and to consider that he might have been a prefect of the Praetorian Guard.[659] The Empress Orbiana must also in this case have been close kin to Q. Sallustius Macrinianus, a contemporary senator, the son or grandson of an eponymous procurator of Mauritania in 194.[660] It is much more difficult to identify a likely Herennius, though, despite there being precious few families of this name in the senate known for the general period, although Herennius Orbianus, who had been a member of the Arval Brethren in the mid-2nd century, is also likely to have been an ancestor.[661] The *Historia Augusta* muddies the water by naming Alexander's wife in one place as 'Memmia daughter of the ex-consul Sulpicius, granddaughter of Catulus' and much later on as the daughter of Macrianus.[662] This has led some to speculate that Alexander must have married three times but, as Fink pointed out, Memmia is clearly a steal from the family of Galba (qv) and his first wife, whilst the second perhaps derives from the recently deposed emperor Macrinus or even from the future usurper Macrianus.[663]

According again to the *Historia Augusta* (with all the reservations that demands), a relative of Gessius Alexianus Bassianus was Catilius Severus, later his advisor.[664] This is presumably Cn. Catilius Severus, suffect consul in 200 and an Arval Brother 213/221 or a son, perhaps the contemporarily attested L. Catilius Severus.[665] Presumably, he was descended from or close kin to L. Catilius Severus Julianus Claudius Reginus consul (ii) 120, who briefly adopted Marcus Aurelius. The consul of 200 was son of an Aurelia – perhaps the association was too much for the compiler of the *Historia*. No credible kinship to Severus Alexander can be detected, however. A tantalising sidelight on Alexander's family history is the *Historia Augusta's* tale that he had a pedigree drawn up showing his descent from the Caecilii Metelli of the Republic.[666] Whilst this is most likely fiction, it is so unlikely a tale that there is always the possibility it is *not* made up. If the story contains any truth, it is probably a remote element of the Empress's pedigree that was drawn up and not Alexander's.

Julia Maesa died in 224, whereupon the less able Mamaea took over, extending her reach accordingly. Hence the marriage of Alexander to an

---

658 ILS 486
659 Syme (1971) 157
660 ILS 3055
661 PIR² H81
662 V. *Sev. Alex.* 20, 3 & 49, 3-4
663 Fink (1939) 329; Suet. *Galba* 3, 4
664 V. *Sev. Alex.* 68. 1
665 ILS 5039
666 V. *Sev. Alex.*, XL. 3

aristocrat of obscure stock seems like an attempt to bolster the unpopular dynasty through an alliance with the metropolitan élite, just as Soaemias had attempted to do with the far less tractable Elagabalus. The ploy failed because Augusta Orbiana, unsurprisingly, put Mamaea in second place by the very nature of her position. Indeed, if we only knew more about her, we might appreciate that she showed some mettle and increasingly kept Mamaea out of things. Added to which, making the father-in-law *caesar* placed at least some control of affairs into hands other than her own. Needless to say, in 227 Mamaea banished the young Empress to Libya and had Seius Caesar killed for allegedly attempting to use the praetorians against her.[667]

Orbiana's other mistake was a result of her relatively enlightened decision to appoint a council of wise men to advise the Emperor, including the jurist Domitius Ulpianus, known to history as Ulpian, whom she appointed one of the Praetorian Prefects with enhanced powers.[668] He introduced some essential reforms and oversaw the reversal of almost all Elagabalus's administrative and religious excesses. Unfortunately, he was not a military man and lost the respect of the Guard, one of his measures provoking three days of rioting setting the praetorians against the people. As a result of this, he felt obliged to execute two Praetorian Guard officers, a step too far. A detachment of the Guard promptly killed him in the imperial palace. This seems to have set an unfortunate precedent, for the soldiers perceived the Emperor as young, weak and even worse, under the control of a woman. Thus, there were periodic outbreaks of trouble throughout the reign, not only in the praetorian camp but in the military provinces as well – an ominous sign.

Nevertheless, the reign has also been hailed as marking a restoration of the gubernatorial diarchy between emperor and senate, although Dio suggests that the relationship was mainly window dressing. Alexander was still advised by a council of senators and promoted Pretorian Prefects to senatorial rank, but his mother did not let go of power to the extent that the senate regained much for themselves. Nevertheless, they still provided the governing élite and were for a time at least mollified.

Another problem was that for all the dynastic instability since Caracalla's eastern campaign, the empire had been at peace. However, the peace was shattered when the 500-year-old empire of Parthia was overthrown by Artaxerxes (Ardashir), a noble subject of the last Parthian king, Artabanus V who, by 226, had re-invented his realm in the guise of the ancient Persian Empire. In 230, he took back the province of Mesopotamia, created by Severus after his capture of Ctesiphon some thirty years before. The restoration of the province was essential to the prestige and future safety of the empire. Preparations began in 231, but were bedevilled by an usurper, probably Taurinus. Diplomacy was tried, reverses were experienced, but a successful outcome was obtained and Artaxerxes finally withdrew from the disputed province, giving guarantees to Alexander – or so we are told. What actually happened is not at all clear, but Roman arms, despite setbacks, must have

667 McHugh (2017) 146
668 PIR² D169

eventually triumphed for so ambitious a sovereign as the first of the Sassanids to withdraw voluntarily. This enabled Alexander to celebrate a triumph.

The armies on the German and Danubian frontiers had been reduced in strength to bolster the anti-Persian expeditionary force and the German tribes seized the opportunity to cause much trouble and destruction. In 234, Alexander led the army across the Rhine and restored order but made the fatal mistake of attempting to reach a negotiated solution that included a substantial grant to the barbarians to keep the peace. Looked at from the perspective of the army, of course, this meant less likelihood of loot and pillage, the spoils of war being a major incentive to discipline and good morale. At the same time, the Emperor was pursuing a policy of financial retrenchment in the military sphere that was already impacting on remuneration.

One of the most senior equestrian officers, a Thracian called Maximinus, is thought to have used this to sow discord and in the resulting mutiny Maximinus was acclaimed by his men on 21 March and the following day Alexander, his mother and their entourage were murdered by a detachment of NCOs at Vicus Britannicus (Bretzenheim), near Mogontiacum (Mainz). Alexander left no issue and suffered a *damnatio memoriae* from his successor, but he was finally deified by the senate after Maximin's death in 238.

SEVERUS (I) see SEPTIMIUS SEVERUS

SEVERUS HOSTILIANUS
?249

Severus Hostilianus was an usurper, mentioned by Zonaras as having been acclaimed by the senate in the reign of Philip I, but he is spurious in the same way as Marcus (II).[669]

SEVERUS II
306, August – 307, March/April

Sir Ronald Syme characterised Severus II as a 'low-born drinking companion of Galerius'.[670] That he probably lacked charisma is underscored by the rapid desertion from him of his troops when he tried to dislodge Maxentius in spring 307. He is the only Tetrarch who was not related (as far as we know) to any of the others. He was born in Illyricum probably around 260 and rose rapidly in the army, being a senior commander before he was chosen as *caesar* by Galerius, taking office on 1 March 305.[671] His promotion to *augustus* as a response to the acclamation in Britain of Constantine probably occurred in August 306. His full original name is not known, but as Emperor

---

669 Körner (2001) 391-393
670 Syme (1971) 212
671 ILS646

he was styled Imperator Flavius Valerius Severus Pius Felix Augustus.[672] He was granted the tribunician and proconsular powers as Caesar and was consul in 307. He does not appear to have been *pontifex maximus*. We do not know the name of his wife, possibly because she had died or been divorced prior to his accession, but they did have a son, [Flavius Valerius] Severianus, who survived him, who later unwisely attached himself to Maximin II Daia but was executed by Licinius after Maximin's fall .[673] Following the desertion of his troops, Severus was taken prisoner by Maxentius in spring 307 and was killed or forced to commit suicide at Rome on 16 September.

SEVERUS III see LIBIUS SEVERUS

SILBANNACUS
?248

A man styling himself Mar[ ] Silbannacus is known only from an extremely rare *Antoninianus* to have been an usurper at about the period of Philip the Arab's fall and the reign of Decius. Some reference books give his name as Marcus but the abbreviation here is undoubtedly a *nomen*, not a *praenomen*, and Marcius or Marius are the only likely alternatives.[674] He may well have been an unrecorded governor of one of the Germanies (and therefore a senator) elevated by the troops on the Rhine frontier as a result of some forgotten crisis. Indeed, if his *nomen* really was Marcius, he might have been a kinsman of Marcia Otacilia Severa, Philip's Empress. The year 248 would appear the most likely place for him, bearing in mind the style of the coin itself.

He adopted the imperial style Imperator Mar[(c)ius] Silbannacus Augustus.[675] The coin's reverse depicts Victory, so he may have inflicted a surprise defeat on a German or Frankish invasion, prompting his men to acclaim him. A second issue features Mars *propugnator* (champion) and was also found in Gaul. Scholarly opinion is divided as to his exact *floruit*, under Decius being one suggestion and another that he preceded Postumus. Harold Mattingly fairly convincingly dated it on style and quality to c. 248/250, however. The likelihood is that he was soon killed by his own troops. His *cognomen* seems Celtic, so he was perhaps a senator of Gaulish or even British extraction. He had no known family or connections.

SILVANUS
355, 11th August – 8th September

Silvanus was an usurper on the Rhone frontier who arose amidst the instability following the defeat of Magnentius and Decentius by Constantius II. Following the overthrow of Magnentius and his brother, Constantius II returned east,

---

672 PLRE I Severus 30
673 PLRE I Severianus 1
674 Körner (2001) 386-389
675 Coin, British Museum, believed to have been found in Lorraine.

leaving trusted lieutenants in charge to settle things down on the more sensitive frontier areas. On the Rhine he left his *magister peditum* (infantry general) Silvanus who had earned his promotion through his desertion from Magnentius to the cause of the House of Constantine. Following an intrigue at his HQ at Milan, he was forced to assume the purple at Colonia Agrippina (Cologne) in August 355. Whether he obtained recognition from the senate at Rome (within his sphere of command) is not known but it seems unlikely, or reprisals would have been recorded once order had been restored, and memories of the events of 350 were doubtless still raw there. As emperor his style was Dominus Noster Imperator Cl[a]udius Silvanus Augustus.[676] The *nomen* Claudius may have been added on accession as a sop to the House of Constantine, but not necessarily.

The imperial claimant was a Christian, the son of Bonitus, a Frank, the commander of the VII[th] Claudian Legion in Moesia Prima under Constantine the Great, who later promoted him to a senior post, probably *dux*.[677] Silvanus was a senior tribune commanding an élite regiment when he defected to Constantius in 351 prior to the Battle of Mursa. The following year he was made *magister peditum* in Gaul and later (it would appear from a decree addressed to him) was promoted to *magister militum*, a relatively new post, combining the offices of *magister peditum* and *magister equitum*, with responsibility for the west. Whilst the Emperor was staying at his base, Milan, with Silvanus at Cologne dealing with the German frontier, his acclamation was provoked by a coterie of corrupt courtiers altering despatches and sowing doubt in the Emperor's mind about Silvanus' loyalty. The end of the revolt came about after 28 days, through an emissary from the Emperor, Ursicinus, betraying the claimant's trust during negotiations, having him dragged from a church service and hacked to pieces. 'Such was the end,' wrote Ammianus Marcellinus, 'of a commander of no small merit, who was driven by fear of the slanders in which a hostile clique had ensnared him in his absence, to adopt extreme measures in self-defence.'[678] His wife and young son were saved, suggesting that the Emperor may have soon afterwards realised that the matter had been unjustly provoked by his own officials.[679]

The whole episode has been doubted by one recent commentator on the grounds that Silvanus issued no coins, but the gates of the nearest mint, Trier, were closed against him and he is named as Augustus in two inscriptions and alluded to in a third.[680]

---

676 ILS748, cf. ILS 1460 where he is merely Silvanus Augustus.

677 PLRE I Bonitus 1, cf. 2

678 *Op. cit.*, 15.5.29

679 The 'young son' was perhaps Silvanus, a *dux* and local governor in Africa in 393: PLRE I Silvanus 5

680 CIL.X. 6946. On him see PLRE I Silvanus 2, also Aur. Victor 42, 16, Zonaras 13, 9 & Eutropius 10, 13

SPONSIANUS
c.248 or 260, June – Autumn

Sponsianus was an enigmatic usurper in the Balkans whose bid for power might have occurred at either of two widely separated dates, and whose very existence, like that of Silbannacus, is known from only two coins.

Sponsianus would appear to have been acclaimed emperor in Moesia (probably Upper Moesia) of which he may have been governor, or an equestrian military commander (*dux*), sometime in the reign of the Emperor Philip I.[681] The events leading up to the acclamation of Pacatianus would seem the most likely context, yet metallurgical analysis published in 2022 suggested rather that he was a *dux* cut off in Dacia in the wake of the capture of Valerian in 260 and who was forced to style himself emperor in order to negotiate with the surrounding tribes. Nothing can be discovered about him in either case, nor can any clues be recovered from his name. There would appear to be no Sponsii amongst the Roman élite to explain it, although three late first-century funerary inscriptions in Rome name a Sponsianus.

Sponsianus first came to notice with the discovery of an *aureus* in Transylvania in 1713 and, like all unique finds, it was long dismissed as a forgery, especially as the coin was cast and not struck; but if you are cut off in a gold-producing area with no mint nearby and wish to buy off some threatening barbarian warlords, you make do. Furthermore, it seems inherently unlikely a forger would choose a name so rare as Sponsianus. 17th- and 18th-century forgeries certainly *were* made, but only in the name of known ephemeral usurpers. The fact that he escaped the attention of the *Historia Augusta* adds much to Sponsianus' credibility.

His coins are unusual in that the imperial inscription occupies both faces of the flan, whilst the reverse bears no 'slogan', consisting only of two figures standing either side of an Ionic column supporting a statue with wheat ears (for plenty) issuant from either side of the base.[682]

STOTZAS (I)
536
541 – 545, October

Stotzas was a serial rebel in Africa under Justinian, who failed to learn the lesson of a first failed *coup* and had a sufficiently large following to leave a successor.

The *magister militum* Martinus was one of the leaders (in his case of the federate troops) of the expedition against the Vandals in Africa in 533 and the commander of his personal guard was an officer called Stotzas. Three years later, there was an army mutiny, and the ringleaders chose this same Stotzas as their leader. They proposed to throw the remainder of the imperial contingent out of the province and seize control. He thereupon besieged

---

681 Körner (2001) 389-390

682 RIC IV Sponsianus 1

Carthage at the head of more than 9,000 soldiers but raised the siege on the appearance of Belisarius, who defeated him, causing him to withdraw into Numidia, where he started a further rebellion amongst the troops there. At one time, almost two-thirds of the Roman forces in North Africa had gone over to him, although significant numbers later deserted when the prince Germanus arrived late in 536 and announced that there would be no reprisals for those prepared to return to the imperial cause.[683] The following year Stotzas, supported by Moorish and Vandal allies, fought Germanus's forces at Scalas Veteres ('Old Steps', a coastal location in the modern suburbs of Tunis), after which he took refuge in Mauretania, where he married the daughter of one of the Moorish princes there and settled.[684]

One chronicler specifically avers that in 541 he assumed the purple in his own name, and he is elsewhere referred to as a *tyrannus*, the normal term for an usurper. It seems odd that he should have waited until five years after his (largely unsuccessful) first revolt to so style himself, and it may be that he assumed the imperial style when first chosen as the leader of the uprising of 536. We have no record of the way he was styled, but it was presumably Dominus Noster Stotzas Pater Patriae Augustus. If there was a provincial *concilium* so soon after the *reconquista* of Africa, it may or may not have acknowledged him.

In 544 Stotzas tried again to assert his control and defeated a Roman force, possibly that of the Pretorian Prefect of Africa, Solomon, at the Battle of Cillium (Kassarine, Tunisia), after which he left Mauretania and plundered Byzacena, where he suborned more recruits from the regular forces there. He went on to plunder other cities in the province of Africa, and he was killed in battle at Thacia in autumn 545 against the *magister militum* Johannes, who also died in the engagement. Amazingly, this did not end the rebellion and he was succeeded by one Iohannes, styling himself Stotzas II. We know nothing of his family.

STOTZAS (II)
545, October – 546

Statzas II was the style of Iohannes, heir to the failed usurper Stotzas I, who allied himself with a second usurper in order to keep his bid alive.

An officer called Iohannes was a commander under Stotzas I, who was elected as his successor on the usurper's death in battle by a motley collection of 500 Romans, 80 Huns and over 400 Vandals. He was henceforth known as Stotzas II or Stotzas Junior. Soon after his elevation, his forces marched on Carthage along with Moorish allies and encouraged a second Roman revolt under Guntharis, allowing him to take Carthage after a battle with the prince

---

683 At this juncture another officer of a gubanatorial bodyguard (that of Germanus and Theodorus the Cappadocian) called Maximinus attempted to establish himself as a breakaway usurper through a mutiny but, failing a placatory promotion, he was anticipated and executed: PLRE III Maximinus 1

684 PLRE III Stotzas; Conant (2012) 216, 301-302

Areobindus, who was killed. After the fall of Guntharis, he was captured and sent in chains to Constantinople where he was crucified.[685]

SYAGRIUS
465, October/November – 486

Syagrius was by inheritance ruler of a breakaway polity in Gaul during the final years of the Western Empire, which he had taken over from his father Aegidius. He allied himself with the Franks in keeping various other barbarian elements under control, but he succumbed to Frankish expansion in the long run.

How he styled himself is lost to us, but as Professor Fanning has pointed out, it would have been anything but *rex* (king) which is often how modern commentators describe him. It may well be that the father made him a *comes* and *magister militum*, although a later source refers to him as patrician. He was born about 430 and therefore succeeded to power aged roughly 35. He may have had the *comes* Paulus as his *magister militum*, for we find this man successfully leading Roman troops and Franks under King Childeric I against the Visigoths and then in 469 defeating Odoacer (later to overthrow Romulus in Italy) and taking Juliomagus (Angers), where he was killed in action.[686]

Syagrius' *imperium,* originally covering most of central and northern Gaul, was reduced by numerous conflicts to an area stretching from the Atlantic coast with the Loire as its southern border and probably excluding Brittany to the Meuse/Scheldt Channel littoral. With Arbogastes in Trier as *comes* as late as 477, it may be that he had managed to re-establish considerable mastery in the east of Gaul, too, no doubt with Frankish support.[687] Later, the western portion was lost and the Seine became the western edge of his empire – mainly the old province of Belgica Secunda with parts of Gallia Lugdunensis and Germania.[688] In 476, after the deposition of Romulus by Odoacer, he and Syagrius sent embassies to Constantinople seeking recognition, which confirms that the Gallic ruler considered himself an emperor (or *tyrannus*) in the traditional sense. In the event, Eastern Emperor Zeno recognised Odoacer as patrician on petition of the senate but rejected the claims of the Gaul.

His alliance with the Franks fell apart after 481 under the rise of the young, energetic and charismatic new King, Chlodovechus (Clovis/Louis I) who was bent on expansion and continuing co-operation with Syagrius had no part in it. In 486, the two sides met in battle near Soissons, the Roman

---

685 PLRE III Ioannes 35

686 PLRE II Paulus 20; he is a prime candidate to have been made a consul of this breakaway polity.

687 PLRE II Arbogastes; he was son of Arigius and a descendant of the Arbogastes who served Theodosius I as *magister militum*. His appointment could have been a Frankish one, but if so, he was an odd choice, with friends like Sidonius Apollinaris: MacGeorge (2012) 75.

688 Some commentators consider his empire rather smaller at its end, eg. James (1988) 67-71

ruler coming off worst, being in the aftermath forced to seek refuge at Tolosa (Toulouse) with Alaric II, King of the Visigoths. This move led to an ultimatum from Clovis to Alaric, who had no stomach to take on the Franks (when he did in 507, he was killed and Visigothic rule in Gaul was effectively ended). He acceded to a demand to hand Syagrius over, who was put under house arrest but was clandestinely executed in 487.

The rule of Syagrius managed to outlast the final emperor of the west by six (or in some estimations ten) years. Clovis was recognised by the eastern emperor as patrician and honorary consul, maintaining the fiction that the west was still united as a sort of federation under the rule of Constantinople.

TACITUS
275, November/December – 276, June/July

Tacitus was an alleged senatorial, short-lived and probable stop-gap emperor, who followed Aurelian and defeated a Gothic incursion before dying on campaign in Asia.

Most of the ancient sources claim that there was a substantial interregnum between the assassination of Aurelian and the elevation of his successor. If so, the name of any *interrex* is unknown; if one was appointed by the senate he would have been the first since Ser. Sulpicius Rufus in 52BC. The period covered would have been October/November to December 275.[689] The next Emperor, Tacitus, is painted as an elderly senatorial nobleman, boasting of his family connections with Cornelius Tacitus, the early second-century historian.[690] Sir Ronald Syme managed to cut through all this, making the point that there was not likely to have been an interval of more than a few days after the assassination.

There is little certain information about this Emperor's family, although the *Historia Augusta* claims him for Interamna Nahars (Terni, Italy) and with estates in Africa.[691] He was certainly no senatorial noble of distinguished lineage, nor any descendant of the historian Tacitus as the *Historia* supposes. One supposed reason for his assassination (if assassination there was) was that a relative called Maximinus had been appointed governor of Syria and his remorseless exactions there had created widespread discontent.[692] He is said to have left behind sons (who would have been senators) and his successor, Florianus, was said to have been his uterine half-brother.[693]

Instead of an elderly nobleman elected by the senate, the new Emperor was almost certainly another Danubian general, but in this case one who

---

689 Aur. Victor 35, 9-12; coins; HA *V. Tac.* 1.1
690 The only attested use of Tacitus as a *cognomen* after the demise of the historian was amongst the Caecina family, who may genuinely have been amongst the author's descendants.
691 HA *V. Taciti* 10, 3, 5 & 15, 1
692 Zonaras 12, 28; Maximinus: PLRE I. Maximinus 1; killed before the Emperor in June 276.
693 HA *V. Taciti* 6, 8, 14, 3 ('many children') & 16, 4

had ended his career with sufficient renown to have been adlected into the senate, probably with the rank of ex-consul, and indeed, he appears on the *fasti* as ordinary consul for 273. The received story we have is of the old boy receiving the news that he had been named as emperor at his residence in Campania and entering Rome in civilian garb to be invested with the purple by the senate.[694] Syme was prepared to accept that he was by this stage in his career a senator, and may very well have been residing in Campania.

Once installed, he assumed the style Imperator Caesar M. Claudius Tacitus Pius Felix Augustus, was acknowledged as *pontifex maximus*, granted the tribunician power and proconsular *imperium*.[695] He was also made consul designate for 276, appointed one M. Annius Florianus as his Pretorian Prefect and punished Aurelian's assassins. He is also reported to have restored the senators' *cursus honorum* – their career path in the governing hierarchy, curtailed under Gallienus.[696] He remained in Rome until the new year when he went out to the Balkans to join the army assembled by his predecessor in order to complete his mission to the east. He advanced into Asia Minor and encountered a strong force of Goths (actually Heruli) which he successfully defeated, an achievement which earned him the epithet Gothicus Maximus.[697] He continued to Tyana (Kemerhisar, Turkey) in Cappadocia where he died in July 276, either from disease, but perhaps more likely through assassination. On his coins he was accorded the title *Restitutor Rei Publicae* (restorer of the Republic), yet strangely, he was neither deified nor condemned by the senate on his death, whereupon Florianus seized the throne on the strength of his alleged kinship with Tacitus.

TAURINUS

231

Taurinus was a short-lived and allegedly reluctant usurper in Syria whose reign was of unknown duration during the reign of Severus Alexander. Taurinus, like Verus, is only a *cognomen* and he was labelled an usurper (*tyrannus*) by Polemius Silvius, but according to Aurelius Victor he was the unwilling choice of the soldiers.[698] The relevant events presumably occurred in 231, when Severus Alexander was amassing forces for his campaign against Artaxerxes of Persia. A former suffect consul, Taurinus was probably acclaimed in Syria, where he may have been governor and on the collapse of his revolt – the length of which is unknown – he subsequently drowned himself in the Euphrates.

Taurinus may well have been called [T.] Statilius Taurinus, for a fuller version of the usurper's name garbled as Verconius Turinus by the *Historia Augusta*, evokes that of the senator attested in 155, Statilius Cassius

---

694 Syme (1971) 237 f., cf. Zonaras 12, 28, Aurelius Victor 36, 1
695 ILS 590; PIR² C1036/PLRE I. Tacitus 3
696 Aur. Victor 37, 6
697 ILS 591 (Cos. II, *trib. pot.* II)
698 Polemius Silvius *Laterculus* II. 30-31; Aurelius Victor 24

Taurinus, surely the brother of the Statilius Taurus who was attested a year later.[699] That Taurinus was a member of the Arval Brethren and a patrician by creation and was very likely the son of another Statilius Taurus who was a senator of praetorian rank in 117. The T. Statilius Silianus who was also an Arval Brother (in the reign of Caracalla or Elagabalus[700]) must have been a close relative, too. Sir Ronald Syme, writing of this whole group of usurpers, says that they 'may have asserted an illustrious ascendance'.[701] It is possible that these Statilii were descended from the Statilii Tauri of the early Empire, although there are two or three generations completely missing between the latter and the senator of 117.

TERENTIUS MAXIMUS
?80

Terentius Maximus was a man who was one of three people in the Flavian period who misguidedly thought they could gain power from their resemblance to Nero.

Maximus shared his name with a respectable procurator of the period but appears not to have been related to him. He came from the consular province of Asia. He decided to cash in on his looks and managed to gather together a sufficiently substantial force of armed irregulars, at the head of which he managed to advance to the Euphrates.[702] How he expected to displace Titus was never apparent. Indeed, from that point on the enterprise seems to have fallen apart, and he was obliged to take refuge in Parthia, where the king had hopes of deploying him in diplomatic discourse for his nuisance value, but nothing appears to have come of it and the man's fate is not known.[703]

TETRICUS I
271, February/March – 274, March/April

Tetricus was the last effective emperor ruling the third century breakaway Gallic empire. He was brought to heel and spared by Aurelian. C. Pius Esuvius Tetricus was Victorinus' governor in Aquitania and probable close relative who, thanks to the decisiveness of Victoria, succeeded to the throne without any problem. He was a man of noble birth who, prior to his service in the breakaway realm, enjoyed senatorial status.[704] His name is undoubtedly Gallic and derives from the Gallic people the Esuvii, and in turn from the deity Esus; he may indeed have been descended from a prince of that people.

---

699 PIR² S523; FS 3128

700 ILS 5039; PIR² S848. The alternative is that he could belong to the (presumably unrelated) Statilii Maximi, a family of greater prominence in the Antonine era.

701 Syme (1971) 159, n. 6

702 PIR² T79, T80

703 Dio, 66, 19.3

704 PIR² E99; PLRE I. Tetricus 1. It was the *Historia Augusta* that claimed he was related to Victorinus's mother Victoria: *op. cit.* 24.2

He was clearly a man whom the troops were prepared to accept, and coin evidence suggests that on the way from his province to Trier he seems to have inflicted a defeat on some German tribes, which had probably attempted an incursion in the wake of the death of Victorinus. The following year, he had to deal with these tribes again, before settling the imperial capital at Trier rather than Cologne.

His style was Imperator Caesar C. Pius Esuvius Tetricus Pius Felix Augustus, and he is believed to have served his first (suffect) consulship in 272 (although it could have been somewhat earlier, as a private citizen), followed by an ordinary one in 273 and a third the year following. His *tribunicia postestas* was renewed four times before his fall.[705] In 273 his son, also called C. Pius Esuvius Tetricus, was nominated *nobilissimus caesar* and thus heir designate as C. Pius Esuvius Tetricus Nobilissimus Caesar and made *princeps iuventutis*.[706] He shared the consulship with his father in 274. His elevation seems to have been preceded by some kind of crisis which was accompanied by a debasement of the coinage, previously running at a somewhat superior weight and fineness than in the Empire at large. The son was never accorded the rank of Augustus, so it is technically incorrect to refer to him (as occasionally happens) as Tetricus II, although coins were issued in his name as *caesar*. The cause of this is not really understood. Drinkwater suggests that by 273 the influence and financial support of Victoria had ended, possibly through her death, and that more coin was required to give the troops an increased donative.

By the end of 273, the Emperor Aurelian had restored order in the east and was in a position to bring the Gallic empire back into a re-united empire. Accordingly, as soon as winter had abated in 274, he advanced into Gaul. Tetricus accordingly moved to meet his forces. Traditionally, the battle at Châlons-sur-Marne has been remembered as an easy victory for Aurelian after which Tetricus and his son were spared. The impression was that they had reached an accommodation with Aurelian and had 'thrown the match' as it were, especially as their men were being suborned by the probable governor of Gallia Belgica, Faustinus (qv). This story is, however, thought to have been much influenced after the event by Aurelianic propaganda. It seems that in fact the battle of Châlons was hard-fought with heavy casualties, and that although Tetricus and his son *were* spared, they were captured, humiliated and displayed in the Emperor's triumph alongside the equally humiliated (but typically defiant) Zenobia.[707] Yet, after the triumph, both men were allowed to resume their places in the senate, the elder Tetricus being soon afterwards being made *corrector* of Lucania – governor of a minor Italian sub-province and thus hardly a promotion – and died many years later.

---

705 ILS 566
706 *Ibid.*, I. Tetricus 2; PIR² E100; ILS 567
707 Drinkwater (1987) 42-43

TETRICUS II see TETRICUS I

THEODERIC
508/511

Between 508 and 511, Theoderic the Amal, Ostrogothic King of Italy since 493, had himself described on an inscription at Tarracina, uniquely, as *semper Augustus*. Whether this qualified him as a usurping emperor is doubted by most commentators. More likely it was a piqued reaction to the Emperor Anastasius' favouring of Clovis, King of the Franks (whom he appointed consul in 508), after his defeat of the Visigoths at this time.[708] We hear no more of this, however, his other inscriptions and coins reverting to the previous style of *Rex Theodericus*. He died in 526 after having ruled Italy in the manner of the better late Roman emperors.

THEODOSIUS I
379, 19th January – 395, 17th January

Theodosius I was one of the more effective later fourth-century emperors, but one who rather let events in the western half of the empire slide, resulting in his having unnecessarily to fight two major campaigns to dislodge rivals.

Theodosius was, as far as we know, the first emperor of Spanish origin since the accession of Hadrian two hundred and two years previously. He was the son of Valentinian I's cavalry C-in-C of the same name who had been executed through the unfortunate machinations of others following his successful overthrow of Firmus in 375. The general's son by Thermantia was born around 346 at Cauca (Coca) in Gallaecia, one of the Spanish provinces, and followed his father into the army. His career seems to have been highly successful, although no doubt aided by the success of his father. He served under his father in Britain with his kinsman Magnus Maximus following the so-called Barbarian Conspiracy from 367, and both almost certainly served under him in Africa, before Theodosius was appointed a *dux* in Moesia Prima c. 374. He retired in 375 after his father's death to his family's Spanish estates, which suggests that the family were certainly aristocratic, if only in local terms. There he married his fellow Spaniard Aelia Flaccilla around 376, and they had two sons. He was summoned back by Gratian I in 378 to be *magister militum* in Illyria in the aftermath of the defeat at Adrianople and acquitted himself well, leading the Emperor to raise him to be his co-Augustus with responsibility for the east on 19 January the following year. He was on the spot, in a strong position and he engineered an opportunist *coup*, possibly with Maximus assisting.[709]

Theodosius took the style Dominus Noster Flavius Theodosius Pius Felix Augustus and was endowed with the tribunician and proconsular powers,

---

708 Heather (1989) 108f.; Moorhead (1992) 186, quoting CIL X 6850-6852; Barnwell (1992) 95
709 PLRE I Theodosius 4

probably automatic by this stage, for a formal vote in the two senates may have become superfluous. He served a consulship in 380 followed by two further terms in 388 and 393.[710] Like Maximus, he eschewed the pontifical title, which thereupon fell into desuetude. On accession, the Empress assumed the additional name of Flavia and was styled Augusta, the first empress to enjoy this rank since St Helena. Like his cousin, the new Emperor was a redoubtable defender of Christianity, but his later soubriquet of 'The Great' was earned on the battlefield. After a four-year campaign, he roundly defeated the Goths in the Balkans, finalising affairs through a treaty reached in 382. This seemed like the end of the problems posed by these particular Goths (the Visigoths) but in fact, by settling them within the empire – the Hunnic pressure to their eastern flank had not abated since a decade before – under the authority of their own king, a risky precedent had been set. Furthermore, should Theodosius have wished to draw upon their military services, it would be as allies, not as integrated units of the army, as before – another complicating factor. It may well be that the measure was conceived as a temporary one which the emperor, taking over after Adrianople from a position of weakness, planned to resolve in the medium term. In the event, this never happened. He also managed to secure a long-lasting peace on the eastern frontier with the Persians. When his kinsman Maximus was acclaimed emperor in Britain – possibly as early as 380, although he only crossed to the continent in 383 – he appeared sanguine about the situation, allowing him to occupy the area of the Gallic empire with full recognition, including eastern coin issues in Maximus' name, with Valentinian II left with Italy and Africa.

In 383 he invested his elder son, Arcadius (qv) as co-emperor. Three years later the Empress Flaccilla died at Constantinople. This was soon followed by the advance of Maximus into Italy, which occasioned the flight of Justina, Valentinian II and his three sisters to the east. The Emperor at first seemed unmoved by their plight, but in time, Justina managed to push forward the elder sister, Galla, for whom the recently widowed Theodosius apparently fell heavily. Justina thereafter cleverly exploited this infatuation to manipulate the Emperor into taking her exile seriously and eventually obliged him to take measures to remove his kinsman and her nemesis, Maximus, in return for permission to marry Galla, with the aim of restoring Valentinian II, legitimising the rule of Theodosius' family and securing a series of familial connections going back to Diocletian. There were two sons of the marriage with Galla, Gratian and Iohannes (who died as infants) and a daughter, Galla Placidia.

Theodosius' continuing strategic military interventions towards the Persians were somewhat diverted by his efforts in 388 to crush Magnus Maximus, which he achieved after an unexpectedly swift and hence successful campaign ending with his former western colleague's death at Aquileia in late summer. Valentinian II was something of a cypher when it came to effective rule, and Theodosius celebrated a tactless triumph in Rome over his kinsman and former colleague and followed this by staying nearly two years in the west. He was allegedly received in Rome with great enthusiasm. Nevertheless, the élite of

---

710 ILS783

this great bastion of paganism were disappointed when, in 392, the Emperor issued an edict banning pagan practices throughout the Empire. Interestingly, he preserved the magnificent temples for other purposes or as works of art: the first known example of a conservation-minded ruler. Unfortunately, his Christian successors failed to emulate his example during the following century.

Eventually Theodosius was forced to hurry back east to resume his Persian campaigning plans and placed affairs in the west in the hands of Arbogastes, his barbarian *magister militum*. One reason for his being favoured was that he was felt unlikely to declare himself emperor, being barbarian, but in this Theodosius overlooked the role of a catspaw claimant being put up by an ambitious general. Eventually, Valentinian began to challenge the decisions taken by Arbogastes and, having challenged his barbarian commander once too often, Valentinian II allegedly committed suicide in 392. Having disposed of Valentinian, Arbogastes needed to retain supreme power, especially as Theodosius was unlikely to acquiesce in his bringing about the ruin of his brother-in-law. The western strong man was both a pagan and a barbarian, so he needed a pliable emperor. He chose Eugenius. For two years Theodosius essentially ignored events in the west whilst dealing with the Persians and building up his forces for yet another inevitable round of civil conflict in the west. He nominated his younger son, the 8-year-old Honorius, as co-emperor with his elder brother to secure the succession.

Whilst all this had been going on, Theodosius had been obliged to take a terrible revenge on the citizens of Thessalonica for uncontrolled rioting over an alleged conviction of rape of a cup bearer by a champion charioteer. The Goth Butheric, the army commander, Illyricum, put the riot down with immense slaughter, which resulted in his immediate excommunication by the Bishop of Milan, St Ambrose, whose authority within the church at the time was unchallengeable, exceeding by force of character and consistency even that of Pope Siricius. The Emperor was forced into the humiliating position of having to do penance for his crime for which he seems to have been prepared to accept responsibility and which was done without repercussions for the redoubtable prelate.

Meanwhile, in 394, his forces having been sent west (mirroring the events of 388) met Arbogastes' army on the river Frigidus, not so far from Aquileia where he had defeated Maximus six years before. Following a two-day battle, which once again tore the manpower heart out of the Roman army, so high were the casualties on both sides, Theodosius prevailed.

The Emperor pardoned the associates of Eugenius (who lost his life in the conflict) along with those of the dead Arbogastes and thereafter made dispositions whereby in the event of his death the empire would be divided by his sons. Probably this was a similar arrangement to that made by Valentinian I, and not intended to be permanent. In the event, the younger son, Honorius, was summoned to Milan at the beginning of 395 with the intention of being formally invested as co-emperor with his elder brother and father. However, Theodosius took ill and died unexpectedly soon after his arrival. The division of the Empire was about to become permanent.

THEODOSIUS II
402, 10th January – 450, 28th July

Theodosius II was grandson of Theodosius the Great. His unprecedentedly long and relatively tranquil reign lasted for nearly 50 years. The son and heir of Arcadius was born on 10 April 401 and was hurriedly raised to the rank of Augustus by proclamation on 10 January 402 whilst still a baby. Shortly afterwards the Eastern Empire came under the control of Anthemius, grandfather of the Emperor Anthemius and a grandson of the Pretorian Prefect of Constantius II, Philippus, himself the son, it was said, of an Egyptian sausage maker. Anthemius was *comes sacrarum largitionum* (keeper of the privy purse) in the east from c. 400, was advanced to *magister officiorum* (chief minister) in 404 and Pretorian Prefect (east) a year later. In 406 he was also made patrician. He was virtual ruler of the Eastern Empire and was noted for his readiness to listen to advice and for his prudent administration. He rebuilt the walls of Constantinople 404-413, hence their name, the Theodosian Walls. He held the consulship in 405 with Stilicho, with whom he had worked when young, in a gesture of solidarity with the western administration. In short, there was no better person to oversee the transition when Arcadius died in 408.[711]

Flavius Theodosius was proclaimed at the age of just seven and took the style Dominus Noster Flavius Theodosius Invictissimus Augustus.[712] He held the consulship in 403 and thereafter no fewer than 17 more times in his reign.[713] Anthemius was displaced after about 14 years in control, probably at the conniving of the Emperor's imperious sister, Aelia Pulcheria. She wielded sole effective power in the east thereafter until her death in 453.

On turning twenty, the Emperor married the daughter of an eminent, recently deceased Athenian pagan Sophist intellectual, Leontius. Her original name was Athenaïs, but she adopted Eudocia instead, after adult baptism. Beautiful, eloquent and an accomplished poet, she had caught the eye of the Emperor's sister Pulcheria whilst staying at Constantinople in pursuit of a legal case relating to her father's estate. They married on 7 June 421, when she assumed the honorific additional *nomen* Aelia. On 2 January 423 she was proclaimed Augusta. Subsequently she appears to have clashed with her sister-in-law Pulcheria. At the same time, she was obliged to cope with her kinswoman Galla Placidia and her children, self-exiled from the questionable attentions of Honorius. Although Placidia returned to the west after the defeat of Iohannes, in the long run Pulcheria triumphed, using her court eunuchs to undermine the Empress, especially after the latter returned from a thanksgiving trip to Jerusalem (undertaken following the marriage of Licinia Eudoxia to Valentinian III) with a great number of Christian relics, having founded two churches. She brought the relics of the protomartyr St Stephen back to Constantinople. Her resentful sister-in-law smeared her with false

---

711 PLRE II Anthemius 2
712 ILS 804. 806, the latter as consul xv (435); *invictissimus* = most unconquered.
713 In 407, 409, 411, 412, 415, 416, 418, 420, 422, 425, 426, 430, 433, 435, 438, 439 & 444.

charges of adultery and she eventually retired to Jerusalem in 443 and died there on 20 October 460.[714]

The Emperor, meanwhile, took no active role in the state, although unlike his father, who had been thoroughly indolent and unlovable, Theodosius was bookish, a talented illuminator of manuscripts, mildly religious, a keen huntsman and personally charming. In anyone other than an Emperor, this would have been no bad thing, but it was perceived as weakness when strength was required. He did take an interest in what was going on, but he was generally content to let his sister and her picked men run the Empire.

Yet the Eastern Empire managed to escape the baleful calamities which encompassed the west. A treaty was arrived at with the Sassanian court in Persia that was intended to guarantee peace for a century and actually succeeded in producing something resembling calm for the remainder of the reign and beyond. On the other hand, the Balkans were constantly in turmoil, with various barbarian tribes making incursions. Yet Theodosius' generals were able to exploit their energies in using the most effective of groupings to hold in check the increasingly troublesome Isaurian tribesmen, who had long been within the Empire but were uncivilised and turbulent.

The reign was also notable for the re-codification of the law. This had not been done since the time of the Tetrarchy and much law had become redundant and more had been formulated through precedent via the court or imperial rescripts (mandatory advisory notes to administrators in the emperor's name). In 429, a commission was set up to regularise the law for both parts of the Empire. A draft was produced in 435, refined and then published as the Theodosian Code in 438, being promulgated simultaneously by the senates of Rome and Constantinople on 15 February. It remained current in the west for a century (although in the Visigothic areas of Gaul and Spain, a revised version of 507 was promulgated) and in the east until a much more root-and-branch revision was undertaken in the reign of Justinian I.

The last decade of Theodosius' long reign was punctuated with renewed challenges on the Danube frontier. The Huns had for some years been paid a modest tribute by the Empire to keep them quiet, but after Attila took over with his brother in 437, attacks and raiding began along the frontier, which by 441 demanded corrective action. In 447 the brother died, leaving Attila to his own devices and he immediately demanded the tribute be doubled. This the Emperor understandably refused, with the result that the Huns unleashed a veritable *blitzkrieg* across the Danube and down through the Balkans to the very walls of Constantinople, by-passing the capital, and into Asia Minor, causing immense damage. Having created a desert, lack of forage led the Huns to drift back to their homelands on what we know as the Hungarian plain for, although exceedingly fierce, the supply side of fighting, the logistics, was not something of which they had the least concept. Subsequent negotiation saw Attila's demands rocket. Imperial intelligence discovered the Huns' intention to attack the west, and the imperial negotiators banked on Attila's reluctance to again raid south and east. Furthermore, there had been

---

714 PLRE II Eudocia 2.

such destruction that there would have been little in it for the Huns had they tried a repeat performance. Thus, in 450, they moved west and the Eastern Empire breathed a sigh of relief. And, thanks to Aëtius, they were never to trouble the Empire so seriously again, east or west. It was in the middle of the negotiations with Attila, that the emperor, out hunting, met with a fall and was killed, to be succeeded by Marcian.

THEODOSIUS III
590, 26th March – 602, 1st/2nd December

Theodosius was the son and designated heir of the Emperor Maurice, whose sole rule can have lasted only days after the murder of his father by the usurping Phocas. Theodosius was born on 4 August either in 583 or 585 (the future Pope Gregorius – St Gregory the Great – was his godfather) and was named after the last emperor to have been *porphyrogenitus*, Theodosius II. He was proclaimed *nobilissimus caesar* sometime in 587 and raised to the purple on 26 March 590, taking the style Dominus Noster Theodosius Perpetuus Augustus. On 8 February 602, he married the Patrician Germanus's daughter, thus cementing his family to the dynasty of Justinian and to that of Anastasius, although it would seem that there was no move at that time to make his wife, whose name in consequently unknown, Augusta. By the time of his death there would appear to have been no issue.

When the revolt of Phocas broke out in November 602, Theodosius was offered the chance to remain emperor if his father abdicated, but he fled instead with his father, being sent on from Chalcedon where they landed to liaise with Chosroes of Persia. Inexplicably, when arrested his father recalled him, which sealed his death warrant and he, too, was apparently killed at Calcedon on his return, accompanied by the patrician Constantinus Lardys, probably in the first few days of December. The words 'apparently' and 'probably' are used advisedly, as some accounts suggest that he did not obey his recall but made his way to Persia. More likely this story derived from the existence of a later imposter sponsored by the general Narses, who soon afterwards rose against Phocas in Mesopotamia, exploiting these rumours. The false Theodosius was then presented to Chosroes by Narses. The Great King claimed to have him with him and recognised him as rightful emperor, although the alleged pretender is subsequently said to have died in Lazica (Eastern Georgia). The Persian King was only too eager to exploit the chaos in the Empire to regain territory lost through the 591 treaty and the war he waged over the following two decades was theoretically to right the wrongs meted out to the unfortunate Maurice.[715]

The dynastic succession which, by the interconnections of descent and marriage could plausibly be said to have originated with the rise of Probus in 274, came to an end with the destruction of the family of Maurice and his son, leaving only a few fortunate survivors, like Germanus, to carry the line

---

715 PLRE III Narses 10, Theodosius 13

into the seventh century. (The reign of Theodosius IV, 715-717, lies outside the parameters of this work.)

TIBERIUS I
14, 19 August – 37, 16 March

Tiberius well understood the constitutional niceties of the relationship of the *princeps* to the senate and ruling élite, but his desire to escape from the day-to-day running of the Empire allowed the rise of two Pretorian Prefects, Sejanus and Macro, whose manipulative and arbitrary rule destroyed any trust between ruler and ruled and led to the decimation of the Imperial family.

Tiberius [Julius] Caesar Augusti f. Divi n. is the style employed on adoption in AD4 by the patrician senator Ti. Claudius Nero, son of the homonymous praetor of 42BC and Livia, who re-married the Emperor Augustus.[716] Tiberius was born in the year of his father's praetorship and was *quaestor Augusti* (that is, in personal attendance as quaestor on Augustus himself) in 23, the start of his senatorial career. He inherited the estate of a childless well-wisher – who could indeed have been distantly related – M. Gallius (one of the praetors in the fateful year of Caesar's assassination), on condition of a testamentary adoption. Suetonius tells us he soon dropped the name M. Gallius Nero Claudianus and reverted to his original style. This would not have affected his patrician status.[717]

Tiberius was praetor in 16BC and thereafter had a distinguished military career in east Gaul, Pannonia (12-9BC) and Germany (9-7BC), proving himself to be a general of more than ordinary competence. Yet things began to go sour for him in 12BC when Augustus' right hand man M. Vipsanius Agrippa died and he became the 'long-stop' heir to Augustus, with only Agrippa's three very young sons to keep him from the highest power. His younger brother Drusus had been long favoured over him, which no doubt rankled. Both, however, were given the proconsular power late in 11BC for five years.

Also in 12BC Augustus, at the prodding of Tiberius' mother, the Empress Livia, obliged him to divorce his wife of many years, Agrippa's daughter Vipsania (they were betrothed in her infancy) in order to marry his own mother-in-law and step-sister, Julia, with whom he did not get on, leading to their parting at an early date. It is said that he could never catch sight of Vipsania thereafter without being moved to tears, although she seems to have re-married C. Asinius Gallus, consul in 8BC, without further trauma.

Tiberius was consul in 13 and again in 7BC (when he was again granted the proconsular power)[718] and in many ways was the obvious successor in terms of effectiveness, prestige and authority, yet was very much overshadowed in

---

716 ILS107; PIR2, C 941. He was, however, occasionally (eg. AD7) styled Ti Julius Caesar Augusti f. Claudianus, cf. CIL vi. 40339, cf. Dio 55.27.3-4.]

717 Suetonius *Tiberius* 6.3; a testamentary adoption strictly speaking did not affect the adoptee's status – patrician or plebeian – or tribe, except with Octavian/Augustus, of course. See Syme (1986) 53-54

718 Dio, LIV, 33, 5 & 34, 4

the longer term by C. and L. Caesar and this seems to have grated, along with the failure of his marriage to Julia. Consequently, he withdrew from public life and went to Rhodes in 6BC, the year Augustus, who doesn't emerge from the ancient sources as really liking Tiberius very much, granted him the tribunician power again. Four years later, Julia was implicated in a shadowy conspiracy, news of which cannot have helped.

With the death of Caius Caesar in AD4, Tiberius had to be recalled, bearing in mind that Agrippa Postumus, who was adopted by the *princeps* at the same time, was quietly sidelined three years later, either because he was the focus of a faction which had previously supported Caius Caesar or because he was considered temperamentally unsuitable. Tiberius was in consequence formally adopted on 26 June by Augustus, and Tiberius was ordered to adopt his brother's eldest son, Germanicus, who thus held precedence over his own surviving son, Drusus, which rankled even further. In 12, he was made *princeps senatus*, given the proconsular *imperium*, earned putting down the Pannonian revolt and repairing the damage in Germany in the aftermath of the disaster of Varus' defeat in the Teutoberger Wald in AD9, and was designated heir.[719]

Tiberius was first hailed as *imperator* in 9BC and then again, a year later, followed by AD6, 8, 9, 11, 13 and 16. He assumed the office of *pontifex maximus* on the death of Augustus, and was granted tribunician power on 26 June, 6BC for five years and then again on 26 June AD4, renewed annually. He adopted, at the same time as he himself was adopted by Augustus, Nero Claudius Drusus, elder son of his brother Drusus, who became his official heir.

Having succeeded, leading to a slight adjustment in nomenclature (to Ti. Caesar Divi Aug[usti] f. Divi n.), it was apparent that he was damaged goods. Always rather aloof, with few real friends, his long disengagements from the political front line, either in exile or at war, put him at a disadvantage. The disappointments and humiliations of the preceding reign seem to have left an indelible mark on his psyche, compounding an inherent failure properly to communicate his feelings either to his family, advisors or the senate. He did not really want the job; Augustus was a hard act to follow and Tiberius was at heart a Republican, but one unable or unwilling to risk any restoration, which could easily have plunged the Empire back into factional warfare.

Nor was the succession a foregone conclusion. Andrew Pettinger has suggested that the transition was really quite fragile and identified M. Scribonius Drusus Libo as the leader of a serious plot to push the new *princeps* aside and either restore the Republic or take power himself.[720] A descendant of Pompey and great-nephew of Scribonia, the second wife of Augustus (by a subsequent marriage), Libo was at the time (AD16) praetor, along with his probable half-brother Scribonius Proculus, whilst his elder brother of the whole blood, Lucius, was one of the consuls for the year. There was an attempt by one of Agrippa Postumus's slaves, Clemens, to impersonate

---

719 Pettinger (2012) 143-145
720 Pettinger (2012) *passim*.

his former master (who had been summarily killed on Augustus' death, but probably not at Tiberius's instigation) and promote himself as *princeps*. This failed and Tiberius, using his first great equestrian minister, Sallustius Crispus (who had probably been the prime mover in Postumus' death) as his spokesman, played down the entire matter. Once apprehended, Clemens was quietly disposed of. With Libo, a very prominent member of the ruling élite, a trial for treason (*maiestas*) had to be staged, and the offending challenger for power neutralised in as near legal a manner as possible. It was not to be the last time a member of Libo's family was to be destroyed by the lure of supreme power, for Camillus Scribonianus (qv), leader of an attempted coup in 42 and Piso (qv), the designated heir of Galba, were both close kinsmen. Ironically though, the Scribonian blood line was also a notable element in the distinguished ancestry of Marcus Aurelius 150 years later.

As a result, Tiberius treated the senate at first with kid gloves, but as time went on and his position seemed increasingly secure, we find hostile prosecutions being launched in the senate almost out of the blue, with senators getting killed or persuaded to suicide for ridiculous reasons. Simultaneously, the Emperor's close advisors acquired increasing amounts of power. Thus, by the time he had retired permanently to Capreae (Capri) in 29, his affairs were in the hands of an increasingly confident Pretorian Prefect with powerful familial links to a number of senatorial families called L. Aelius Seianus, known to history as Sejanus. By the time he was finally toppled in 31, much permanent damage had been done, many distinguished lives lost – and more in his bloody downfall. In spite of this, his successor, Q. Naevius Sutorius Macro, was hardly an improvement.

These events and the gradual attrition of the Imperial family by death and misadventure tend to disguise the fact that administratively Tiberius' reign was predominantly peaceful and prosperous. At his death at Circeii on 16 March 37, he left a healthy realm to an exceedingly unhealthy survivor of the holocaust he had visited on his immediate family: the Emperor Caligula.

TIBERIUS II
578, 26th September – 582, 14th August

Tiberius II was the designated successor of Justin II who proved to be a steady pair of hands, but whose expenditure levels were to store up problems for his successor. Tiberius was a Thracian and was born c. 530, becoming a *notarius* (civil servant), soon entering the service of the future Justin II. He was made *comes excubitorum* (commander of the guard) before the accession of his patron, a post he held until 574. Shortly after Justin's elevation, in 569 he was made *magister militum* (master of the soldiers, unattached) and the following year, after conducting negotiations with the Avars (which broke down due to the obduracy of the Emperor), he soundly defeated them in Thrace, although the following year he suffered a defeat at their hands. Through adroit diplomacy and tact he managed to secure a satisfactory peace. After the end of 573, he assumed control of affairs at the behest of the Empress Sophia.

Quite early in his career he became betrothed to the daughter of an army adjutant called Johannes and of his wife Ino, but both Johannes and the girl died, quite possibly of the plague, and he instead married the widow, Ino. When he became Emperor, she was given the name Aelia Anastasia.[721] She came originally from Daphnudium, probably an island off the Black Sea coast of modern Turkey. The Empress Sophia disliked Ino and excluded her from the palace whilst Justin II lived, but on his death, she moved in with Tiberius and Sophia was set up separately in her own heavily protected household elsewhere. Ino was proclaimed Augusta by her husband in the wake of his sole accession and retained the style until her death in 593. One of their three children had died before Tiberius assumed the purple. The marriage of their daughter Constantina secured the succession, whilst that of their younger daughter Charito to the Justinianic prince Germanus incorporated Tiberius' family into that of Justinian and Anastasius.

On 7 December 574 Tiberius was adopted as his son by Justin II, proclaimed *nobilissimus caesar* and given the additional name of Constantinus. Nearly four years later, he was raised to the rank of co-Augustus on 26 September 578, and he succeeded as sole ruler on the emperor's death on 5 October. From thence his style was Dominus Noster Tiberius Constantinus Perpetuus Augustus, although on some coin issues he is styled Constant[inus] Viv[at] Felix Au[gustus] ('Emperor Constantine, may you live in good fortune') which marked a radical change from the normal formula. More conventionally, another issue styles him D[ominus] N[oster] Tib[erius] Constan[tin]us P[er]p[etuus] Aug[ustus]. He held the ordinary consulship in 578 and again the following year. His accession was disputed by the patrician Justinianus, the great nephew of Justin I (greatly encouraged by the dowager Empress), but an assassination attempt organised by him right at the beginning of the sole reign failed miserably. Justinianus was forgiven and his son (presumably Germanus, for no other son is known) was betrothed to Charito.[722]

One problem Tiberius faced in the east he solved by making peace with the Persians, but at the expense of infuriating the Khan of the Turks, whose people enter history at this point. They had been promised an alliance by the Persians which promptly collapsed, leaving them exposed; they seized the Chersonese (Crimea) in revenge and proved difficult to dislodge.

Tiberius himself was a steady pair of hands, relatively popular and a pragmatist. His only Achilles heel was to overcompensate for the parsimony of his predecessor and indulge in an excess of liberality (which probably explained his popularity); his first act was to remit 25% of all taxes for a year, which was rash indeed. On the other hand, he ended the persecution of the Monophysites (although he remained antipathetic to the Arians, mainly because most of its adherents were barbarian). He also cultivated the Greek-speaking provinces, realising that the stability of the empire depended on this core element of which he himself, as a Thracian, was a representative.

---

721 PLRE III Anastasia 2

722 Greg., HF *v*.30. Germanus and Charito were the parents of Germanus (qv).

He also spent much of his reign strengthening the army, depleted by recruitment problems (a legacy of the plague of four decades before) and the thrifty inclinations of Justin II.

He died on 14 August 582, probably as a result of complications following food poisoning but, as with the demise of his more famous imperial namesake, it was rumoured that his repast of mulberries concealed a fatal potion. Perhaps the culprit was his *Comes Sacrarum Largitionum* (Keeper of the Privy Purse), desperate to stem losses to the treasury through the Emperor's ill-advised open-handedness.[723]

Be that as it may, on his deathbed he adopted as his successor the successful *magister militum* Mauricius, who had returned three days beforehand from the east and whom he made *nobilissimus caesar* a mere eight days before expiring. There was, as a result, a smooth transition of power.[724] (The reign of Tiberius III, 698-705, lies outside the parameters of this work.)

TIBERIUS see also MAURICE

TIBERIUS GEMELLUS see GEMELLUS

TIMOLAUS
267

Timolaus was one of the two alleged younger sons of Odaenathus of Palmyra, whom the *Historia Augusta* claims were made Augusti with their father, a happenstance unattested elsewhere, as indeed are the two boys. He was killed, apparently, along with his father in circumstances not wholly understood, in 267.[725] There is no confirmation of all this outside the *Historia Augusta*.

TITIANUS
145

Titianus was an enigmatic co-conspirator in a plot against Antoninus Pius who was tried before the senate but who committed suicide in the face of the senators' judgement. The *Historia Augusta* tells us that a senator was tried before the senate for 'attempted usurpation' in 145.[726] He was subsequently condemned and suffered a *damnatio memoriae* – his name being erased from monuments and the consular lists *(fasti)*. From other sources we know he had an accomplice and that both committed suicide.

The senators in question were Atilius Titianus and Priscianus, identifiable as T. Atilius Rufus Titianus, consul in 127 and M. Cornelius Priscianus,

---

723 We do not have the name of this official for 582, unfortunately.
724 PLRE III Tiberius 1
725 HA *Tyr. Trig.* XXVII & XVIII
726 HA *V. Pii* VII, 3-6

also an ex-consul. The latter was condemned for 'hostile action disturbing the peace' – from which it seems reasonable to conclude that Atilius was probably the would-be usurper and 'beneficiary'.[727] The acclamation seems to have occurred in Hispania Tarraconensis and the motivation is completely lost to us. The likelihood is that they were brothers-in-law, Titianus being married to a sister of Priscianus, their father probably being L. Cornelius Priscus, suffect consul in 104. Atilius's second *cognomen* may also link him, albeit not particularly closely but perhaps enough to enhance his motivation, to the Imperial family of the time. The name suggests that his mother may have been a Titia, as was the mother of L. Epidius Titius Aquilinus, brother-in-law of L. Ceionius Commodus, Hadrian's short-lived first choice as heir. The identity of the two postulated Titias is more problematic, however.

Titianus was presumably the grandson of T. Atilius Rufus, a suffect consul of c. 75 who died in 84, a man probably of north Italian origin. We are told that Antoninus spared and supported his son – whose full name has not survived – and Corneliuis Priscianus, a senator of praetorian rank by 166, may well be a son of Atilius's co-conspirator, similarly spared. The entire episode is shrouded in mystery and like Saturninus (qv), the attempted usurpation had not progressed as far as to be accompanied by an issue of coinage.

TITUS
79, 23 June – 81, 13 September

Titus was the popular and seemingly well-balanced elder son and right-hand man of Vespasian, whose reign was cut short by an unexpected but natural death. Titus Flavius Vespasianus was born on 30 December AD39 at Rome and whose uncontested claim was that he was brought up at court with Claudius' ill-fated son, Britannicus, whom he befriended and on the occasion of whose death he was present.[728] He had a very successful career as a military tribune in Britain and Germany, thereafter opting for jurisprudence. He was elected to a quaestorship for 64, later accompanying his father to Palestine as his legate, in which role he proved himself uncommonly competent.

On his father's accession, his style changed to T. Caesar Aug. f. Vespasianus and he was granted the tribunician and proconsular power on 1 July 71. After the fall of Jerusalem in September 70, which he had besieged and captured, he had been hailed as *imperator* by his troops, and consequently by 72/73 he was styled Imperator Titus Caesar Augusti f. Vespasianus.[729] He was consul for the first time with his father to open 70, holding office again in 72, 74, 75, 76, 77 and 79. Vespasian appointed him – irregularly, since he was a senator and not an equestrian – Prefect of the Praetorian Guard, hitherto one of the two most senior equestrian positions in the Empire, surely feeling that a totally reliable person in charge of that turbulent unit was essential after

---

727 PIR² A130; Syme (1958) II. 596 n. & (1971) 38
728 Suetonius, *Titus*, 2
729 Syme, RP III (Oxford 1984) 1071

Titus, marble bust, part-ancient,
Chatsworth. (Courtesy of the
Trustees of the Chatsworth
Settlement)

the excesses of the previous twelve months. Titus, in this position, was able
to do a great deal of his father's dirty work. His role under his father was to
act as his executive assistant.

On 23 June 79, Titus succeeded his father, when he added Augustus to his
style and also succeeded him as *pontifex maximus*. He was consul again –
with his younger brother – in 80, and by the time of his death had been
acclaimed *imperator* 16 times.

Titus' love life was a trifle tangled. He married first, c. 63, Arrecina
Tertulla, younger daughter of M. Arrecinus Clemens, Praetorian Guard
commander from AD40 until he was executed in the over-reaction resulting
from the murder of Caligula, for complicity. The family was probably already
related to the Flavii, probably through Vespasian's grandmother Tertulla.
Arrecina died c. 65. Titus re-married, before 66, the socially much more
distinguished Marcia Furnilla, probably the daughter of Q. Marcius Barea
Sura, a relatively undistinguished senator, of a family which appears to have
entered the senate early in Augustus's reign. Her grandfather Q. Marcius
Barea Soranus had come late to a (suffect) consulship in AD52. She derived
her second name from her mother, Antonia Furnilla.[730] Antonia was the
daughter of an otherwise unknown A. Antonius and in all probability a
descendant of C. Furnius, consul in 17BC, a member of an obscure senatorial

---

730 ILS 953

Titus destroyed the Temple and burned Jerusalem in 70. The Arch of Titus shows the Temple treasures being carried off.

family, whose father had been a triumviral praetor.[731] It seems highly likely that a sister – another Marcia – was the mother of the future Emperor Trajan, which could explain why that Emperor's father, M. Ulpius Traianus, was first appointed to command one of the legions against the Jewish rebels (with Titus commanding another), was made suffect consul on Vespasian's accession and later (in 74) raised to the patriciate.[732]

Titus divorced Marcia shortly after the birth of their daughter, having fallen for Julia Berenice, a daughter of M. Julius Agrippa I, Tetrarch, later King, of Judaea, who had died in 44. She had already had three distinguished husbands, the last of whom, who had died in 63, was none other than Polemo II, king of Pontus and Cilicia, a great-grandson of Mark Antony through his daughter, who had married Pythodorus of Tralles. Berenice came to Rome with him but was immensely unpopular – the example of Cleopatra should have served as a warning – and was ordered home to Judaea on Vespasian's instructions in 75, after which Titus seems to have rapidly got over her.

Several Roman emperors on succession gave every appearance of being likely to make a good fist of the job, but turned out to be monsters – Caligula, Nero and Domitian spring to mind. Yet Titus came to the throne with a louche reputation and as hated for his effectiveness as praetorian commander as for his predilection for Berenice, but somehow transformed himself almost on the instant into a good-natured and benevolent ruler, greatly lamented on his premature demise – like his father, at Aquae Cutiliae (Terme di Cotilia, near Cittaducale) – on 13 September 81 after a reign of 2 years and 2 months. He was deified by the senate almost immediately after his death.

TITUS see also *QUARTINUS*

TRAJAN
98, 27 January 98 – 117, 9 August

Trajan was a competent soldier-emperor whose reign steadied the ship of state after the upheavals of Domitian's reign and the uncertainties of that of Nerva. He prepared the way for a century of stability – Rome's so-called Golden Age.

Trajan was effectively emperor from the moment of his adoption by the elderly Emperor Nerva in the autumn of 97, although it was not until three months after the Emperor's death that he deigned to visit the imperial capital. He was always the soldiers' emperor – himself a soldier but of a sufficiently senatorial background to understand the subtleties of government by carrying the senate with him. He was one of the greatest and most memorable of emperors and under him the Empire reached perhaps its greatest extent. Apart from his undoubted military genius, he was also endowed with good sense, tact and restraint – perhaps better expressed as patience. This enabled the reign to be remembered as an age of expansion – and hence prosperity – and

---

731 Dio, lii. 42,4
732 Jones (1992) 11, 59, 201; Birley (1987) 242

civil tranquility. It was only in old age, towards the end of his reign, that the Emperor's relations with the senate suffered a sharp deterioration. Even so, compared with the well-remembered excesses of Domitian's last years, it was only a relatively minor perturbation.

M. Ulpius M. f. Traianus was born on 18 September AD53, son of M. Ulpius Traianus, who had served as one of Vespasian's first consuls in 70, and Marcia, probably the sister of the second wife of the Emperor Titus. One of his great aunts was the grandmother of Hadrian; his sister Ulpia Marciana was the grandmother of Hadrian's wife Vibia Sabina.

The Ulpii claimed to have originated at Tuder in Umbria, but migrated during the Republic to Italica in Baetica, one of the Spanish provinces, where Scipio Africanus had settled the veterans of his army during the second Punic war.[733] Trajan's family develops a whole new existence in the *Historia Augusta*, which attributes the Emperor Aurelian with a senatorial mentor and adoptive father called Ulpius Crinitus, 'who used to assert that he was of the House of Trajan'.[734] This man was the supposed son of Ulpius Crinitus, allegedly suffect consul in AD238. Crinitus himself, we are told, was suffect consul before 255, in 257 and in 270 – all fictional consulships – and he apparently had 'consular descendants'. The *Historia* also claims Crinitus as the parent of Ulpia Severina, wife of L. Domitius Aurelianus, allegedly suffect consul in 258, and Augustus as the Emperor Aurelian.[735] Roman law would in reality exclude the possibility of an adopted son marrying his father's natural sister. The entire matter is unconfirmed anywhere else and may confidently be taken to be fiction.

Trajan served as military tribune under his father in Syria 73/76, reached the quaestorship in c. 78 and, as a patrician, missing out on the next stage in the promotional ladder, the aedileship or tribunate of the people, proceeding to a praetorship in c. 84, following which he was a legionary legate in Hispania Tarraconsensis, from whence he became involved in the measures taken by Domitian to put down the rebellion of Saturninus. He was suffect consul in 91, after which we hear almost nothing of him (bar his being sent to govern Germany), until his accession. He either went into hibernation in Domitian's last, dangerous period, or else served loyally and with the necessary low profile. He was adopted by the Emperor Nerva in October 97, becoming Caesar Nervae f. Nerva Traianus Germanicus, but remained in Upper Germany, where he was provincial governor, as appointed on the Emperor's accession.

It took Trajan well over a year to return to Rome from campaigning in the east, setting a precedent for a trend much more noticeable in the later third and fourth centuries, when it became clear that Rome's importance to the Empire's governance was considerably less than might have previously been supposed. The intervening period had been profitably spent, however, with the new Emperor embarking upon a tour of inspection of his northern

---

733 See *ibid*. I. 30; II. 604, 605, 785-786
734 HA *V. Aureliani* 10.3f., 11. 1-8, 12.1, cf. Syme (1971) 4, 100-101
735 PIR² D135

and eastern frontiers. He must have felt extremely confident in the loyalty of the senate and praetorians, far away in Rome, for as events in later eras demonstrated, the first few months were the most dangerous ones in a new reign, before a regime could be properly established.

Trajan's conduct thereafter was largely exemplary, although we are somewhat influenced by the younger Pliny's *Panegyricus* delivered before the senate, when its author assumed the suffect consulship in September 100. Trajan himself was a master of tact in his dealings with the governing classes, despite exercising power more directly than most of his predecessors. His success was down to his compliance with convention, his appreciation of the delicate balancing act between *princeps* and senate, and his emollience.

The new Emperor acceded to the principate, was elected *pontifex maximus,* acclaimed *imperator* for the first time and was granted the tribunician and annually renewable proconsular powers on 28 January 98. On the deification of his predecessor a short time later, he took the style of Imperator Caesar Divi Nervae f. Nerva Traianus Germanicus Augustus,[736] rapidly adding *pater patriae* after, and *optimus* before 'Augustus'.[737] He was then already ordinary consul (for the second time) holding the consular *fasces* again in 100, 101, 103 and 112.

He was a soldier to his core, and a capable one at that. Even when not campaigning he appears to have been happiest indulging in pastimes like hunting, in which he could express his *machismo*. He was almost certainly bisexual and, if Dio is to be believed, with paedophilic predilections. He was a more than competent administrator, a fine general and superb tactician.

His next opportunity to flex his military muscles was in 101 when he set out to subdue the Dacians, a Balkan people who occasionally caused serious trouble on the Danubian frontier of the Empire and who managed to hold off a major offensive by Domitian in the later 80s. A partial annexation in that year was followed by another campaign in 105 and within 18 months Dacia had become a new Roman province, the struggles between the participants being immortalised in bas relief on Trajan's Column in Rome. He added the name Dacicus in 102 and Parthicus in 114, receiving further imperial acclamations in 101 and 102 (three altogether), 105, 106, and a further seven between 113 and 117, mainly on the field of battle.[738]

A final campaign was against Parthia, after the Parthians had interfered in the client kingdom of Armenia in 114. Trajan annexed Armenia and then Mesopotamia, ending with the capture of the Parthian capital at Ctesiphon a year later. Thereafter the eastern campaign began to go awry, with a Mesopotamian revolt and Trajan's failure to capture the crucial stronghold of Hatra. Perhaps a whiff of defeat reached North Africa, for almost simultaneously, the Jewish populations in Cyrenaica, then Cyprus and Egypt rose up in a particularly bloody revolt. There was also news of further trouble in Germany, causing Trajan to break off his campaign in the east

---

736 ILS 282
737 ILS 305
738 ILS 286, 304

and hurry back to Rome, despite a circulatory complaint which he is said, in some sources, to have attributed to poison. He was forced by a worsening of his condition to pause at Selinus in Cilicia (subsequently Traianopolis), apparently wrote out a declaration of adoption of his successor and kinsman, Hadrian and expired on 9 August 117.

During his reign, Trajan arranged for the deification of his father M. Ulpius Traianus and the elevation to the rank of Augusta of both his sister and his wife in 105. In c. 75, he had married Pompeia Plotina from Nemausus (Nîmes) in Gaul, about whose family nothing is known, although Syme suggests that she might have been a kinswoman of her husband.[739] The young Trajan's wife might perhaps have been connected to another rising senatorial family; possibly she was the daughter of the Gallic senator L. Pompeius Vopiscus, whom the Emperor Otho had nominated to a suffect consulship in AD69, although there is not enough information about him to be at all sure, though he came from the province in which Nemausus lay. Either way, there were no children, and the succession passed, probably through the astute machinations of the Empress, who died in 123, to his closest male relative, P. Aelius Hadrianus, already serving alongside her husband, virtually as his deputy, in Mesopotamia. Theoretically, Trajan lived long enough to adopt him, but the credibility of this adoption is widely doubted by modern scholarship.[740] Anthony Birley considers that 'The adoption was, at best, by a dying man and stage managed by the Empress.'[741] He was 64 when he died, after a reign of nineteen and a half years, and he was later deified by the senate.

TREBELLIANUS
260/268

Trebellianus was a 'governor' of Isauria according to the *Historia Augusta*, who briefly seized power in that mountainous region before being killed by the commander Camisoleus on the orders of Gallienus.[742] Nothing more is known of him, nor of the events surrounding his supposed bid for power.

TREBONIANUS GALLUS
251, 1ˢᵗ June – 253, August

Gallus was the man on the spot when the Emperor Decius died fighting Kniva and his Goths on the Danube at the end of May 251. He was proclaimed following his predecessor's demise and attempted to rule with the senate but fell foul of another usurper before he was able to stabilise a chaotic situation.

C. Vibius Trebonianus Gallus was, like most of his predecessors, a distinguished and aristocratic member of the senate. The family came from

---

739 Syme (1958) II. 604, 794 and see below.
740 Syme, *op. cit.* I. 239-241
741 Birley (1997) 77
742 HA *Tyr. Trig.* XXVI.1-4

Perusia (Perugia) where he was born, as did that of his wife, the Empress Baebiana. It may be that he was fairly closely related to Julius Caesar's lieutenant, C. Vibius Pansa (consul in 43BC) who also came from Perusia, and Professor Wiseman adds that C. Vibius, a moneyer in c. 39BC, was also from there and was probably related to Pansa, that all were in the Tromentina voting tribe, as were the Vibi Vari, from which family it is thought Gallus descended.[743] A probable ancestor was Ap. Annius Trebonius Gallus, consul in 108, son of Civil War general Ap. Annius Gallus (suffect consul and made a patrician 68) who was related by marriage to the Athenian senator, the magnate and patron of the arts Herodes Atticus.[744]

Gallus was born in about 206, becoming quaestor around 235, probably aedile or people's tribune c. 237, praetor 240 and consul in 245. He had served as a legionary legate in Thrace 235/6. In 250 he was appointed governor of Upper Moesia. On the death of Decius and Etruscus at the Battle of Abrittus, on or around 1 June 251, Gallus successfully managed to extricate his remaining forces from the chaos, regrouped and was acclaimed emperor by the relieved soldiers. Whether he encompassed the doom of his predecessors, as was alleged in some sources, seems on the whole, doubtful.

As with Philip the Arab and others, desperation to consolidate his position at Rome led to the conclusion of a hasty treaty. Kniva was allowed to re-cross the frontier not only with his booty but with his Roman captives, many of them of high status, and an annual subsidy was to be paid. Probably Gallus expected to be able to mount an expedition soon afterwards to rectify these matters, but in the event this never materialised.

Gallus thus returned to Rome and obtained recognition from the senate. His Empress, however, was denied the title Augusta by the ever-correct Gallus, because the mother of the surviving son and co-Augustus of Decius, Hostilianus, was still alive and bore the title. He also adopted Hostilianus and recognised him as co-emperor (but without him being *pontifex maximus*), creating his own son Volusianus *caesar* and *princeps iuventutis*. He also persuaded the senate to deify his predecessors: in other words, he did everything by the book, including paying elaborate respect to the senate, somewhat side-lined since the death of Gordian III. On recognition, he took the style Imperator Caesar C. Vibius Trebonianus Gallus Pius Felix Augustus; he added Invictus not long afterwards, being granted the tribunician and proconsular power and the office of *pontifex maximus*.[745] As with many of his shorter-lived predecessors, we do not know how many imperial acclamations he received, although there was invariably one at the beginning of the reign. He was consul for the second time in 252. He had married Afinia M. f. Gemina Baebia, in all probability a descendant of L. Afinius Gallus, suffect consul in 62, also, like the empress, a Perusian; her maternal grandmother was probably Baebia M. f. Nigrina.[746] Later,

---

743 Wiseman (1971) no. 490
744 Birley (1987) 113; PIR² A653, 692, 654
745 ILS 522; PIR² V403 & cf. AE (2006) 1249-50
746 ILS 527

November 251, his co-Augustus Hostilianus died of plague and Gallus thereupon replaced him as Augustus with his son Volusianus. Gallus also had a daughter, Vibia Galla.

The treaty with Kniva did not hold for long and the Danube frontier was again plunged into chaos. Worse, Sharpur I, King of Persia, emboldened by his apparent easy victory against Philip I and seeing that the Empire was in turmoil, decided to try and destroy it, in the east at least. He was aided, as he no doubt calculated, by an outbreak of plague which began about this time and decimated civilian populations and the army alike. Thus, at a moment of political weakness, the Empire was suddenly made much more vulnerable by a drastic loss of manpower and an economic downturn. The result for central government, which seems to have largely continued to run the Empire perfectly well despite of the perturbations at the highest level, was a drastic drop in tax revenue, just when the army was continually having to be paid donatives and generally expanded to meet the external threats, themselves fuelled by the perceived internal chaos. It was a classic vicious circle. Sharpur's campaign was successful; he had overrun the entire province of Syria by 253 and clashes in the east continued for a decade before being brought under control; the plague rampaged through the Empire for even longer.

Gallus comes over as a traditionalist at a time when traditions of all kinds where under threat. In his two years in power, he had little time to consolidate his regime. As a senior senator, his attempt to rule with the senate (many of the reverses of his fairly numerous coin issues bear the letters S C for *senatus consultum*) was perhaps misplaced. At the beginning of 253 he revived Decius' persecution of the Christians, possibly as a means of diverting attention away from (or finding scapegoats for) the crises which beset his rule. Either way, the next effective usurper, Aemilian, put paid to his well-intentioned efforts and his persecution, catching the capital by surprise.

Aemilianus, governor of Lower Moesia, having successfully brought the Goths to heel after Gallus' treaty had broken down, was acclaimed by his army and, as was *de rigueur*, immediately set out for Italy. Gallus, in response, called on the former right-hand man of Decius, P. Licinius Valerianus, now governing Germany, to travel south and help him deal with Aemilian, but he arrived too late to do anything for Gallus. Heading a much inferior force, his soldiers killed Gallus and his son at Interamna Nahars (Terni), just north of Rome early in August 253. Gallus' men went over to the challenger mainly because, with the example still fresh of the demise of Philip at the hands of Decius, which had resulted in heavy loss of Roman lives inflicted by other Romans, no soldier wanted to kill comrades in arms. Valerian still managed to deal with Aemilian but, on this occasion, to his own advantage and at a time of his own choosing.

URANIUS

?231

Uranius, who was said to have been of servile origin, is identified by Zosimus and Georgius Syncellus as an usurper in Edessa during the run-up to Alexander Severus' Persian expedition, and thereby assumed he was the father of the later usurper at the same city (Uranius) Antoninus (IV).[747] This was once thought to be reinforced by coin typology, but subsequent scholarship has demonstrated otherwise.[748]

URANIUS ANTONINUS (IV)
253–254

Uranius Antoninus was a locally connected usurper who established himself in Emesa in the upheavals that saw Valerian and Gallienus succeed and gradually stabilise a very volatile situation.

L. Jul[ius] Aur[elius] Sulp[icius] Ura[nius] Antoninus appears to have seized power in Emesa in order to protect it from the depredations of the rampant Persian invaders, taking advantage of the tumult at the heart of the Empire and in the Balkans.[749] That he was successful must stand to his credit both as a commander and as a ruler. However, he was by no means a tyro, as he was also the priest-king of the city state – the conical black stone brought to Rome by Elagabalus appears on one of his coins – and a successor of the psychotic Severan, clearly implying fairly close kinship. He also appears at an earlier juncture in Zosimus' account as an usurper; it has subsequently emerged that this is a chronological misplacement of the man caused by numismatists' disagreements over the dating of the coin types.[750] If the later chronicler John Malalas is to be believed, he is to be identified with the Emesan High Priest of Aphrodite, Samsigeramus, certainly a name to be found amongst the members of the family of Elagabalus.

Some of Antoninus' gold coins just give his name with *Conservator Aug.* or *Fecunditas Aug.* on the reverse, almost as if he was deliberately playing down imperial style. Despite that, however, he is shown wearing a wreath but styles himself merely L. Jul[ius] Aur[elius] Sulp[icius] Ura[nius] Antoninus – no 'Imperator Caesar' nor 'Augustus', although he probably was so styled officially – claiming the tribunician power and the consulate ('Co[nsuli]s I'[751]) although these are unlikely to have been ratified by the senate in Rome. Some reverses also include the formula 'AUGG' confirming his imperial style and that he was either recognised briefly, probably by Valerian, or was claiming that he had been.[752]

Accounts differ as to his fate. Those who suggest that he abdicated and was accorded an honourable retirement ring truest, for he had saved the situation in Syria long enough for Valerian to get there in force and begin to roll the Persians back. If that was the case, it is possible Antoninus was accorded

---

747 Zosimus 1.12; *op. cit.* p. 674
748 Fink (1939) 329; but for a doubt about this see Syme (1971) 159, cf. Settipani (2000) 443
749 PIR² I195; Syme (1971) 202
750 Frank (1939) 329; Zosimus I. 12, 2 who wrongly claims he was of slave descent.
751 RIC 7
752 *Saeculares Augg*, RIC 7

some form of recognition by the senate which has – as has so much during this period – escaped record. Furthermore, he may well have been a senator and a former (suffect) consul in the first place, as had the scions of various eastern potentates from the second century.

Zosimus records an Antoninus (qv) as one of those who rebelled against Gallienus at the same time as Memor and Aureolus. He is most likely to be identifiable as this man, too, although the possibility must be entertained that he was left in charge at Emesa by Valerian and rebelled again during the chaos following Valerian's capture, perhaps in cahoots with (or even in opposition to) the Palmyrans.[753]

URBANUS
?271

Urbanus was an usurper in the reign of Aurelian. Neither the time nor the location of his elevation has survived, nor have any coins (if any were minted), and nothing is known of the man. He was presumably rapidly suppressed.

VABALLATHUS
271, late or 272, early – 272, 28th August

Vaballathus was a Palmyrene usurper in the east under Zenobia, who was deposed by Aurelian along with his mother. L. Julius Aurelius Septimius Vaballathus Athenodorus was the eldest son of Zenobia, ruling the east under her (for he was only 10 when he succeeded and 16 when he was deposed) as the recognised official proxy for the Empire at first as *Rex regorum corrector totis orientis* (King of Kings and governor of all the East) and later as *consul imperator* and *dux Romanorum*.[754] After the death of Claudius II, he seems to have largely gone independent, assuming the style *imperator*. When faced with the prospect of being neutralised by Aurelian, however, under his mother's auspices he burnt his boats and by around February 272 had assumed the title of Augustus, becoming a fully fledged usurper, being styled Imperator Caesar Vhabalathus Augustus (*sic*), or (on a milestone) Imp[erator] Caes[ar] L. Julius Aurelius Septimius Vaballathus Athenodorus, a status briefly accepted by Aurelian according to papyri found in Egypt. Less than a year later, however, he was captured and deposed when the Emperor took Palmyra, at the end of his fourth regnal year there as *rex regorum*.[755] He is assumed to have survived in Rome with his mother and the rest of the family. He, or one of his brothers, may have married and had issue, for St Jerome tells us that there were descendants in Rome in his day, in the early 5th century, and a little earlier, Libanius wrote of a descendant in one of his letters.[756]

---

753 Zosimus I. 38, 1; PLRE I. Antoninus 1
754 PLRE I. Athenodorus 2
755 Millar (1971) 16 & n. 164
756 Thus supporting HA: *posterior etiam nunc Romae inter nobiles manent* (27.2)

VALENS (I)
251, March – April

Valens was an ephemeral usurper in Rome following the departure of Decius for the Balkans to deal with Kniva's Gothic incursion. The appearance of the usurper Valens must have constituted a serious loss of face for the future Emperor Valerian, when the latter was left behind by Decius as home supremo, especially as he was a fellow senator and even possibly a kinsman. Worse, he was actually proclaimed at Rome with support of a faction of the senate, although we do not know what events brought this about; perhaps the contrast between the austerity of Decius after the munificence of Philip. According to Aurelius Victor, this incident was a riot of sorts fomented or led by Julius Valens Licinianus, who 'seized imperial power at the urgent insistence of the common people' but who was killed in short order thereafter.[757] The date seems to have been late March 251.

[Ti.] Julius Valens Licinianus was a senator in 251 and because he does not seem to have been particularly well connected, we do not know much about his family. Although the combination of names is not at all uncommon, he may have been descended from the younger Pliny's equestrian friend Julius Valens.[758] If so, a couple of generations thereafter are missing before we reach the usurper's probable grandfather, [Ti.] Julius Licinianus, a senator in 188/189.[759] He was father of Ti. Julius Licinianus, a senator in 223, when he was one of the patrons of Canusium (Canosa di Puglia).[760] Thus, he in turn is thought to have been the father of Valens. We know nothing of wife nor children, but two generations down the line, Julius Valens, although of equestrian rank – he was a *vir perfectissimus* – was governor (*praeses*) of Nearer Spain under Diocletian and could have been a descendant. In this period, anyone who wanted an official career needed to avoid the senate, members of which, since the time of Gallienus, had been largely relegated to roles of minimal influence. Thus, the connection is plausible, although the frequency of both names leaves a large element of doubt. Valens must at least have been fairly senior, without doubt a former suffect consul, and he lasted days rather than weeks before being killed by the mob.[761]

VALENS (II)
261–262

Valens was an obscure usurper in northern Greece who was allegedly eliminated by an equally poorly attested neighbouring governor, himself suppressed by yet another usurper on his way to contest power with Gallienus.

---

757 HA *Try. Trig.* XX; Aur. Victor, 29.8

758 *Ep.* 5, 21, 2; PIR² I 609

759 PIR² I 379

760 PIR² I 380; ILS 6121

761 HA *Tyr. Trig.* XX (where he was inserted out of sequence solely in order to pad out the number of usurpers in Gallienus's reign); Aur. Victor, 29, 3; *Epitome* 29,5; PIR² I610 cf. I380

Proconsul of Achaia or Macedonia in 261, Valens appears to have raised the standard of revolt possibly as a result of successfully defending Thessalonica from the marauding Goths, according himself the epithet Thessalicus. As he appears in the *Historia Augusta*, one might be tempted to view him with some reservations, were it not for the fact that he also appears in two other sources, thus confirming his existence, but not his his actions. The *Historia* claims he was disposed of by Piso, probably in 262.[762] Yet, as this Piso is said by the *Historia Augusta* to have been sent to put down the revolt by Macrianus and to have become an usurper in Valens' place – an usurper putting down another usurper who had eliminated a previous usurper – it all rather epitomises the chaos of the mid-third century and the equal chaos of this source. The identity of Valens remains elusive, although the same source claims him as a great nephew of Valens I.[763]

VALENS (III)
316, October – 317, 8th January

Valens was the co-ruler with the tetrarch Licinius, elevated through expediency and who was promptly disposed of by his colleague when his services were no longer required. This man, whose original name may well have been [M.] Aurelius Valens, was a senior army officer serving Licinius as *dux limitis* (border commander) in Dacia. He was appointed co-ruler with Licinius a few days after the battle of Cibalae (Vinkovci, Croatia) on 8 October 316 against Constantine's forces, taking the style Imperator Caesar M. Aurelius Valerius Valens Pius Felix Augustus. To him fell the tasks of re-grouping Licinius' army acting as a decoy for his colleague to mount a second attack. His generalship probably led to the welcome stalemate between the two antagonists. His reward, however, once the ensuing peace agreement had been made, was to be disposed of – permanently.[764] Whether this took place before the end of the year when the hostilities actually ceased, or on 1 March 317 when the treaty between Licinius and Constantine was actually signed, is not entirely clear. In either case, he lived long enough to issue coins. Nothing is known of any family.

VALENS (IV)
364, 28th March 364 – 378, 9th August

Valens was the self-indulgent and incompetent younger brother of Valentinian I, who looked after the Eastern Empire for his brother but lost much of his army and his own life at the Battle of Adrianople against the Goths.

Whilst his brother Valentinian I hardly sent Roman biographers into ecstasies over his character, abilities and habits, Flavius Valens was universally

---

762 HA *Gall.* II.2 & *Tyr. Trig.* XIX.1. *Epitome* 32.4 7 Ammianus Marcellinus 21,16.10; PLRE Valens 2

763 HA *Gall.* II.2-4; *Tyr. Trig.* XIX-XXI; on the relationship of Valens I & II, XX. 2. PLRE Piso 1

764 PLRE I Valens 13

regarded as the inferior man, in looks, capability, deportment and disposition. He was born c. 328, the younger son of Gratianus, the Emperor Constans' *comes rei militaris* in Africa and later in Britain in the 340s. Valens enjoyed a fairly torpid military career before, in the early 360s, he was appointed a middle-ranking officer in the Imperial Guard (*protector domesticus*). On his acclamation, Valentinian made him *tribunus stabuli*, a military court appointment with oversight of the procurement of mounts and draught horses for the army everywhere. He was plucked from these none-too-heavy responsibilities on 28 March 364 by his brother and made co-ruler, later with responsibility for the eastern half of the Empire. On his accession he was already married to Domnica, and they had one son, Valentinianus Galates, and daughters Carosa and Anastasia.

Valens seems to have been recognised along with his brother in all the usual powers of the emperor and also seems to have been acknowledged as *pontifex maximus.*[765] His style was Imperator Caesar Dominus Noster Flavius Valens Semper Augustus, although he later added 'Victoria ac Triumfator', placed before 'semper', like his brother.[766] He also held six consulships, in 365, 368, 370 and 373 (all jointly with his brother) and in 376 and 378 as well. He was unswervingly loyal to his brother, which contributed much to internal stability. The beginning of his reign was, however, marred by the emergence of Procopius, an usurper with ties of kinship to the House of Constantine. This occurred at Valens' capital, Constantinople, which he had just left to deal with a breakdown in Jovian's peace treaty with the Persians. This diverted the Emperor until the following spring. As a consequence of their support of Procopius, there was now the problem of an influx of Goths, which took until 369 to sort out, resulting in a treaty agreed following a ruinous defeat of the barbarians.

Thereafter Valens was able to re-apply himself to the problems of the east, which had been exacerbated by Shapur, the Persian King, taking advantage of the problems caused by Procopius to seize control over Armenia, then under the rule of a Roman client king, Arsaces III, formerly married to Olympias, daughter of Constantine's Praetorian Prefect, Ablabius (making him a first cousin by marriage of the future Emperor Theodosius I and a kinsman of the imperial claimant Firmus), demonstrating the Empire-wide reach of the new aristocracy created by the reforms of Constantine. The only other claimant with whom Valens had to deal was a senior civil servant called Theodorus who had the misfortune to be told by an oracle that he would succeed Valens, which led to the young man's execution for treason. He never had any pretensions to become an imperial claimant.[767]

Although Shapur was roundly defeated, the problem of Armenia continued to simmer in the background, keeping the Emperor in the area, whilst he sent a *comes*, Lupicinus, to deal with problems amongst the Goths on the Danube, seriously compounded by the westward surge of the Huns from the Steppes,

---

765 FS1715; PLRE I Valens 8
766 ILS760
767 PLRE I Theodorus 13. This incident took place in 371/372.

which spooked the Goths into seeking to re-locate across the river. Aided by the *dux* of Moesia, Maximus (not to be identified with the future emperor Magnus Maximus), the transfer was so appallingly mishandled that the Goths rebelled and Valens was obliged to rush back to the Balkans to deal with it. His brother had also just died, but his successor, the pious and rather unwarlike Gratian, scored a substantial victory on the Rhine and diverted some troops to aid his uncle. Unfortunately, before they could link up, Valens, very poorly advised, got himself into a position where conflict was inevitable, and in the ensuing (second) Battle of Adrianople (Edirne, European Turkey), the under-strength Roman force was completely annihilated by a hugely superior army of Goths. The Emperor himself was killed. The date was 9 August 378 and the defeat was regarded as the most catastrophic since Cannae in 216BC. It utterly emasculated the Roman army in the eastern part of the Empire and triggered a *coup*, leading to the acclamation of Theodosius I.

VALENTINIAN I
364, 26th February – 375, 17th November

Valentinian was a short-tempered Pannonian soldier-emperor who strengthened the Empire and founded a new dynasty, but who injudiciously made his brother Valens ruler of the eastern half of the Empire.

There was a ten-day interregnum after the unexpected death of Jovian – had he been done away with, a conspirator would have surely been proclaimed immediately. The generals and courtiers met to decide on a successor. Their choice, after much deliberation, fell on a former *comes* of Julian whom the Emperor had banished, but who had been recalled by Jovian and appointed a senior tribune in Galatia. Having been summoned to the conclave and having accepted, this *comes*, Valentinian, took a month before astounding the army high command by selecting his portly, sluggish and illiterate younger brother Valens as his co-ruler.

The new Emperors were the sons of Gratianus, a giant of a man of humble origin from Cibilae in Pannonia (Vincovci, Croatia), who had risen through the ranks to become a senior commander (*comes rei militaris*) in Africa and later in Britain under Constans. Valentinian himself was born in 321 and seems to have served with his father before being appointed to a tribunate in Gaul in 357, after which Constantius II promoted him and posted him to Mesopotamia c. 360 before Julian made him a *comes*, although after his recall he reverted to the rank of tribune. He was married to Marina Valeria Severa at the time of his elevation and had a son. After he had become Emperor, he divorced Marina and made a political match to secure his dynasty by marrying Justina, the widow of the usurper Magnentius. Such an alliance would hardly be thought likely to secure the dynasty, bearing in mind the nature of her previous husband, but Justina seems to have been the daughter of a senator, [Vettius] Justus. More importantly, her mother is thought to have been Julia, a daughter of Julius Constantius, consul in 335, half-brother of Constantine, an attachment to whose family would indeed have brought cachet to the house of Valentinian. By Justina, he had another son and three daughters.[768]

The new Emperor took the style Imperator Caesar Dominus Noster Flavius Valentinianus Pius Felix Maximus Victor ac Triumfatori Semper Augustus and this was acknowledged by the senates at Rome and Constantinople, which granted both Emperors tribunician and proconsular powers.[769] Although an orthodox Christian, he also took the office of *pontifex maximus*. He held a modest four consulships, in 365, 368, 370 and 373, all jointly with his brother. A few months after his accession, the two brothers split the empire between them along the same lines as had Valerian in 253, Diocletian in 286, and Constantius II in 340, Valentinian taking the west and his brother the east. He spent almost all of the reign campaigning and, in having to pay for the increased military requirements, began squeezing the civilian population remorselessly, also launching a series of treason trials against the plutocratic but largely politically impotent western senators – the old aristocracy – not because (as he alleged) that they were using pagan magic and soothsayers to hatch plots against him, but because he needed to sequestrate their estates in order to raise cash to pay the army. This epitomised the way that the imperial administration had begun the move to rehabilitate the senatorial class under the House of Constantine, but then, after 363, all this went into reverse as this military clique took over and governed much more pragmatically and to some extent reactively. Where a smattering of members of recently ennobled families could have expected high bureaucratic and military appointments before, now most such positions went to Pannonians, rather as they had to Illyrians in the post-Gallienus period.

Valentinian fought a whole series of campaigns on the Rhine, mainly with considerable success, securing the frontier for a generation, making treaties, launching punitive expeditions, and strengthening forts, garrisons and cities. During this period he was also forced to deal with a serious crisis in Britain caused by barbarians running amok in 367, followed by an usurper, Valentinus, all sorted out by his able *comes*, Theodosius, who later went on to quell a series of revolts in North Africa, provoked by flagrant corruption in the administration and which culminated in the acclamation of yet another self-proclaimed emperor, Firmus. These events led to the Emperor to add to his formal style, Germanicus Maximus, Alemannicus Maximus, Francicus Maximus and Gothicus Maximus. The latter is a reminder that, having settled the Rhine, Valentinian then turned his attention to the Danube, where he was obliged to fight more campaigns than he needed to because of his lack of diplomatic skills and quick temper. Indeed, a manifestation of the latter before a stubborn delegation of Sarmatians caused a stroke which killed him on 17 November 375.[770] His eight-year-old son by his first wife, Gratian

---

768 Settipani (2000) 330; PLRE I Constantius 7; Julius Constantius was made patrician and was killed in 337.

769 ILS760, 771

770 PLRE I Valentinianus 7

(qv), had been proclaimed co-ruler with him on 24 August 367 and at 16, succeeded him as sole (Western) Emperor.

VALENTINIAN II
375, 22nd November – 387, October
388, 28th July –392

Valentinian II was a child emperor who was made co-ruler with his elder half-brother Gratian at a tender age and whose first period of rule was dominated by his Arian and aristocratic mother Justina, and whose second period in power was dominated by a barbarian *magister militum*.

The younger son of Valentinian I by his second marriage was born on 2 July 371 at Trier and was named after his father. He was proclaimed Augustus on 22 November 375, five days after his father's death.[771] For most of his life he was under the influence of the dowager Empress Justina, various ministers and, after 379, his older and much more experienced co-ruler Theodosius I. Furthermore, during his reign, the eastern part of the Empire began to gain predominance over the west. Valentinian II was recognised as Emperor by the court, the army and, no doubt, by the two senates. He was given the style of Imperator Caesar Dominus Noster [Flavius] Valentinianus Pius Felix Semper Augustus.[772] He was made consul in 376 and again in 378, 387 and 390. On the death of Valens (when he was still only eight) he succeeded as sole Augustus in the east, his rule being exercised by a close-knit group of courtiers who had either avoided or survived the Battle of Adrianople. Yet the entire east was in turmoil: there were Goths rampaging through Thrace and the Balkans, and only a modest force had been sent by Gratian's advisors to help – prudently, as it turned out, from the point of view of the security of the west. This led to the senior Emperor (still only nineteen himself) appointing Theodosius I as his half-brother's co-ruler at the beginning of 379. From then on, the older man was to make all the running; Valentinian was assigned as co-emperor in the west, with Italy and Africa under his aegis, most of the rest remaining under Gratian. Increasingly, he tended to become a cipher, representing the continuity of the regime and Imperial family, although the senior man eventually married his colleague's sister Galla in the wake of his deposition by Magnus Maximus. A complicating factor was that the Emperor was an Arian Christian, taking his lead from his mother – the widow of the Arian usurper, Magnentius – earning him the disapprobation of the charismatic St Ambrosius, Bishop of Milan, whose implacable opposition finally prevailed.

Once Magnus Maximus had become established in the West – essentially reviving the Gallic empire of 120 years before – Valentinian's faith became a stick with which to beat him for both Theodosius and Maximus, ambitious kinsmen united in their detestation of the youthful ruler's lack of orthodoxy. Then, in September or early October 387, Maximus moved south from

---

771 PLRE I Valentinianus 8
772 ILS781 & coins.

Trier to Milan and deposed Valentinian, allowing him to escape with his mother and sister, Galla, to the east. After some months Justina eventually managed to goad a seemingly reluctant Theodosius into action towards her son's restoration by deploying the charms of Galla on the recently widowed emperor, who eventually agreed to move against Maximus in the summer of the following year, after Justina had given permission for him to marry Galla. Shortly after that, Justina died, and Theodosius was able to persuade Valentinian to return to the Orthodox faith.

Theodosius' generals led a remarkably rapid advance on Italy through the Balkans, narrowly defeating the forces of Maximus twice, and forcing his kinsman's surrender and death at Aquiliea at the end of July 388. Consequently, Valentinian II was restored, but much of the running of the empire lay in the hands of a triumvirate of very able and highly motivated Frankish generals, led by Arbogastes, fiercely loyal to Theodosius and openly contemptuous of the young Emperor. Consequently, when the by now adult Valentinian attempted to assert himself and exercise his *imperium*, he was found dead in his apartments on 15 May 392. Officially it was suicide, but nobody was fooled. Theodosius was again sole ruler, although his subsequent failure to recognise Arbogastes' nominee to the purple, Eugenius, resulted in yet another costly civil conflict.

VALENTINIAN III
425, 23ʳᵈ October – 455, 16ᵗʰ March

Valetinian III was the child-emperor whose long reign saw the inexorable increase of the influence of *magistri militum*, who presided over the loss of most of Africa, much of Gaul and Spain and the eventual defeat of Attila the Hun.

Placidus Valentinianus was born on 2 July 419, son of the patrician and briefly Honorius' co-emperor, Constantius III by Galla Placidia, the daughter of Theodosius I by his second wife, Valentinian II's sister Galla. The infant prince was recognised by Honorius as his heir when he was accorded the style of *nobilissimus caesar* in 421/422, although this was not at first recognised by the eastern court, but shortly afterwards he was taken to Constantinople by his mother, the dowager Empress Galla Placidia, in 422. After Iohannes had become Emperor, he was at last recognised as the potential Western Emperor by being recognised as *nobilissimus caesar* at Thessalonica en route back to Italy on 23 October 424. After the fall of Ravenna and the death of Iohannes, he remained in a kind of constitutional limbo until proclaimed emperor in the autumn of 425.

By this time, measures were fully in place to restore the Western Empire. Ravenna had been sacked in retribution for the events of the reign of Iohannes and it had been rendered uninhabitable, so the imperial capital moved back to Rome, for the first time since the 3ʳᵈ century, whilst Ravenna was put to rights. Eventually, on October 23 425, the six-year-old Valentinian was acclaimed Emperor. He never really came into his own though, being intellectually weak, martially and maritally inadequate, as well as personally indecisive.

He took the style Dominus Noster Placidus Valentinianus Invictissimus Pius Felix Augustus and his mother, made Augusta for the second time (Honorius is believed to have stripped her of the style in 422/423), acted as regent for him until around 438/440.[773] He served as consul, first in 425 as a belated ordinary consul (Iohannes' tenure not having been recognised) then in 426, 430 and after that at five-yearly intervals: 435, 440, 445, 450 and 455. His thirty-year reign marked the final descent of the west into a pale shadow of its former self. The enmity between the army commanders Aëtius and Bonifatius led to endless intrigue, with the latter coming perilously close to usurping power himself whilst serving as C-in-C Africa. Bonifatius also reinforced his sparse forces with an army of Vandals to defend the province, which ultimately in 439 meant the barbarians overran all of the northern African provinces up to and including Africa Proconsularis, in the process establishing an autonomous kingdom, which lasted until it was reclaimed under Justinian in 530.[774] One result was that Rome's grain supply had either to be bought at a premium from the Vandal kingdom or from other imperially controlled outlets, adding to the problems the west was already experiencing, like a drastic fall in taxation revenue.

Meanwhile, Gaul was still seething with barbarian groups. In command there, Aëtius had his work cut out for over a decade trying to reconcile the expectations of mercenary groups like the Burgundians, whilst trying to confine the Visigoths to Spain and keep the remaining parts of Gaul free from raids and sieges by the unwanted guests. On the whole, he did tolerably well, but never quite managed to subdue and settle the entire Diocese. Even the British called upon him in the later 440s to come to their aid against 'Saxons', but he was too tied up with events between the Rhine and the Pyrenees to be able to help. His greatest test was the invasion of the Huns, provoked by the appalling behaviour of the Emperor's sister, Justa Grata Honoria, whose dealings with Attila, the Hunnic chieftain, caused him to mount an invasion of Italy in order to claim her as his bride. The Huns had been a serious threat to the stability of the east up until then, but their departure westwards allowed the east some respite. At first, diplomatic means were tried, including the grant to Attila of the honorary rank of *magister militum*. Nothing worked and the threat grew. Eventually, Aëtius managed to cobble together a large force of disparate barbarians (mainly Visigoths) along with regular troops, and defeated Attila decisively at the Battle of the Catalaunian Plains (Châlons-sur-Marne) in southern Gaul in 451. The contemporary poet Sidonius Apollinaris described how 'Suddenly the barbarian world, rent by a mighty upheaval, poured the whole North into Gaul…' The Hun tried again in 452, taking Aquileia and Mediolanum (Milan) before agreeing to withdraw after the personal intervention of Pope Leo. Fortunately for

---

773 ILS 804, 806, 816. PLRE II Valentinianus 4

774 PLRE II Bonifatius 3. He divorced his first wife, Pelagia (allegedly a barbarian), by whom he had a daughter who promptly married Aëtius, giving him a son Gaudentius, and probably also a daughter.

practically everyone, he died of a stroke the following year and his empire began to crumble.

Valentinian had been betrothed as a child to the daughter of Theodosius II, Licinia Eudoxia, whilst still living in Constantinople, and eventually married her there on 29 October 437 when she was aged fifteen. They had two daughters, Eudocia and Placidia.[775] She was proclaimed Augusta at Ravenna (by this time rebuilt) in 439.

The distinguished senator Petronius Maximus – quite possibly a grandson of Magnus Maximus – plotted the downfall of Aëtius, whose power he coveted, especially as in early 454 the *magister militum* had agreed with the Emperor to a marriage between their children, which would have virtually guaranteed Aëtius, or his son, the succession. As a result of a plot of fiendish complexity, the great general was killed in the palace by the Emperor's own hand on 21 or 22 September 454. The crowning irony was that when he demanded appointment to Aëtius's vacant posts himself, Maximus was refused. The Emperor's own assassination on 16 March, in the Campus Martius at Rome in the following year, by a pair of barbarian officers, could therefore be seen as inevitable.

VALENTINUS

368

Valentinus was an enigmatic usurper in Britain who seems to have attempted to take power against the backdrop of the so-called Barbarian Conspiracy in 367/8 – or who conceivably engineered the rebellion in the first place in the hope of profiting by the chaos.

Nothing is known of this Valentinus' background except that he was a Pannonian and thus probably one of those who owed rapid promotion to the accession of Valentinian I; indeed, as a Pannonian with a derivative name, he may have been a kinsman. The likelihood therefore is that he was a senior officer of some sort, promoted by the Emperor or his brother. Having committed some serious offence, instead of being executed, his brother-in-law Maximinus, then Pretorian Prefect, persuaded the Emperor to exile him to Britain where, with other exiles, he may well have planned a rebellion.

Quite how closely this was linked to the 367 barbarian-led rampage is not known, but there certainly seems to have been a link. Maybe Valentinus was hoping to stir unrest and then triumphantly put it down, seeking to benefit from the mayhem or its aftermath. The rebels obtained the support of elements of the army in Britain, but it is not made clear if he was actually styled augustus or not. It would seem very unlikely that any rising would have worked if he hadn't, but the whole affair was subsequently hushed up, so the information may have been lost as a result. There are no coins, however, and after a relatively short period he was captured with the other

---

775 PLRE II Eudoxia 2, Valentinianus 4

ringleaders by the *comes* Theodosius and handed over to the C-in-C for the Diocese, the *dux* Dulcitius, for execution.[776]

VALERIAN
253, c. October – 260, June

Valerian was the successor of Aemilian, in the turbulent years following the death of Philip the Arab. Valerian steadily began to end the upheavals taking place throughout the empire, along with his son Gallienus as co-emperor, until his unfortunate capture by the Persians in 260, which led to further outbreaks of anarchy and barbarian incursions that took his son the remainder of his reign to reduce.

P. Licinius Valerianus Colobius was born around 195, but whilst the sources all seem to agree that the branch of the Licinii from which Valerian and his family stemmed was noble and Etruscan, it is difficult to pin his ancestors in the male line down.[777] Even Valerian's father's name is unknown and it is his wife's family, the Egnatii, who are provably distinguished. This particular inclination to favour kin when bestowing offices, especially the consulship, may provide a guide to the further reaches of Valerian's family, however. Gallienus's father-in-law enjoyed a second consulship in 260, and the fact that the otherwise obscure C. Salonius Lucullus held the ordinary consulship in 265 may well be explained if we postulate that he was the Empress Salonina's uncle. Again, contemporary senator P. Egnatius Marianus' name strongly suggests that he must have been closely related to Gallienus and that he was consul in 268 would appear to confirm it. The *Historia Augusta* gives Valerian an unattested 'noble kinsman' called Valerius Flaccinus.[778]

Valerian may have married twice, since his presumed elder son bore none of the names associated with the family of the mother of Gallienus. If so, the marriage must have been c. 215 and very brief. The Emperor's second wife, whom he married c. 217/218, was [Egnatia] Mariniana, daughter of Q. Egnatius Victor Marinianus, suffect consul before 230.[779] In 251, Valerian, who by this time had certainly served a suffect consulship, was appointed *censor* by the senate – the first non-imperial holder of this important office for centuries – and was *princeps senatus* or 'father of the senate', which suggests that he was the most senior surviving ex-consul. That suggests he served his consulship sometime around 230; the problem is that this information only appears in the *Historia Augusta*. Probably he was merely an ex-consul serving in various expected capacities in the provinces, as one might expect. Thus in 251-252 he was governor of a Danubian province, since he was fighting Goths and, by 253, he was governing Rhaetia, unless he had been given an unspecified overall command by Gallus, holding the fort for Gallus when Aemilianus took over.

---

776 PLRE I Valentinus 5
777 The *signum* Colobius is provided by *Epitome* 32, 1
778 HA *V. Prob.* 5.3
779 PIR² E37 & E39

He was acclaimed by his troops in October 253 shortly before deposing Aemilian and was recognised by the senate within days of the death of his predecessor, doubtless with the unspoken reservation that he was likely to last little longer and any of his three predecessors. The senate also pronounced a *damnatio memoriae* upon poor Aemilian, which might seem a little harsh for a man who had ruled, respectful of his fellow senators, for only just over three months. In the event, any cynicism about the likely length of the new Emperor's reign was soon dispelled, for Valerian, although a senator of aristocratic background, set about putting the Empire back on its feet and, had it not been once again for the intervention of Shapur, King of Persia, he might well have succeeded.

Valerian, described (by the *Historia Augusta*) as careful, modest and serious, was recognised by the senate, granted proconsular and tribunician power and was made *pontifiex maximus*, taking the imperial style Imperator Caesar P. Licinius Valerianus Augustus, later expanded to Pius Felix Invictus Augustus. He also began to be styled *Dominus* ('Lord') presaging his son's adoption of the style *Dominus Noster*, which became the norm over the succeeding years for emperors right up until the seventh century.[780] He was consul again in 254, also in the following year and finally in 257. His wife Mariniana was made Augusta, but seems to have died shortly afterwards, being deified by the senate.

Having settled matters at Rome, the new ruler was obliged to tackle a full-blown crisis. The frontiers were in a shambles: the Persians had captured Antioch and most of Syria, Armenia and Mesopotamia, and the Danube had seen two, possibly three armies removed and marched off to Rome and whilst most detachments no doubt were sent back, elements would have remained to bolster each succeeding emperor: Decius, Gallus, Aemilian and now Valerian, leaving the frontiers at acute risk.

Valerian immediately appointed his 35-year-old son Gallienus – a competent general – as co-emperor. In the face of mounting crises in both the northern frontiers and the east, the empire was divided between them, although not formally, in 256, Valerian at the same time appointing Gallienus' son Valerian junior as *caesar*, although when he died in 258 his younger brother Saloninus was appointed in his place.

Gallienus set out to restore the situation on the Danube and Rhine frontiers, which he did with some success, earning both emperors the additional style Germanicus Maximus in 257. Valerian went east to tackle the Goths who had become bold enough to begin raiding Asia Minor by sea and had even penetrated to the Crimea, disrupting Roman corn supplies in the process.

Meanwhile, taking advantage of the instability in the Empire, the Persians resumed their campaigning in the east. From events such as the capture and abandonment of Antioch, it is clear that Sharpur's main objectives were not to take over the eastern portions of the Empire, but to take booty. Antioch had fallen in 256, but Valerian recaptured of the city in the following year. The reality of Sharpur's alleged puppet emperor, Cyriades – really a criminal

---

780 PIR² L258

chancer called Mareades – may safely be discounted an as example of the *Historia Augusta* conjuring usurpers out of thin air to people his 'Thirty Tyrants' section.[781] Thereafter, Valerian set about slowly clearing the entire area of Sharpur's forces and garrisons.

Even so, he had a hard time with the Persians, who were bolstered by success, lack of serious opposition and good morale. Whilst two civil wars were raging in the west, the Persians had made serious inroads into the east with the result that [Uranius] Antoninus (IV), a successor of Elagabalus as priest-king of Emesa had been constrained to offer himself as an imperial claimant with a mandate, at the very least, to keep Sharpur from sacking Emesa. On arrival, Valerian's first move was to put down Antoninus, who may have abdicated rather than been killed. Thereafter operations were hampered by poor morale, a devastated countryside and an increasingly widespread outbreak of plague. The Emperor's capture, probably through betrayal rather than through a military failure, at Edessa in May/June 260, marks the low point in the entire history of the Empire prior to the collapse of the west in the fifth century. News of it set off a rash of usurpation in the empire.

Valerian was taken to Persia where various chronicles recount that he lived on in ignominy, being either used by Sharpur as a mounting block or being covered with the skin of an ass. Later sources claim that he was flayed, either alive or after his death, and a straw-stuffed mannequin fashioned from the result, thereafter on display for generations in one of the most important temples in the Persian capital. Professor Grant suggests that he may in fact have sought sanctuary with Sharpur after an army mutiny, making all the subsequent tales merely smokescreens of dubious veracity.[782] If that is what really happened, the matter would have had to have been kept quiet in order to shore up the reputation of Gallienus, who duly succeeded him as sole emperor, although hardly unchallenged.

VERUS (II)
218, c. November – 219, January

The usurper rose to power amid the upheavals in Syria following the elevation of Elagabalus and the destruction of Macrinus. Verus was an usurper at Tyre in Syria in the months that followed the elevation of Elagabalus in winter 218-219 and was thus what might be termed a Macrinus continuity candidate. He was said to have risen from the rank of centurion to the senate (probably through adlection by Caracalla to fill in gaps left by his depredations) and was in 218 legate of IIIrd Legion Gallica in the East. He was probably faced with troops reduced to mutiny by news of the excesses of Elagabalus, despite his legion having been amongst those who supported the Emesan youth initially. The rising was put down early in 219, Verus being presumably killed and the Legion disbanded. Marcius Veracilius Verus, an early 3rd-century

---

781 HA *Tyr. Trig.*, 2
782 Grant (1985) 165

suffect consul is the most likely candidate to be identified with this usurper, but what was he doing serving as a legionary legate if he had been consul?[783] Nothing is known of the family.

VERUS see LUCIUS VERUS (I)

VESPASIAN
69, 20th December 69 – 79, 23rd June

Vespasian was the general who finally brought to end the Year of the Four Emperors, stabilised the body politic, carried out necessary reforms and strengthened the Empire, founding a new dynasty in the process.

The victory of Vespasian over Vitellius and the establishment of the Flavian dynasty marked the end of some eighteen months of civil war, upheaval and uncertainty. T. Flavius [T. f. T. n. Quir.] Vespasianus, was born on 17 November 9AD at Falacrinae (Falacrine), near Reate. In 39 he married Flavia Domitilla the elder, probably his second cousin whose own status had to be regularised before the marriage could take place.[784] After her death she was retrospectively accorded the rank of Augusta.

Once established, Vespasian, ably assisted by his elder son Titus, ruled moderately and with a sure touch. The senate was replenished with loyal supporters of the dynasty, other senatorial families were raised to the prestigious status of patrician (giving a fast-track to the highest offices); a *modus vivendi* with the traditional governing élite was established which satisfied both sides, and in due course a series of military victories, like the Emperor's own in Judaea, and those of Cn. Julius Agricola – the father-in-law of the senatorial historian Cornelius Tacitus – in Britain, helped to consolidate the Empire.

The Imperial family itself descended from a family of middling sort from Reate (Rieti), the first to hold the purple not of ancient patrician stock of the Republic, bar the relatively ephemeral Otho and Vitellius, although as we have seen, even they were patrician by creation. Yet compared to them, the Flavian dynasty's origins were, to put it kindly, unassuming. Furthermore, Vespasian was the first emperor to be a *novus homo* – a new man – without even a senatorial father.

The first family member of whom we know anything concrete had served as a centurion – an élite one, nevertheless, a *primus pilus* – who had fought under Pompey at the Battle of Pharsalus in 49BC. There was also a story going around at the time of Vespasian's bid for power that this man, his grandfather, was the son of a Gaul, who had settled in Reate and was an agent for hiring labour from his native land to gather in the Italian harvest. Levick points out that his grandfather's *cognomen* – Petro – is of Gallic

---

783 Dio 80. 7
784 Jones (1984) 3

origin, so there may indeed have been at least a grain of truth in what was clearly intended at the time as a slur.[785]

The family, despite burgeoning wealth, never quite managed at this stage to aspire to equestrian rank and both Vespasianus' mother and grandmother were higher up the social scale than the Flavii themselves. The former, Vespasia, was a senator's sister and equestrian's daughter and the latter, Tertulla, was of also of equestrian stock.[786] Once established, links were forged with the previous dynasty by the marriage in AD70 of Domitian – albeit in predicably disreputable circumstances – with Domitia Longina, the daughter of Nero's general Cn. Domitius Corbulo by a daughter of C. Cassius Longinus.[787]

Prior to that, however, Titus seems to have become brother-in-law to the future Emperor Trajan's father. This link to the following, Antonine, dynasty was later strengthened by two further marriages amongst the descendants of Vespasian's elder brother T. Flavius Sabinus. His daughter Flavia Sabina married twice and her descendants from both alliances – the Pedanii Fusci and the Caesennii Paeti – made Antonine connections, including a marriage with Hadrian's sister.

Although a late-starting senator of good reputation, the new Emperor was of the first generation of his family to enter the *curia*. His career, which began under Tiberius, owed something to flattery of Caligula and much to his successor's freedman, Narcissus. It was, nevertheless, one of unchecked military competence and success, starting with a junior command during the invasion of Britain in which he covered himself with glory. The only setback was that Agrippina did not like anyone connected with Narcissus, yet Vespasian was chosen to accompany Nero on his tour of Greece, when he famously caused displeasure by dropping off during one of the Emperor's dramatic recitations; miraculously, he and his reputation survived.

It is well known that Vespasian, aided by his elder son Titus as legate, was engaged in putting down the Jewish revolt about the time that Nero died. Between then and the accession of Vitellius, Vespasian had crushed most resistance, taken Jerusalem and destroyed the temple. The events of AD68-69 were not lost on the general in Palestine: the power base had swung from a senatorial and familial one to one firmly rooted in the military, although family ties still played a part, bearing in mind that both Galba, Otho and Vitellius had fairly close links to the Julio-Claudian dynasty. Nevertheless, military competence and a good reputation throughout the legions looked to be an excellent start.

The success of the Jewish War, as the author Josephus called it, put Vespasian in a position pre-eminent to avenge Galba, spurred on by the accession of the venal Vitellius, whom Vespasian would have known personally perfectly well,

---

785 Levick, B., *Vespasian* (London, 1999) 6-7

786 Suetonius, *Vespasian*, 2, 1; 5, 2

787 Cassius was suffect consul in 30 and had been married to Junia Lepida, a great-great-granddaughter of Augustus, although Domitia may have been the offspring of a later marriage: CIL.IX.3426; PIR² D181; Suet. *Divus Titus* 10; Syme (1958) I. 300 & II. 560 n.

for it is worth bearing in mind that all the protagonists were drawn from the same élite and were acquainted as well as being, in some cases, related.

What exactly Vespasian had in mind as his *modus operandi* for securing power when he was acclaimed does not seem apparent for, as we have seen, the impetuous commander Antonius Primus got the show on the road before anyone seems to have realized it. By 20 December 69, Vespasian was in control, albeit at the cost of the life of his valued and wise elder brother, T. Flavius Sabinus, killed out-of-hand by Vitellius' supporters on 18 December in the run-up to the fall of the Rome. Vespasian's first style on succession from December 69 was Imperator T. Flavius Vespasianus Caesar, but within two months it was changed to Imperator Caesar Vespasianus Augustus. He also received the tribunician power, to which were added later that year (70) *pater patriae* and *pontifex maximus* – all *in absentia*.

Although there was a year's mopping up to be done in the Holy Land – including the reduction of Masada – Vespasian had sufficient confidence in Titus to finish the job well and appointed him as his replacement before heading first for Alexandria and then Rome, where he arrived two months short of the first anniversary of the fall of his predecessor.

He found that the Empire had functioned perfectly well throughout all the upheavals, run by the less glamorous 'B' list members of the élite, those not necessarily connected to the former dynasty nor the ancient aristocracy. These men Vespasian promoted, attempting through a combination of shrewdness, ruthlessness and administrative adroitness in forging a new élite out of the best elements of the old, especially as he found himself distrusting the survivors of the coterie behind the ousting of Nero, like senator Helvidius Priscus, an early casualty of the new regime. The new emperor was, in a sense, the first since Augustus to understand the delicate balancing act that had to be maintained between the ruler and the senate, and he managed it rather well. A good sense of humour seemed to have helped.

Modelling himself on Claudius, he had the senate elect him censor for 73/74 and not only replenished the ranks of the senate from the more senior and competent members of the equestrian order – especially those whose services to himself and his family had commended them – but also nominated a group of prominent and loyal senators for adlection into the patriciate, almost all from new or emergent families. He reformed aspects of the administration, especially the fiscal side, for he had taken over a desperately depleted treasury. This only served to enhance his reputation for meanness with money. He resorted to tax rises, new taxes and other, less straightforward means of replenishing the fisc.

He died in his bed at his villa at Aquae Cutiliae (near Citta Ducale) on 23 June 79, the first to do so without hint of foul play since Augustus 65 years before, quipping on his deathbed, 'I think I am becoming a God.' He was succeeded by his son Titus – rather than an adopted heir – the first such father-to-son succession ever, leaving aside the unfortunate Britannicus, and one of the few successful ones. Needless to say, he was subsequently deified by the senate.

VETRANIO
350, 1st March – (?)November

Vetranio was an usurper in the Balkans who stood against Magnentius and came to a bloodless accord with Constantius II. Vetranio was of peasant birth from Lower Moesia and apparently illiterate, despite having risen to high command as *magister peditum* in Illyria and having been *en poste* for a considerable time, being elderly when he was acclaimed at the very end of February 350 by the army at Sirmium (Sremska Mitrovica, Serbia). This was as a result of the news reaching the troops that Constans had been deposed and killed by Magnentius. His imperial style (from coins) was D[ominus] N[oster] Vetranio P[ius] F[elix] Aug[ustus], although on a single issue he is styled *nobilissimus caesar* only, suggesting an attempt to style himself as the official heir of Constantius II. Subsequently, he negotiated unsuccessfully with Magnentius for recognition, but when the army of Constantius II had approached Serdica (Sofia), the latter appealed, as a son of the great Constantine, to the usurper's army. Vetranio thereupon cast off his diadem, declared that he had only assumed power to stand against Magnentius and opened negotiations to end the stand-off. This resulted in his being allowed to abdicate and retire honourably, the Emperor realising that the old commander's acclamation had helped his own cause in tying up Magnentius whilst he disengaged himself from the east and moved to the Balkans. This probably occurred late in the year, perhaps November. After his abdication he retired to Prusa (Bursa, modern Turkey) and died in 357. Nothing is known of his full name or his family.

VICTOR
384 – 388, c. 1st August

Magnus Maximus named his young son Flavius Victor as co-augustus, probably in 384.[788] He adopted the style Dominus Noster Flavius Victor Invictus et Perpetuus Augustus.[789] After his father was captured and killed, Victor managed to escape but only for a few days, when he, too, despite his allegedly tender years, was hunted down by Arbogastes, taken and summarily dispatched.

VICTORIA
271, February/March

Victoria was the powerful mother of Gallic emperor Victorinus, who appears to have seized control following the murder of her son (and, allegedly, grandson) and minted two issues of coins in honour of her deified son before engineering the succession of Tetricus and retiring. She also features – looking strikingly youthful – on the reverse of one of her son's coin issues.[790] Her

---

788 PLRE I Victor 14. And see footnote 438.
789 ILS788; PRE I Maximus 39
790 *Tyr. Trig.* VI-VII

name is rendered Victorina and elsewhere Vitruvia in some sources; either the latter was her *nomen* and only used occasionally, or is just an error for Victori[in]a.

VICTORINUS (I)
269, June – 271, March

Victorinus seems to have been the right-hand man of Postumus and may indeed have been his intended successor. He probably started out as Postumus' Pretorian Prefect, but can be assumed to have moved on by 267, in which year he served as (Gallic empire) ordinary consul with Postumus.[791] The additional indication that he was probably not Pretorian Prefect in the later part of the reign was that if he had been, he would probably have been on the spot during the unfortunate events at Moguntiacum in March 269, when Postumus put down the rebellion of Laelianus but was himself deposed and killed by the usurper Marius after refusing to allow his troops to sack the city. Had Victorinus been there, he would undoubtedly have either been killed or his accession would have followed seamlessly without the intervention of either the usurper or his ephemeral nemesis. As it is, he held back and kept his powder dry. Two days after the assassination of Marius, he was acclaimed emperor at Trier.

His origin probably lay amongst the higher echelons of the Gallic nobility, and his full name, M. Piav[v]onius Victorinus suggests possible Celtic and certainly western provincial ancestry, especially the double 'v', rendered without fail on his coins, although not elsewhere, making his name well-nigh unique.[792] He styled himself officially Imperator Caesar M. Piavonius Victorinus Pius Felix Augustus. He served a second consulship in 271 and renewed his tribunician power twice after his accession.[793]

It was on Victorinus' watch that Claudius II's general Placidianus managed to re-assert control over most of Spain and some of Southern Gaul, causing the once great Gallic nation of the Aedui to go over to the new Emperor at Rome. Victorinus determined to put an end to this piece of insubordination and to bring the Aedui to heel, if only to prevent more Gaulish *civitates* from attempting to break away. This he achieved, although at the expense of a seven-month siege of the cantonal capital, Augustodunum Aeduorum (Autun), which was subsequently sacked and its more important inhabitants scattered into exile. The Emperor returned in triumph to Colonia Claudia Ara Agrippinensium (Cologne).

Beyond that, Victorinus' achievement was to consolidate what remained of his Empire, and in this he was successful. The Rhine frontier remained quiet and in the end his undoing was excess. He was apparently something of a philanderer, mainly targeting other officers' wives and, in the spring of 271, went too far with the spouse of an official called Attitianus who arranged

---

791 The year of the consulship could have been 266: Drinkwater (1987) 120
792 Drinkwater, *op. cit.*, 125-126
793 PLRE I Victorinus 12; the fictional child is *ibid.*, Victorinus 1a

his assassination. The *Historia Augusta's* suggestion that he had a son, also Victorinus (qv), whom he made *caesar*, is generally thought to be spurious.[794]

At this stage, the late Emperor's mother Victoria (or Vitruvia) took a hand. Whether Attitianus or anyone associated with him expected to be elevated to the purple we shall never know, for his mother acted with commendable speed and single-mindedness. She issued a generous donative to the army out of her own pocket, secured the deification of her son, resisted the temptation to emulate Zenobia and thus brought about the acclamation of the governor of Aquitania, Tetricus, who was almost certainly a close kinsman of his predecessor. It was the nearest the Gallic empire ever got to a dynasty.[795]

VICTORINUS (II)
271

Victorinus was allegedly the young son of Victorinus supposedly made *caesar* by his father on the day of his assassination and listed by the *Historia Augusta* as one of the author's Thirty Tyrants. His place amongst the usurpers of the empire is regarded by most scholars as entirely baseless.[796]

VINDEX
67, c. October – 68, March

C. Julius Vindex was an aristocratic Gallic rebel whose insurrection had supposedly been prompted by the conspiracy of Piso against Nero and which acted as the catalyst for the revolt of Galba and the fall of Nero the following year.

An Aquitanian, Vindex was adlected into the senate by Claudius, probably in his *lustrum* of 48. In late 67, he was pro-praetorian governor of Gallia Lugdunensis, although he had previously survived by a narrow margin in a conspiracy of 59, snuffed out with the demise of Nero's mother Agrippina. Dio described him as 'powerful in body and of shrewd intelligence ... skilled in warfare and full of daring for any great enterprise; and he had a passionate love of freedom and a vast ambition.'

He struck bronze coins with *libertas* on the obverse and SPQR on the reverse. Galba, having heard of Vindex's actions, astutely held back from interfering, allowing him to be dealt with by neighbouring provincial governor, L. Verginius Rufus, before declaring his own hand. Vindex, defeated in battle, committed suicide.[797]

VITELLIUS
69, 16th April – 20th December

---

794 *Tyr. Trig.* VII 1-2. He was put into make up the number thirty in the title.
795 Aur. Victor 33.14 cf. HA *Tyr. Trig.*. VI. 3, VII. 1-2 He may have been a son-in-law or nephew. Coin as deified: Sear, 11273
796 *Tyr. Trig.* VII
797 Dio 63, 22. 1-2

Vitellius was the venal senator who made an effective bid for supreme power in the Year of the Four Emperors against Otho, but whose lack of charisma and other shortcomings ensured that he was no match for his nemesis, Vespasian.

The origins of the third short-lived emperor of 69, who briefly held power in the hiatus between the reigns of Nero and Vespasian are rather similar to those of Otho: he was a member of a local family in Italy making good and sending a son to the senate. Suetonius, however, gives space to a tale from Elogius that Faunus, legendary King of Latium, married a demi-goddess called Vitelia and that their posterity later became regal patricians, one being the wife of L. Junius Brutus the regicide; to counteract this, he also points out stories of humbler – but equally suspect – origins. Yet in the case of the Vitellii, the founder of the dynasty from Nursia (Norcia) sent four, possibly even five, sons into the early first-century senate – quite an achievement. The marriage of this Emperor's daughter allowed his blood line to survive into the 3rd century.

Aulus Vitellius was born on 7 (or possibly 24) September AD14 and is credited by Suetonius with having been one of the youths Tiberius gathered around him on Capri in his declining years.[798] He thus acquired the unsavoury *cognomen* of Spintria (rent-boy), which rather set the tone for the rest of his career as a somewhat louche character, although had his accession to the principate been successful in the long term, the reportage of his life might have been rather different. Nevertheless, he managed to keep on the right side of Caligula, Claudius and Nero, which was something of an achievement, although one accomplished in the shadow of his powerful father, Lucius, a 'safe pair of hands' who served three consulships. He was consul in 48 (his brother Lucius succeeding him as suffect the same year) and governed Africa from 55 to 57 with every sign of probity and success. He walked with a limp acquired in a youthful chariot wreck whilst racing with Caligula. He was very tall, but his gluttony led to his becoming heavily paunched.

He married firstly his cousin Petronia, daughter of P. Petronius, the suffect consul of 19 by Plautia, daughter of A. Plautius, consul in 1AD.[799] They divorced in 62 having had a son who died in uncertain circumstances before the couple parted. In the same year, Vitellius re-married; his bride was Galeria Fundana, daughter of a man who had been praetor before 54 and who was probably called – if her daughter's name is anything to go by – Galerius Fundanus. Her grandfather was probably the Prefect of Egypt from 16 to 31, C. Galerius, who was married to the author Seneca's maternal aunt, Helvia.[800]

Vitellius was acclaimed on 2 January 69, a day after the army in Germany had refused to take the oath to Galba and acceded fully to the purple on the death of Otho on 16 April, following his victory in the first battle of

---

798 Suetonius gives both birth dates and the year but says he was 56 at his death, which would make the year 13: *Vitellius* 3

799 Tac. *Ann.* iii. 49.1; Levick (1999) 15; A. Plautius had married Vitellius' aunt; their son, Aulus, led the invasion of Britain in 43.

800 Griffin (1992) 453-454; Vitellius's new sister-in-law married C. Calpurnius Piso, the leader of the plot against Nero of 65: Griffin, *op. cit.* 96 & n. 2

Cremona. Not that the gluttonous, venal and unmilitary Vitellius was present; he remained in comfort in Gaul and stayed there until his two generals, A. Caecina Alienus and Fabius Valens, had captured Rome, before – fatally, as it turned out – slowly moving to the capital and enlivening the journey with unpalatable displays of triumphalism, drunkenness, venality and indiscipline, both amongst his forces and his entourage. They arrived to celebrate a totally inappropriate triumph in late June, although the transition of power went unexpectedly smoothly.

Vitellius' bid for supreme power was without doubt based on his own hyper-inflated view of his abilities, spiced with a dash of vanity. He had a link with the Julio-Claudian dynasty through his brother Lucius' second marriage to Junia Calvina, Augustus's great-great-granddaughter (being the offspring of M. Junius Silanus, consul in AD19, and Aemilia Lepida, daughter of the younger Julia and L. Aemilius Paullus). Although this link had by 69 been broken through divorce (Junia Calvina survived until very old, to AD79), it without doubt played a part in Vitellius's thinking. But even upon his arrival in Rome, Vitellius's hold on power was clearly becoming tenuous.

He persuaded the senate to ratify his succession, to grant him the tribunician and proconsular power and bestowed upon him the office of *pontifex maximus*, along with four major priesthoods that went with it in all legitimised successions. He took the style of A. Vitellius Germanicus Imperator Augustus, tactfully eschewing the name Caesar, which reflects creditably on him, suggesting a diplomatic element of modesty his biographers entirely fail to mention. On the other hand, he had not earned the 'Germanicus' by successfully campaigning against the Germans; he had merely been a rather reactive governor there.

Meanwhile, on 1 July, Vespasian, fresh from the Jewish revolt, was unexpectedly acclaimed emperor in Judaea and within a week or two Vitellius was made aware of this. Yet before Vespasian's friend and supporter C. Licinius Mucianus could really start out to the west to face Vitellius down, Antonius Primus, a legionary commander in Pannonia – much closer to Italy – and Fuscus, the powerful procurator of neighbouring Illyricum, had also declared for Vespasian and had already started for the Po.

Vitellius found himself defending more or less the same ground as had Otho that April and, on 24-25 October was soundly defeated at the second battle of Cremona, which was followed by an appalling four-day sack of the city. He made a less than effective strategic withdrawal southward and part of his army, sent against the Flavians at Narnia (Narni) on 17 December, went over to the enemy. The game was up. Vitellius retreated to Rome, which fell on the 20th. He was killed on the same day, having fled to his mother's house whence he was eventually flushed out and crudely butchered. Only his mother, widow and daughter survived the carnage. The daughter Vitellia Galeria Fundana married the senatorial grandee Libo Rupilius Frugi and was thus the distaff grandmother of Antoninus Pius and great-grandmother of Marcus Aurelius.[801]

---

801 On Libo Rupilius Frugi ('Rupilius Bonus' in HA *V. Marci* I.4): Birley (1987) 244

VOLUSIANUS
November 251 – August 253

Volusianus was the son of the Emperor Gallus, raised to the purple to replace Hostilianus, who had died of the plague in November 251.

C. Vibius C. f. Afinius Gallus Veldumnianus L. Volusianus was at the time of his elevation probably an adult and possibly already a senator. As Emperor, he was styled Imperator Caesar C. Vibius Afinius Gallus Veldumnianus Volusianus Pius Felix Augustus and was given the supreme pontificate jointly with his father and all the other usual powers.[802] He held the consulship in 252 and again in 253, but he was killed with his father by elements of their troops at Interamna Nahars (Terni), en route to try and suppress the revolt of Aemilianus (qv).

ZENO
474, 9th February – 481, 9th April

Zeno was a politically adroit eastern ruler from a somewhat untamed part of the empire, whose regime was much beset by usurpers, mainly encouraged by his predecessor's widow, by the problem of the collapse of imperial authority in the west and by the problem of the Monophysite heresy.

The successor to emperor Leo I was an Isaurian, one of a people long within the Empire and since 212 Roman citizens, dwelling in the mountainous interior of southern Asia Minor and noted for their savagery and turbulence. They had first been subdued by Sulla's ally, P. Servilius Vatia (consul 79BC) in 76-75 who, being acclaimed *imperator*, was accorded the honorary *agnomen* Isauricus and celebrated a triumph for their suppression in 74.

Originally called Aricmesius Tarasicodissa, Zeno was born in 425 at an unlocated place called Rhusumblada, but we only know the name of his mother, Lallis. Neither is his early career at all clear but it was probably military, and in 466 he was sent to Constantinople on a delicate diplomatic errand and remained in the capital, having been rewarded with a senior commission in the guards as *comes domesticorum*. He changed his name because he realised that it would aid his career and probably also because the patrician Zeno was an Isaurian and was then greatly respected.[803]

Zeno was by this time married to Arcadia, mother of his son, also Zeno, and possibly of two daughters, Hilaria and Theopiste. He had an illegitimate son (whose name is not known) who married and had a daughter (again anonymous) who, some time after 474 (chronology would suggest c. 477/478 at the earliest), married Hermineric, the youngest son of the patrician Aspar and a very youthful consul in 465; they lived in exile in Isauria until they returned to Constantinople from 491.

Inevitably, after his appointment a number of Isaurians were attracted to Constantinople and formed the core of the reconstituted armed forces

---

802 ILS 522

803 That they were father and son or even closely related is doubted: cf. Crawford (2019) 29-30

initiated by Leo I. Zeno's wife had presumably died by this time and he married the Emperor's daughter Ariadne in 467. He was shortly afterwards appointed *magister militum* for Thrace and held a consulship the following year (469), before the end of which he was to command the whole army of the Eastern Empire. He may have been behind the murder of Aspar in 471, although if so, he saved the life of his future grandson-in-law, the patrician's youngest son, Hermineric. He was made patrician and in 473 appointed commander-in-chief at court. On the death of Leo, his six-year-old son, who succeeded as Leo II, supposedly proclaimed Zeno emperor on 9 February 474, probably with the connivance of his mother.

The new Emperor adopted the style of Dominus Noster Flavius Zeno Perpetuus Augustus, and he held a second consulship in 475, adding one more consulship in 479. In 475, he encouraged the eminent senator Severus to negotiate a highly advantageous peace treaty with the Vandals, almost concurrent with that negotiated by Orestes from the western court. Elevated to the rank of patrician to lend *gravitas* to his mission, Severus secured the return of large numbers of Roman captives and arranged freedom of worship for orthodox Christians in Arian Carthage.

The first crisis arose through the Empress Verina having taken a lover, Patricius (not Aspar's son of that name but a senator who had been *magister officiorum* under Leo I), whom she intended to marry and raise to the purple once she removed her son-in-law. As the Isaurians had turned out to have been less than a blessing in the capital – reverting to type on frequent occasions – their unpopularity had rubbed off on the emperor. The dowager Empress therefore colluded with her brother Basiliscus to depose him, which she did by persuading Zeno to escape to Isauria with his family by a crude stratagem on 9 January 476. However, Basiliscus, aided by Zeno's friend, the *magister officiorum* and patrrican Illus (qv), seized control of the situation, and made himself emperor whilst having the sense to have Verina's admirer Patricius liquidated. However, due to the sheer incompetence and lack of authority of the usurper, most of his supporters gradually switched their allegiance back to Zeno, who was restored in August 477.

Zeno pardoned his mother-in-law (unwisely) and eventually banished her to Isauria. A period of calm and reconstruction followed, during which the Emperor declined to assist Nepos in regaining possession of Italy (and the rather sleight-of-hand recognition of Odoacer as patrician there). Then, in 479, another usurper in the shape of Anthemius' son Marcian II seized power and Zeno was only saved by a last-minute intervention by the patrician Illus, who drove the claimant and two of his brothers out of the City. They renewed their bid once safe in Asia Minor but were ultimately unsuccessful. At this stage, Nepos was assassinated and Zeno became ruler of a united Empire, albeit with little direct control over the west. Yet his ability to impose his authority was still being constantly challenged, not only by his distantly exiled mother-in-law but by his own wife, who was behind an attempt to kill Illus in 482. Illus suspected the Emperor was also behind the plot and fled east to join forces with the man sent to dispose him, the patrician Leontius (qv), the latter ironically ending up as an usurper himself at Antioch before being driven out by an expeditionary force of Goths led by Iohannes and Theodericus, the latter a future King of Italy. Despite this, they managed to hole up in Isauria, which became thenceforth for a while a breakaway mini-empire for four years before being crushed in 488, the dowager Empress included in the general slaughter.

According to the historian of the Goths, Jordanes, when the ruler of Italy Odoacer was threatened by the advance of the Ostrogoths under Theoderic in 487, Zeno wrote commending the newcomer to the (western) senate and Roman people.[804] The idea was that Theoderic, as *magister militum*, should rule Italy in place of Zeno until such time as the Emperor could arrive and re-establish full imperial authority in the west. In the event, Zeno died before the operation was complete and before his successor's authority was properly established, Theoderic had dug in. Nevertheless, at the time it was understood that there was one Empire, of which Theoderic's kingdom was a part.[805]

A final running sore which affected the reign was the Monophysite heresy and the Emperor's inconclusive attempts to find a compromise which would avoid the fragmentation of Christendom. He died with the matter unresolved after a period of waning faculties, on 9 April 491, leaving the succession to be decided by his widow.

ZENOBIA
271, August – 272, August

Zenobia was apparently the daughter of a Palmyrene magnate called Septimius Antiochus and claimed descent from the Kings of Syria, Mark Antony and Cleopatra VII of Egypt.[806] She assumed power in the east on the death of her husband Odenathus, rather as Victoria had done for Tetricus, the difference being that whilst Tetricus was an adult, her son Vaballathus was only a child of about 10 or 11. She therefore had to secure the succession and act as regent for the boy. Until 270, she made no claim to imperial power, either for herself or for her son, and in that she differed from previous would-be usurpers in the east, like Antoninus (IV) and the Gallic emperors, in not attempting an independent polity. Thus, matters proceeded smoothly and thereby allowed first Gallienus and thereafter Claudius II to deal with problems elsewhere without having to worry about the stability of the east.

In 270, however, there was a change. For some reason, probably related to the security of her core dominions, Zenobia extended her control to encompass Arabia, southern Asia Minor and Egypt itself. Early in 272 (or possibly any time after later summer 271)[807] she finally assumed the style of a Roman ruler, styling herself Septimia Zenobia Aug[usta] and simultaneously elevated her son to the purple as well. In May 272, Aurelian managed to recover Egypt.

---

804 Moorhead (1992) 249

805 Barnwell (1992) 137

806 PLRE I. Zenobia 1. HA provides her with younger sons, Herennius and Timolaus, the former, inevitably, said to have been styled Augustus; *op. cit.*, 15, *passim*

807 See the discussion of the matter in Southern (2008) 119-120

Zenobia in chains by Harriet Goodhue Hosmur, c. 1859. (Courtesy Saint Louis Art Museum, public domain)

A month earlier he had prepared an expeditionary force to re-take the rest of the east, starting at Byzantium (Constantinople) and going on towards Palmyra via southern Asia Minor, where he paused briefly to invest Tyana (near Kemerhisar, Turkey); otherwise, he met with little resistance until he reached Syria, where he was obliged to join battle with the forces of Zenobia near Antioch at Immae (Reyhanli, Turkey), at Daphne (Antioch, Syria) and at Emesa (Homs, Syria). Zenobia was not a weak opponent, although Aurelian spared most defeated cities and captured soldiery, thereby making it easier for backsliders to desert the Empress. Thus, when the final confrontation took place at Palmyra itself, the Emperor's clemency facilitated the capitulation of the city once Zenobia had fled east and been captured, presumably with Vaballathus.

After her defeat, Zenobia was brought to Rome, paraded in Aurelian's triumph and then allowed to retire with honour, allegedly marrying again (to an unnamed Senator) and living to a considerable age.[808] The claim by Zosimus that she died on the way from Palmyra to Rome may be discounted.[809]

---

808 She was probably only in her early 30s when captured.
809 Zonaras, *loc. cit.*, supported by St Jerome; Zosimus 1, 59

Appendix I

Chronological List of Entries in the Dictionary

Emperors serving between 395 and 476 are suffixed E for specifically Eastern Empire rulers and W for specifically western rulers. Regnal years separated by dashes indicate an unbroken period in power between two certain dates; those separated by a slash indicate the rule took place at an unknown date within that period. A date preceded by a question mark indicates some uncertainty regarding the precise date concerning the person's regime. Usurpers (italicised) and uncanonical entries are indented.

JULIUS CAESAR (48-44BC)
[*Republic: Second Triumvirate*
43-32
32-30 M. Antonius, E & Octavian, W
30-27 Octavian/Augustus]
AUGUSTUS (27BC-14)
  AGRIPPA POSTUMUS (14)
TIBERIUS I (14-37)
  GEMELLUS (37)
CALIGULA (37-41)
  GAETULICUS (39)
  CAMILLUS I (41)
CLAUDIUS I (41-54)
  BRITANNICUS (54-55)
NERO (54-68)
  VINDEX (67-68)
  MACER (68)
GALBA (68-69)
  SABINUS (68)
PISO I (69)
OTHO (69)
VITELLIUS (69)
  CIVILIS (69-70)
VESPASIAN (69-79)

TITUS (79-81)
  TERENTIUS MAXIMUS (?80)
DOMITIAN I (81-96)
  SATURNINUS I (89)
NERVA (96-98)
TRAJAN (98-117)
HADRIAN (117-138)
ANTONINUS (I) PIUS (138-161)
  TITIANUS (145)
LUCIUS VERUS (161-168)
MARCUS (I) AURELIUS (161-180)
  AVIDIUS CASSIUS (175)
COMMODUS (180-192)
  PRISCUS I (185)
PERTINAX (193)
DIDIUS JULIANUS (193)
  PESCENNIUS NIGER (193-194)
SEPTIMIUS SEVERUS (193-211)
CLODIUS ALBINUS (195-197)
CARACALLA (198-217)
GETA (210-211)
MACRINUS (217-218)
DIADUMENIANUS (218)
  MAXIMUS I (218-219)

VERUS II (218-219)
ELAGABALUS (218-222)
SEVERUS ALEXANDER (222-235)
   CAMILLUS II (?230)
   TAURINUS (231)
   URANIUS (?231)
MAXIMIN I THRAX (235-238)
   MAGNUS (235)
   QUARTINUS (235/236)
GORDIAN I (238)
GORDIAN II (238)
PUPIENUS MAXIMUS (238)
BALBINUS (238)
GORDIAN III (238-244)
   SABINIANUS (240)
PHILIP I THE ARAB (244-249)
PHILIP II (247-249)
   PACATIANUS (248)
   IOTAPIANUS (248-249)
   SILBANNACUS (?248)
   SPONSIANUS (?248/?260)
   MARCUS II (?249)
   SEVERUS HOSTILIANUS (?249)
DECIUS (249-251)
ETRUSCUS (251)
HOSTILIANUS (251)
   VALENS I (251)
TREBONIANUS GALLUS
  (251-253)
VOLUSIANUS (251-253)
AEMILIAN I (253)
VALERIAN (253-260)
   CYRIADES (253)
   URANIUS ANTONINUS
   (253-254)
GALLIENUS I (253-268)
   INGENUUS (258-259)
   PRISCUS II (259)
   REGALIANUS (260-261)
   ANTONINUS V (260/262)
GALLIENUS II (260)
   SALONINUS (260)
   MACRIANUS I (260-261)
   MACRIANUS II (261)
   QUIETUS (260-261)
   GENIALIS (260)
   BALLISTA (260)

PISO II (260)
SATURNINUS II (260/268)
TREBELLIANUS (260/268)
POSTUMUS I (260-269)
   VALENS II (261-262)
   CELSUS (260/268)
   AEMILIAN II (261-262)
   MEMOR (262)
   ODAENATHUS (266-267)
   HERENNIANUS I (267)
   HERODES/HERODIANUS (267)
   MAEONIUS (267)
   TIMOLAUS (267)
   AUREOLUS (267-268)
CLAUDIUS II GOTHICUS
  (268-270)
   POSTUMUS II (?269)
   CENSORINUS (?269)
   LAELIANUS (269)
   MARIUS (269)
VICTORINUS I (269-271)
QUINTILLUS (270)
AURELIAN (270-275)
   URBANUS (?271)
   SEPTIMIUS (271)
   DOMITIAN II (271)
   ZENOBIA (271-272)
   VABALLATHUS (271-272)
   VICTORINUS II (271)
   VICTORIA (271)
TETRICUS (271-274)
   FIRMUS I (272)
   ANTIOCHUS (273)
   FAUSTINUS (274)
TACITUS (275-276)
FLORIANUS (276)
PROBUS (276-282)
   HERENNIANUS II (280)
   SATURNINUS III (280-281)
   BONOSUS (280)
   PROCULUS (280)
CARUS (282-283)
CARINUS (282-285)
   NIGRINIANUS I (?282/284)
NUMERIANUS (283-284)
   JULIAN II (283-285)
   JULIAN III (284)

DIOCLETIAN (284-305)
CARAUSIUS I (285-293)
MAXIMIAN (286-305, 308, 310) W
AMANDUS (286)
ALLECTUS (293-296)
DOMITIAN III (296-297)
ACHILLEUS (297 – 298)
EUGENIUS I (303)
GALERIUS (305-311) E
CONSTANTIUS I CHLORUS (305-306) W
CONSTANTINE I (306-337)
SEVERUS II (306-307) W
MAXENTIUS (306-312) W
LICINIUS I (308-324) E
ALEXANDER (308-310)
MAXIMIN II DAIA (310-313) E
VALENS III (316-317) E
LICINIUS II (317-324) E
MARTINIANUS (324) E
CALOCAERUS (334)
DALMATIUS (337)
HANNIBALIANUS (337)
CONSTANTINE II (337-340) W
CONSTANS I (337-350) W
CONSTANTIUS II (337-361)
MAGNENTIUS (350-353)
VETRANIO (350) W
NEPOTIANUS (350)
NIGRINIANUS II (350)
DECENTIUS (353)
POEMENIUS (353)
CARAUSIUS II (354/358)
GENCERIS (354/358)
SILVANUS (355)
JULIAN IV THE APOSTATE (360-363)
SALUTIUS (363 & 364)
JOVIAN (363-364)
VALENTINIAN I (364-375) W
VALENS IV (364-378) E
PROCOPIUS (365-366) E
MARCELLUS I (366) E
GRATIAN I (367-383) W
VALENTINUS (368) W
FIRMUS II (372/3-375) W

VALENTINIAN II (375-387, 388-392) W
THEODOSIUS I (379-395)
SERVATUS (?378/379)
MAGNUS MAXIMUS (380/383-388) W
ARCADIUS (383-408) E
VICTOR (384-388) W
EUGENIUS II (392-394) W
HONORIUS (393-423) W
THEODOSIUS II (402-450) E
MARCUS III (406-?407) W
GRATIAN II (407) W
CONSTANTINE III (407-411) W
ATTALUS (408-410 & 414-415) W
MAXIMUS (IV) (409-411 & 419-421) W
CONSTANS II (410-411) W
JOVINUS (411-413)
SEBASTIANUS (412-413) W
HERACLIANUS (412-413) W
CONSTANTIUS III (421) W
IOHANNES I (423-425) W
VALENTINIAN III (425-455) W
MARCIAN I (450-457) E
PETRONIUS MAXIMUS (455) W
AVITUS (455-456) W
MARCELLUS II (457)
MAJORIAN (457-461) W
LEO I (457-474) E
LIBIUS SEVERUS III (461-465)
AEGIDIUS (461-465) W
SYAGRIUS (465-486) W
ANTHEMIUS (467-472) W
ROMANUS I (470) W
OLYBRIUS (472) W
LEO II (473-474) E
GLYCERIUS (473-474) W
JULIUS NEPOS (473-480) W
ZENO (474-481) E
ROMULUS AUGUSTUS (475-476) W
BASILISCUS I (476-477) E
MARCUS IV (476-477) E
BASILISCUS (II) *LEO* (477-478) E
MASTIES (?477-516) W
MARCIAN II (479, 480, 484)

OVIDA (480-482) W
ILLUS (484-488) E
LEONTIUS I (484-488) E
ANASTASIUS I (491-518)
    BURDUNELLUS (496) W
    PETRUS (506) W
    THEODERIC (508/511) W
JUSTIN I (518-527)
    STOTZAS I (536, 541-545)
    STOTZAS II (545-546)

JUSTINIAN I (537-565)
    HYPATIUS (532)
    MAXIMIN III (539)
    GUNTHARIS (545-546)
JUSTIN II (565-578)
TIBERIUS II (578-582)
MAURICE TIBERIUS (582-602)
THEODOSIUS III (590-602)
    GERMANUS (602)

Appendix II

Abbreviations of Names

Roman Praenomina

A.	= Aulus	N.	= Numerius
Ap.	= Appius	P.	= Publius
C.	= Caius	Q.	= Quintus
Cn.	= Gnaeus	Ser.	= Servius
D.	= Decimus	Sex.	= Sextus
K.	= Kaeso (archaic)	Sp.	= Spurius
L.	= Lucius	T.	= Titus
M.	= Marcus	Ti.	= Tiberius
M'.	= Manius	V.	= Vibius (archaic)

From 212, the system of using three names (*tria nomina*), of which the first was (usually) drawn from the list above, began to break down, and by the earlier part of the fourth century it was mainly only the senatorial aristocracy who still used them, although the conventions behind the *tria nomina* had by then also become largely ignored.

Bibliography

Abbreviations used to identify some works in the footnotes are provided at the end of the relevant entry.

1. Ancient Sources

Anon., *Scriptores Historiae Augustae,* 3 Vols., Trans. Magie, D. (Harvard & London 1954/1960)   [HA]

Anonymous Valesianus, Pts I & II (Loeb, 1939)

Aurelius Victor, Sex., *De Caesaribus* trans. Bird, H. W. (Liverpool 1994)

Avitus of Vienne, *Letters,* ed. & trans. Shanzer, D & Wood, I. (Liverpool 2002)

Caesar, C. Julius, *The Civil War,* Trans. Mitchell, J. F., (London 1967)   [Caes. *BC*]

Cassiodorus Senator, Magnus Aurelius, ed. & trans. Bjornlie, M. S. *Epistolae Variae* (Oakland, California 2019)

Dio Cocceianus, M. Cassius, *Roman History,* 9 Vols., Trans. Cary, E., *et al* (Harvard & London 2000)   [Dio]

Eusebius, *History of the Church,* Trans. Williamson G. A. (London 1965)

Eusebius, *Vita Constantini,* Trans. Cameron, A & Hall, S. G. (Oxford 1999)

Eutropius, *Breviarum ab Urbe Condita,* trans. Bird, H. W. (Liverpool 1993)

Evagrius, *Ecclesiastical History* (Amsterdam 1964)

Gregory of Tours, *History of the Franks* Trans, Thorpe, Lewis (London 1976)   [Greg. HF]

Herodian, *History of the Empire,* Trans. Whittaker, C. R., 2 Vols. (Harvard & London 1969)

Inscriptions:

Corpus Inscriptionem Latinarum, ed. Mommsen, T. *et al,* (Berlin, from 1863)   [CIL]

Inscriptiones Latinae Selectae, ed. H. Dessau 5 Vols. (Chicago 1979-80)   [ILS]

Remains of Old Latin: Vol. IV Archaic Inscriptions, ed. E. H. Warmington (London & Cambridge, Mass. 1967)   [CIL I²]

Josephus, Flavius, *Antiquitates Judicae* Trans., Whiston, W. (Ware 2006)   [Jos. *AJ*]

Josephus, Flavius, *The Jewish War,* Trans. Thackeray, H. St. J., 3 Vols. (Harvard & London, 1997-2001)   [Jos. *BJ*]

Juvenalis, [Ju]nius, *Satires,* Trans. Green, P. (London 1967)   [Juv. *Sat.*]

Plinius Caecilius Secundus, C., *Letters* Trans. Radice, B. (London 1963)   [Plin. *Ep.*]

Plinius Secundus, C., *Natural History* 10 Vols. (Loeb, Harvard)   [Plin. *NH.*]

Plutarchus, L. Mestrius, *Parallel Lives* 6th edn., 6 Vols., Trans. Langhorne, J & W. (London 1795)   [Plut.]

Procopius, *De Bello Vandalico* Trans. H. B. Dewing (London 1916)   [Proc. *BV*]

Procopius, *The History of the Wars,* 5 Vols. Trans. H. B. Dewing (Harvard & London, 1928)   [Proc. *HB*]

Procopius, *The Secret History* Trans. G. A. Williamson (London 1980)   [Proc. *SH*]

Pseudo-Dionysius of Tel-Mehre, *Chronicle Part III* Trans. Witakowski, W. (Liverpool 1996)

Ruricius of Limoges *et aliis, Ruricius of Limoges and Friends: A Collection of Letters from Visigothic Gaul,* Trans. Mathisen, R. W. (Liverpool, 1999)

Sozomenus, Salminius Hermias, *Ecclesiastical History* (New York 1890)

Suetonius Tranquillus, C., *Duodecimi Caesares* Trans. Graves, R. (London 1957)   [Suet. + *name*]

Tacitus, Cornelius, *Annals of Imperial Rome* Trans. Grant, M. (London 1966)   [Tac. *Ann.*]

Tacitus, Cornelius, *The Histories,* Trans. Wellesley, K. (London 1964)   [Tac. *Hist.*]

Valerius Maximus, *Memorable Doings & Sayings* 2 vols., Trans. Shackleton-Bailey, D. R. (Harvard & London, 2001)   [Val Max.]

Velleius Paterculus *Historiarum Libri Duo,* ed. W. S. Watt, 2nd edn. (Stuttgart 1978)

Zonaras, J., Trans. & ed. Bandich, T. M. & Lane, E. N., *Prologue and History from 222-395* (Abingdon 2009)

Zosimus. *Historia Nova,* Trans. Buchanan, J. & Davis, J. (San Antonio, 1967)

2. Secondary sources

Arnheim, M. T. W., *The Senatorial Aristocracy in the Later Roman Empire* (Oxford 1972)

Arnold, J. J., *Theoderic and the Roman Imperial Restoration* (Cambridge 2018)

Bagnall, R. S., Cameron, A., Schwartz, S. R., & Worp, K. A., *Consuls of the Later Roman Empire* (Atlanta, 1987)

Barbieri, G., *L'Albo senatorio da Settimio Severo a Carino, 193-285* (Rome, 1952)

Barnes , T. D., *Some Persons in the Historia Augusta* in *Phoenix* 26 (1972) 140-182

Barnes, T. D., *The Sources of the Historia Augusta* (Brussels 1978)

Barnish, P. J., *Transformation and Survival in the Western Aristocracy c AD400-700* in *Proceedings of the British School at Rome* LVI (1988) 120-155

Barnwell, P. S., *Emperor, Prefects and Kings: The Roman West, 395-565* (London 1992)

Birley, A. R., *Two Names in the Historia Augusta* in *Historia* 15 (1966) 249f.

Birley, A. R., *The Fasti of Roman Britain* (Oxford, 1981)

Bowersock, G W., *Roman Arabia* (Cambridge, Mass. 1983)

Breed, B. W., Damon, C. & Rossi, A. (eds.), *Citizens of Discord: Rome and its Civil Wars* (Oxford 2010)

Brown, T. S., *Gentlemen and Officers: Imperial Administration & Aristocratic Power in Byzantine Italy* (Rome 1984)

Burgess, R. W., *Chronicles, Consuls and Coins: Historiography and History in the Later Roman Empire* (Farnham 2011)

Burnett, A., *The Coinage of Allectus* in *British Numismatic Journal* LIV (1984) 21-40

Cameron, A., *Gratian's Repudiation of the Pontifical Robe* in JRS (Journal of Roman Studies) LVIII (1968) 97

Cameron, A., (ed.), *Fifty Years of Prosopography: The Later Roman Empire, Byzantium and Beyond* (Oxford, 2003)

Cancik, H. & Schneider, H., (eds.), *Der Neue Pauly: Enzyklopädie der Antike,* Vol. 11 (Stuttgart 2001)   [DNP]

Carroll, M., *Romans Celts & Germans: The German Provinces of Rome* (Stroud 2001)

Chausson, F., & Wolff, É., *Consuetudinis Amor: Fragments d'Histoire Romaine (IIe-VIe siècles) Offerts à Jean-Pierre Callu.* In *Saggi di Storia Antica, 19* (Rome 2003)

Collins, R., *The Arab Conquest of Spain* (Oxford 1989)

Collins, R., *Visigothic Spain* (Oxford 2004)

Conant, J., *Staying Roman: Conquest and Identity in Africa and the Mediterranean, 439–700* (Cambridge 2012)

Craven, M. A. J. B., *The Imperial Families of Ancient Rome* (Stroud 2020)

Dessau, H., Stein, A., Groag, E., *et. al., Prosopographia Imperii Romani* 2nd Edn (Berlin, from 1933-2006)   [PIR^2]

Di Giuseppe, H., *I Bruttii Praesentes, Proprietari e Produttori in Val D'Agri,* in Russo, A., *et al., Dalla villa dei Bruttii Praesentes alla Proprietà Imperiale. Il Complesso Archeologico di Marsicovetere* Siris 8 (2007) 105-114

Drinkwater, J. F., *The Gallic Empire; Separatism and Continuity in the North Western Provinces of the Roman Empire AD260-274* (Stuttgart 1987)

Drinkwater, J. F. & Elton, H. (eds.) *Fifth-Century Gaul: A Crisis of Identity?* (Cambridge 1992)

Drinkwater, J. F., *The Alemanni and Rome 213-496: Caracalla to Clovis* (Oxford 2007)

Eherenberg, V. & Jones, A. H. M., *Documents Illustrating the Reigns of Augustus & Tiberius,* 2nd edn (Oxford 1955)

Elton, H., *Defence in Fifth Century Gaul* in Drinkwater & Elton (qv, Cambridge 1992).

Fanning, S., *Emperors and Empires in Fifth Century Gaul,* in Drinkwater & Elton (qv, Cambridge 1992).

Fauber, L. H., *Narses, Hammer of the Goths* (Gloucester 1990)

Fink, R. O., *Lucius Seius Caesar, 'socer Augusti'* in *American Journal of Philology* LX (1939) 329

Gelzer, M. (ed. & trans. Seager, R.), *The Roman Nobility* (Oxford, 1969)

Grainger, J. D., *The Roman Imperial Succession* (Barnsley, 2020)

Grant, M., *The Roman Emperors* (London 1985)

Grant, M., *The Climax of Rome* (London 1993)

Griffin, M. T, *Seneca: A Philosopher in Politics* (Oxford 1976)

Haarer, F. K. (ed.), *AD 410: The History and Archaeology of Late and Post-Roman Britain* (London 2014)

Haegemans, K., *Imperial Authority and Dissent: The Roman Empire in AD235-238* (Leuven 2010)

Haldon, J. F., *Byzantium in the Seventh Century* (Cambridge 1990)

Haldon, J. F., *The Fate of the late Roman Senatorial Elite: Extinction or Transformation* in *The Byzantine & Early Islamic Near East,* Vol. VI (ed. Haldon, J. & Conrad, L. I. (Princeton 2004)

Handley, M. A., *Death, Society and Culture: Inscriptions and Epitaphs in Gaul and Spain,* BAR International 1135 (Oxford 2003)

Harries, J., *Sidonius Apollinaris and the Fall of Rome AD407-485* (Oxford 1994)

Heather, P., *The Fall of the Roman Empire: A New History* (London 2005)

Hekster, O., *Emperors and Ancestors: Roman Rulers and the Constraints of Tradition* (Oxford 2015)

James, E., *The Franks* (Oxford 1988)

Jaques, F., *L'ordine Senatorio Attraverso la Crisi del III Secolo* , in *Societa Romana e Impero Tardo-antico* , ed. Giardina, A. (Rome 1986) pp.81-225 & 650-664

Jones, A. H. M., *The Later Roman Empire: A Social and Economic Survey* 3 Vols. (Oxford 1964).

Jones, A. H. M., Martindale, J R & Morris, J., *Prosopography of the Later Roman Empire,* 3 vols in 4 (Cambridge, 1971, 1980, 1992)   [PLRE]

Jones, B. & Mattingly, D., *An Atlas of Roman Britain* (London 1990)

Kaldellis, A., *The Byzantine Republic: People and Power in New Rome* (Cambridge, Mass. 2015)

Kennedy, D., *C. Velius Rufus* in *Britannia* XIV (1983) 183-196

Kent, J. P. C., *The Revolt of Trier against Magnentius* in *Numismatic Chronicle* 9 (1959) 105-108

Kiilerich, B., *Visual Dynamics: Reflections on Late Antique Images* (Bergen 2015)

Kirk, M, with Kelley, D. H., Mommaerts, T. S. & Stone, D. *Reply to note by Settipani, C.,* (New Jersey 2001)

Knight, J. K., *The End of Antiquity: Archaeology, Society and Religion AD 235-700* (Stroud 2007)

Kulikowski, M., *The Career of the Comes Hispaniarum Asterius* in *Phoenix* 54 (2000) 123ff.

Lancon, B., *Rome in Late Antiquity* Trans. Antonia Nevill (Edinburgh 2000)

Livermore, H. V., *The Origins of Spain and Portugal* (London 1971)

Llewellyn, P., *Rome in the Dark Ages* (London 1993)

MacKenzie, A., *Archaeology in Roumania: The Mystery of the Roman Occupation* (London, 1986)

Mabbott, T. O., *A Newly Found Coin of Bonosus* in *The Numismatist* LXVIII (Oct. 1955)

Mathisen, R. W., *Roman Aristocracies in Barbarian Gaul: Strategies for Survival in an Age of Transition* (Austin, Texas, 1993)

Mathisen, R. W. & Shanzer, D., *Society and Culture in Late Roman Gaul: Revisiting the Sources* (Aldershot 2001) .

Matthews, J., *Continuity in a Roman Family: The Rufii Festi of Volsinii* in *Historia* 16 (1967) 484-509

Matthews, J., *Western Aristocracies and the Imperial Court* (Oxford, 1975)

Mattingly H. & Sydenham, E. A., et al., *Roman Imperial Coinage* 10 vols. in 11 (London 1923-1933, reprinted 1965-1994)   [RIC]

McEvoy, M. A., *Child Emperor Rule in the late Roman West AD367-455* (Oxford 2013)

McGeorge, P., *Late Roman Warlords* (Oxford 2002)

Mennen, I., *Power and Status in the Roman Empire AD193-294* (Leiden & Boston 2011)

Millar, F., *Paul of Samosata, Zenobia and Aurelian* in JRS LXI (1971) 16ff.

Moorhead, J., *Theoderic in Italy* (Oxford 1992)

Münzer, F., *Roman Aristocratic Parties and Families* (new and rev. edn, trans. Ridley, T. (Baltimore 1999)

Musset, L., *The Germanic Invasions: The Making of Europe 400-600AD* (New York 1965)

Norwich, Viscount, *Byzantium: The Early Centuries* (London 1989)

Novak, D., *Anicianae Domus Culmen Nobilitatis Culmen* in *Clio* 62 (1980) 473-494

Patterson, J. R., *The City of Rome Revisited: from Mid-Republic to Mid-Empire* in *JRS* C (2010) 210-232.

Pettinger, A., *The Republic in Danger* (Oxford 2012)

Pflaum, H. G., *Deux Familles Sénatoriales des IIe et IIIe Siècles* in *Journal des Savants I* (1962) 106-121

Potter, D. S., *The Roman Empire at Bay AD180-395* (London 2004)

Rohl, D. M., *The Lords of Avaris* (London 2007)

Roller, D. W., *The World of Juba II & Kleopatra Selene: Royal Scholarship on Rome's African Frontier* (London 2003)

Rufino, A. C., *Los Senadores Hispanorromanos y la Romanización de Hispania*, 2 Vols (Seville 1990)

Rüpke, J. & Glock, A., Trans. Richardson, D. M. B., *Fasti Sacerdotum* (Oxford 2008)   [FS]

Salway, B., *What's in a Name? A Survey of Roman Onomastic Practice from c 700BC to AD700* in JRS LXXXIV (1994) 124-145

Salzman, M. R., *The Falls of Rome* (Cambridge 2021)

Scott, R., *Byzantine Chronicles & the Sixth Century* (Farnham 2012)

Seaby, H. A. *et al.*, *Roman Silver Coins, Arranged According to Cohen*, 5 Vols (London 1952-1978)

Settipani, C., *Continuité Gentilice et Continuité Senatoriale dans les Familles Senatoriales Romaines a L'époque Imperiale: Mythe et Réalité*, 2 Vols, Vol. II (Oxford 2000)

Sherwin-White, A. N., *The Roman Citizenship* (Oxford 1973)

Shiel, N., *Carausius et Fratres Sui* in *British Numismatical Journal* XLVIII (1978) 7-11

Stech, B., *Senatores Romani qui Fuerint inde a Vespasiano usque ad Traiani Exitum* in *Klio* X (1912)

Swift, E., *The End of the Western Roman Empire: An Archaeological Investigation* (Stroud 2000)

Syme, Sir R., *The Roman Revolution* (Oxford 1939)   [RR]

_____ *Personal Names in Annals I-VI* in JRS XXXIX (1949) 9

_____ *Marcus Lepidus: Capax Imperii* in JRS XLV (1955) 22-33

_____ *Antonine Relatives: Ceionii and Vettuleni* in Athenaeum 33 (1957) 306-315

_____ *Tacitus* 2 Vols (Oxford 1958)

_____ *Ammianus and the Historia Augusta* (Oxford, 1968)

_____ *Ten Studies in Tacitus* (Oxford 1970)

_____ *Domitius Corbulo* in JRS LX (1970) 34-39

_____ *Emperors and Biography: Studies in the Historia Augusta* (Oxford 1971)

_____ *The Crisis of 2BC* (Munich 1974)

_____ *Roman Papers, III*, Ed. Birley, A. R. (Oxford 1984)   [RP III]

_____ *Roman Papers IV*, Ed. Birley, A. R. (Oxford 1985)   [RP IV]

_____ *Roman Papers, VI*, Ed. Birley, A. R. (Oxford 1991)   [RP VI]

_____ *Roman Papers, VII*, Ed. Birley, A. R. (Oxford 1991)   [RP VII]

_____ *The Augustan Aristocracy* (Oxford 1989)   [AA]

Taylor, L. R., *The Voting Districts of the Roman Republic*, Papers and Monographs of the American Academy in Rome XVI (Rome 1960)

Taylor, N. L., *Roman Genealogical Continuity and the 'Descents from Antiquity' Question* (review of Settipani (2000)) in *American Genealogist* 76 (April 2001) 129-136

Thomas, B., *Laterculi Praesidum*, 3 Vols (Gothenburg 1972-74)

Thompson, E. A., *The Visigoths in Spain* (Oxford 1969)

Townend, G., *Some Flavian Connections* in *Journal of Roman Studies* LI (1961)

Webster, G., *The Roman Imperial Army* (London, 1969)

Weinand, J (ed.), *Contested Monarchy: Integrating the Roman Empire in the Fourth Century AD* (Oxford 2015)

Whitby, M., *The Emperor Maurice and his Historian: Theophylact Simocatta on Persian and Balkan Wars* (Oxford 1998)

Williams, S. & Friell, G., *The Rome that did not Fall: The Survival of the East in the Fifth Century* (London 1999)
Wiseman, T. P., *New Men in the Roman Senate* (London 1971)
Wiseman, T. P., *The Myths of Rome* (Exeter, 2004)

Imperial Biographies

Alföldi, A., *The Conversion of Constantine and Pagan Rome* Trans. Mattingly, H. (Oxford 1948)
Arrizabalaga y Prado, L. de, *The Emperor Elagabalus: Fact or Fiction?* (Cambridge 2010)
Astarita. M. L., *Avidio Cassio* (Rome 1983)
Barrett, A. A., *Caligula: The Corruption of Power* (London 1989)
Birley, A. R., *Marcus Aurelius: A Biography* (London 1987)
Birley, A. R., *The African Emperor: Septimius Severus* (London 1988)
Birley, A. R., *Hadrian, The Restless Emperor* (London 1997)
Cameron, A., *The House of Anastasius* in *Greek, Roman and Byzantine Studies* Vol. 19 (1978) 259-276
Casey, P. J., *Carausius & Allectus: The British Usurpers* (London 1994)
Craven, M. A. J. B., *Magnus Maximus: A Forgotten Roman Emperor and his British Legacy* (Stroud 2023)
Crawford, P., *Roman Emperor Zeno* (Barnsley 2019)
Drinkwater, J. F., *The Usurpers Constantine III (407-411) and Jovinus (411-413)* in *Britannia* 29 (1998) 269-298
Goldsworthy, A., *Caesar: The Life of a Colossus* (London 2006)
Grant, M., *The Antonines* (London 1994)
Hartley, E., Hawkes, J., Henig, M. & Mee, F., *Constantine the Great, York's Roman Emperor*, York Museum Exhibition Catalogue, (York, 2006)
Holland, R., *Nero, The Man Behind the Myth* (Stroud 2000)
Jones, B. W., *The Emperor Titus* (London 1984)
Jones, B. W., *The Emperor Domitian* (London 1992)
Kokkinos, N., *Antonia Augusta* (London, 1992)
Körner, C., *Philippus Arabs* (Berlin 2001)
Leadbetter, W. L., *Galerius and the Will of Diocletian* (London 2009)
Levick, B., *Claudius* (London 1990)
Levick, B., *Vespasian* (London 1999)
McHugh, J. S., *Emperor Alexander Severus: Rome's Age of Insurrection AD222-235* (Barnsley 2017)
Morgan, G., *69AD: The Year of the Four Emperors* (Oxford 2006)
Murdoch, A., *The Last Pagan: Julian the Apostate and the Death of the Ancient World* (Stroud 2003)
Murdoch, A., *The Last Roman, Romulus Augustulus and the Decline of the West* (Stroud, 2006)
Opper, T., *Hadrian, Empire and Conflict,* British Museum Exhibition Catalogue (London 2008)
Peacock, P. B., *Usurpers under Elagabalus* (Washington 2000)
Pohlsander, H. A., *The Emperor Constantine* (London 1996)

Rebenich, S. & Wierner, H. U. (eds.), *A Companion to Julian the Apostate* (Leiden 2020)

Seager, R., *Tiberius* (London 1972)

Shiel, N., *The Episode of Carausius & Allectus* BAR 40 (Oxford 1977)

Shlosser, F. E., *The Reign of the Emperor Maurikios (582–602): a Reassessment* (Athens 1994)

Sivan, H., *Ausonius of Bordeaux: Genesis of a Gallic Aristocracy* (London 1993)

Southern, P., *Augustus* (London 1998)

Southern, P., *Empress Zenobia: Palmyra's Rebel Queen* (London 2008)

Syvänne, I., *The Reign of Emperor Gallienus: The Apogee of Roman Cavalry* (Barnsley 2019)

Turton, G., *The Syrian Princesses* (London 1974)

White, J. F., *Restorer of the World: The Roman Emperor Aurelian* (Staplehurst 2005)

Williams, S. & Friell, G., *Theodosius, The Empire at Bay* (London 1994)

Index of Persons Excluding the List
of Biographical Entries

Abbreviations: dau. = daughter, Fl. = Flavius, gr. = governor (used loosely); jr. = junior, PPO = later imperial praetorian prefect, PUR = Prefect of the City of Rome.

Duplicated (and some other) names are qualified by a brief descriptive to distinguish one from another or to locate them in time; no distinction is made between suffect and ordinary consuls.

Letters 'I' and 'J', 'U' and 'V' are treated separately, as in English usage, rather than Latin, where in both cases they are one and the same: 'I' & 'V'.

Romans are indexed under their *gentilicia* except where those do not apply and thereafter under the name under which they are best known.

Ablabius, consul 331 84, 93, 141
Abnun, Persian grandee 132
Acacius, father of Empress Theodora 169
Acilii Glabriones 45
Acilius Attianus, *eques* 138
Acilius Glabrio, M'. 232
Adminius, British ruler 262
Aelia Anastasia/Ino, empress 291
Aelia Eudoxia, empress 34
Aelia Flaccilla, 1st wife of Theodosius 282
Aelia Galla, empress 191
Aelia Marcia Euphemia 30, 198
Aelia Paetina, wife of Claudius 68
Aelia Verina, empress of Leo I 52-53, 150, 164, 173-174, 175, 198-199, 258, 325-326
Aelius Hadrianus Afer, P. 138, 200
Aelius Marullinus, triumviral senator 137-138
Aelius Seianus (Sejanus), L. 11, 55, 68, 112, 288-290
Aelius Tubero, Q. 68

Aemilia Lepida 68
Aemilia Lepida, dau. of L. Paullus 323
Aemilia Lepida, wife of Galba 114, 242
Aemilius Lepidus, M., triumvir 9, 11, 38, 41, 114, 221
Aemilius Lepidus, M., consul 11, 114
Aemilius Lepidus, M., conspirator 57, 112-113
Aemilius Paulus, L, lover of Julia 39, 41, 323
Aeneas, Prince of Troy 158
Aëtius, Fl. 21, 48, 49, 149-150, 193, 197, 237
Afranius Burrus, Sex. 221
Afranius Hannibalianus 21, 141
Agrippa, *see* Julius Herodes, Vipsanius
Agrippinus, *magister militum* 20
Ahura Mazda, god 132
Alaric I, Visigothic king 34, 35-36, 141-142, 144-146, 153
Alaric II, Visigothic king 278
Alexander the Great 61, 151, 235-236, 264
Allobichus, *magister militum* 87

Alypia, dau. of Anthemius 30, 198
Amantius, eunuch 165
Ambrosius (Ambrose) St. 65, 110, 190, 284
Anastasia, sister of Constantine I 81
Anastasia, Constantinian princess 29
Anastasia Constantina 29
Andragathius, *magister militum* 135, 190
Anicia Juliana 227
Anicia Juliana, dau. of Olybrius 227
Anicii 15
Anicius Faustus, *duumvir* 236
Anicius Faustus, Q. consul 198 236
Anicius Faustus Albinus Basilius, Fl., 169
Anicius Probinus, senator 192
Anicius Probinus, consul 395 236
Annaeus Seneca, L. 221, 323
Annia Aurelia Galeria Faustina 107
Annia Aurelia Galeria Lucilla, empress 180
Annia Faustina, Claudia, empress 107
Annia Galeria Faustina, empress 32-33, 46-47, 203
Annius Afrinus, M. consul c. 67 200
Annius Faustus, *delator* 200
Annius Faustus, consul 121 200
Annius Flavius Libo, M., consul 204 259
Annius Fuscus, alleged father of Niger 234n
Annius Libo, M., consul 160 259
Annius Sabinus Libo, M. 104n, 259
Annius Scapula, Spaniard 200
Annius Vinicianus, M., plotter 57-58
Annius Verus, M. thrice consul 33, 200
Annius Verus, M. consul 140 202
Anthemiolus, son of Anthemius 30
Anthemius, comes 285
Anthemius brother of Marcian (II) 198
Anthemius of Tralles 171
Antinöus, favourite 139
Antiochus VIII Gryphus, king of Syria 151
Antonia L. f. Saturnina 262
Antonius, M., triumvir 9, 38, 39, 110, 160-161, 221, 223, 264, 326
Antonius Primus, general 318
Antonius Saturninus, L., *duumvir* 261
Anullinus, senator 99

Apollodorus of Damascus 137
Apronia Caesiana 112
Apronius, L., consul 8 112
Arabia, dau. of Justin II 167
Arbogastes, *magister militum* 109-110, 144, 277n, 284, 319
Arbogastes, *comes* 277
Arborius, tutor 78
Arcadia, 1ˢᵗ wife of Zeno 324
Ardaburius, father of Aspar 196
Ardaburius, son of Aspar 174
Areobindus, consul 506 227n
Areobindus, *magister militum*, Africa 136, 277
Ariadne, Aelia, twice empress 27-28, 29, 173-174, 1980-199, 325
Arigius 277n
Armatus, consul 476 52, 53, 258
Arria Fadilla 216n
Arrius Pacatus, C., senator 262
Arruntius, L., consul 6AD 58
Arsenius, monk 34
Artabanus, king of Parthia 271
Artabanus, *dux* 136
Artaxerxes/Ardashir, king of Persia 271, 280
Annius Libo, M., consul 160 259
Artemisia, wife of Procopius 249
Ascanius (Iullus) 158
Asellius Aemilianus 72-73, 235
Asiaticus 57, 260
Asinius Gallus, C., consul 8BC 289
Asinius Sabinianus, M., consul, c. 225 259
Aspar, Fl. Ardaburius, 30, 173, 174, 196, 198, 325
Aspaeus, Palmyrene 31
Asterius, *comes Hispaniarum* 219
Athaulf, Visigothic king 36, 91, 145, 153-154, 264
Athenogenes, bishop of Petra 208n
Attitianus, officer of Victorinus 321
Attalus, king of Asia 107
Attila, Hun ruler 49, 163, 197, 286-287
Aurelianus, gr. in Cilicia c. 300 43
Aurelii 32, 42
Aurelius Annius Verus, M. 204
Aurelius Cleander, M. 77
Aurelius Commodus Pompeianus, L. 180n

Aurelius Pius 32n
Aurelius Symmachus, Q., senator 35, 191
Aurelius Thedotus, *dux* 24
Aurelius Victor, Sex. 18, 53
Ausonius, Decimius Magnus 21, 78, 87n, 134
Avidius Heliodorus, C. 46
Avidius Nigrinus, C. 140
Avienus, father of Pope Severinus 259n
Avitus, Bishop of Clermont-Ferrand 48

Babylas, St., bishop of Antioch 240
Baduarius, *cura palatii* 167
Barbaria, probable wife of Romulus 259
Barbia Orba Orbiana, Cneia Seia etc. 270
Basilina 156
Bassianus, nephew of Constantine 178
Batea wife of Dardanus 158
Bauto, Fl. 34, 190
Belisarius, Fl., *comes* 166, 171
Bonifatius, *comes* 149
Bonitus, Frankish commander 274
Bonitus, St. 48
Boudicca, queen of the Iceni 222
Brutus *see* Servilius Caepio Brutus
Bruttia Crispina 76-77
Bruttius Praesens, C. 76
Bucius Lappius Maximus, A. 261
Butheric, army commander 284

Caecilia Paulina, empress 214-215
Caecilii Metelli 270
Caecina Alienus, A. general 323
Caecinae 278n
Caelius Calvinus, L. consul 51
Caelius Honoratus, Q. consul 105 51
Caesar, *see* Julius
Caesaria, mother of Hypatius 147
Caesarion, Ptolemaeus XV of Egypt 161
Caesennii Paeti 317
Calocerus, bishop of Byzantium 247
Calpurnia, widow of Caesar 161
Calpurnia, wife of Quartinus 254
Calpurnius Piso, senator 120
Calpurnius Piso, C. plotter 11, 222, 224, 323n
Calpurnius Piso Caesoninus, L. 161

Calpurnius Piso Frugi Licinianus, L. 242
Calvia Crispinilla 115-116, 181
Calvisius Sabinus, C. consul 26 112
Cantianilla, St. 65
Cantianus, St. 65
Cantius, St. 65
Capellianus, gr. Numidia 129, 259
Carausius of Penmachno 63
Casperius Aelianus, praetorian prefect 224
Cassiodorus Senator, Magnus Aurelius 256
Cassius Longinus, C. assassin 102, 200
Cassius Longinus, Q., gr. Baetica 200
Cassius Regallianus, C., consul c. 200 256
Castinus, *magister militum* 148-149, 219
Catilius Severus Julianus Claudius Reginus, L. 202, 270
Catilius Severus, Cn. Consul 200 270
Caunius Priscus 245
Cavades I, king of Persia 28
Cecropius, *dux* 121
Ceionia Fabia 202
Ceionii 72, 179-180
Ceionius, *praefectus fabrum* 179
Ceionius Albinus, M. Nummius 180
Ceionius Commodus, L., consul 136 140, 202
Ceionius Rufius Volusianus, C. 25
Ceionius Silvanus, M. 180
Celsus 33n
Charito, wife of Jovian 153
Charito, dau. of Tiberius II 123, 291
Charlemagne, emperor 22n, 167
Childeric I, king of the Franks 277
Chosroes II, king of Persia 208-209, 287
Christodorus, poet 29
Claudia, dau of Nero 222
Claudia, half-sister of Probus 247
Claudia Aquillia 107
Claudia Constantina 71
Claudia Octavia, dau. of Claudius I 222
Claudii Nerones 68
Claudii Pulchres 67, 251n
Claudius Candidus, Ti. 235
Claudius Julius Pacat[ia]nus 230

Claudius Marcellus, M., Augustan heir 39

Claudius Nero, Drusus 39, 289

Claudius Nero, Ti., praetor 42BC 40, 288

Claudius Petronius Probus, Sex. 227, 236

Claudius Pompeianus, Ti., consul 46, 232

Claudius Pompeianus Quintianus, Ti. 77, 180n

Claudius Postumus Dardanus, PPO 154

Claudius Pulcher, C., consul 92BC 39

Claudius Severus, Cn. 107

Claudius Severus Proculus, Ti. 107

Claudius Solemnis, Ti., consul c. 230 230

Clemens, slave 290

Cleopatra VII, Queen of Egypt 9, 161-162, 326

Cleopatra Selene 110

Cleopatra Tryphaena 151

Clodia, 1st wife of Augustus 38

Clodius Galba, D. *eques* 72

Clodius Hermogenianus Olybrius, Q. 227

Clodius Pulcher, P, killed 52BC 38

Clodius Pupienus [ ], L. 252

Clodius Rufus, L., consul 7BC 182

Clovis/Chlodovechus, Frankish king 164, 278, 282

Cocceia, sister of Nerva 224

Cocceius Balbus, C., consul 39BC 223

Cocceius Nerva, L., legate 41BC 223

Cocceius Nerva, M., consul 36BC 223

Consentius of Narbo, rhetor 153

Constans III 194n

Constantia, dau. of Hannibalianus 141

Constantia, wife of Gratian 90, 157

Constantina, dau. of Constantine 80, 90, 141

Constantina, dau. of Tiberius II 208, 291

Constantinus Lardys, patrician 287

Constantius, praetorian prefect 211

Cornelia, wife of Caesar 161

Cornelia Orestina *see* Livia Orestilla

Cornelia Salonina Chrysogone 118

Cornelia Supera, C., empress 23

Cornelii Cethegi 252 & n

Cornelii Lentuli 56

Cornelius Balbus Theophanes, L 51, 137

Cornelius Cossus, L. 112

Cornelius Dolabella, P., consul 44BC 116, 162

Cornelius Dolabella, P., consul 56 242

Cornelius Lentulus, Cossus, consul 1 112

Cornelius Lentulus Caudinus, L. 112

Cornelius Lentulus Marcellinus, Cn. 38

Cornelius Macer, senator c. 300 254

Cornelius Saecularis, P., consul 260 118

Cornelius Scipio Africanus, P. 137

Cornelius [Scipio], P. consul 35BC 39

Cornelius Scipio Orestinus, senator 56

Cornelius Sulla, L., dictator 82BC 8, 114, 157, 200, 267, 324

Cornelius Superus, C. 23

Cornelius Tacitus 18, 47, 278

Cornificia, sister of M. Aurelius 200

Cornificius, L., consul 33BC 200

Crassus, *see* Licinius Crassus

Creusa 158

Crispus, brother of Claudius II 71

Crispus, Fl. Julius 80, 83, 178

Cupresennius Gallus 94

Dalmatius, supposed father of Probus 247

Dalmatius, ex consul 57

Dalmatius, the elder 141

Dalmatius, *see also* Maximus

Damiana dau. of Iannina 208

Dardanus, mythic hero 158

Decebalus, king of Dacia 256

Decimius Rusticus, PPO 87, 154

Decius Vindex, Q., 94

Demetrius, nephew of Probus 247

Didia Clara, dau. of Didius Julianus 98

Didymus 218

Didius Severus, *eques* 97

Dio Cocceianus, M. Cassius, historian 18

Dionysius of Alexandria 24, 240

Domitia Longina, empress 56, 102

Domitia Lucilla, mother of M Aurelius 97

Domitianus, *dux* 183

Domitius, supposed brother of Probus 247

Domitius, supposed son of Probus 247

Domitius Ahenobarbus, Cn. 68, 221
Domitius Corbulo, Cn., marshal 56, 102, 222
Domitius Lucanus, Cn. 138
Domitius Ulpianus, jurist 271
Drusus, *see* Claudii, Julii, Livii
Dulcitius, father of Justin II 166

Ecdicius, *magister militum* 163
Eclectus, freedman 232
Edobichus, *magister militum* 86-87
Egnatius Rufus, conspirator 41
Ela-Gabal, god 106-108
Ennia Thrasylla, wife of Macro 55, 56
Ennodius, St. 47, 126, 257
Eros, private secretary to Aurelian 44
Eucherius, son of Stilicho 145
Eudocia, Aelia/Athenaïs, empress 285-286
Eudoxia, Licinia, empress 237, 237, 286
Eugenius, minister of Theoderic 227
Euric, Visigothic king 30-31, 162, 258
Eusebia, empress 90
Eusebius, Fl., consul 347 90
Eusebius, Fl., junior 90
Eutharicus Cilliga, Fl., consul 519 124, 165
Eutropia, empress of Maximian 21
Eutropia, dau. of Constantius II 219, 220
Eutropius alleged father of Constantius I 71, 88
Eutropius, eunuch 34-35
Eutropius, chronicler 53
Eutychianus (Gannys) 106
Exuperius, rhetor 141

Fabia Orestilla, empress 129
Fabius Chilo, L. Severan marshal 235
Fabius Titianus, PUR 220
Fabius Valens, general 323
Faunus, king of Latium 322
Fausta, empress of Constantine 78, 80, 83, 89, 210
Faustina, *see* Annia
Faustina, wife of Constantius II 90
Felicissimus, rebel 44
Firminus Licerius Lupicinus, Fl. 126
Flavia, alleged dau. of Carausius (II) 64
Flavia Aprilla, wife of Numerianus 226

Flavia Maxima, 1st wife of Gratian 134
Flavia Maximiana Theodora 89, 141
Flavia Sabina, niece of Vespasian 317
Flavia Titiana, empress of Pertinax 233
Flavius Aper, L. kinsman of Severus I 267
Flavius Aper, M., 267
Flavius Aper, L., praetorian prefect 66, 99, 211, 226
Flavius Clemens, T., consul 95 104
Flavius Clemens, T., jr. 104
Flavius Romulus, consul 343 258
Flavius Sabinus, T., uncle of Titus 102, 224, 317-318
Flavius Claudius Sulpicianus, T. 98, 233
Flavius Vitellius Seleucus, M. 264
Fulvia, wife of P. Clodius 38
Fulvia Plautilla, Publia, 59
Fulvia Prisca 183
Fulvii Rustici 151
Fulvius Macrianus, P. 254
Fulvius Plautianus, P. praetorian prefect 59, 184-185
Fulvius Plautius Hortensianus, C. 61, 267
Fulvius Quartinus, T., senator 254
Fulvius Rusticus Aemilianus, C. 97
Furii 58
Furius Camillus, M., consul 8AD 58, 68
Furius Sabinius Aquila Timisitheus, C. 130-132, 230, 239

Gaïnas, general 34-35
Gaiseric, Vandal king 29-31, 48-49, 52, 174, 176-177, 194, 227-228, 258
Galeria Fundana, 2nd wife of Vitellius 323
Galeria Fundana, dau. of Vitellius 33
Galeria Valeria, dau. of Galerius 211
Galerius, C., gr. Egypt 16-31 323
Galla, 2nd wife of Theodosius I 283
Galla Placidia, princess 36, 91, 145-146, 149-150, 154, 193, 283, 286
Gallius, M., adopts Tiberius I 288
Gaudentius, son of Aëtius 21, 237
Gellius Maximus, L., *medicus* 217
Germanus, husband of Charito 291
Germanus, patrician 123, 217, 276, 287-288, 291n

Germanicus, *see* Claudii, Julii
Gerontius, *magister militum* 79, 86-87, 218-219, 269
Gildo, Moorish leader 189
Goar, Alan leader 153-154
Gratianus, son of Theodosius I 283
Gregory of Tours, historian 21
Gregory the Great, pope 209, 287
Gunderic, Vandal leader 219
Gundobad, king of the Burgundians 31, 125-126, 228
Guntarius, Burgundian leader 153-154

Habiba, alleged mother of Maximin 214
Hadrianus, nephew of Probus 247
Haius Diadumenianus, Cn., *eques* 185
Hecebolus, gr. Libya 169
Helen of Troy 158
Helena, Flavia Julia, St. 81, 88-89, 192, 283
Helena, dau. of Constantine I 80
Helena, sister of Constantius II 156
Helvidius Priscus, C. 318
Helvia, Seneca's aunt 323
Helvius Pertinax, P., jr. 233
Heraclianus, praetorian prefect 121
Herculanus, brother of Romulus 257
Herodes (Herod) the Great 139
Herodes Atticus, senator 128
Herennia Cupressinia Etruscilla 94
Herennianus son of Proculus 251
Herennius Etruscus, Q. 94
Herennius Orbianus, Arval brother 270
Hermineric, consul 465 324
Hesychius, Gallic noble 48
Hesychius, Fl., *comes* 48
Hieronymus/Jerome, St. 240
Hilaria, supposed dau. of Zeno 325
Hordeonius Flaccus, M. 67
Hunila, wife of Bonosus 54
Hypatius, Fl. 90

Icelus, freedman 114
Illidius, St. 192
Illus, king of Troy 71
Illus, patrician 53, 198-199, 325-326
Illus Trocundes, Fl. Appalius 199
Iohannes, son of Theodosius I 283
Iohannes, son of Theodora 169
Iohannes, officer 291

Iohannes, *magister militum* 276
Iohannes, grandson of Hypatius 147
Iohannes *qui et* Athalaricus 124, 326
Iohannes, consul 576 172
Isidorus of Miletus 171
Isis, god 95
Iullus/Ascanius 158

John Chrysostom, St. 35
John the Cappadocian 170
John, nephew of Vitalianus 172
Jovinus, Fl., consul 367 153
Julia, mother of M. Antonius 159
Julia, dau. of Caesar 161
Julia, dau. of Augustus 25, 288-289
Julia, grand-dau. of Augustus 39, 68
Julia, granddaughter of Tiberius I 223
Julia, widow of T. Flavius Sabinus 104
Julia Agrippina, the elder 68, 221
Julia Agrippina, the younger 221, 317
Julia Aquillia Severa empress 107
Julia Avita Mammaea 108
Julia Cornelia Paula, empress 106
Julia Domna 12, 61, 105, 124-125, 185-186, 265-266
Julia Drusilla, dau. of Caligula 56-57
Julia Fadilla 215
Julia Maesa 108, 186, 269-270
Julia Mamaea 215, 269-71
Julia Soaemias Bassiana 96, 106, 108, 215, 269
Julianus, son of Constantine III 79, 87
Julii Maiores 264
Julius, N. 158
Julius Agricola, Cn. 47, 262, 268
Julius Antiochus Epiphanes, C. 264
Julius Antiochus Seleucus 264
Julius Aquillius Tertullus, M. 107
Julius Asclepiodotus 26
Julius Bassianus, father of Julia Domna 265
Julius Caesar, C. heir apparent 14, 39, 289
Julius Caesar, Drusus 289
Julius Caesar, Germanicus 123, 221, 289
Julius Caesar, L., consul 90BC 159
Julius Caesar, L., Caesar's father 159
Julius Caesar, L., consul 64BC 159
Julius Caesar, L., heir apparent 14, 39, 289

Julius Caesar, Nero 123
Julius Caesar, Sex., consul 157BC 159
Julius Callistus, C., freedman 56, 260
Julius Clatius Severus, T. 107
Julius Constantius 83, 84, 141, 156
Julius Fortunatianus, C. *eques* 263
Julius Gallienus, Q., caesar 119
Julius Herodes Agrippa, M., king 55, 107
Julius Ingenuus, C., military tribune 148
Julius, Iullus 158
Julius Iullus, C. 159
Julius Iullus, Vopiscus 159
Julius Juba, C. 110-111
Julius Lupus, P. 216n
Julius Patricius, son of Aspar 174
Julius Paullus, Batavian 67, 107
Julius Paullus, jurist 106
Julius Priscus, C., brother of Philip (I) 151, 239-140
Julius, Proculus 158
Julius Ptolemaeus, C., Numidian ruler 110
Julius Saturninus, C. 263
Julius T. f. Fab. Saturninus, T. 263
Julius Severus, C., consul 109 107
Julius Ursus Servianus, C. 140-141
Julius Verus Maximus, C. 215-216
Junia Calvina, wife of L. Vitellius, jr. 323
Junia Claudilla, 1st wife of Caligula 56
Junia Lepida 317n
Junius Balbus, father of Gordian III 130
Junius Balbus, C., *eques* 130
Junius Brutus, L., regicide 322
Junius Silanus, C. Ap. 57
Junius Silanus, D. lover of Julia, jr. 39
Junius Silanus Torquatus, M., consul 19 56, 323
Jupiter, god 158
Justina, Neratia empress 183, 188, 191, 283
Justinianus, *magister militum* 85-86
Justinianus, *patrician* 291
Justinus, Fl., consul 540 166
Justus, *magister militum* 79, 86
Justus, son of Justin II 167

Keindrech, possible empress 192

Kniva, Gothic commander 22, 23, 95-96, 108, 246
Laeta, empress 134
Laetus, praetorian prefect 231-232, 266
Lagodius 218
Lallis, mother of Zeno 324
Laodice Thea Philadelphia 151
Leo I, pope 238
Leontia, dau. of Leo I 173, 198, 199
Leonita, wife of Phocas 210
Leontius, Sophist 285
Leontius, general 199
Licerius, senator 126
Licinius Crassus, M., triumvir 9, 33, 160-161, 242
Licinius Crassus Frugi, M. consul 27 242
Licinius Lucullus, L., consul 74BC 259
Licinius Mucianus, C. marshal 323
Livia Drusilla, Augusta 14, 24, 39-41, 56, 114, 288
Livia C. f. Livilla 39
Livia C. f. Pulchra 39
Livia Medullina Camilla 68
Livia Ocellina 113
Livia Orestilla, 2nd wife of Caligula 56
Livii Ocellae 56
Livius Drusus, C., triumviral senator 39
Livius [Drusus] M. 39n
Livius Drusus, M., tribune 91BC 39
Livius Drusus Claudianus, M., 39
Livius Drusus Libo, M., consul 15 58
Locusta 69
Lollia Paulina, 3rd wife of Caligula 56-57, 260
Lollia Saturnina 56
Lollius, M., consul 21BC 56
Longinus, brother of Zeno 28
Longinus of Cardala 28
Longinus, exarch of Italy 167
Lucilla, dau. of M. Aurelius 77
Lucillianus, father-in-law of Jovian 249
Lucina 237
Lupicina Euphemia, empress 164, 166, 169
Lydius, Isaurian brigand 248

Macedo, officer 253-254
Macedonius, patriarch 28
Macrinus son of Diadumenianus 184
Macro, *see* Naevius Cordus

Maecenas, C. 11, 39
Maecia, wife of Avidius Cassius 47
Maecia Faustina, sister of Gordian II 130
Maecianus, kin to Proculus 251
Maecilius Fuscus, gr. Britain 48
Maecilius Hilarianus, consul 332 48
Maecilius Nepos, yr. Pliny's friend 48n
Maecius Gordianus, praetorian prefect 132
Magna, dau. of Olybrius 227
Magna, sister-in-law of Anastasius 29
Magnia Urbica, empress of Carus 65
Maiorianus, *magister militum* 193
Manlia Scantilla, empress 98
Marcellinus, general of Aurelian 31
Marcellinus, *magister officinorum* 220
Marcellinus, Gallic *magister militum* 162
Marcellinus, Dalmatian warlord 164, 174
Marcellus, PPO Gaul 194 & n, 196
Marcia Otacilia Severa, empress 239-241, 273
Marcianus, *dux* 121
Marcianus, son of Anthemius 30
Marcius Rutilus, C. censor 351BC 8
Marcus, son of Basiliscus 52
Maria, wife of Hypatius 147
Marina Severa, mother of Gratian (I) 134
Marius, C., consul 107BC etc., 8, 10, 157
Marius Maximus, L., historian 235
Martin of Tours, St., 192
Martinus, *magister militum* 275
Massinissa, king of Numidia 111
Matasuntha 124
Maternus, officer 77, 266
Mauricius, decurion 127
Mauricius (II), usurper 208n
Maximinus, general 111-112
Maximinus, gr. Syria 278
Maximinus, would be usurper 276n
Maximus/Dalmatius, father of Probus 247
Memmius Regular, P, consul, 31 56
Meriades 92
Merobaudes, *magister militum* 134
Mevius Silus Crescens Fortunatianus, C. 263
Micca, supposed parent of Maximin (I) 214

Milonia Caesonia, 4th wife of Caligula 56-57
Minervina 80
Mithras, god 95
Mithridates I Callinicus of Commagene 151
Mummia Achaïca 113
Mummius Achaïcus, L. 113
Mundus, general 171
Mustafa Kemal Pasha/Atatürk 171

Naevius Cordus Sutorius Macro, Q. 11, 55-56, 288, 290
Narcissus, freedman 317
Narses, Exarch of Italy 167, 171-172
Narses, general 287
Nebiogastes, *magister militum* 85-86
Neratii 183
Neratius Junius Macer, L. 183
Nigriniaus, *caesar* 220
Nonia Celsa, empress 185
Nubel, king of Mauretania 110
Numerianus, gr. in Gaul 65
Nummius Senecio Albinus, M. 233
Nunechia, wife of Gerontius 218
Nymphidia 56, 260
Nymphidius Sabinus, C. 57, 114

Oclatinius Adventus, M. 185
Octavii 37
Octavia, sister of Augustus 68
Octavius, Cn. 37
Octavius Laenas, Ser[gius], consul 97 223
Odenathus, husband of Zenobia 326
Odo[v]acer 52, 126, 164, 176, 199, 230, 258-259, 277-278, 326
Ofilius Valerius Macedo, C. 254n
Olybrius, Anicius, PPO Italy 503 227
Onoulfus, brother of Odovacer 52
Opellius, legionary legate 184
Orestes, *magister militum* 163, 257-258, 325
Orestes, *see also* Rufius
Oriuna, alleged empress of Carausius (II) 64
Ovinius Camillus 58
Ovinius Rusticus Cornelianus, L. 58
Owein ap Macsen Wletig 87

Pacatus Drepanius, Latinius, panegyricist 191
Paccia Marciana, 1st wife of Severus I 265
Palladius, son of Petronius Maximus 237
Papirius, *primus pilus*, 181
Patricius, consul 500 168
Patricius, ally of Verina 325
Paulina, dau. of Carus 65, 225
Paulus, *comes* 277
Paulus, brother of Orestes 257, 258
Paullus, brother of Anastasius 29, 227n
Paullus, father of Mauricius 207
Paullus, Gallic aristocrat 21
Pedanii 317
Pedanius Fuscus, Cn. 140
Peducaeus Plautius Quintillus, M. 72-73
Perperna, M. consul 92BC 94
Pescennius, C. republican senator 234n
Pescennius T. f., L. 234n
Pescennius Niger, P., Arval brother 234
Petillius Cerealis Caesius Rufus, Q. 67
Petronia, 1st wife of Vitellius 322
Petronii Mamertini 267
Petronius, P., consul 19
Petronius Didius Severus, L. 97
Petronius Annianus, consul 314 227
Petronius Probianus, consul 322 236
Petrus, brother of Maurice 209
Philagrius, Gallic noble 48
Philippus, PPO 285
Philostratus, philosopher 128
Phocas, emperor 124, 209-210, 287
Pisidius Romulus, Fl., PUR 406 257-258
Placidia, empress of Olybrius 227, 237
Placidianus, general of Claudius II 320
Plautia, A. f. 322
Plautia Urgulanilla, 68
Plautius, A., consul AD1 322
Plautius, A., consul 29 322n
Plinius Caecilius Secundus, C. 12
Poemenius, *dux* 93
Pompeia, dau. of Pompey 161
Pompeius, bro. of Hypatius 147, 165, 171
Pompeius, son of Hypatius 147
Pompeius Macer 182

Pompeius Magnus, Cn. Triumvir 9, 33, 38, 114, 159-161, 242, 290
Pompeius, Sex. 9, 38
Pomponius Bassus Faustinus, Ti. 42
Poppaea Sabina, Ollia 222, 229
Porcius Cato, M., censor 221
Porcius Cato Uticensis, M. 161
Praeiecta, widow of Areobindus 136
Praeiecta, sister of Justin II 147
Priam, king of Troy 158
Prisca, empress 100
Priscianus poet 29
Priscillianus, bishop 190
Probus, cousin of Hypatius 147, 171
Probus, nephew of Anastasius 147, 165
Procopius, historian 19
Procopius Anthemius, consul 515 198
Procopius, son of Marcian (II) 198
Procopius, *magister militum* 30
Procopius, gr. of the Islands 199n
Ptolemaic kings of Egypt 151, 161
Pudens, brother of Laetus 266
Pulcheria, Aelia, empress 91-92, 196, 285-286
Pyrallis, concubine 56

Quinctilius Varus, P. consul 13BC 38, 289
Quirinus, god 158

Remistus, Visigoth 50
Ricimer, Fl., *magister militum* 29-31, 47, 49-50, 173, 176, 192-195, 198, 227, 228, 257-258
Romanus, *comes* 111
Romula 117
Romulus, king 7, 158
Romulus, son of Maxentius 210-211
Romulus, brother of Marcian (II) 198
Romulus, *comes* 257, 258
Rufinus, Fl. PPO (E) 34
Rufius Gennadius Probus Orestes 259
Rufius Magnus Faustus Avienus 259
Rufius Opilio, Fl., consul 524 165n
Rupilia 33
Rupilia Faustina 200
Rupilius Frugi, Libo 33, 324
Rusticiana, wife of Symmachus 141

Sabbatius, brother-in-law of Justin I 166, 168

Sabinia Furia Tranquillina, empress 131
Sabinus, 2i/c of Heraclianus 142
Sallustius, brother of Jovinus 153
Sallustius Lucullus 262
Sallustius Macrinianus, P., gr.
  Mauretania 270
Sallustius Macrinianus, P. senator 270
Sallustius Passienus Crispus, C. 24
Sallustius Saturninus, *procurator* 263
Salonius Longinus Marcellus, M. 118
Salvius Julianus Aemilianus, P, jurist 97
Salvius Otho Titianus, L. 228-229
Salvius Otho, M., people's tribune 43BC
  228
Salvius Titianus, L. 224
Saoterus, favourite of Commodus 77
Sarus, *magister militum* 85-86, 154
Saturninius Secundus *signo* Salutius 152
Scamander, river god 158
Scribonia 2nd wife of Augustus 38, 58,
  69, 290
Scribonii Libones 33, 289-290
Scribonius Drusus Libo, M., *praetor* 16
  289-290
Scribonius Libo, L, *eques* 38
Scribonius Libo, L., consul 34BC 38
Scribonius Libo, L., consul 16 290
Scribonius Proculus, senator 290
Scipio *see* Cornelius Scipio
Secundinus, senator 147
Seius Caesar, L. 270-271
Seius Fuscianus, P., consul (ii) 188 270
Sejanus, *see* Aelius Sejanus
Seleucus IV Philopator, king of Syria
  264
Sempronii Gracchi, 127
Septimius Antiochus, father of Zenobia
  326
Septimius Flaccus 265
Septimius Geta, P., consul 203 124
Septimius Herennianus/Hairan 142
Septimius Severus, C. cousin to Severus
  I 265
Sergius, patrician 136
Sergius Catilina, L., rebel 9, 157-158
Sergius Paullus, gr. Cyprus 227
Sergius Paullus, L. consul 167 227
Servilia, alleged paramour of Caesar
  162
Servilius Caepio Brutus, Q., assassin
  162

Servilius Vatia Isauricus, P., consul 79BC
  324
Servius Tullius, king 8
Severianus, brother-in-law to Philip I
  239-240
Severianus, Fl. Valerius 273
Severinus, pope 640 259n
Severus, patrician 324
Severus Hostilianus, fictional usurper
  204
Sextia, empress of Pupienus Maximus
  252
Sextius Africanus, T., gr. Africa 252
Sextius Africanus, T., consul 112 252
Sextius Lateranus, T., consul 197 252
Sharpur, king of Persia 119, 120-121,
  131-133, 254
Sidonius Apollinaris, C. Sollius 47, 49,
  87n, 177, 193, 194n, 194, 277n, 312
Silius, C. 54, 68
Silvanus, praetorian prefect 119
Silvanus, *dux* 274n
Simon bar Kokhbar 139-140
Siricius, pope 190, 284
Sol Invictus, god 42
Solomon, patrician 136, 276
Sophia, empress 167, 291
Sosius Pompeius Falco, Q. 233, 266
Sozomen, author 18
Statilia Maxima 252
Statilia Messallina, wife of Nero 222,
  230
Statilii 280 & n
Statilius Cassius Taurinus 280
Statilius Silianus, T., Arval brother 280
Statilius Taurinus, T. 280
Statilius Taurus, 2nd-century senator 280
Stephen, St., protomartyr 286
Stilicho, Fl. 34-35, 91, 142, 144-146,
  285
Suetonius Tranquillus, C., historian 12
Sulla, *see* Cornelius Sulla
Sulpicia Dryantilla, wife of Regalianus
  256
Sulpicius Galba, C. 113
Sulpicius Rufus, Ser., *interrex* 52BC
  278
Syagria, wife of Theodatus 48
Syagrius, Fl., consul 21
Syagrius, consul 21

Tacfarinas, African ruler 58
Tatulus, officer 257
Terentius Varro Murena, A., conspirator 41
Tertullus, consul 410 36
Themistius, philosopher 34
Theocritus, *comes* 165
Theodatus, Gallic noble 48
Theoderic, gothic king 48-49
Theoderic Strabo, *magister militum* 198
Theoderic, king of Italy 28, 126, 171, 259, 326
Theodora, empress 147, 164-165, 167-172
Theodorus, brother of Avitus 48
Theodorus the Cappadocian 276n
Theodorus *qui et* Tzirus 172, 217
Theodosiolus 218
Theodosius, *comes* 111, 134, 282-283
Theopiste, supposed dau. of Zeno 325
Thermantia, mother of Theodosius I 282
Thermantia, 2nd wife of Honorius 144
Tigidius Perennis, Sex., praetorian prefect 77, 245
Tmisitheus, *see* Furius
Timotheus, Bishop of Alexandria 53
Tonantius Ferreolus, PPO Gaul, 451 22
Totila, king of Italy 171
Trebonius Garutianus, 116, 181
Tribonianus, jurist 170
Trocundes, brother of Zeno 150
Tyrius Septimius Azizus of Palmyra 143

Ulpia Severina, empress 43
Ulpius Crinitus 43
Ulpius Pupienus Silvanus, M. 252
Ummidius Quadratus, M. 77
Ursicinus, emissary of Constantius II 274

Valeria, dau. of Diocletian 100, 117
Valeria Maximilla 117, 210
Valeria Messalina, empress 54, 56, 68

Valerii Messallae 257
Valerius Alexander 25
Valerius Asiaticus, D., consul 35 32n, 56
Valerius Hermonius Maximus, senator 257
Valerius Poplicola, praetor 375 258
Valerius Sabinus, C., mint master 44
Varronianus 152
Varronianus, Fl., son of Jovian 153
Vercingetorix, Gaulish leader 160
Verconius Taurinus 280
Verginius Rufus, L. 114, 222, 322
Verianus 218
Verina empress *see* Aelia Verina
Verrius Gratus Sabinianus, C. 259
Viator, *comes* 163, 230
Vibia Sabina, empress, 139-140
Videmer II, Ostrogothic king 126
Vigilantia, sister of Justin I 166
Vigilantia, mother of Justin II 166
Vigilius, pope 166
Vipsania, 1st wife of Tiberius I 288
Vipsanius Agrippa, M. 11, 24, 39, 41, 288
Virius Lupus, general 74
Virius Nepotianus, consul 336 219
Vistilia, matriarch 56
Vitalianus 28, 147, 166, 169, 172
Vitelia, demi-god 322
Vitellia Galeria Fundana, dau. of Vitellius 324
Vitellius, L, thrice consul 69, 322
Vituriga *alias* Samso 251
Volaginius, soldier 58
Vortigern, British leader 87n

Walia, Visigothic king 91, 145

Zenas 25
Zeno, son of Zeno 325
Zenonis, wife of Basiliscus 52-53
Zonaras, author 28, 51, 328n
Zosimus, author 18, 33, 328